East End 1888

*To Michael

with personal regards

William J. Fishman*

To my beloved Doris

East End 1888
A year in a London borough among the labouring poor

William J Fishman

Five Leaves Publications

www.fiveleaves.co.uk

East End 1888

by William J Fishman

Published in 2005 and reprinted in 2009
by Five Leaves Publications,
PO Box 8786, Nottingham NG1 9AW
www.fiveleaves.co.uk

Copyright © William J Fishman 2005 (1988)

ISBN: 9780907123859

First published in 1988 by Gerald Duckworth & Co. Ltd.

Five Leaves acknowledges financial assistance
from Arts Council England

Five Leaves is a member of Inpress
(www.inpressbooks.co.uk),
representing independent publishers

Design and typesetting by
Four Sheets Design and Print
Printed in Great Britain

Contents

Foreword *by Richard Cobb*	1
Preface	5
Chapter 1: The Image and the Reality	9
Chapter 2: Housing, Health and Sanitation	38
Chapter 3: The Unemployed and the Sweated	67
Chapter 4: Paupers and "Bastilles"	107
Chapter 5: Women and Children	147
Chapter 6: The Ghetto	166
Chapter 7: Crime and Punishment	223
Chapter 8: The Saints	286
Chapter 9: Politics	330
Chapter 10: Leisure	374
Select Bibliography	401

Foreword

W.J. Fishman's history is social history as it should be: *walked* (and *what* a walker he still is), seen and heard. His awareness of locality is unrivalled, and one senses the contribution of the powerful combination of family loyalty, childhood and adolescent memory and tenderness: the memory, too, of the scene of some of the most violent political confrontations of the 1930s, and his ability to recreate an urban topography of one of the most distinctive and unusual quarters of any of the great cities of the late nineteenth century.

He is himself an *enfant du quartier*, his ear uniquely attuned to its successive, or in some cases overlapping, forms of speech: East End cockney and Yiddish, both languages rich in imaginative evocation, as if to compensate for the generally grinding poverty of the physical surroundings. One feels too that his totally arresting account, most of the time a bleak chronicle of deprivation and misery, owes much to filial affection: his father was an independent tailor who had battled his way up — not very far — in the confined and steamy world of the sweatshop. We can follow him through the so-often lethal winter fogs of the docks, without any danger to our own lives or limbs, and, through his perceptive eyes, we can see streets cut in two by the vast fortifications of the railway embankments, and so losing their unity, creating between the inhabitants of the two halves, a frontier, moral and physical, as effective as any later Berlin Wall. Here are figures huddled against the winter cold beneath the dripping arches of the Great Eastern Railway (itself the principal network of poverty on the move on the cheap). His descriptions of housing conditions reach out beyond the purely statistical though statistics are there, including the exorbitant levels of rents to the physical sensation of the St George's slum: dark, sunless, cold, filthy, overcrowded. Yet a study devoted to what must have been one of the most deprived areas of any great city — London's *quartier du Temple* or La Chapelle, Belleville perhaps, save that it is so high up — is illuminated as much by affection, and even a timid, flickering ray of hope (there may indeed be a future, things may even get a little better) as by often justified indignation at the callousness of so many public authorities (the author gives short shrift to the Chief Rabbi and to the sitting MP of the late 1880s). We can see through his eyes the grim barrack-like structures of the workhouses, huge sentinels towering over the tiny houses and casting the shadow of an imminent and dreaded future over so many of the inhabitants. He has that peculiar local insight which enables him to read signs recognisable to a population largely illiterate: "The houses there were not numbered, but each door had a hieroglyph upon it, unless it was known by an old boot in the first floor window, or a coloured rag that waved on a stick above the entrance" (here is the mastery of the truly observant social historian). And he fully shares the reluctance of the slum children to leave the freedom, and the dangers, of the open street for the regimented horrors of the charitable institution. There is a compelling description of "the infamous Jago". "Aldgate," he writes, "is plagued by open slaughter-houses in the main and side streets, with blood and animal innards splattered on the sidewalks."

East End 1888 was not the sort of place where one might live long. Indeed many lives would be very brief, and death could quite often be public, especially in winter, though there is an account of a cleanly-clothed man picked up in the street in the summer who died of starvation on admission to the London Hospital (itself an object of popular dread). There was no mortuary in Whitechapel, and bodies, including those of children, had to be housed temporarily in a shed. Death is ever present, especially in the popular fear of hospital or workhouse, places one would never come out of alive: better, at least, to die among one's own. And yet it is also a landscape peopled by a varied humanity: wry, resourceful, violent, drunken, thieving, tenacious, ingenious, rich in comic inventiveness, supportive — as well as despairing, defenceless, rejected and hopeless. This is a book about *people* and, as such, the very opposite of some mechanical excursion into bleak economic tables. It is carried, from start to finish, by an abiding compassion for the victims, that is, *most* people, especially the most vulnerable: women and children, the deaf and dumb, the physically handicapped, the bewildered "greener" just off the boat, the seasonally unemployed and the recent immigrants from the areas of extreme agricultural depression from the 1870s: North Essex, Suffolk, Norfolk.

One of the most moving chapters is about women and children: the former subjected to regular Saturday-night beatings-up, driven into prostitution, embarked as cheap labour in the sweatshops or, if lucky (if that is lucky) and supported by the right sort of references from charitable institutions, found places as overworked domestic servants in middle-class households in the increasingly fashionable north-west districts of London. The children cannot speak for themselves, but much of the marvellously eloquent illustrative material provided informs at least about their predicament and about a bleak future — it was at least a future — narrowly confined to the rules and the constraints of a Home, to the *Exmouth*, a training ship, to enrolment in Army Bands as boys, or to group emigration to Canada. Here we have poor little mites of 9, 10 and 11 "consenting to emigrate to Canada". There is something equally bleak about the official word used for such operations: "disposal". Still, even "disposal" could offer them some possibility at least of survival. This harrowing chapter is one of the best in the book, illustrating the author's ability to use to convincing effect a whole series of personal "case histories", most of them brutal in their brevity and repetitiveness — "Orphan", "Deserted", "Child of Widow" — but still providing tiny windows of hope on a future however predictable and collective. As Fishman insists, often the mere fact of survival was at least a positive step.

There is an excellent chapter on the ghetto, and in the chapter on crime the author manages not to become too deeply embroiled in the endless speculation as to the identity of Jack the Ripper. We are in Ripper country throughout, a terrain the historian knows better than anyone, but the Ripper remains very much on the periphery of his preoccupations; he is much more interested in the Ripper's victims, who are among the most tragic of the case histories with which the book is so liberally and intelligently packed.

There is a chapter on politics, about which I cannot speak with any knowledge, but I much enjoyed the chapter on leisure. On the saints, Fishman shows himself characteristically unfashionable: he admires General Booth and Dr Barnardo, and even the eccentric Frederick Charrington, on the simple, and to me convincing, grounds, that their intervention often made the difference between life and death. The Homes were no doubt rigorous — the late Frank Norman could write of his institutional childhood with bitterness — but most of their inmates survived to manhood. Fishman emphasises the extreme devotion and boundless courage of the female Salvationists in their dealings with the poor, the needy and the hopeless.

Centenaries are best avoided. I don't think 1888 in the East End has much to tell us about 1988, and I am sure the bicentenary of 1789 would be best left uncommemorated; but it won't be. The middle classes of 1888 had little need to live in fear of revolution, and the Salvation Army certainly did much more to alleviate the immediate sufferings of the poor in the East End than the fashionable doctrinaire radicals. This is a very good book, not merely because it is compassionate, but because it is most unrevolutionary.

Boots and warm clothing were a better protection than any provided by political theory or doctrinal orthodoxies. *"Schwer und bitter is dos Leben"*, the Jewish lament that could have been the subtitle of this compelling book, did at least speak for life, of whatever little expectancy. For death, one would have to go somewhere else. I can take pride in the fact that, along with Christopher Hill and the late Jack Gallagher, I tried to persuade Bill Fishman to write up his fantastic knowledge of the history of the Tower Hamlets, so much of it then conveyed to us in unforgettable verbal form. This is a book that helps to warm the human spirit.

Richard Cobb

Preface

In this book I try to present an overall picture of life among the labouring poor of East London in Victorian times. To achieve focus, I concentrate on a single year, 1888, and a single borough, Tower Hamlets.[1]

It is with mixed feelings that I came to the end of seven years of exploration, particularly within that legendary area where my own formative years were spent: relief from the burden of writing, regret for parting from that lost world that more than marginally resembled my own, forty years on.

From the mass of sources, certain definitive images and attitudes emerged. One was a universal dread and loathing of the Workhouse. This was a legacy of the 1834 Poor Law Amendment Act which consigned both the genuine and the reckless indigent to these grim, massive battlements, the *Bastilles* of the poor. At the point of entry human warmth and sympathy vanished. Families were parted, wives and children permanently incarcerated in separate barrack-like wards. Conditions were deliberately made to deter: strict discipline, bland food as bare sustenance and dull, monotonous labour, all geared to the principle that the inmate must earn his keep. (Annual profitability was sacrosanct where the cash nexus reigned supreme!) Although, as recorded here, there were acts of benevolence, dependent upon the individual Guardians concerned, for the poor East Ender the Workhouse was the ultimate horror; the final degradation being a pauper's grave with the loss of one's identity as an individual human being. Hence, for him, rather starvation or the prison cell than the local "Work'us". Until recently many of the old survivors even shunned the relatively more humane services of Social Welfare, which to them, bound by childhood memories, was associated with the hated institution that had only just been legislated away (in 1929).

Other striking features emerged: the wit, perspicacity and lively presentation of local journalists with their excellent command of the English language; the self-sacrificial devotion, whatever their motivation, of those once despised middle-class philanthropists, secular or religious, radical or apolitical, who laboured ceaselessly to alleviate suffering among the poor; the illusions of contemporary, self-righteous pundits of *laissez-faire* shattered, thanks to the social aberrations revealed by "happenings" in East London. (This message, however, appears *not* to have been received by certain modern politicians, who know little of, and care less for, the lessons that might be learned from the social, economic and political exposes in East London that year).

I must express my gratitude to those who helped me on the way. To Professor Richard Cobb for his generous advice and concern, his work on the "marginal" poor providing both a model and a stimulus for my own, and to Professor Trevor Smith for his continuing devoted and practical aid. I am always indebted to my old friends and mentors, Professors Theo Barker and Harry Hearder, who originally set me off in the direction of historical research; to my colleagues in the Political Studies department of Queen Mary College, particularly Dr Elizabeth Vallance and Dr Wayne Parsons, for putting up with my constant verbal ramblings with patience and understanding; to historians Professor George Rudé and Raphael Samuel (the latter generously offering me access to his own material on local crime).

For sources and illustrations my thanks to the following: Chris Lloyd and Harold Watton of the Tower Hamlets Local History Library; Ralph Hart of the GLC Records department; the staff librarians of the British Library; Terry McCarthy, Director of the National Museum of Labour History; those senior citizens of Tower Hamlets who, through personal reminiscences and memorabilia helped me to bring to life many of the subjects and incidents recorded here. Finally, I shall always be grateful to the Barnett Shine Trust — to Barney, Sybil and Barbara — and Martin Paisner, who gave generously to facilitate my research; to Mrs Evelyn Lockington for her impeccable work on the typescript and advice on syntax. Again my deepest gratitude is to my wife Doris whose cajoling, but rare devotion throughout, enabled me to finish the task.

The reader will respond to this according to his or her own values. As for myself, I leave the last words to Jack London, written long after his earlier investigative account of East End life in *The People of the Abyss* (1903): "No other book of mine took so much of my young heart and tears as that study of the economic degradation of the poor!"

W.J.F.

[1]The borough of Tower Hamlets in 1888 included the following areas: Whitechapel (including Spitalfields), Stepney, St George's-in-the-East and Wapping, Limehouse, Poplar, Mile End Old and New Town, Bow and Bromley. It was bounded by the River Lea to the east, Hackney and Shoreditch to the north, the City of London to the west, and the River Thames to the south.

Those who do not remember the past are doomed to relive it.
Santayana,
Life of Reason, 1905-1906

Chapter 1
The Image and the Reality

> The City is of Night, perchance of Death,
> But certainly at Night, for never there
> Can come the lucid morning's fragrant breath ...
> JAMES THOMSON, THE CITY OF DREADFUL NIGHT

> The East End of London is the hell of poverty. Like an enormous black, motionless, giant Kraken, the poverty of London lies there in lurking silence and encircles with its mighty tentacles the life and wealth of the City and of the West End.
> J.H. MACKAY, THE ANARCHISTS

Long before 1888 the image of the East End of London — in fact and fiction — was already vividly established. Observations on this great Wen had been voiced in their own time by Dickens and Mayhew, and brilliantly reinforced by the sombre illustrations of Doré. Barely five years had elapsed since the horrific revelations of an outraged priest, conveyed by William C. Preston in *The Bitter Cry of Outcast London* (1883), had shaken the complacency of the Victorian church-going middle classes. 1888 would bring a sharper focus to an area which, according to established mores, constituted a permanent threat to the social order.

It had also became a national institution: a reservoir of constant fantasy, to be drawn upon, with profit, by both religious and secular "salesmen".

A perceptive correspondent informs us:

> Invention about 1880 of the term "East End" was rapidly taken up by the new halfpenny press, and in the pulpit and the music hall ... A shabby man from Paddington, St. Marylebone or Battersea might pass muster as one of the respectable poor. But the same man coming from Bethnal Green, Shadwell or Wapping was an "East Ender", the box of Keating's bug powder must be reached for, and the spoons locked up. In the long run this cruel stigma came to do good. It was a final incentive to the poorest to get out of the East End at all costs, and it became a concentrated reminder to the public conscience that nothing to be found in the East End should be tolerated in a Christian country.[1]

How could this dehumanisation of such a vast body come about, as though a whole people had been cast off from the mainstream of civilisation? One major cause was the accident of location, which had brought the area into the front line of the revolution in transport and communications to meet the expanding financial and trading interests of the City and the Port of London:

> One great effect of railway, canals and docks in cutting into human communities [is] a psychological one... East Londoners showed a tendency to become decivilised when their back streets were cut off from main roads by railway embankments. The police found that by experience! Savage communities in which drunken men and women fought daily in the streets were far harder to clear up, if walls or water surrounded the area on three sides, leaving only one entrance.[2]

By 1888 the constituents of Tower Hamlets shared a common socio-economic definition: "a strong continuing tradition of small workshops industrially important in the aggregate, sited in deteriorating slum property, largely dependent on the traditional skilled labour of local families". But to the predominantly middle-class outsider the individual East Ender was a creature beyond the Pale. Professor Julian Huxley, that same year, voiced this sentiment: "I have seen the Polynesian savaging and in his primitive condition, before the missionary or the blackbirder or the beachcomber got at him. With all his savaging, he was not half so savage, so unclean, so irreclaimable, as the tenant of a tenement in an East London slum."

Overall, for the layman, the East End conjured up "a nursery of destitute poverty and thriftless, demoralised pauperism, in a community cast adrift from the salutary presence and leadership of men of wealth and culture, and ...a political threat to the riches and civilisation of London and the Empire".[3] It was the dangers accruing from the latter that prompted the attention of Charles Booth and urged him to choose the area for his first exploratory studies into the conditions of the labouring poor. He gauged the fears of his class, while he sought the methodology to effect accurate social reporting. Ostensibly to refute what he regarded as "exaggerated statements as to the situation of the poor", he selected this particular "piece of London [which] is supposed to contain the most destitute population in England...

the focus of the problem of poverty in the midst of wealth". But the clue, it could be argued, lay elsewhere.

1886 had been a terrible year for labour: everywhere reductions of wages, everywhere increases in the unemployed, and 1886/7 a cold, hard, winter.[4] Hunger, not Socialism, brought the London workless on the march to Trafalgar Square, the traditional centre of protest. On 8 February 1886 a Social Democratic Federation (SDF) demonstration headed by H.M. Hyndman and H.H. Champion moved on to Hyde Park when, provoked by the jeers of gentlemen onlookers at the Carlton, a breakaway group went on the rampage, smashing windows and looting shops well-stocked with food and luxuries — an additional goad to starving men and women. In the minds of the respectable, suspicion turned to fear of a social upheaval before these outbreaks of violence, and "the rush to contribute to successive Mansion House Funds owed its inspiration to panic rather than pity". The Lord Mayor's Show that year (21 November), "a mockery, a wanton display of misapplied wealth, in the face of direst poverty", according to the radical *Reynolds News* on the preceding Sunday, provoked a simultaneous demonstration organised by the SDF at Trafalgar Square, which drew a crowd of over 7,000. A follow-up leading article (28 November) in the same journal was ominously entitled "The Coming Social Revolution!"

Against this background, in May 1887, submitting his first findings on Tower Hamlets labour,[5] Booth concluded that, though an unexpectedly high proportion of the total population, 35 per cent, had been found living, at all times, more or less in want: "This is a serious state of things, but not visibly fraught with imminent social danger, or leading straight to revolution!" Short-term comfort indeed for the established classes, who, only six months later (13 November), in experiencing the affair of Bloody Sunday,[6] were fearfully anticipating exactly that. More so, as the funeral procession of its only martyr, Alfred Linnell, on 18 December was the greatest seen in London since the funeral of the Duke of Wellington in 1852. A parade one-and-a-half miles long, comprising 120,000 people, marched from Great Windmill Street, via Kings Street, Covent Garden and the Strand, and ended up, significantly, at the East End Bow Cemetery. Sinister were the overtones of the eulogy at the graveside, the "Death Song" by William Morris, delivered by thousands of voices:

> Here lies the sign that we shall break our prison
>
> Not one, not one nor thousands must they slay
> But one and all if they would dusk the day.

Yet Booth was, instinctively, correct. Atomised Labour was as threatening as a paper tiger. Morris, lamenting "There was to me something awful... in such a tremendous mass of people, unorganised, unhelped, and so harmless and good tempered", acknowledged this. By the new year (1888) it was quite safe for Booth to proceed further with his investigations in the East End.

His first "summary of evidence" was acquired with the help of 34 School Board visitors, chosen to gather source material since they had been "working in the same district for several years and thus having extensive knowledge of the people". The principal object of the district inquiry was to show the conditions under which the people lived, but also to give their employment and thus build up the dual picture of family and overall community life-styles. The result, even at the purported "cold scientific level", was more dramatic than he anticipated. In his terms, part of the object of the exercise was to refute the "ill-founded and exaggerated claims" of the SDF publication in 1885 declaring that as much as 25 per cent of the population was living in extreme poverty, a view currently backed up by sensational slum-to-slum revelations in the *Pall Mall Gazette*. Booth had concluded "judging by his own experience [that] the mass of people who lived in what were dubbed "the slums" were by no means all wretched and unhappy".[7] The application of the stern scientific method brought a rude awakening. The Jeremiahs and the sensationalists would prove much nearer the mark than Booth's arrogant presumptions. For the results of his own quantitative appraisals bore this out. From a total population of 456,877, according to his team's findings,

> 65% lived above the poverty line.
> 22% lived on the poverty line.
> 13% were chronically distressed "for whom decent life is not imaginable",
> i.e. those who daily faced starvation.[8]

Thus over one third (35 per cent) of the people of Tower Hamlets were constantly living on or below the margin of subsistence. It was this proportion that would appear to evidence the qualifying image of the East End as an "Empire of Hunger": an impressive figure of want. Booth, by categorising in terms of human units for his measure of mass poverty, produces — almost, but not quite — a chronicle of dry bones. The crowd is there, etched out in some detail, but where is the face in the crowd? Where the flesh, blood and soul of individual human beings that must be exposed in order to present the totality of poverty and degradation? It is certainly not conveyed by the calculations of a "dessicated adding machine". They are arguably useful to reinforce qualifying realities, as footnotes, quantifying the extent of suffering.[9] It is to the impressionistic accounts on the spot of the philanthropists, priests, radicals, journalists, novelists and the like — middle-class interlopers — who came in to labour earnestly in the vineyards, that we must turn. William Morris, no stranger to the East End, wrote at the end of 1888:

> I should like the impressions of London given by one who had been under its sharp-toothed harrow. From him I should like a true tale of the City of Dreadful Night.[10]

There were many that year who had been, and their tales confirm Morris's lurid title. Booth's objective, to show "the conditions under which the people live", particularly the labouring poor, would be more convincingly revealed by the articulate, who chose to dwell among them. For conditions of places, people and life-styles, faithfully recorded, we walk with the explorers who "lived in".

Margaret Harkness — socialist, feminist and novelist[11] — was one of these. The East End in 1888 is brought to life in a series of brilliant vignettes portrayed in her early novels (written, significantly, under the male pseudonym John Law): *Out of Work* (1888) and *In Darkest London: Captain Lobo, Salvation Army* (published in 1889). Snapshots of the social milieu of Whitechapel ("the East End in the East End", according to contemporary observer J.H. Mackay) are presented to us in stark outline:

> [Captain Lobo] turned into the familiar Whitechapel Road, and walked on past the flaming gaslights of the costermongers, the public houses and the street hawkers. An old woman offered him pig's feet; a newspaper man shouted the last ghastly details of a

> murder, tipsy men and women rolled past him singing East End songs set to Salvation music. He caught sight of the slum lassies in a public house, and listened at the door while one of them argued with an infidel...
> Turning away he stumbled over two half naked children who were waiting for their drunken parents. A woman with a sickly infant on her breast asked him for money to find a night's lodging. A small boy tried to trip him up, and ran to join some gutter children.[12]

Aldgate, city entrance into Whitechapel, is plagued by open slaughter- houses in the main and side streets, with blood and animal innards splattered on the side walks. This was a constant subject for complaint by the Vicar of St. Jude's, the Rev. Samuel Barnett, who voiced his concern for the moral consequences, especially for the children of the poor, of this open peep-show of cruelty to animals. Captain Lobo, i.e. Harkness, evokes the scene but suggests that cruelty is endemic in both rich and poor.

> He... saw a herd of frightened sheep being driven over the sawdust into the slaughter house. Their bleating was piteous! At their feet ran a dog barking. Men in blue coats drove them along with sticks, callous of their terror and distress. Many people in the East End enjoy these sights. Some will climb up walls to see a bullock stunned with a pike, or a calf s throat cut. There is in every one of us a deeply seated love of cruelty for its own sake, although the refined only show it by stinging words and cutting remarks. So let no one think the scum worse than the rest. The scum is brutal, the refined [are] vicious.[13]

A bird's eye view of the topography of the streets, variable according to place and architecture, revealed a superficial unity. Mile End Old Town and select parts of Bow proved the obvious exception: the most respectable, "nothing to be called poverty here" according to Booth's notes, since they contained the maximum concentration of shop assistants, clerks, sub-officials, and petty entrepreneurs, dwelling in neat, clean, recently built two- or three-storied houses, located in quasi-fashionable "Squares" or "Greens". Elsewhere, in between the major thoroughfares of East London from west to east,[14] was a network of narrow streets, courts and alleyways, with offshoots often ending in rookeries: a maze of rabbit warrens, mainly topsy-turvy, one-storeyed, leprous, grey-bricked hovels, interspersed here and there with gaunt red battlements, which, in a few years, would be converted into foetid *Bastilles*. That year, Beatrice Potter, research assistant to Booth, would be appalled at "the Industrial Revolution [that] had thrust hundreds of thousands of families into the physical horrors and moral debasement of chronic destitution in crowded tenements in the midst of mean streets",[15] an understandable reaction by a sheltered outsider first exposed to these horrors during her assignments in the streets of Whitechapel and Bethnal Green.

Other observers proffered sharper etchings to emphasise the sordid. Between Shoreditch High Street and Brick Lane lay the infamous Jago, recorded for posterity by the chronicles of its famous priest, the Rev. A. Osborne Jay. He had chosen, voluntarily, to minister to "this Shoreditch parish of 8,000 people, with a death rate four times that of the rest of London, with 17 public houses and no church of any kind at all, a parish with a record of criminality which none could surpass or even equal, a parish which was described in the newspaper, as 'the sink of London'... worse than barbarian".[16] The Old Nichol mob, "sunken and degraded", were a marginal "tribe" who inhabited old, decayed cottages, "originally built below the street level, and, in some cases, some rooms as disclosed in the *Builder*, as long back as 1860, were mere underground cellars; in others, the houses were so constructed that no light of the sun ever reached portions of the premises, whilst a fruitful source of evil had been the employment of a material called 'billy sweet' in place of mortar, which was incapable of properly drying". By 1888 the Rev. Jay could vie with his more southerly-placed colleague, the Rev. Barnett of St. Jude's in Tower Hamlets proper, for the dubious honour of incumbent of the "worst parish" in the Bishop of London's diocese.

Yet in Spitalfields, even after the demolition, instigated by the Metropolitan Board of Works, of the foulest rookeries in the Flower and Dean Street area, most of the festering slums remained.[17] The surviving alleys and culs-de-sac, though in more advanced stages of decay, would still be as Henrietta Barnett found them:

> None of these courts had roads. In some the houses were three storeys high and hardly six feet apart, the sanitary accommodation being pits in the cellars; in other courts the houses were lower, wooden and dilapidated, a stand pipe at the end providing the only water. Each chamber was the home of a

family who sometimes owned their indescribable furniture, but in most cases the rooms were let out furnished for 8d a night. In many instances broken windows had been repaired with paper and rags, the banisters had been used for firewood, and the paper hung from the walls which were the residence of countless vermin...[18]

Such unpalatable descriptions of habitations for the labouring poor would be repeated *ad nauseam*, from Aldgate Alley to Burdett Road, from the Jago to Ratcliffe Highway and beyond to the "islands" of Wapping and the Isle of Dogs.

By 1888 the problems of poverty and housing were interdependent. Housing was a disaster area in the East End experience. Joseph Loane, Medical Officer of Health for the Whitechapel District, in his annual report on sanitary conditions in 1889 which embraced data relevant to the preceding year, stated the case bluntly, but with rare commonsense. He was no sentimentalist. Rehousing the poor was:

> the most difficult social problem of the day. Philanthropists are often devoted individually to schemes for "improving the welfare of the poor", and each person has pet schemes to suit some particular class... The matter of house accommodation? Let me state the case. A large area is cleared of wretched hovels to make way for the large piles of cleanly-looking buildings. What has become of the people who were dislodged? Are they re-housed in the new Model Dwellings? Certainly not. In the first place the rents demanded are above their means and in the second place, the caretakers overlook them in their careful plan of selection. It follows that they must drift into other rooms in houses, perhaps already sufficiently occupied. It is thus clear that the very class of persons requiring most urgently some better accommodation is the class for which the large building trusts have not provided... It is useless to expect that the rents which this class could afford would pay for lands and buildings, and then enable a four per cent dividend to be declared ...[19]

Was this a fair or over-simple summary of the difficulties past and present?

On 30 April 1875 the Artisans and Labourers Dwelling Act (the Cross Act) was passed "to allow and to encourage slow clearance on a larger scale, the purchase and demolition by the local authority of large areas of 'unfit' property". The urgency of these reforms had been prompted by a petition, drawn up by

Barnett for the Whitechapel Guardians, and presented to Parliament. It revealed that the death rate, in certain portions of Whitechapel, was 40 in 1,000 and that 80 per cent of the paupers came from condemned homes. Dilapidated, insanitary houses bred disease which, as the cholera epidemics demonstrated, showed little respect for class boundaries. Bad housing constituted a threat to society. The need for demolition and rebuilding, to rehouse the itinerant poor, was paramount.

Whitechapel was, accordingly, the first area earmarked for improve- ment. On sound *laisser-faire* principles and the economic precept of profitability, Parliament would not readily support local or central government responsibility for re-housing and, therefore, opposed public-sector subsidies. Local authorities could use public money by raising rates or borrowing, but in no circumstances must this entail loss to ratepayers. "It was still imagined that the local authority could purchase slums, lay out land, and build houses for the poor, without loss!"[20] Private investment was the answer. The profit motive would overcome. Building speculators would provide the will, the money, the skills, given the right incentive. Quite so. But not in building for the poor.

For, by 1888, there was no rapid improvement in housing. There was a noticeable time lag between demolition and rebuilding. The causes were diverse, although the common thread running through all was the greed of property owners. There were inbuilt disincentives, such as the apathy of local councils, the fear of offending the ratepayers and vested interests. Land was sold; old dwellings were torn down, but not readily replaced by the less lucrative houses for the poor. (Vast plots remained vacant for nine years in the parish of St. Jude's, except for the erection of two new pubs — much to the chagrin of the vicar!) Instead schools, commercial structures and warehouses, especially in Whitechapel and Stepney, rose up to cut the skyline. The Metropolitan Board of Works refused to sell some demolished sites in Spitalfields, on the premise that more profit would be attained from the building of warehouses rather than homes.[21] Under the terms of the Act slum landlords saw the possibilities of making easy money. When the surveyors came to assess compensation, they overpacked their premises with lodgers to claim the maximum for lost rents. To add to the misery of tenants of property awaiting demolition, landlords were unwilling to spend on improvements, or even on basic repairs.

The inevitable evictions and displacements were soon manifest. But local officials were also hesitant to order slum clearance, which increased homelessness. The delay was particularly noticeable during the current recession, the consequences of which bore heaviest on the East End. The volume of the displaced was reaching a peak, while demographic pressure increased because workers needed to live near their place of employment. Thus, just as the local poor were violently opposed to demolition, which robbed them of their homes whatever their condition, the authorities feared the threats to society posed by a growing army of the homeless and dispossessed. William Booth, with his usual perception observed:

> There is a depth below that of the dweller in the slums. It is that of the dweller in the street, who has not even a lair in the slums which he can call his own.
> The existence of these unfortunates was somewhat rudely forced upon the attention of society in 1887, when Trafalgar Square became the camping ground of the Homeless Outcasts of London.[22]

The Nineteenth Century underlines the message, repeating medical officers' reports that owing to demolitions to make way for railways "the spectacle has been seen in the East End of London of a number of families wandering about since Saturday night with their scanty worldly goods on their backs, without any resting place but the workhouse."[23] Later that year Mr Karanelli, member of the Whitechapel District Board of Works, voiced the alarm of his colleagues at the change in Whitechapel during the last few years resulting from the influx of homeless outsiders. "Whitechapel [is] now the resort of the residuum of the whole country and the refuse of the Continent."[24]

The previous year had witnessed the culminating point of the troubles, in which an apparently militant unemployed was mobilising for an attack on the social order. "Everybody above the levels of the poorest felt threatened by the existence of this unsafe sort of people. Opinions about how to meet the threat differed widely, but as the strength of the working-class vote began to be assessed, the need to gentle this unsafe people into docility by improving their condition began to seem urgent." The construction of high-rise buildings in areas of need could serve a dual purpose, namely to accommodate the homeless in a confined space, thereby making it easier for the authorities to discipline and control them. The Peabody Trust Buildings had proved the model, but there were glaring deficiencies. The high price of 5s 6d for a two-roomed tenancy proved too expensive for the ordinary worker, while the lower-paid were repelled by the high rent, the lack of single rooms for the unmarried, and rules against sub-letting.[26] The Rev. Barnett, ensconced in an area in which recent demolitions had left large vacant plots ready for development, took up the challenge.

In 1883, frustrated by the local delay in implementing the terms of the Cross Act, Barnett called together at his vicarage a group of four public-spirited investors led by a Mr and Mrs Murray. The result was the formation of the East London Dwellings Company "to be launched with preliminary promises of £36,000" in order to buy, rehabilitate or rebuild on slum properties. Barnett's concern was to bring shelter to the poorest of the poor on the principle of humane consideration for the individual against the fashionable authoritarian regimentation inherent in the tenement blocks, structured as lodging "boxes" for the working class by entrepreneurs mainly concerned in cheap construction and high rents. But, in accordance with sound business principles, this was no exercise in philanthropy. Dividends would be paid at 4 per cent. By 1886, the Company's rebuilding in Spitalfields had advanced to such an extent that a jubilant Barnett could report that "The rebuilding of the poor has been going on apace, replacing the net of squalid courts and filthy passages... Brunswick Buildings in Goulston Street and Wentworth Buildings in Wentworth Street are inhabited." His example stimulated a spate of local construction, including that initiated by Rothschild, who sponsored the erection of the Charlotte de Rothschild Dwellings (opened 2 April 1887), and later the Nathaniel Block, thereby ousting the labyrinthine warrens with their troglodyte inhabitants in Thrawl and Flower and Dean Streets. In 1888 a healthy inroad had been made on the slums, but over the whole of Tower Hamlets the urban blight remained almost intact.

What did this mean in human terms? Perhaps the realities of life of the "submerged" inhabitants of Tower Hamlets (Charles Booth's 35 per cent, i.e. almost 160,000 living on the margin) are better conveyed by middle-class observers. In spite of their overtones of "do-gooding" and occasional lack of compassion, it is they who best recall for us the living portraits of the poor.

The poor were not a homogeneous class, At the bottom of the pile was the "loafer", the street scavenger, whom Charles Booth purported to define: "He lives without labour and is the major recruit to the criminal or semi-criminal classes." His life was brutal and, more often, short. His face is brought to life by Harkness:

> Among the foreigner lounges the East End loafer, monarch of all he surveys, lord of the premises. It is amusing to see his British air of superiority. His hands are deep down in the pockets of his fustian trousers, round his neck is a bit of coloured rag or flannel, on his head is a battered cap. He is looked upon as scum by his own nation, but he feels himself to be an Englishman and able to kick the foreigner back to "his own dear native land" if only Government would believe in "England for the English" and give all foreigners "notice".[28]

Beatrice Webb found these men "low looking, bestial, content with their own condition",[29] and Booth tried to elaborate the picture by isolating the way of life peculiar to them — which raises difficulties since differences between their life-style and that of the next "class" up — the casuals — were often marginal. His description, however, is convincing. It was not easy to estimate how they lived (beggary, burglary, pickpocketing, prostitution?). On the other hand:

> What is got is frequently shared; when they cannot find 3d for their night's lodging, they are turned out at night into the streets, to return to the common kitchen in the morning. These are the battered figures who slouch through the streets, and play the beggar or the bully, or help to foul the record of the unemployed; these are the worst class of corner men who hang round the doors of public houses, the young men who spring forward on any chance to earn a copper, the ready materials for disorder when occasion serves. They render no useful service and create no wealth; they oftener destroy it. They degrade whatever they touch ...

Those designated unemployable, especially the young street predators, provided a regular supply of recruits. The girls "take almost naturally to the streets; some drift back from the pauper and industrial schools, and others drift down from the classes of casual and irregular labour... a number of discharged soldiers are... found in these sections".[30]

One step up the ladder, the "casuals" were the day-to-day labourers, mainly in the docks and markets. In his first report (1887) Charles Booth estimated 9,842 adult men (7.7 per cent of the total) in this category. Though few in number at that time, they would act as a "distress meter", as more unemployed flowed in from outside. The docks were the magnet for those desperately seeking work; and the docker, symbolic figure of Labour in the local tradition, was the major victim of the casual system.

Early in 1888, the *East London Observer*, in a leading article "East End Docks in Difficulties", confirmed that this had been so for some years, but now:

> East and West India Docks are unable to find sufficient to pay even the interest on debenture stock, and the London and St. Katharine's Company can, by close work, only manage to pay a dividend at the rate of 1 per cent per annum. With a capital of about £6 million in all, the East and West India Dock Company shows a balance of income over expenditure for the past year of not more than £29,534 and taking the general position of the Company, it is worse off by some £200,000 than in the preceding year. The cause of this is the Tilbury Docks (opened by the East and West India Dock Company in a rail war of rates against London and St. Katharine's in order to intercept the trade for the Port of London). The reason — the dock is too far from the City — "the mart of the trade" and though railways may do the work of transporting ever so smartly, there is a sense of distance which cannot readily be overcome.[31]

The difficulties confronting employees in a shrinking industry were to have a harsher impact on those armies of labour daily mobilising at the dock gates. Beatrice Webb's own reaction to the casuals seeking work was, initially, cold and uncompassionate. She noted in her diary:

> A look of utter indifference on their faces; among them the one or two who have fallen from better things — their abject misery. The mass of the rejected lounge down to another dock or spread themselves over the entrance to the various wharves. About 100 of the lowest will congregate in the "cage" in Nightingale Lane

waiting for the chance of a foreman needing them as odd men. If
a man weary of ennui and an empty stomach drops off to sleep,
his companions search his pocket for the haphazard penny.

Moreover she accepted the opinionated observations of
Kerrigan, School Board Visitor for the Stepney Division,
verbatim:

> The worst scoundrel is the cockney-born Irishman. The woman
> is the Chinaman of the place: drudges as the women of savage
> races; she slaves all day and night. Describes the communism of
> this class. They do not migrate out of the district, but they are
> constantly changing their lodgings "they are like the circle of the
> suicides in Dante's Inferno: they go round and round within a
> certain area". They work for each other, hence the low ideal of
> work. They never leave the neighbourhood. From the dock gates
> they lounge back to the streets "treating" and being "treated",
> according to if they have earned a few pounds. Live chiefly on
> "tobacco" which is a compound of sugar, vinegar, brown paper
> and German nicotine. The teapot is constantly going — bread
> and a supply of dried haddock which goes through a domestic
> preparation: dried in the chimney and acquiring a delicate
> flavour by laying between the mattresses of the beds. They never
> read. Except Catholics, they never go to church. On the Bank
> Holiday the whole family goes to Victoria Park.[32]

Of course there were class divisions between the dock workers
themselves, mainly between those regularly and those
temporarily employed. The former would include administrative
and gate staff; and a minority of socially-conscious stevedores.
Beatrice Webb gives them their due: "Permanent men might be
classed just above the artisan and skilled mechanics. They read
Herbert Spencer and Huxley, and are speculative in religious
and political views" (*MS Diary*, May 1887). This accords with
Harkness's description of a free-thinking bookish dock labourer
in the Albert and Victoria Docks.[33]

Between the casuals and the regulars were the irregulars
working — from one to two days, to a full week's employment.
They were the toughest in build, always first in line to be taken
on. "A man will very quickly earn 15s or 20s but at the cost of
great exhaustion, and many of them eat largely and drink freely
till the money is gone, taking very little of it home" (C. Booth).
There was little evidence of dovetailing of employment. They
took things as they came. Booth complained of their

improvidence, of the mounting of debts in winter, of buying on "tick" and repayment in summer. Yet there are many cases of savings, in the form of weekly subscriptions from ¼d to 2d a head for, say, death clubs (to be buried correctly by meeting the cost of a grand cortege on the day and thus avoiding the final horror — the ignominy of a pauper's grave), goose clubs or benefit societies. Collections were generally held in the local pubs, where, Booth noted laconically, "the encouragement to thrift is doubtful!"

The stern appraisals of Charles Booth and his entourage are modified by other contemporary observers, who transformed his dry figures (9,842 adult male casuals and 3,934 irregulars) into living, pulsating individuals subjected to a society acting on the sacrosanct principles of economic efficiency, the cash nexus, and *laisser-faire*. More sympathetic reporting by William Booth (the founder of the Salvation Army) and others, evokes the social afflictions suffered by the casuals. An ex-artilleryman returns to his "native town", London, from the north to seek work:

> He has had no regular employment for the past eight months. His wife and family are in a state of destitution, and he remarked "We had only 1lb of bread between us yesterday". He is six weeks in arrears of rent and is afraid that he will be ejected. The furniture which is in his home is not worth 3s and the clothes of each member of his family are in a tattered state and hardly fit for the rag bag. He assured us he had tried everywhere to get employment and would be willing to take anything.[34]

He joins the hundreds on early vigil by the riverside. Awaiting the "call-on" for a day's work has brought in an army of the desperate. The dehumanising effects of the struggle for work are recalled in sober fashion by John Law:

> The London dock gates [were] thrown open early "to the mob" who go there to "pick up a living" ...the crowd talking until the bell commenced ringing. Then a dash was made by the ragged crew for the entrance. Some of the contractors had taken possession of the little wooden pulpits, others had ensconced themselves behind iron railings. (Footnote: These iron railings have now been replaced by wooden bars, because some of the men were, according to the words of the labour master "nearly cut in two" in their attempts to get tickets.) The marks of a dock-labourer's fist embellished the countenance of one contractor, and he seemed to have a wholesome dread of brickbats, for he

threw anxious glances at the hands of the men while he distributed his tickets; another looked down on the herd that swarmed about his pulpit and listened to the angry growling of the men with apparent indifference; a third took on his "preference" men and let the rest scramble for his remaining tickets... Then those men who were "not wanted" went sulkily away... their struggles... often sharp and fierce before they tried to drown their misery in gin-shops.

With economy of language, but with no lessening of effect, William Booth describes the hell at the dock gates, where the "terrible scene of men, six hundred of them, waiting the chance of a job, but less than twenty of these get engaged... No sooner is the foreman seen, than there is a wild rush to the spot and a sharp mad fight to "catch his eye".[36] But the sheer brutality of men fighting to survive daily was vividly exposed by Ben Tillett, who had personally suffered the obscenities of the cage. As the "caller-on" walked up to select the daily work gang, men flung themselves at the bar of the cage, struggling to get to the front so as to catch the eye of their tormentor, who strutted up and down casually noting and selecting the most ravenous that is, the potentially cheapest candidates for the labour ticket. Tillett then recalls:

> Coats, flesh and even ears were torn off. The strong literally threw themselves over the heads of their fellows and battled... through the kicking, punching, cursing crowds to the rails of the "cage" which held them like rats — mad human rats who saw food in the ticket. [37]

Degradation begat degradation. Tillett remembers how certain contractors retained hired thugs who "hounded and whipped the men... Young men were put to run old and weaker men down, either carrying loads or running trucks. Dreadful furies were let loose on the docks. I have often heard the... curse... 'Kill the old sod!'."[38]

All this — for what? The answer given by R.P., a regular docker, to a Salvationist investigator, is revealing: "We get 5d an hour... I would earn 30s a week sometimes, and then perhaps nothing for a fortnight. That's what makes it so hard. You get nothing to eat for a week scarcely, and then, when you get taken on, you are so weak that you can't do it properly." This accords with a report on "Dockers Wage" in the *Commonweal*[39] showing the rapid decline in earnings. In a statement to the Select Committee of the House of Lords on Sweating, the Secretary to the Dock Labourers' Union emphasised that there were currently "more dock labourers than there was work for. Sixteen years ago they could earn on average 24s or 25s a week, now they can only average 7s." Reality for most was two hours' work a day at 5d an hour. With those on a full day's stretch, Tillett shared memories of weak, exhausted men collapsing at the pay box or others dying on their own doorstep still clutching their miserable pieces of blood money. Early in 1888 there is an account in the *East London Observer* of a dock worker found dying at the kerb side:

> 11th January: Inquiry in London Hospital under coroner, Eastern Division of Middlesex, Mr. Wynne E. Baxter, on death of James Butler, aged 43, labourer, lately living in a lodging house in Thrawl Street, Spitalfields. Brother tells how at one time deceased was a very strong man, but lately he had become weak. He was a London Dock Labourer. William Jones, a carman, deposed that at 7 o'clock on the morning of Saturday, 31st December, he was going along the Cannon Street Road when he noticed deceased sitting on the pavement, apparently very ill. Witness, with assistance, removed deceased on a barrow to the London Hospital, where it was found deceased was dead... Verdict — Heart Failure![40]

Extra occupational hazards were inherent in dock work. By the end of the year the *Lancet* "discovered that in the course of five years' work, more than half the dock labourers got wounded or otherwise seriously injured".[41] There were many cases, including fatalities. On 9 January a fog "of almost phenomenal density" fell on London for nearly a week, such that "navigation on the river was almost suspended".[42] *The East End News* in a strong article deploring the high numbers of dockers drowned during that fog, "with no ark of safety in the shape of a stationary floating buoy to which they might cling", was moved to point out:

> Had the men drowned lately belonged to a better class of society, the clamour at their death would have changed the insouciance of the dock authorities into active measures for the prevention of a similar recurrence but
>
> > "Rattle his bones over the stones;
> > He's only a docky whom nobody owns."

> Each winter brings in its train a record of the loss of both men and boys, i.e. telegraphic and other messenger boys who *nolens volens* must, no matter how thick the gloom or dangerous the footways, proceed with their despatches through a perfect labyrinth of death traps without a single aid to proper guidance, or chance of rescue in case of stumbling — victims are not confined to casual workers — but are to be found even amongst old dock hands who notwithstanding a lengthy knowledge of the localities and their most dangerous parts frequently fail to reach the gates alive...

A person falls in and cries for help, but

> help is impossible to render owing to hearer's inability to find the spot where he had fallen. A simple life line attached to the quay wall could have saved his life, as it would have saved many another in the past.[43]

Poplar Hospital, receptacle for injured dockmen for generations, was very familiar with the dangers. On board even the cautious and toughest would make a false step on the narrow plankings, slip and be crushed under their own load; while the half-starved casual, a prisoner of his physical weakness, was naturally more accident prone. In the last issue of the old year's *East London Advertiser* we are told of the following:

> Samuel Henry Cootes of 29 Elthorpe Street, Poplar, died of injuries received by falling down the hold of the S.S. Selembia on September 30th 1887. Dr. Bonehill deposed that the deceased was admitted to Poplar Hospital suffering from a broken backbone. He was a very powerful man, with a good constitution, or he could not have lived for such a length of time as he did with such an injury as he sustained.
> Verdict accidental death![44]

A sombre note with which to start the New Year. It would be the first of many reported in 1888. Towards the end of the year, the radical *Commonweal* communicated the plea from the Secretary of the Tea Operatives and General Labourers Association to the press from 19 Huntslett Street, Bonner Lane in Bethnal Green:

> Will you kindly assist us in the matter of calling the attention of the dock and riverside labourers that the Lord Commission is inquiring into the grievances under sub-contract? Any one who

has any information to give that would explain the evil need not fear publicity...[45]

Apparently the *Lancet* did not. For it was moved to protest loud and clear:

> Competition, the desire for cheapness, the struggle for profits, seem to have wrought their worst in the docks. Here men have been known to work for 2½d an hour. Here men faint from over-exhaustion and want of food. Here lives are needlessly squandered; men are ruptured, their spines injured, their bones broken, and their skulls fractured, so as to get ships loaded and unloaded a little quicker and a little cheaper. In other departments of enterprise the commercial greed of this century has produced the same callous indifference for human life, but the State, sooner or later, has interfered to protect the weak and helpless.

The *Lancet* was never prone to exaggeration, but, in 1888, its criticism was to no avail. The following year would register a movement from below, as the wretched ones were finally roused to act in unison against the worst evils. The great Dock Strike of 1889 would be the first round in the long, hard struggle for civilised conditions in the docks.

Other ephemeral folk who drifted in and out of the East End streets, from the "Pump" to Bow Bridge, from the Red Church to Wapping High Stairs, were the petty dealers — street traders or costers (constituting 1,354 heads of families, according to Charles Booth, but this, for obvious reasons, is scarcely an accurate figure!). One could catch sight of a motley crew of street performers anywhere along the main thoroughfares. "You have seen me swallow fire. You have seen me swallow coal. Now you will see me swallow sawdust," came the hoarse cry of the toothless sword-swallower, inheritor of a family skill, entertaining vast crowds on the Waste or Poplar High Street well into the 1920s. Then there were the organ grinder and his monkey, kerb acrobats or professional beggars "flogging" penny notions from a bag in the street; newspaper and song-sheet hawkers. Among the general dealers could be seen the antique book buyer for "translating", the old clothes man (shabby Irish or Jewish), and the old iron collector, whose day-to-day existence was dependent on the limited demands of the very poor. They were the "marginal" men, difficult to quantify, since they were wanderers, many of no fixed abode, recruited from unemployed musicians, costermongers without capital, street glaziers, wood sellers and the like. They lived from hand to mouth, sometimes scarcely distinguishable from the "loafers" or unemployed countrymen come to town as "casuals" seeking heavy portering in the markets or a "pick-up" at the dock side. For these, operating in a Hobbesian world, the over-riding imperative was the problem of daily survival.

For both "submerged" and labouring poor, displaced by recent demolitions,[47] there was the other necessity for survival — shelter. This meant pressure on scarcer accommodation before there was rebuilding to fill the vacuum. Overcrowding increased in areas nearest to the unsettled. As we have seen, the aftermath of the 1875 Act had led, locally, to "the people cleared from the destroyed slums [being] sifted away into the interstices of the remaining slum".[48] The slum was, therefore, self-perpetuating. Mainly petty speculators, with a little spare capital or saving to invest, caught on to the profitability accruing from the need to house the poor. Charles Booth noted the proliferation of the building of workshops in garden spaces, which "obstruct light and shut out air", and that these extensions eventually tied houses back to back. A mass of evidence was accumulated by the reforming architect, Robert Williams, confirming that "the poor being good rent payers" attracted a host of predators. Easy money could be made in buying up small vacant plots which were overlooked by the large-scale developer:

> Men get hold of a piece of land — working men are like others in this matter and forthwith they "develop" it, make it "ripe for building", as the phrases of these men go — they slice their bit of land into the narrowest strips, and cram as many dens upon them as they dare.[50]

The slums were being extended by greedy entrepreneurs "building up crops of cottages in back gardens which could produce a surer and larger income than a bed of cabbages or a bank of beautiful flowers". Thus any open land was crammed with rows of small dwellings, the old rookeries supplanted by new and worse ones with greater concentration of families exposed to less light and air. Booth described Tongue's Alley in Fieldgate Street, off the Whitechapel Road, where nearly all the gardens were covered with workshops, warehouses and buildings approached by a single "small tunnel of an entrance 31¾ inches wide. Yet the poor people pay large rents — some 5s a week — and they contain but two rooms, 'One up and one down.'"[51] Nearby, a court slum dwelling houses...

> a tailor's sweatshop and wife and children in a three roomed house, where all eat, sleep and work (8s per week rent)... like demoniacs under some terrible strain they labour incessantly, for, more regular than the sun (in that court) comes the agent for the rent every Monday morning, and mark you, he is a wily man. He enters the amount in the tenant's rent book, which contains neither name nor address, for which piece of cunning he has, doubtless, a deep reason. Perhaps he does not care to have his whereabouts blazoned forth in a tenant's rent book, lest an over zealous sanitary inspector may see and make a note thereof. Fifty pounds sterling is about all this slum house cost, and the tenant pays £20 16s a year for it.[52]

Exorbitant rent was the rule and was accepted as such. H.W. Lawson, President of the Leasehold Enfranchisement Association, in a lecture given at the Bow and Bromley Reform Club, condemned the evils inherent in a process within the law, where "a species of land crab ate up the foundations of the people's houses" and where "the system of building upon leasehold land led directly to overcrowding, overbuilding and excessive rents and... directly to want of interest on the part of the occupier in the house he inhabited". Concurrently Charles Booth was recording conditions in the chronically deteriorated habitations in the "evil quarter mile" of Spitalfields, and confirmed Lawson's allegation. In the infamous, festering Dorset Street dilapidated "three storey houses are let out in single rooms. Front rooms 5s. Single back rooms 3s and 4s." Within the Fashion Street complex of enclosed side courts and alleyways, one-storied rickety cottages with stairs in the corner of the living room leading to one bedroom above were priced at 4s a week. These were inhabited by two parents and, sometimes, six children.[54]

How could one expect normal civilised standards to prevail in such holes? Robert Williams rightly contended that "want of room is as conducive to want of cleanliness as want of air and light; but when you get a combination of the three evils... it is downright heartlessness to rail at the slum dwellers — as many do — because they and their abode are dirty. It is like grumbling at a sweep for being black."[55] He quoted Dr Hurley's dictum that "to be supplied with respiratory air in a fair state of purity every man ought to have at least 800 cubic feet of space to himself. This is the minimum space and represents a room 10ft × 10ft × 8ft. But this space generally has an average of 2½ [people] and in the extreme up to 12!"[56] And within the vast black spots of Tower Hamlets the extreme was the norm. The following press reports, just two of many, exemplify the issue: one, naturally, pertaining to Spitalfields, the other to the equally insalubrious parish of St. George's. Of St. George's we read

> Mr Woontow, the Sanitary Officer, reported among other cases of overcrowding, that at 12 Langdale Street, a man with his wife and four children were living in one room, and had taken in a young man lodger. An order was made to remove them.[57]

Of Spitalfields:

> At an inquest held by Dr Macdonald, in Spitalfields, upon the death of a baby four months old, evidence was given that the parents and their seven children lived all together in one room about 12 feet square, for which they paid 4s 6d a week. Dr Hume deposed that the child had been suffocated, most probably by overlying. The jury returned a verdict of accidental death, but added a rider to the effect that the sanitary authorities were most lax in their duties to allow a family of nine to live and sleep in so small a room, and that the overcrowding which prevails in the East End ought to be inquired into and something done to alleviate it.[58]

A worthy plea, but to no avail. At a meeting of the Whitechapel Board of Works on 9 July a strong remonstrance was mounted protesting at the indefinite delay in undertaking demolition and reconstruction in the Bell Lane area — "the worst area in all London".[59] In October the same Committee repeated its attack on the Metropolitan Board of Works for "again refusing to take the initial step towards removing a plague spot from Spitalfields. The matter in question is one of long standing, for as far back as 1877, the Medical Officer of Health reported that... Bell Lane and Pearl Street areas were unfit for human habitation."[60]

Further protests were registered by a member, Mr Barham, at continuing neglect by the central body. "He noticed that the Metropolitan Board has now introduced a Bill in Parliament for widening High Street, Kensington, an improvement that could wait for ten years, while the district of Spitalfields was urgently needing attention."[61] A deputation of concerned dignitaries, including Lord Rothschild, Viscount Cross and the Bishop of Bedford, failed to stir the authority and "ended in a fiasco... Two weeks elapsed in making preparation for the interview and time being 'of the essence of the question' it became too late for the Metropolitan Board to give the necessary legal notices. So the only thing to be done is to await until the County Council [i.e. the new LCC] is in operation. That the Spitalfields area is a scandal to the hub of the civilised world there can be no doubt."[62] It was far more acceptable to legislate for marginal road improvements in the fashionable West End, than for the life and death need for improved working-class housing. Pockets of "vile dens, fever haunted, and stenchful crowded courts" existed right across the borough. Commenting on the investigative report of Home Office Commissioners on the "condition of Bethnal Green", the *East London Observer* noted the incidence among 560 houses of "damp... badly paved yards, defective roofs, broken floors, dirty walls and ceilings, broken plasters, dilapidated window frames, faulty gutters, the absence of water supply in closets, and dilapidated dustbins..."[63] This could be repeated *ad nauseam* in other clusters of geriatric dwellings, festering in Wapping, St. George's, Poplar and the Isle of Dogs.

We may well ask "Where is the 'Home, Sweet Home', of Victorian song and legend?" Certainly not here. Focusing on the slum dwellers, a host of contemporary impressionistic texts present the grim realities. It was in 1888, during her first explorations into this "proletarian" area (falling within her father's definition), that Karl Marx's daughter Eleanor was moved to be actively involved with the East End poor. "From now on the seal was set upon her friendship with working men and women... Eleanor had never known real hunger: debts and duns and short commons, yes, and sometimes 'doing without', but not the ravening need of those clinging to the brink of survival who asked for bread and were given a stone."[64] Here the hard cold statistics of her research findings were transformed into visible human suffering. Thenceforth her sensitivity would lead her, through her own bruised spirit, beyond passionate commitment to a virtual self-identification with the poorest of the poor.

> Sometimes I am inclined to wonder how one *can* go on living with all this suffering around one. One room specially haunts me. Room! — cellar, dark, underworld — in it a woman lying on some sacking and a little straw, her breast half eaten away with cancer. She is naked but for an old red handkerchief over her breast and a bit of old sail over her legs. By her side a baby of three and other children — four of them. The oldest just nine years old. The husband tries to "pick up" a few pence at the docks — the last refuge of the desperate — and the children are howling for bread... that poor woman who in all her agony tries to tend her little one. But that's only one of thousands and thousands.[65]

Kaleidoscopic images are projected by others coming in from outside into the fringes of human survival in a milieu of hunger and decay where myriads of "vermin render night unbearable". Eleanor's companion, Margaret Harkness, responded with more restraint to the horrors confronting both. Inside Aldgate Alley she observed:

> The houses there were not numbered but each door had a hieroglyph upon it, unless it was known by an old boot in the first floor window, or by a coloured rag that waved on a stick above the entrance. The alley was paved with large, uneven flag stones, between which sprouted weeds and grass that had a sickly appearance. On the stones were scores of ragged children. Some scooped up the dirt with oyster shells to make mud pies of it; some lay on their backs, catching the water that dripped into their dirty hands from an old pump. Three small boys sat on the pump handle, regardless of angry voices that issued from the surrounding window, and half-a-dozen girls craned their necks to see a thrush in a cage near the entrance.[66]

Elsewhere, a gloomy cul-de-sac, where strangers dare not enter, is nevertheless a boon to the rapacious landlord:

> The place is lined on either side by dark-looking houses. The postman seldom pays it a visit. If he arrives there boys and girls hail his advent, and the person for whom he has brought a letter is fetched down to meet him. Policemen are little known here. They prefer to keep away when a fight is going on, for the people are rough, and more than once boiling water has been thrown over constables by intoxicated women.
> Eight families live in that place. They rent rooms at 5s, 4s, and 3s a week, unfurnished apartments with broken windows and choking chimneys. The landlord makes quite a nice little fortune, for he can go to bed although his houses are

overcrowded, and he can sleep knowing that his tenants have empty pockets. He sends an agent to collect the rents and salves his conscience by giving a donation to some charity when he hears that so-and-so has been evicted. His wife begs him not to talk about the poor things, because their sorrows are quite too much for their feelings, and she entreats him not to go near the place for fear that he should bring home smallpox![67]

A more trenchant insight into the insalubrious diversities of slum life is conveyed by J.H. Mackay, from his labyrinthine journeying from the Jago into Whitechapel via Brick Lane. He and a companion had penetrated a no-go area where everywhere "the neglect of hunger... daily fights a frightful battle with death"; and caught the tension, bitterness and hatred felt by the "natives" towards the well-breeched outsiders. The couple made their way down the middle of a street, for a venture on to the pavement meant danger:

> Sometimes a window was half-opened, a bushy head thrust out, and shy, curious eyes followed half in fear, half in hate, the wholly unusual sight of the strangers. A man was hammering at a broken cart which obstructed the whole width of the street. He did not respond to the greetings of the passers-by: stupefied, he stared at them as at an apparition from another world; a woman who had been cowering in a dark corner, motionless, rose terrified, pressed her child with both hands against her breast hardly covered with rags, and propped herself, as if to offer resistance against the wall, not once taking her eyes off the two men...[68]

Cruelty and insensitivity infected the young. Mackay was shocked by a group of young children "amusing themselves by the sight of the dying fits of a cat whose eyes they had gouged out, and whom they had hanged by the tail. When the bleeding, tortured animal jerked with his feet to get away, they struck at it with the cruel awful pleasure children take in visible pain." Caught, as though suspended in time, is the following extraordinary tableau of Brick Lane, which in part is still today as it was yesterday:

> It is a long walk down Brick Lane... Enormous warehouses, looming up in the distance, vaulted railroad tunnels of the Great Eastern Railway, broke the monotony of the crowded rows of streets. Odours alternated: decaying fish, onions and fat, pungent vapours of roasted coffee, the foul air of filth, of

decaying matter... Shops with bloody meat, stuck on prongs — "cats meat", at every street corner a "wine and spirits" house; torn posters on the walls, still in loud colours; a crowd of young men passes by — they shout and sing; down the sidestreet a drunken form is feeling its way along the wall, muttering to itself and gesticulating, perhaps overcome by a single glass of whiskey.[69]

Footnotes

[1]*The Nineteenth Century* XXIV(1888) p. 262.
[2]Ibid. p. 260
[3]Gareth Stedman Jones, *Outcast London* (London 1971) pp. 15-16.
[4]Reiterated by Annie Besant in *An Autobiography* (London, 1893) p. 316.
[5]Charles Booth, "The Inhabitants of the Tower Hamlets (School Board Division), their Conditions and Occupations. Time Span Winter 1886 — early 1887", paper read before the Royal Statistical Society, May1887.
[6]Bloody Sunday, 13 November 1887. A planned series of demonstrations and marches organised by the Metropolitan Federation of Radical Clubs to protest against coercion in Ireland, were broken up with much violence by the police before reaching Trafalgar Square (banned for public meetings by the Police Commissioner on 8 November). Eleanor Marx, who was in the thick of the action at Parliament Street, records "I have never seen anything like the brutality of the police; the Germans and Austrians who know what police brutality can be, said the same to me." The Victorian *bourgeoisie* really believed that they were confronted with the most serious danger to public order which has menaced it since the Chartist rising of 1848!
[7]T.S. and M.B. Simey, *Charles Booth: Social Scientist* (Oxford, 1960) pp. 56, 66-9.
[8]Booth defined the poverty line as 21s per week for "a moderate sized family". For analysis in detail see "The Inhabitants of the Tower Hamlets" (cited above, n.5). With this as a yardstick, it is argued that the Whitechapel (Spitalfields) area had a poverty level of about 45 per cent. See Raymond Sibley, "Aspects of social deprivation in Whitechapel in the late 19th century" Loughborough University M.A. thesis, September 1977. The St. George's district had the highest percentage of poverty according to Charles Booth in his following *Life and Labour of the People of London*, vol. 1, *East London*, p. 62. Of 47,000 inhabitants 23,000 were living in poverty by his definition.
[9]It could be argued that statistical evidence is useful to reinforce the qualifying image, but not always convincing if offered as the only evidence.
[10]*Commonweal*, 15 December 1888, Notes and News.

[11] Margaret Harkness was born on 28 February 1854, the daughter of Robert Harkness, curate of Trinity Chapel, Great Malvern. She certainly must have lodged in the East End, from her vivid description of minor streets which were familiar to me as a boy. A biography, the first ever, is at present being undertaken by Irene Snatt.
[12] John Law, *In Darkest London: Captain Lobo, Salvation Army* (London, 1889) p. 239.
[13] Ibid. p. 14.
[14] From north to south: Shoreditch High Street; Bethnal Green Road; Whitechapel Road leading on to Mile End and Bow Roads; Commercial Road, leading to East India Dock Road.
[15] Beatrice Webb (née Potter), *My Apprenticeship* (London, 1926) p. 297.
[16] Rev. A. Osborne Jay, *A Story of Shoreditch* (London, 1896) p. 5. Also later subject of classic social novel *A Child of the Jago* by Arthur Morrison (London, 1896). In 1889 the death rate was as high as 41 per 1,000. (See T.H. Smith in *East London Papers*, vol. 11, no. 1, p. 41).
[17] For a scholarly account of the background to the demolitions see Jerry White, *Rothschild Buildings* (1980) pp. 6-20.
[18] H.O. Barnett, *Canon Barnett: his life, works and friends*, 2 vols. (London 1918), vol. 1, pp. 73-4.
[19] Annual Report on the Sanitary Condition of the Whitechapel District (with vital statistics) for the year 1889, pp. 20-1.
[20] Enid Gauldie, *Cruel Habitations* (London, 1974) pp. 276-7. This view is still noticeably prevalent among Conservative "radical reformers".
[21] Royal Commission for Housing of Working Classes, 1885, qu.5002.
[22] William Booth, *In Darkest England* (London, 1890) p. 25.
[23] *The Nineteenth Century* XXIV (1888) p. 252. See also Enid Gauldie, *Cruel Habitations*, p. 277. The poor rendered homeless by slum clearance were increasing overcrowding by moving into neighbouring streets. "Medical Officers were, therefore, reluctant to recommend closure and demolition."
[24] *East End News*, 5 October 1888. Report on the Board of Works meeting of 1 October.
[25] Enid Gauldie, *Cruel Habitations*, p. 286.
[26] Against the trend of price decreases "the high rents were the product, primarily of the relentless pressure of people upon houses, and the increasing costs of land and house building" (A.S. Wohl, "The Housing of the Working Classes in London, 1815-1914", in *History of Working Class Housing* ed. S.D. Chapman [London, 1971] p. 27).
[27] Booth obtained their number "by adding the estimated number from inmates of common lodging houses and from the lowest class of streets" ("The Inhabitants of the Tower Hamlets", pp. 14-15.)
[28] *In Darkest London*, p. 3.
[29] *My Apprenticeship*, p. 255.
[30] "The Inhabitants of the Tower Hamlets", p. 15.
[31] *East London Observer* (hereafter *ELO*) 28 January 1888, and follow up notice on 4 February 1888.
[32] *My Apprenticeship*, p. 256.

[33] John Law, *Out of Work* (London, 1888) pp. 59-62.
[34] William Booth, *In Darkest England*, p. 38.
[35] *In Darkest London*, pp. 175-9, and a similar description in *Out of Work*, pp. 130-1.
[36] *In Darkest England*, pp. 36-7.
[37] Ben Tillett, *A Brief History of the Dockers Union* (London, 1910) p. 12.
[38] Ben Tillett, *Memoirs and Reflections* (London, 1931) p. 173.
[39] Dated 1 December 1888.
[40] *ELO* 14 January 1888.
[41] *Justice* 22 December 1888, commenting on the recent *Lancet* report in *Tell Tale Straws*. See also *East London Advertiser* (hereafter *ELA*) 15 December 1888, "The Dockers' Bitter Cry — Perils of Dockwork".
[42] See *The Echo*, 9/10 January 1888. For details of accidents, *ELO* 14 January 1888. Details of "The Weather in 1888", in *The Times Register of Events in 1888* (published by Times Office by George Edward Wright, 1889) are also informative.
[43] *East End News* 7 February 1888, "Death Traps or A Cry for the Drowning Dockman".
[44] *ELA* 29 December 1887.
[45] *Commonweal* 15 December 1888.
[46] *ELA* 15 December 1888 on the *Lancet* report
[47] See above, p.9.
[48] Enid Gauldie, *Cruel Habitations*, p. 288.
[49] "The Inhabitants of the Tower Hamlets".
[50] Robert Williams, *London Rookeries and Colliers Slums* (London, 1893).
[51] Ibid., pp. 23-6.
[52] Ibid., pp. 20-1. See also his pamphlet *The Face of the Poor or the Crowding of London's Labourers*, p. 15, where he confirms that the "Royal Commission of 1884 proved that the average rent of weekly tenements was 3s 10¾d per room per week, but calculated at 3s only. These poorest of London's toilers provide the money for a magnificent rent roll of £1,345,515 12.0d! The poor one-room dweller pays double the rent the dweller in the pleasant suburb pays... the poor workers part with a fourth and often a third of their wages in rent."
[53] In a lecture delivered at the Bromley Vestry Hall on "The Housing of the Poor" 8 February 1888, and reported in the *ELO* 11 February 1888.
[54] *Booth Collection*, third series, vol. 7, Group B 343 (Whitechapel) pp. 18-24.
[55] *London Rookeries*, p. 22.
[56] R. Williams, pamphlet: *The Face of the Poor*, p. 16. Many, though not all, of the new tenement authorities paid little heed to this health hazard. Williams informs us that "by 1895, in Whitechapel more than a quarter (25.3%) of deaths in block dwellings were due to diseases of the respiratory system due to crowding, therefore insanitary conditions".
[57] *ELA* 3 November 1888, "The Young Man Lodger".

[58]*ELA* 15 September 1888, "Overcrowding in Spitalfields".
[59]*East End News* 13 July 1888.
[60]*ELA* 27 October 1888, "The Last Sentence in Spitalfields". We are further informed that "The Bell Lane area... found living accommodation for 600 people per acre, or deducting certain open spaces in the district, 800 human souls per acre, while the Pearl Street area holds 500 per acre. This is a fearful state of overcrowding when it is remembered that for the Whitechapel district the population is 176 or for the whole metropolis 50 per acre."
[61]*ELA* 3 November 1888.
[62]*ELA* 1 December 1888.
[63]*ELO* 23 June 1888.
[64]Yvonne Kapp, *Eleanor Marx* (London, 1976) vol. 11, pp. 261-2.
[65]Letter of Eleanor Marx to Laura, 24 June 1888. (International Institute of Social History)
[66]*In Darkest London*, p. 126.
[67]Ibid., p. 61.
[68]J.H. Mackay, *The Anarchists* (Boston 1891) p. 163.
[69]Ibid., p. 170.

Chapter 2
Housing, Health and Sanitation

Even in poverty East Enders could probably claim a permanent roof over their heads. However, by 1888 Tower Hamlets was already an over-congested ghetto of displaced labour with housing at a premium. Sub-letting within sub-letting was rife. As we have seen, this brought to the attention of the authorities innumerable cases of overcrowding — well beyond the statutory limits. Temporary accommodation was vital to meet the influx of the homeless. This was met by another source of easy money for the sharp investor — the lodging houses.

Shaftesbury's Lodging Houses Act urged borough councils to undertake their provision.[1] Funds could be obtained by raising a rate, or by borrowing either from the Public Works Loan Commissioners or through a mortgage on the rates, and used to buy or rent empty land and repair old property for conversion. "Model Lodgings" was the phrase. But "the housing of the kind of people who, in 1851, were living in the dens he [Shaftesbury] wanted to abolish, *could never be profitable*".[2] There was therefore little activity on the part of local councils to remedy the need until the Ripper murders of 1888 forced action upon them. Instead the expansion of lodging houses, or doss houses, was undertaken by middle-class house buyers who themselves lived well outside the area but who employed paid "wardens" or "keepers" on the premises to exercise day-to-day control. These were often unscrupulous ruffians, living on the margin of the law. (Many a clergyman's daughter with a little capital invested in lodging house deals, since returns in the long term were good and regular, but they often had no idea where or how their property was run and most of them never came near it!) It is no wonder that the doss houses added to the disreputable image of East London. In this context the *East London Advertiser*[3] appealed for a minister "worthy of the cloth" to take up the unpopular and long-vacant living of Christ Church, Spitalfields "to redeem the masses from the Slough of Despond in which they are sinking. The parish abounds with common lodging houses and thieves' restaurants."[4]

The most horrific conditions were attributed to those lodging houses catering for the casual poor. At best they were free of criminals, prostitutes and vermin. The majority, located in Spitalfields, St. George's and along the docks, were not. Harkness describes a typical cheap "doss" priced at 4d single for the night. A gloomy, decaying, two-storied house is divided into "dormitories", i.e. "rooms full of small iron bedsteads, covered with a grey blanket. They were arranged in two rooms against the wall, and were so close together that it was almost impossible to move between them." The doss-house keeper explains:

> "We're under Mayhew's Act... The police walk in and out as they like. We've clean sheets once a week and a wash house in the back. They're damn particler, are the police. They come after me and my missus like ferrets."

Downstairs, in the main kitchen, police or no police, gambling went on, while:

> men and women stood there cooking their supper; emptying into tins and saucepans bits of meat, bones, scraps of bread and cold potatoes they had begged, stolen or picked up during the day. Hungry children held plates ready for the savoury messes and received blows and kicks from their parents when they came too near the fire, or interfered with the cooking arrangements.
> Crouching on the floor, gnawing a bone, was a hungry man. His face was sodden with drink. He had swollen features, palsied hands, and trembling feet. He had probably begun life in this Christian country as a homeless boy in the streets and would most like close his day in the casual ward of some workhouse. Then
>
> > Rattle his bones over the stones,
> > He's only a pauper who nobody owns!
>
> The lodgers threw him scraps, and laughed to see him tearing his food to pieces, devouring it like a dog, on the ground.[5]

This probably exemplified a more "respectable" establishment. Others served as a rendezvous for prostitutes and the underground. Dr Barnardo cites the case of a young teenager, Jenny Wren, one of many whose "mother, lost to every sense of shame, pursuing an evil life in the common lodging house... anxious to save her (child) from the black future", voluntarily handed her over to Barnardo's care.[6] Three of the Ripper victims at one time lodged in the same house in Flower and Dean Street. The doss was over the cover for a thieves' kitchen, where only the Salvationist slum lassie could enter without fear and no policeman dare venture alone. Again, Harkness conveys details of a scene with obvious familiarity.[7] Young Salvationist girls, armed with *War Crys*, descend a deep flight of stairs to an underground place at the end of a long passage:

> Half a dozen men sat there by the fire, doing nothing. If they had any dinner, the remains of the feast had been cleared away. Not a plate, nor a crust stood upon the table. Only a black cat licked its paws and purred as it looked at the slum saviours. (However hungry such men may be, they never let the pet of their establishment remain famished.)
>
> They were a savage looking set of men. No policeman ever entered alone into their kitchen. A clergyman found his way in one Sunday evening. He was stripped, in order that the men might see if he was a detective. Finding all his linen marked with the same name, and nothing in his pockets, they kicked him out, advising him never to come there again unless he was plentifully supplied with soup tickets.

Only the slum lassies were allowed to intrude into their closed world:

> There they sat, doing nothing, when the slum saviours opened the door. Bits of pipe, ginger-beer bottles, pots and refuse lay upon the earthen floor. A lamp hung from the ceiling. They were glad to have a *War Cry* to break the monotony of their Sunday afternoon, and they greeted the slum saviours.
>
> They sang a hymn and the thieves joined in the chorus!!

Again the Salvationists were the only privileged outsiders allowed into the hideout of the sham cripples, those "who make up as deaf and dumb, lame, blind and infirm" to solicit handouts. Certain lodging houses were a cover for gambling dens, but here too the girls entered without fear. (It was accepted that there were no "coppers' narks" in the Salvation Army.) Harkness posits a curious dialogue between the Salvationists and a loner watching the game, who responds to their religious overtures with well-versed scepticism:

> "Are you saved, brother?" they asked a man with a white face and bloodless lips, whose clothes hung loosely on his emaciated body.

"If starving will save me, I ought to have been saved long before this," the man answered.

"You must give up your sins: then God will send you food," was the reply.

The man shook his head, and said, "The Bible calls God a father, and no father would starve his son for sinning. He would give him food first and speak about his sin afterwards."

"God is merciful and just," said the slum saviour.

"Let him send me work," the man said. "Then I'll believe in Him."

"Every breath you draw is a gift from God. He has let you live so long. He might have cast you into hell years ago, brother. Give up your sin. Come to Him."

"It's hell to live in a place like this," the man answered, looking round the dark room, and at the face of the lodgers. "Have you any money? Give me food first. I'll attend to salvation afterwards."

"Gold and silver have I none," was the girl's reply; "but what I have, that I give unto you."

"Then my lass, you can carry your preaching somewhere else. Don't come here to talk of salvation to a man like me. I'm hungry."

Mayhem, notably violence, was inherent in life in a lower doss, which also operated as an open working-mart for prostitutes. One of many cases involving both violence and prostitution was reported fully in the *East End News* for 5 October. At Worship Street police court a charge of face-stabbing was made against a Mary M'Carthy by a Mrs Ann Neason. The Prosecutrix was deputy of a Spitalfields lodging house and, during the course of the trial, spoke of a dwelling in George Yard owned by W. Knot, a baker of Brick Lane, who was also proprietor of two other common lodging houses in Wentworth Street. Total vacancies included 28 single beds at 4d and 24 doubles at 8d a night. The magistrate, Mr Williams, was quick to seek clarification on a woman ordering a double bed:

Mr Williams: And the woman can take any man she likes? You don't know if the couples are married or not?
Witness: No, Sir. We don't ask them.
Mr Williams: Precisely what I thought. And the sooner these lodging houses are put down the better. They are the haunts of the burglar, the home of the pickpocket, and the hotbed of prostitution. It's time the owners of these places, who reap large profits from them, were looked after.

Asking whether the accused who hired a double bed was married:

Witness: No, I don't think so.
Mr Williams: Then the place is a brothel!

Later Mr Williams, commenting further:

> "In my humble judgement they are about as unwholesome and unhealthy as well as dangerous to the community as can well be. There are places among them where the police dare not enter, and where the criminal hides all day long..."

Not only the criminal, but that curious déclassé figure, the gentleman "slummer", was a frequent inhabitant. Initially drawn to the East End for his first experience of cheap and easy sex, and to savour the colour and vibrancy of the pub and music hall, he stayed, permanently hooked. For instance, we read of "A Strange Taste" in the *East London Advertiser* — one of many, though they were usually suppressed to prevent a family scandal:

> Reports on death at the London Hospital of one John Boyle, alias Benjamin Ryan, aged 40, said to be a gentleman of considerable means, who was discovered lying in an unconscious condition outside a common lodging house in Brick Lane, Spitalfields on Sunday last and who died in hospital. A witness who knew the deceased said that he lived at various common lodging houses in the neighbourhood of Whitechapel and Aldgate. Some time ago he had a fortune left him. He belonged to a good family, his sisters occupying a large house in Cavendish Square. When he wanted to see his friends, he used to dress up stylish and appear respectable. Death, it was found, was due to alcoholism accelerated by acute pneumonia.[8]

Other high class, even aristocratic, intruders came in for other reasons. Slumming had its charitable side, which could be an exercise in satisfying one's curiosity and conscience in one, as the following might testify:

> On a recent evening, the lodging house known as the "Globe Chambers", situated at No 12, Wellclose Square, was the scene of unusual gaiety on the occasion of the visit of a distinguished company of ladies and gentlemen, brought down to the East of London by the Hon. Lady Beauchamp. The kitchen of the

lodging house was tastefully decorated by the lodgers, the decorations being given by Mr Paris, the proprietor. A substantial tea consisting of bread and butter, meat pies, cake and tea was provided by her Ladyship for the lodgers. The room was decorated with paper chains, the gas pipes tastefully ornamented with pink and white ruffles and the pillar in the middle of the room displayed the Jubilee colours from the floor to the ceiling. Round the room were placed texts, mottos and conspicuous among them were to be seen over the mantelpiece two shields bearing these inscriptions: "A hearty welcome!" and "New Year's Greeting". After grace had been said by her Ladyship, the men were invited to "wire in", which they did, and the good things rapidly disappeared. When the tea was over, and the tables cleared, some singing etc. followed, and the Hon. Miss Beauchamp sang a solo. Her Ladyship then spoke to the men very earnestly, and presented each of them with a Testament before she left.[9]

From which they might derive some spiritual uplift, on top of a good feed and a bed for the night. They were more fortunate than the night people who, penniless and homeless, slept in some passageway or beneath the rail arches along the Great Eastern Railway; that is, unless moved on by the policeman on the beat, The East End was the depository of those "with no fixed abode". The Ripper murders focused the issue, especially for women, and a spate of *ad hoc* night shelters was instituted by philanthropic or voluntary concerns. Since they attracted tramps and the destitute, they were always overcrowded and created a health hazard. A report by Dr Taylor to the Sanitary Committee of the Mile End District illustrated the dangers arising from ill-devised local schemes:

Since the recent calamity in the east of London, several benevolent persons have come forward to provide night shelters for the outcast men and women. One of the shelters is... situated at 59 Mile End Road, a few doors from Cleveland Street. Being given to understand that this shelter is occupied nightly by about 150 people, I considered it my duty to visit these premises, which I did on the 20th last at 11pm. The shelter comprises two compartments which are separated by a curtain. In the front portion which measures 80ft long, 12ft wide and 9ft high, were huddled together about 100 men; in the rear portion which measures about 20ft square, were about 60 women in the same condition as the men; the rooms are badly ventilated and there is only one WC which the women alone are allowed to use. I found the cubic space of air per head to be about 76ft, whilst the minimum space should be 300. Whilst sympathising with such a philanthropic object it is from a sanitary point of view most unhealthy, and to my mind it becomes a nuisance under the Sanitary Act of 1866, Sec. 19, which provides "That any house or part of a house so overcrowded as to be dangerous or prejudicial to the health of its inmates is a nuisance." This is clearly a case in which the Vestry is called to act without delay.[10]

The Vestry did. It ordered closure, and thereby removed one haven for the night folk.

By 1888, at the other end of the scale the building revolution in the form of functional, high-rise block dwellings, was making its impact locally. Reporting back in 1889, the Whitechapel Union alone recorded 23 model dwellings already erected, totalling 2,546 apartments and accommodation for 9,429 tenants. (5,486 adults and 3,943 children). Barnett's efforts had borne fruit. In 1887 the College Buildings near Toynbee Hall were ready for habitation. These were to operate as an experiment in self-government, where tenants' committees "will be parties to the management of the building who, after paying the landlord 4 per cent on his outlay, will divide the surplus among the tenants in proportion to the rent paid". Throughout 1888 it proved a success, with Barnett jubilantly proclaiming that "co-operative tenancy showed good financial results, each tenant getting a dividend of £2 10s!" But the snag was the tenants' reluctance to allow their dividends to accumulate (ie to save), so that eventually they would become collective owners of the property. They refused, and Barnett could never understand why. It was evident that the East Ender, traditionally facing a daily struggle for survival, would opt for "the cash in hand and waive the rest".[11]

Any evidence of Barnett's aim to administer "without petty rules or unjust interference" appeared marginal in those tenements controlled by his company. Elsewhere regulations were stern, even repressive. "The philanthropy which provided Rothschild Buildings was far from unconditional. With it went a detailed programme of class control."[12] Rents were still not cheap enough, even for the regularly employed.[13] It is, therefore, arguable whether such schemes *did*, as Charles Booth suggested, help to depress rents in the immediate locale. Strict conditions of tenure were laid down, especially in hygiene: they included an insistence on vaccination, the maintenance of cleanliness, and a fixed number per flat to prevent overcrowding. The *East London Observer* (9 June 1888), enthused over the new block or square of Artisans Dwellings erected off Royal Mint Street, in which 367 rooms were "divided off into one, two and three rooms". These were sited near the older Charlotte's Buildings and were there to provide for "a better class of person" by offering the most up-to-date conveniences. Harkness gives us a rare insight into the mores of the earlier building dwellers and their reaction to the new environment.

The Charlotte block near the Mint had been built for casuals: dock labourers, Billingsgate porters, hawkers and costermongers, people who might make a reasonable deal one day and nothing the next. The wives supplemented the meagre income by charing, tailoring and sack-making, besides cooking and housework. Octavia Fry's lady collectors were everywhere in evidence. Most of the tenants believed that the buildings were the women's property. They provoked animosity in the men, who claimed that the buildings were built "cheap and nasty [because] women don't understand business, [and] some West End ladies fluked money in them". Old-time building workers concurred, deriding "such jerry work" as they "watched the walls springing up, windows appearing as if by magic, and all the cheapest inventions brought to fill in this artisans' dwelling".[14] Certainly the scale of "petticoat" authority was seen to be imposing:

> Several times in the week ladies arrived in the Buildings armed with master-keys, ink-pots and rent books. A tap at a door was followed by the intrusion into a room of a neatly-clad female of masculine appearance. If the rent was promptly paid the lady made some gracious remarks, patted the head of the children and went away. If the rent was not forthcoming, they took stock of the room (or rooms), and said a few words about the broker.
> "She takes the bread out of a man's mouth, and spends on one woman what would keep a little family," grumbled a tenant.
> "I pity her husband," responded a neighbour.
> "Females like 'er don't marry," mumbled a misanthropic old lady.[15]

Nevertheless opinions on the model dwellings remained divided. The earlier supporters claimed that they decreased mortality rates, especially for infectious diseases, discouraged crime and immorality, and *enforced* orderly living. As developments increased, radical critics attacked them on their own grounds. They explained the low mortality as due to the higher class of occupant than those originally designated or, contrarily, accused them of contributing to the spread of disease, of obscene goings-on on the staircases and of blocks terrorised by gangs of toughs. Hemmed in by authoritarian "rules and wrought iron railings... they would become the burial place of the individual man".[16] Certainly by this time a Barnett interest, the George Yard Dwellings (erected in 1875 to provide single rooms for the very poor), was losing caste. The poor could not afford, nor did they welcome, the irksome restrictions imposed by the owners. Here, in 1888, scene of the Ripper murder of Martha Turner, there were already unlet rooms. (In 1890 the block was finally converted into student accommodation and re-named Balliol House.) Walter Besant fulminated against these "big barracks [where] children go slow of sight. They have nothing to exercise their eyes upon." Given that they were already there, he recommended a vital safeguard for improvement — tenants' control! "It has not yet occurred to the managing bodies of these barracks that the tenants who are entrusted with the votes for the government of the country might also very well be entrusted with the government of their own dwellings." Architect Robert Williams added his own criticism that block buildings were built only for investors' profit, and also that they they were conducive to more, not less, overcrowding.[17] But what did the tenants themselves feel? Though they have left no written comments, other evidence suggests that in general they were much happier in their block apartments than in rented slum cottage rooms or lodging houses. Harkness underlined this strongly:

> Whatever the rich thought about it, the poor liked the Buildings; at any rate they liked them for a time, just as rich people enjoy hotel life for a season. The children played about the court, the mothers gossiped in the doorways, the men smoked and talked politics on the balconies. Moreover, the rooms were cheaper than ordinary lodgings and if the tenants were "kept under" by female despots, the despots were kind enough. Many a sick baby was cured, many a girl was sent into service, many a boy was started in life by the ladies who collected the rents. Some tenants grumbled against petticoat government, but others liked it; and all agreed that "an eddicated female was a phenomenon to be much watched, criticised and talked about".[18]

Standard and style of building differed. But the new "Rothschild" tenants concurred with the dwellers near the Mint. They, too, quickly adapted to high-rise living and from the beginning "had it very nice", making of their small two-roomed apartment a real home. In those in which a particular ethnic group predominated — Jewish or Anglo-Irish — they helped to forge a caring community, with the poor helping the poor.

Hunger and want provided their own outriders. The ragged, emaciated flotsam, who with fanatical courage resisted the pull of the workhouse, could be found stretched underneath the sodden railway arches, or moving trancelike, night and day, along the walls of the major thoroughfares and side-alleys. That year an army of the hungry mustered in Tower Hamlets. Charles Booth, in his second enquiry (May 1888), which included Hackney, purported to quantify them. In his report to the Royal Statistical Society he estimated that in both boroughs, "the very poor... number about 100,000... On the whole St. George's in the East (having 23,426 or 49 per cent in poverty) is the poorest parish, but it is run very hard by Bethnal Green in this unenviable race." Booth offered a rather superficial analysis of the causes of extreme poverty, attributing much of it to the competition between the very poor. He concluded, however, with a more positive suggestion for its alleviation, one which smacked of the heresy of voluntary State involvement.

> The entire removal of this [very poor) class out of the daily struggle for existence, Mr Booth believes to be the only solution of the problem of poverty... that they are a constant burden to the State; and suggests that the time has arrived when some means should be found of carrying voluntarily on our shoulders the burdens which otherwise we have to carry involuntarily round our necks.[19]

But what of the actual condition of that "featureless crowd, who suffered silently, repined or struggled?" What kind of fate could so many of them expect? It was the other Booth — William, the Salvationist — who understood, in human terms, to whom he was referring when he pleaded the urgency of a solution. He demanded succour for those who:

> (1) having no capital or income of their own, would in a month be dead from sheer starvation were they exclusively dependent

upon the money earned by their own work, and (2) those who by their utmost exertions are unable to attain the regulation allowance of food which the law prescribes as indispensable even for the worst criminals in our gaols.[20]

For starvation was rife. Harkness's East End doctor, who had dedicated himself to the task of ministering to the poor, since few of his profession would, was pessimistic about any hope of alleviation:

> The whole of the East End is starving. What the people want is food, not physic... I dare not give the people, drugs that are used by West End physicians; for if I did the poor wretches would be killed outright. They have no constitution, only flabby flesh and blood with scarcely any oxygen in it. All I can do is colour water with something or other and hand it over the counter. The poor things drink it directly they get outside the dispensary and call it "comforting". I do not mean to say they have no bread. But they are all underfed. Why, it is brutal to make children go to school without a proper breakfast, to force the brains of boys and girls who have empty stomachs. IF THE POOR WERE NOT SO WONDERFULLY GENEROUS TO ONE ANOTHER THE RESULT WOULD BE A GENERATION OF IDIOTS. It is this cardinal virtue of theirs which makes them so attractive. I bring into the world scrofulous children; I bolster up diseased patients; I let people down easily in the grave; I do no good, but I cannot go away. The misery I see binds me here as a parish doctor.[21]

Non-payment of rent was a common hazard. As William Booth explained, for the honest poor "it meant every week they contrive by pinching and scheming to raise the rent, for with them it is pay or go; and they struggle to meet the collector as the sailor nerves himself to avoid being sucked under by a foaming wave." Captain Lobo, Salvation Army officer, came across a dying woman who "tried to explain why they [her family] were all so hungry... the husband had been out of work for nine months and, during that time, they had sunk lower and lower. One thing had followed another to the pawnshop, until at last nothing was left not even a blanket." Then why not enter the workhouse? It was the fear of being separated from her husband and children that kept them together until the inevitable finale.[22] Death by starvation in the street was not uncommon. The incident, based on fact, of a corpse found in an alleyway is described with horrifying familiarity by Mackay:

The body was frightfully emaciated; the ribs of his chest protruded sharply; the joints of his hands and feet were so narrow that a boy's hand might have encircled them. His cheeks were fallen in, and his cheek bones stood out prominently; his nose was sharp and thin; his lips entirely bloodless, and a little opened as if in pain; the projecting teeth apparently in good condition. The temples and the region of the throat were deeply sunken — the corpse appeared as if it had been lying for a month in a dry place, so thin and tight the yellowish skin covered the bones.

The observer inquired of the policemen standing by the body, "Starved?"
The policeman nodded, stolid and indifferent. Starved!

Dr Barnardo, replying to a naive, obviously affluent contributor who asked, "Can people *ever* starve in London?", cited one instance among many that "reach me almost daily of incredible suffering endured to starvation point by young and old". It was contained in a letter to *The Times* relating to a happening at the People's Palace:[24]

Sir,
A little before 2 o'clock on the afternoon of Wednesday the 17th [of November 1888], a poorly but respectably dressed old man, cleanly in appearance and with well-blacked shoes, staggered into the premises of the People's Palace, dying of starvation. Too weak to coherently explain his condition, he was led into the office, and supplied by the clerks there in attendance with a basin of soup and some bread which, however, his famished stomach refused to retain for a moment. He was then placed in a cab and conveyed to the London Hospital, where he lingered for about an hour and died, the coroner's jury subsequently returned a verdict of "Death from starvation".

Such an incident as this shocks our very feeling, and occurring as it does, in a city literally swarming with charitable agencies, gives rise as to the real condition of the respectable, uncomplaining poor around us. These people shrink from the workhouse to the last, and, unwise as their silent endurance may be, the fact of its existence should be faced, and some steps taken to prevent the repetition of such saddening occurrences as that at the People's Palace on Wednesday week. There is something especially sad in the case — the poor uncomplaining old man making his way into the People's Palace — his palace, built to brighten the lives of such as he — and dying of starvation almost on its doorstep. The life of John Weal, who appears to have come from Lincolnshire, and to have been entirely without friends or relations in the world, will not, however, have been poured out entirely in vain, if his death serve to direct renewed attention to the difficult problem presented in the efficient relief of the respectable poor.

Yours faithfully, C.

Was the global picture of Tower Hamlets, as Hell's Kitchen sustained by an unmitigated flow of human misery, justified? William Booth appears to support the view. He ventured the hope that "every honest worker on English soil will always be as warmly clad, as healthily housed and as frequently fed as our criminal convicts!" He was pessimistic about the foreseeable future when human beings will be cared for "to the standard of the London Cab Horse... a very illustration of broken down humanity; he usually falls down because of overwork and underfeeding." At least "every cab horse has three things: a shelter for the night, food for its stomach, and work allotted to it by which it can eat its corn." "How can we take the census of those who have fallen below this standard?" asked the Salvationist leader.[25] His namesake, Charles Booth, purported to do so by the scientific method. From his findings 65 per cent lived above the poverty line, thus invalidating any of the former's dicta on working-class conditions.[26] To suggest that the area was one huge midden is a travesty. There is enough evidence to confirm diversity: in trades employing full-time labour, in life-styles, in culture and social milieu according to class and ethnicity.

For instance, Goade's Plan for London, under preparation in 1887, listed for Whitechapel alone 35 occupations both in large-scale factories (a few) and in small light industry (the majority), which accorded with Charles Booth's accounting on the regularly employed.[27] Following his analysis the social picture varied, roughly improving as one proceeded eastward from Whitechapel. ("Tom Tiddler's ground — the El Dorado of the East — a gathering together of poor fortune seekers: its streets are full of buying and selling, the poor living on the poor [and] the Jews... seeking their livelihood under conditions... on the middle ground between civilisation and barbarism.") Stepney was essentially the abode of labour, for here both casuals (11 per cent) and regularly paid workers (24 per cent) reached a maximum. Labour divisions were reflected in the contrast between the modern two- or three-storied terraced houses built to accommodate the "respectable" and "responsible", ie those who could regularly meet payment of rent, and the decaying cottages in squalid streets and courts inhabited by the "feckless" casuals. Poplar, the largest district constituting the eastern border, with a variety of labour contingents, housed the largest proportion of artisans (26 per cent) as compared with the rest of Tower Hamlets, as well as railway servants, seamen, professional classes (clerks etc) and dockers — the last relegated to the lowest grade, the poor. Mile End, extending into Bow, which registered the maximum concentration of shop assistants, clerks, sub-officials and independent traders, was the area at its most salubrious, where beautiful open squares (Tredegar, Coborn, Beaumont and the like), enclosed in parts by solid Georgian houses, witnessed the absence of poverty. It is no coincidence that the *East London Observer's* only recording of wills left by locals is of two wealthy men who had both lived and worked in this specific district.[28] While St. George's-in-the-East, hemmed in on the river side, and cut off from St. Katherine's Docks by Wapping, with some demolition but little rebuilding and a greater irregular labour force at large (9½% per cent as compared with Whitechapel's 4%), would appear to confirm Charles Booth's prognosis that it could be the most poverty-stricken of all.

The peripheral parish of Bethnal Green vied with the last for the dubious honour of highest in the "impoverished" category. It warranted a special report by the Home Office Commissioners instigated by the Mansion House Council. One revealing item was the dramatic decline in the number of hand-loom weavers since 1842, to be replaced by new industries, such as matchbox-making and fish-curing. Another disturbing feature for the authorities was the high incidence of early marriages which had led to a higher birth rate. Blame was attributed to "the Red Church in its system of accomplishing marriage at a cost of only a few pence to the bridegroom", such that "the birth rate in Bethnal Green in 1881 was 41.2 per cent per 1,000, while in London it was 34.7 per cent per 1,000".[29] Since this was apparently continuing unabated, it brought on a stern pronouncement from the Archbishop of Canterbury while he was opening the Oxford Hall in Victoria Park Square on 18 February. The *East London Observer* soberly reported his firm views on the second greatest social evil — early reckless marriage — with no comment on his astonishing statement that:

> Early marriages did not take place among the upper classes, for he had heard it said that young men seemed inclined to give up the idea of marriage... But in his part of London it almost made his blood run cold to think of the many early marriages... Self-restraint was that which the Christian men and women of Bethnal Green must bring to bear upon their fellows.

This was followed by his firm conviction of the mutual uplift resulting from the wealthy classes' self-denying contacts with the poor:

> It was good for the rich and educated people to become associated with the poor, and never were they richer and more happy than when they knew that both their leisure and their money were trusts which they were bound to use for this world's benefit... There was only one way by which men could obtain a fair share of God's good things, and that was by the road of diligence, industry and thrift.[30]

Like beauty, poverty was in the eye of the beholder. Among the labouring poor, regular and irregular, many were quick to define their own status within the class of the "respectable", always to the detriment of those "below" them. It was one way in which the secure worker aped the mores of his class superiors. This would suggest some form of caste division among the local workers, which is evidenced by Harkness's own shrewd observation:

> People who live in Shoreditch, or St. George's in the East, are apt to be confounded with their poorer neighbours by the uninitiated, although the initiated know that there is a greater distance between a dressmaker and a charwoman than between a countess and the wife of a successful merchant. It is a royal failing to see no difference between a nobleman and a lackey; so the uninitiated must be pardoned for their total ignorance in confounding together shopkeepers, artisans, labourers and casuals. The initiated are aware how wide is the step which separates these people one from another.

A certain house in a certain square or street denoted status. Moving up the scale was to cross the frontier northwards into the clean, sturdy two- or three-storied cottages flanking the wide streets bordering Victoria Park, where, as was asked,

> "Who can doubt the respectability of a person occupying a little house in Hackney? A little house with Venetian blinds in the windows, and a brass knocker on the door must hold respectable people who pay their bills, go to chapel and eat meat on Sunday."[31]

Among the lower echelons, boots, at the least, advertised solvency. They were, therefore, as Dr Barnardo found to his cost, saleable assets. A family, permanently shod, making its way to church or chapel on Sunday, could command recognition and respect from the lesser endowed. An artisan household with a maid (from the country) demanded it. In a legendary "high-class" neighbourhood square, the Salvationist in *In Darkest London* posits the effect of class changes resulting from social mobility:

> Legend says that years gone by the square was inhabited by "real gentry". "Middling folks" live in it at present — people who own small factories or large shops, who are in trade or business. These "middling folks" talk of the "lower classes" and it is difficult to say whereabouts in the social scale "middling folks" come exactly... It suffices to say that "middling folk" bestow old clothes and soup on the "poorer classes" just as the "real gentry" visit the "deserving poor" when down in the country, and give donations to charities during the season in London.

It could be argued that there were mutually conceded "class" differences between workers themselves, where, in some parts of Tower Hamlets, diversity, rather than homogeneity, in socio-cultural attitudes could be found.

There were, however, common patterns in the responses, of the middle classes to the poor. Canning Town's Rev. F. Newlands, speaking on the subject of "Work amongst the East End Workers", was convinced that "the poverty that existed was due largely to intemperance. In the space of three hours one Saturday night 1,538 people — men and women — were seen to enter a public house, and in another, nearly 2,000. All this went, therefore, to show preventable poverty."[32] Harkness's genteel-born Salvation Army officer "could not see that the people take pleasure in their filthy existence; he could not understand the satisfaction they got by fuddling their brains in public houses and by coarse love-making." (Sex, to him, was perhaps merely a boring pre-requisite for procreation!) His reaction to a band of

East End hop-pickers was that they were a mindless flock. "They feel as masses not individuals... Those who know them well will recognise their individuality, but for all political and social purposes they are like a herd of sheep; only, of course, they are of less value than sheep in the money market."[33] The gentleman Radical Arthur Grant, on interviewing a beautiful young tailor's machinist, "was wondering how a face like hers came to be in Whitechapel, and congratulating himself in this confirmation of his Radical opinions, for he believed that with the help of a good tailor, and a little polish, Whitechapel might sit down to dinner in Brook Street!"[34]

A patronising attitude often went hand in hand with a compassionate one. A sensitive and sympathetic journalist commenting on a Harvest Thanksgiving service conducted by the Rev. Samuel Barnett at St. Jude's, Whitechapel, catches the mood of pathos and gentle dignity evoked by the occasion:

> A special order of service had been prepared for the festival, and in the paper were such proverbs and texts as "Life is Low", "The Tree that God plants, no winds hurt it"... After the Old Testament lesson the choir gave a splendid rendering of the anthem "The wilderness and solitary place shall be glad for them; and the desert shall rejoice and blossom as the rose"... The congregation were of the lower middle class and many of them were very poor: and how sympathetically chosen was this hymn with those beautiful words "Though dark my path and sad my lot, let me be still and murmur not" could be seen with a glance round at the poorly clad kneeling figures who had fared so ill "in life's rough way".[35]

Concern for the poor was rarely divorced from stern criticism of their life-style, implying that their situation was as much a result of weakness of character as of forces beyond their control. F.N. Charrington, William Booth, Dr Barnardo and the Rev. Samuel Barnett were, each in his own way, more *sympathique* in recognising the more potent effects of external, that is economic and social, determinants on the condition of labour. A more representative view was put before the Sweating Commission of the House of Lords by the Rev. W. Adamson, Vicar of Old Ford. Adamson lamented the fact that his parish of 11,066 souls "contained no middle class" and thus, presumably, the lack of sobriety and thrift which brought about poverty. Their deterioration was assured by pauper immigration and early marriages. As for the remedies, "he would impose a poll tax on foreigners, and would inflict a penalty on men marrying before 21 and girls before 18 years of age!"[36] In 1888 such expressions of contempt as "loafers" and "hangers-on" came too readily from the lips of the well-breeched in their appraisal of East End workers. Such terms, as Justice forcibly argued, might be "more properly applied to the middle and upper classes and their parasites" whose own easy living was derived from the exploitation of that same labour.[37]

The other global image of Tower Hamlets, to the outsider, was of a vast malodorous midden which bred disease and early mortality. Bad hygienic conditions in large pockets of the local parishes were hardly surprising, considering that poor sanitation was the norm. "Even the drains at Buckingham Palace stank in hot weather and sheets soaked in chloride of lime were put across the riverside windows of the House of Commons." If such negligence was acceptable in the habits and dwellings of the great, what improvements could be expected in the slums? Since Mayhew's revelations, little practical action had been undertaken to effect better sanitation, although this was sanctioned by section 343 of the Public Health Act of 1875. This compelled local authorities to impose sanitary requirements by law, and petty sessional courts could deal with owners of "any premises in such a state as to be injurious to health or a nuisance". A parish-by-parish self-evaluation of maintenance and improvements in public and private facilities (sewage, dust disposal, public baths, etc) gives us a clue, since works claimed to be undertaken were published, and therefore subject to audit and legal scrutiny. These may be gleaned from reports submitted by both the local Medical Officers of Health and the District Surveyors.

Whitechapel provided ample evidence of health hazards. Previously the *Lancet* (27 January 1883) had exposed one source of danger. Of 525 houses inspected in that area, 37 per cent had shown direct communication between drain soil pipes and drinking systems which bred epidemics. For two years before the Ripper murders, the *Lancet* had published a number of articles on the poor sanitary arrangements in Spitalfields and demanded improvements according to legal statute. Yet there are records which suggest that the local authorities were taking measures to counteract these conditions. In the Surveyor's report ending on

Lady Day 1888 there is a comprehensive account of new works undertaken entailing repairs and cleansing. For instance, in places of maximum concentration of street garbage, such as the main Whitechapel Road, Wentworth and Old Montague Streets, large sewers were cleansed and flushed by hand labour. We learn of active means employed to counteract effluence:

> Smaller sewers such as 18in, 2ft back barrel and 12in pipes subjected to periodic flushing by means of hose and standpipe is often efficient to the saving of much labour and expense. This has accordingly been done in many cases throughout the district. It is not, however, always successful, for in the following places the ground had to be opened to perform the work thoroughly, viz. Elder Street, Whitechapel Road, Quaker Street, Angel Alley, Raven Row, Gun Street, Gowers Walk etc.
>
> Gowers Walk — All defective sewers perfected concurrently with paving operation. 33 new private drains to sewers helped to construct.
> Gully Pipes — Opened, cleansed, relaid to sewers helped to construct.
> Summer — Courts and alleyways flushed with water and gullies flushed with disinfecting mixture of carbolic acid, sulphate of iron and water leading to gullies being free from offensive smells.[39]

The innovation of a mechanical dust-destructor in Wentworth Street the year before proved a mixed blessing. Operating continuously throughout the year, except Sundays and holidays, it disposed of 12,501 wagon loads of dust and refuse plus 268 van collections of street sweepings. But it also filled the surroundings with a "shower of fine grey ashes... choking the roof gullies" and, in fact, "adding appreciably to the dust and dirt of the district". Barnett regarded it as a dust distributor rather than destroyer.[40] Public amenities to instil personal hygiene were instituted and expanded. In 1888 Goulston Street Baths (opened since August 1878) showed a record intake. For the poor there were second-class cubicles, priced at 2d a warm, 1d a cold bath. Admission records in the annual report showed that first-class users had increased to 29,843 and second-class to 89,316. One could argue that this would have had only marginal impact on hygiene since many of the bathers would have returned to unhealthy living conditions. Also, in spite of the cleansing department's efforts, street sanitary hazards persisted. One of many complaints was that of Mr Bartram, sanitary inspector, concerning obstructions to public highways which were widespread, and particularly objectionable in Tenter Street, east, south and west, and Great Alie Street:

> In one case there is deposited on the highway soldiers' old clothes, which were thrown from the upper windows to be sorted previous to removal. The road is also frequently blocked by immense quantities of coconuts, which are there deprived of their shells, so that a greater portion of the street is rendered useless to the general public.[41]

Another glaring deficiency, according to legal requirements, was a mortuary. The post mortem on Ripper victim Polly Nichols revealed the *ad hoc* use of a shed adjoining the workhouse in Old Montague Street, with the job of mortuary attendant detailed to an epileptic pauper, whose tasks included the cleansing and laying out of the body for the autopsy.

Similar obligations in renovation and construction carried out in other districts of Tower Hamlets are certainly evidence of a sense of public responsibility on the part of parish administrators. St. George's emerged as bottom of the league in public works and prospects of improvement. The annual report of Dr Rygate, Medical Officer of Health, is significant. The district had the lowest marriage rate (10.4 per 1,000 as against 16.2 in the metropolis — the lowest on record!), the highest birth rate (always found in the poorest and most densely populated areas) of 39.5 per 1,000, and the highest death rate of 28 per 1,000 in the borough. The Medical Officer explained that "the same causes ... are still affecting our death rate, viz that the parish is a poor are, for the most part, consisting of the labouring classes many of whom are engaged at the waterside and the co-existing high birth rate and consequent death rate amongst children". The difficulty of implementing sanitary improvements was that, in addition to suffering "the general depression of trade from the specially low state of the dock interest and sugar interest", he blamed "the influx of pauper foreigners, mostly Jews, who coming from countries where ideas of sanitation are primitive, render sanitary measures very difficult of execution, especially as regards cleanliness and to prevent overcrowding".[42] The latter statement was probably a response to the recommendation of the Sewers Committee (23

February) which, among other suggestions, called for legislation concerning registration of lodging houses, the duties of lodgers, infectious diseases, powers of entry for inspectors, and penalties that "would be of advantage to the health of the parish and would prevent the continued immigration of foreign poor". One positive hope for improving personal cleanliness was the opening of the Betts Street baths on 31 March "to accommodate the 70,000 residents of St. George's, Wapping, Shadwell and Ratcliff".[43]

Proceeding eastwards, sanitation improvements and therefore health prospects, appeared brighter. In Limehouse District new works included the introduction of 624 feet of piping, in parts to replace defective brick sewers, with drainage connections to 68 buildings. Later an additional 790 feet of sewage pipe would replace deficient conduits in 94 buildings, which included 36 new structures and eight blocks of Artisans' Dwellings. Public urinals, essential in a pub-infested, heavy-drinking area were flushed and cleaned each day and more often in hot weather. Carriageways and footways throughout the principal streets were swept and cleaned daily and side streets on alternate days. To prevent "nuisances" from noxious effluvia issuing out of the main sewers, the Metropolitan Board of Works was requested to deodorise the sewage by the "application of Sulphurous Acid for the neutralisation of offensive gases".[44] It would appear that this District, according to its own records, was well served, and, being near the docks, it needed to be. Yet we learn that the persistence of sewer gas at the Shadwell Fish Market "rendered the cessation of the nuisance a matter of the first importance. All knew that this was the Metropolitan Water Board's responsibility, but there was little hope from the Metropolitan Board to whom they had sent communications year after year, and received cautious acknowledgements but nothing else."[45] Later the Medical Officer, on inspecting Victoria Court, Dellow Street, Shadwell, found the premises "in a deplorable and insanitary condition. Three closets out of ten... stopped and the filth and liquid overflowing over the backyard. The houses... very dirty and dilapidated; they form a portion of the Cable Street area reported on to the Metropolitan Board as an area unfit for habitation." As always, we must treat the official records with caution, since the unsavoury image of Limehouse District, with its foul, congested courts and culs-de-sac, particularly those of Pennyfields, Wapping and St. George's, would be sustained until the 1930s and not without cause!

It is apparent that the eastern border — Poplar District including Bow and Bromley — was the most promising area. Its Board of Works report in 1888 suggests a vast number of provisions and improvements for the benefit of its citizens. These included such important amenities as:

> 32 urinals in the district, cleansed twice daily.
>
> *Disinfecting Houses*
> 2 in the district: one in Bickmore Street, the other in Old Ford Road, Bow, used for the purpose of disinfecting wearing apparel and linen brought from houses where infectious disease has existed.
>
> *Public Lamps*
> Lighting performed by the Commercial Gas Company who under contract supply gas, repair the lamp columns and lanterns once a year... the number (of columns) in each parish is
>
> | | |
> |---|---|
> | Poplar | 615 |
> | Bow | 409 |
> | Bromley | 537 |
>
> *Building and Drainage*
> Notices presented and approved for building and draining new houses and erections viz
>
> | | |
> |---|---|
> | Poplar | 181 |
> | Bow | 19 |
> | Bromley | 50 |

Records on sewage, however, seem less definite.[47] Costs of work executed since 1883 totalling £502 18s 9d suggests a gross underestimate. However, the annual reports of the Medical Officer of Health for the South District of Poplar appear to bear out the results of reasonable maintenance of public sanitation. His statistical survey in 1887 of death rates in the various divisions of Tower Hamlets is self-explanatory.

Sanitary areas	Estimated population	Annual rate per 1000 living Births	Annual rate per 1000 living Deaths	Physical zymotic diseases	Deaths of children under 1 year of age to 1000 births
Bethnal Green	130,619	39.1	26.5	4.3	182
Whitechapel	67,865	36.9	25.2	2.9	173
St. George's-in-the-East	46,316	39.8	26.4	2.8	148
Stepney	58,716	33.2	25.9	3.8	227
Mile End Old Town	113,017	34.8	19.5	3.8	130
Poplar	182,706	31.6	18.8	2.6	144

It proved, beyond doubt, that the death rate in Poplar, including Bow and Bromley, compared with those of the other sanitary divisions, was strikingly low, not only in gross mortality, but in death resulting from zymotic (infectious) diseases. What is interesting is that the rate could be reduced by deducting deaths by accident to healthy men while at work, which included 19 from severe bodily injuries and 36 from drowning, ie where dock work took its toll.[48] Nevertheless there was still evidence of health dangers, with a typhoid epidemic at Bromley due to a dairy purveying infected milk that resulted in 40 suspected cases from 25 houses along the High Street; also a threat posed by a large accumulation of refuse at Limehouse Hole, Emmett Street "used by human beings in place of a water closet", such that all openings in the offices of Messrs Young and Dowson sited opposite the heap had to be closed when the foul odour wafted across in high winds.[49] Towards the end of the year we read of a protracted health nuisance from the River Lea resulting from the discharge of foul sewage into Bow Creek, which was contaminating the water between Old Ford and Bromley. The West Ham Sewage Company was deemed responsible, and legal action was being contemplated against West Ham Corporation.[50] On 8 November, London Hospital house physician Dr Debenham struck a note of alarm when "cases of diphtheria had, within the last few days, reached the proportion of an epidemic. So numerous had they become that it was found expedient to forbid the hospital official to admit any but extreme cases." A father of a child who had succumbed to the disease confirmed that "where he lived there were no sewers, the sewage being drained into cesspools at the rear of the houses. Each cesspool was common to several houses, and at times the stench was horrible."[51] We are forced to question the adequacy of official claims to meet the necessary improvements when such cumulative reports of filth and disease occur right across Tower Hamlets.

Hospitals were among other local institutions which provided an additional practical dimension to social welfare for the poor. For example the legendary London Hospital in the Whitechapel Road had a long tradition of research and medical advance which could be explained by its fortuitous location among a ready supply of the sick. The locals feared it. Their attitude, as to the workhouse, was "Abandon Hope, all Ye who enter Here!" Dr Frederick Treves, patron of the Elephant Man and an intern in 1888, explained the reasons why:

> The hospital in the days of which I speak was anathema. The poor people hated it. They dreaded it. They looked upon it primarily as a place where people died. It was a matter of difficulty to induce a patient to enter the wards. They feared an operation and with good cause, for an operation then was a dubious matter. There were stories afloat of things that happened in the hospital, and it could not be gainsaid that certain of these stories were true.

Medical treatment was marked by rough brutality, with little concern for any pain inflicted on the patient:

> The surgeon was rough. He had inherited that attitude from the days when operations were carried through without anaesthetics, and when he had need to be rough, strong and quick, as well as indifferent to pain. Pain was with him a thing that had to be. It was a regrettable feature of disease. It had to be submitted to.

Many common measures of treatment involved great suffering. Bleeding was still a frequent procedure, and mediaeval means were still observed. Treves in his ignorance entered the door directly into the area where the operating theatre stood:

> There was a man on the table who was shrieking vehemently. The surgeon taking me by the arm said. "You have a strong back; lay hold of that rope and pull"... there were already two men in

front of me and we all three pulled our best. I had no idea what we were pulling for. I was afterwards informed that the operation in progress was the reduction of a dislocated hip by compound pulleys. The hip, however, was not reduced and the man remained lame for life.

The chronicler goes on to inform us that antiseptics were not in use. "Sepsis was the prevailing condition in the wards. Practically all major wounds suppurated. Pus was the most common subject of concern... It was classified according to the degree of vileness." Thus cleanliness was considered irrelevant, indeed out of place, "finicking and affected. An executioner might as well manicure his nails before chopping off a head. The surgeon operated in a slaughter house" in a frock coat of black cloth stiff with blood and the filth of years. The more sodden it was the more forcibly did it bear evidence to the surgeon's prowess. Perhaps, through faulty memory, Treves may have exaggerated in portraying the London Hospital as a human abattoir. Yet a contemporary account of a girl who died as a result of an operation involving amputation would appear to support him. Her father's public complaint was that "they regularly butchered her in hospital".[53] This was the opinion of the girl herself, voiced to the visiting parish doctor before her death. Certainly the cold facts of the case presented by the doctor, an impartial witness at the inquest, were by themselves disturbing. They were related in full in the *East London Observer*:

HOW A BRAVE GIRL DIED

Mr Joseph Boxall deposed that in July last his daughter (the deceased) whilst attempting to save a child from being run over was kicked by a horse. She was taken to the London Hospital, and was sent from there to a convalescent home at Folkstone, from which witness took her on the 11th instant. She died, however, on Wednesday last...

Evidence from a Dr Edward Birdoe deposed that on Thursday the 14th, he was called to the deceased on an order from the relieving officer. He saw the deceased who, with her friends, seemed rather embittered at what they considered the bad treatment she had received at the London Hospital. The deceased told him that the doctors put her under chloroform, for the purpose of, as they said, examining her leg. Instead of doing merely this, however, they amputated her leg just above the knee. This was done without the consent of the deceased or her parents. A short time afterwards it was found that to save her life, it was necessary to amputate the rest of her leg and this was done with the consent of the deceased. Witness advised her to go in the infirmary, but she refused, on the grounds that she had a horror of going into any more public institutions. She sank and died on Wednesday last. The cause of death was shock consequent upon the second operation. A juryman said the consent of the parents of the girl ought to have been obtained for the first operation. Nobody was present from the hospital, but the jury refused to adjourn the inquiry, one saying that the second operation caused the death — the jury returned a verdict in accordance with the medical evidence.[54]

And that was that. No follow-up, no criticism and, therefore, no excuses. After all, it was only one more of the anonymous poor, who had little choice but to consign her last days to the doctors — on their part to be arbitrarily dealt with, as a case, not a human being, who must have bled in body and spirit every moment during the inevitable submission to what she *knew* was to be a frightful end.

Poplar Hospital, on the other hand, appears to have developed a vastly different image. Located nearer to the docks, over the years it had built up a reputation of caring service among the poor, especially among the dock workers, who daily faced physical danger. For it was a hospital specialising in accidents. That year, in financial need, it issued an appeal, backed by the *East London Advertiser* in a moving and informative editorial:

> The hospital at Poplar is an institution of which East London is deservedly proud... Situated at the very doors of the docks, and in the midst of the factory life... its wards are always ready to receive the wage earner struck down by accident, and to afford him the best surgical treatment and most tender nursing. Many a working man at the East End has reason to remember with thankfulness the existence of so excellent an institution. That this gratitude takes a practical form is shown in the fact testified by the subscription list that the pence and shillings of the artisans and labourers find their way into the treasury of the hospital equally with the guineas and bank notes of the better-to-do sections of society. The Poplar Hospital for Accidents can boast of no endowments...
>
> There are no expensively paid officers. A lynx-eyed committee of management control the expenditure, and see that for every pound subscribed there are 20 shillings well spent... there are no sensational appeals or statements thrown at the public from

time to time. Hence it is that the committee appeal for new subscribers and fresh donors to help in the work... The hospital has the strongest claims on the mercantile classes of London. The men who meet with accidents and find succour at the Poplar Hospital are the servants of the shipowners, merchants and manufacturers and it therefore behoves on them to subscribe liberally to an institution which confers such benefits on a class whose labour, in a very large degree, goes to make up the wealth of this great city.[55]

* * *

Such was the complex tapestry of peoples and institutions that constituted the irregular face of Tower Hamlets. The grim somnolence of "a city of dreadful night", where poverty seemed endemic, was certainly there in fact and fiction. However, such "sordid uniformity, utter remoteness from delight" and "dismal lack of accent" (Arthur Morrison), was relieved by spacious middle-class enclaves, well defined, which attracted little interest on the part of those social investigators and philanthropists immediately concerned with the misery and horrors endured by the local poor. The normality of the dull majority the respectable and secure — was to them an irrelevance and, in another context, less newsworthy. Nevertheless a society which allowed nearly 40% of its citizens within one borough to live on the margin of existence deserved censure. It was necessary to focus on those other features of poverty making. The events of 1888 provided the opportunity.

Footnotes

[1] The Lodging Houses Act, 8 April 1851.
[2] Enid Gauldie, *Cruel Habitations*, p. 242.
[3] *ELA* 29 September 1888, "Here and There" column.
[4] The Medical Officer of Health's report for Whitechapel in 1888 listed 36 streets containing 141 lodging houses in that district alone.
[5] *Out of Work*, pp. 108-11. See also *In Darkest London*, pp. 28-9 for a good description of conditions in a doss-house.
[6] Dr Barnardo, *Night and Day* November 1888, p. 105, "Child Dangers".
[7] *In Darkest London*, pp. 46-9.
[8] *ELA* 12 May 1888.
[9] *ELO* 28 January 1888.
[10] *ELA* 27 October 1888, "Night shelters for Outcasts — A Bad State

of Affairs".
[11]H.O. Barnett, *Canon Barnett*, pp. 139-40.
[12]Jerry White, *Rothschild Buildings*, pp. 54-5.
[13]At College Buildings 2 rooms were priced at 4s 6d. At Blackwell Buildings 2 moms were priced at 5s. At Rothschild Buildings 2 rooms were priced at 4s 6d, and 3 rooms at 6s. (See Booth Collection, third series, vol. 7 [handwritten] Group B.343 [Whitechapel], pp. 18-22.)
[14]See John Law, *A City Girl*, pp. 9-11, and *Out of Work*, pp. 82-3.
[15]*A City Girl*, p. 10.
[16]Jerry White, *Rothschild Buildings*, p. 32.
[17]See his *The Face of the Poor*, pp. 4-6. Also his criticism in *London Rookeries and Colliers Slums*, pp. 1-2, where he points out that these high-rise mansions did not take into consideration that as "artisans, carters and dock labourers are not gifted with wings, they find it a sore burden when tired and weary after a day's work... to crawl into these high-placed compartments called rooms... they are human packing cases befouled with carbonic acid constantly given off from the lungs and skins of the people crowded in them...".
[18]*A City Girl*, p. 11.
[19]*ELO* 19 May 1888, "The poor who are 'always with us'".
[20]*In Darkest England*, p. 18.
[21]*In Darkest London*, pp. 83-4.
[22]Ibid.
[23]*The Anarchists*, p. 179.
[24]Dr Barnardo, *Night and Day: a record of Christian missions and practical philanthropy*, November 1888, pp. 102-3.
[25]*In Darkest England*, pp. 19-20.
[26]See "The Inhabitants of the Tower Hamlets", pp. 20-5, in which he divides these into trades and occupations.
[27]Occupations listed varied from acetic acid production to yeast making. A major industry is omitted, namely tailoring, perhaps because of its sub-division into so many small workshops which were unaccountable.
[28]*ELO* 10 March 1888 reports the will of John Simpson Ashbridge, late of 568 Mile End Road, 1 Waterloo Terrace, Commercial Road, East, and 49 and 51 Mile End Road, who died on 13 January, proved on the value amounting to "upwards of £30,000"! On 31 March it reports the will of a Harry Perry late of Tredegar Works, Bow and Mostyn Villa, Bow, builder and contractor, who left £33,765 10s 9d!
[29]*ELO* 23 June 1888, "On Condition of Bethnal Green". It also reports that in 1881 the proportion of marriages per 1,000 in Bethnal Green was 20.5% while in the whole of London it was only 9.0%.
[30]*ELO* 25 February 1888, "The Archbishop of Canterbury on the Evils of Bethnal Green".
[31]*Out of Work*, pp. 42-3.
[32]*ELO* 7 April 1888.
[33]*In Darkest London*, pp. 211-13.
[34]*A City Girl*, p. 45.
[35]*ELA* 13 October 1888.

[36] *Commonweal* 12 May 1888.
[37] *Justice* 3 March 1888, "Labour Notes".
[38] See P. Metcalf, *Victorian London* (London 1972) pp. 76-7.
[39] Surveyors Department Report: 32nd Annual Statement from Lady Day 1887 to Lady Day 1888.
[40] For complaints on the destructor see *ELA* and *ELO* of 10 March 1888; also *Canon Barnett*, vol. 1, p. 195.
[41] *ELO* 30 June 1888.
[42] *ELA* 18 August 1888. Precis of 32nd Annual Report of Vestry of St. George's. Annual Report of Dr Rygate, Medical Officer of Health.
[43] *ELA* 7 April 1888.
[44] See Board of Works for the Limehouse District: Statement of Accounts, Reports etc., from Lady Day 1887 to Lady Day 1888 and from Lady Day 1888 to Lady Day 1889. Limehouse District comprised the parish of Limehouse, the hamlet of Ratcliff and the parishes of Shadwell and Wapping.
[45] *ELO* 30 June 1888. According to report to Limehouse Board of Works by Medical Officer of Health on 27 June.
[46] *ELA* 22 December 1888. Limehouse Board of Works report on "Unsanitary Dwellings of the People".
[47] Board of Works for the Poplar District: Surveyor's Report and Summary of all contracts entered into and works commenced during the year ending Lady Day 1888.
[48] See Report of Dr F.M. Corner, Medical Officer of Health to the Board of Works of Poplar — South District (1887) including "Death Rates", Tower Hamlets Division Comparison, 1887.
[49] *ELO* 21 July 1888.
[50] See *ELA* 24 November 1888 and 22 December 1888.
[51] *ELA* 10 November 1888.
[52] Sir Frederick Treves, *The Elephant Man and other Reminiscences* (London, 1923) pp. 54-5.
[53] *ELO* 30 June 1888, "How a Brave Girl Died."
[54] *ELO* 30 June 1888.
[55] *ELA* 24 March 1888.

Chapter 3
The Unemployed and the Sweated

> For loss of self respect, bitterness, the loosening of all social restraints, the lifting of that dam called civilisation which keeps the passions of men from making beasts of them are the results of telling a human being, "There is no work for you to do; you are not wanted!"

> ...ranks of the great army [of unemployed] that goes marching on heedless of stragglers, whose commander-in-chief is laisser-faire, upon whose banners "Grab who can" and "Let the devil take the hindmost", are written in large letters... drink and crime follow close on the steps of laisser-faire's army...
> JOHN LAW, *OUT OF WORK*

> Those firms which reduce sweating to a fine art, who systematically and deliberately defraud the workman of his pay, who grind the faces of the poor, and who rob the widow and the orphan, and who for a pretence make great professions of public spirit and philanthropy, these men nowadays, are sent to Parliament to make laws for the people. The old prophets sent them to hell but we have changed all that. They send their victims to hell, and are rewarded by all that wealth can do to make their lives comfortable.
> WILLIAM BOOTH, *IN DARKEST ENGLAND*

The unemployed

"It is symptomatic that the word unemployed used as a noun is first recorded by the *Oxford English Dictionary* from the year 1882; the word unemployment from 1888!"[1] William Booth later reported that during that year "the average daily number of unemployed in London was estimated by the Mansion House Committee at 20,000. This vast reservoir of unemployed labour is the bane of all efforts to raise the scale of living, to improve the condition of labour." An interesting letter dated 31 December 1887, sent by S. George, Secretary of the Unemployed Registration Committee, to the Local Board of Works in each district of the Metropolitan Poor Law Union, supports this:

> Referring to our Register we find that we have already collected the names of over 25,000 adult males out of work, and when those dependent on them are reckoned, we have the particulars of over 100,000 men, women and children plunged into the direst destitution resulting from want of work... These men, one and all, prior to entering their names on our books, declared their willingness to labour upon useful public works, should any such undertakings be commenced.

He urged that the way to meet this universal cry for work was to start relief projects similar to those undertaken by the Chelsea Vestry in 1886, "which not only afforded employment for many destitute men... but turned out to be a credit to the Vestry" itself.[2] The situation was aggravated by deteriorating conditions in agriculture affecting Essex and the Eastern Counties which had "not been so depressed since the Crimean War". The crisis arose as much from the long-term effects of mechanisation as from the length and severity of the current winter, such that every week "the struggle for existence [w as] getting more keen".[3] Geographically vulnerable, Tower Hamlets was the nearest and easiest to receive the rapid inflow of dispossessed folk seeking bread and jobs and swelling the numbers of workless. An unemployed operative catches their mood in a poem reproduced by *Punch*:

> It may not be "exceptional" perhaps
> That many thousands of us labouring chaps
> Can find no labour.
> Goschen may see in arithmetic quest
> No end of intellectual interest,
> I know there's misery in my home nest
> That in my misery I've many a neighbour;
> And that's enough
> To make me sick of mere statistic stuff.[4]

Locally, the impact was great on both casual and regular employment. An informative piece on the extent of that pressure was evoked in a March issue of the *East London Advertiser*. Poplar required an assistant relieving officer at a salary of £80 a year. Eighty candidates applied, "amongst them being members of professions, shopkeepers, clerks and artisans, the whole batch consisting for the most part of men of good education, and with the best of testimonials... Not a few were clerks in employ of the

East and West India Dock Company, who, owing to reduction of staff, are under notice to quit."[5] Proceedings at the Mile End Old Town Vestry in late April were equally revealing. The surveyor was concerned that "the pressure for casual work was greater than any period of the winter". The threat of outside workless was implicitly recognised when "a strong feeling was expressed that, as regards hands wanted for sweeping and casual work, an endeavour should be made to give first option to the parish". He reiterated that need in May, pleading for more work to be provided, one suggestion being the replacement of machines by manual labour for breaking Guernsey stone![7] Declining demand for dock labour, administrative as well as unskilled, due to closures, and the oversupply of casuals at the gates, helped to reinforce the army of the workless mobilising in the East End, so that by the end of the year *Justice* could, with conviction, proclaim that "we are convinced by personal observation that the number of unemployed is greater and the distress more terrible than was the case last year".[8]

How can we assess the personal humiliations, the terrors suffered by the honest labourer seeking work? Again we rely first on Harkness for a brief entry into their world. She describes a builder's "pig-market", where hundreds were lined up on a selection parade for a handful of jobs:

> On the foreman... depended their chance of carrying home a little money that evening. He came slowly out again. He called on half-a-dozen men, and told the rest they were not wanted. 200 men stood there and only six were required — six skilled hands who a few years before had commanded twice the money they could earn on that jerry building.[9]

Of these, William Booth contends, "most... do more exhausting work in seeking for employment than the regular toilers do in their workshops, and do it, too, under the darkness of hope deferred which maketh the heart sick".[10] Harkness, in some brief vignettes, shows the pattern of life imposed upon the jobless: hungry men lounging off "to be on the benches about squares, and on the grass in the parks"; others hanging around pubs to spend their last penny and "to concoct at the bar some plan of doing something, when a glass of gin had changed grim realities into possibilities of better things, had thrown a veil over dramas at home such as hungry wives and starving children, who could not go out of doors because their rags of clothes were in pawnshops". The comradeship of the poor, their practical mutual aid, was, and still is, exemplified in the sharing of their scarce resources:

> It was "Ulloa, Tom!" and "Well, Bill!" at every platform, a desire to share tobacco, to show kindness and receive favours. These men exist by the generosity of their fellows: and the only good thing that comes of being unemployed is "I help you, and you help me, because we've no place in society". This is the *one*, the only good thing among the legion of evils which are the outcome of forced idleness.[11]

It was ironic that in 1888 it paid better to be born a monstrosity, and therefore more readily employable as a penny gaff entertainer, than a normal man possessed of nothing but his labour. "The former can make £5 a night by standing still to be stared at, the latter is a drag on the market."[12]

So they were too, according to the opinion of certain economic pundits, such as the Labour Correspondent of the Board of Trade, who in scrutinising eighteen societies found that the current number of unemployed, in November 1888, was 3.5%, as compared with 8.5% the year before, and 10% in 1886. Pontificating on his result, he declared solemnly, "It may also be concluded that those still unemployed are so because of some disability of frame or temperament, that, in practice, there is employment for all!"[13] Since his findings were deduced from a limited number of skilled trades, they took no account of the legitimate unemployed concentrated in East London, the victims of slackness in local trades as well as those who had gravitated there as the result of the co-existence of an industrial slump with an agricultural one, which had spread unemployment into other sectors of the London economy. And this mobilisation of the unemployed in an area of legendary lawlessness and disorder perpetuated the fear that gripped both government and society — the fear of revolution. This overriding menace is detected in private correspondence as well as public pronouncements throughout the year. Margaret Harkness, as usual, caught the mood from the bottom end:

> First they grow reckless, then they become hopeless, finally they take to drinking. Starvation prevents them from doing mischief

at present: but they add to the seething mass of discontent that is even now undermining the whole of society. Only those who go amongst them, who know them intimately, are aware of the bitter hatred which they express for "the upper classes", the angry feelings which they smother while ladies and gentlemen roll by in carriages. People will not listen to the warning voice which is again and again lifted by those who associate with starving men and women... to let thousands of men and women in enforced idleness is dangerous."[14]

Such sentiments were made more plausible by the insensitive reaction of Lord Salisbury to a delegation of unemployed, which earlier that year brought forth strong criticism from a perceptive letter writer to the *East London Observer:*

Not content with completely swallowing promises that he had made when out of office to support a scheme for employing them in public works, he goes a step further, and roundly declares that he is convinced that state-provided employment would cause more distress than it could cure... The matter does not stop here however, for men and their families are hovering on the brink of starvation, and there is grave reason to fear that a social revolution is impending.[15]

From the rival *East London Advertiser* came a stern editorial warning under the heading "The Existing Distress":

This much is certain, if our governors do not settle the question soon the governed will adopt measures of their own to solve it. We have already had a foretaste of those methods — a foretaste, which we trust the government will keep in its mind, and make haste to prevent from developing into a full and unrestrained realisation.[16]

Murmurings of *la grande peur* grew in intensity during the course of the Ripper murders. The *East End News* monitored the utterances of the prophets of doom, carefully selecting those of the clergy ensconced in the district. A paper with radical sympathies, it used the Church, whenever possible, to underline its own political stance. On 21 September it printed a precis of a sermon by the Rev. W.E. Kendall at Harley Street Chapel, Bow, on the "Moral and Social Aspects of the Murders". Again a warning of pending disaster unless the government acted quickly to alleviate the problem of unemployment. Drawing upon an ominous historical analogy, Kendall demonstrated the reality of the social dangers ahead:

> Next year Paris celebrates the centenary of her great revolution. He (Kendall) feared the French people are more than one hundred years ahead of us in revolutionary experience. Unless something was done and done soon, for the destitute masses of London and other great cities of this Empire, we should have, not a centenary of revolution, but a revolution itself. It was all very easy to drive 10,000 men and boys before you; but when a half-million or a million people spring up, there would be another kind of reckoning. We must see that those in high authority dealt with this matter, and that the people be not driven to excesses in their despair.

On 19 October the *East End News* quoted from a paper delivered by the Rev. F.W. Newlands, an East End Missionary, even more disturbing in its implications. Another Job's comforter, he prophesied a social upheaval, of which the Ripper murders were a forewarning:

> A lurid light has recently been thrown upon the state of walks in some parts of the East End. I do not hesitate to say that in this seething residuum there is a chronic danger to the Commonwealth; we are living at the crater of a volcano which at any moment may overwhelm the community as with a torrent: it needs very little to bring about a crisis and a catastrophe.

The only hope lay in the therapeutic properties of the Christian witness in a time of political ills, which could "undermine the power of the demagogue and turn men from deeds of violence to paths of quiet and constitutional reform". In fact the authorities, especially the proponents of law and order, did take the threat of civil strife, even revolution, seriously. In September *Justice* revealed that "strict orders have been given to the police to break up all the processions of the unemployed should any attempt be made to march through the streets". Noting the ineptitude of police methods in trapping the Ripper, the journal questioned their motives. "Of what consequences are a few murders more or less in Whitechapel so long as polite society is secure from the denunciation of socialists? The unemployed are clubbed into silence, and the Red Flag is dragged from the hands of starving men lest it; should offend the susceptibilities of the well-to-do."[17]

For all that year there had been cause for alarm. When the "respectable" press like *Punch* (18 February) was quoting from poems of an unemployed operative, implying that the refusal of society to recognise the poor man's right to share in the good things of this world was putting a dangerous weapon into the hands of the revolutionists, and the *East London Observer* (11 February) was printing letters with mildly seditious utterances, ("What counsel can be given to the workless? I don't hesitate for a moment to tell them to besiege the workhouse doors and force the officials to receive them or the police to lock them up!"), it was no wonder that the government, faced with subsequent social disturbances, was moved to punitive action, particularly against local radicals. Violent manifestations from the forces of law and order were no cure for unemployment. In 1888 other solutions were posited, though none could guarantee success. For, as events proved, they tackled the symptoms rather than the disease.

One scheme, devised by the resourceful Warden of Toynbee Hall, was to arouse national interest and debate. It was put forward on 24 January to the Whitechapel Board of Guardians by the Rev. S. Barnett in terms of setting up local Agriculture Training Centres under the aegis of the Poor Law. How and where it was to be instituted was outlined in an incisive report by the *East London Observer*:

> That the Guardians of London represented by the central authority under the Metropolitan Poor Act, or an existing Board of Guardians, purchase uncultivated land in the neighbourhood of London. That such Guardians provide in or near this land accommodation for indoor poor, either in existing buildings or in sheds built for the purpose. That the Local Government Board be asked to issue a special order to administer the country settlement, so that its arrangement may be adapted to the training of the inmates in country work without forcing them to conform to rules which are suggestive of the workhouse. That the guardians offer able-bodied men of good character and of apparently solid determination residence in the country settlement, their wives and families to receive relief during the time of training, and they themselves to get the fixed tenure of land in England or the colonies at the expiration of their time.[18]

The idea, Barnett argued, was an extension of one already adopted in the Whitechapel Workhouse at South Grove. There, he reckoned, they were training men in industrious pursuits, notably bootmaking, carpentry and the like, rather than perpetuating the normal, less productive tasks of picking oakum or breaking stones.[19] Such a scheme was imperative because of the large numbers of unskilled labourers "thrown out of work by the employment of machinery and the influx of immigrants" already concentrating locally. Here he came to the major thrust of his argument. "They had not begun to enter the workhouse yet, it was true, but they were already knocking at our doors" when the increased demand for 'outdoor relief' would be ruinous to the applicants and the ratepayers!" Since Whitechapel had pioneered the establishment of district schools and training ships, it was no wonder that his scheme was unanimously adopted at the meeting of the full board on 20 March. However, as at that time the supply of workhouse accommodation was more than equal to the demand, they proposed to meet in conference to consider the possibilities of joint implementation.[20] Although the venture was aired in the national press, in the short term nothing practical emerged. An attempt at an all-London conference of unions was, apparently, unsuccessful. (The last entry on the subject in the Whitechapel minute book is dated 29 May, when the clerk was instructed to write to assenting unions to agree to convene a meeting at the boardroom of the City guardians. Whether it eventually transpired is not recorded.) Certainly there were no countryside "settlements" that year, although in November Barnett, arguing his case with greater sophistication in *The Nineteenth Century*, made an eloquent plea for experimentation, stressing that "the existence of the unemployed is conducive to class warfare and constitutes a danger to the wealth and well-being of the community".[21] William Booth got the message. He responded by calling on state intervention for their regimentation into such colonies. This solution was shared by Charles Booth, who urged the depositing, under government directions, of those casual poor who "from mental, moral and physical reasons are incapable of better work", into labour camps outside London, where they would exchange "their half-fed and half-idle and wholly unregulated life for a disciplined existence, with regular meals and fixed hours of work (which should not be short!)"[22] It was Poplar that gave practical realisation to the idea by opening two farm colonies at Laindon and at Hollesley Bay in Essex under the auspices of its Board of Guardians.

The other proposed solution was emigration to offset the continuing decline of prospects in the local labour market. The agricultural and industrial disasters of 1866/7, plus a harsh winter, had sent 850 Poplar unemployed abroad, mainly to Canada. This was in accord with the social imperialism of the age with its concomitant state-aided colonisation schemes. East End emigrants caused problems from the start, especially as many of the unwelcome "residuum" of casuals, loafers or the unemployable managed to slip thraugh the net. Objections were voiced that the metropolis was dumping its "human sewage" from Whitechapel on to them. Throughout 1888, in spite of overseas obstacles, emigrant numbers rose. In April the *East London Observer* described the despatch of a genuinely respectable group of unemployed, sponsored by a Tower Hamlets emigration aid society:

> On Wednesday night (18th April) from Mr Charrington's Hall, the first batch of emigrants this season left at 10.30 for Euston en route for Canada. Mr Charrington states that the past success of those sent out by him previously is such that he has no hesitation in still advocating Canada as a country for the honest unemployed. The present party consists principally of families, and nearly all were going to friends formerly sent out by Mr Charrington, and, therefore, will find work on landing. After a hot supper, they left the hall with Capt. Alexander Hamilton, the hon. secretary of the Tower Hamlets Mission Emigration and Colonisation Fund...[23]

It was this same Hamilton who, commenting previously on another emigrant to Canada — a failure "since he kept on complaining and changing jobs which were constantly too hard for him" — remarked that "he would go back to the Paradise of Loafers — Whitechapel Road!"[24]

A major source of supply to the colonies was Dr Barnardo who, by December, had despatched 3,773 boys and girls to Canada. His first organised party had gone out in 1882, since when he claimed to select "the flower of the flock". An enthusiast for colonial resettlement, Barnardo argued that by training the boys in the mechanical arts he could only place them in local employment at the expense of men already ensconced there. By removing them abroad he reduced potential competition in an already tight labour market, and transferred them to a healthier location and economy, where, demand for farm labour was "practically unlimited".[25] Other juveniles were recruited from the borough workhouses, and the social and psychological effects of what was virtually a forced exodus of the young are still to be assessed.[26]

The children had few outlets through which to register their dissatisfaction or protest at maltreatment or neglect. (Inspectors were notoriously thin on the ground in that vast territory where the child emigrants had been dispersed.) Nor were they or their adult counterparts always welcome. By 1888, Canadian attitudes towards them were hardening. In May, Barnardo reported "an increase in the cost of all future parties going to Canada... owing to several causes... government assistance began to be decreased." His explanation revealed the underlying reasons for the growing opposition to the newcomers:

> Canadian confidence has been shaken by an immense amount of improper emigration from this country. Poor men and women from the East End, people of the poorest class... have been sent out to Canada in shoals, without an atom of the necessary supervision en route, except, perhaps, the perfunctory and intermittent care of those worthy clergymen who consented to "conduct a party of emigrants".

These temporary guardians, ignorant of the qualifications and requirements needed for selection, were bringing out with them those members of the residuum who

> carrying in with them their old vices and evil habits, and finding Canada was not the El Dorado of their dreams, soon degenerated into loafing, idle paupers, incapable of self-effort, dependent on charity for support, and driven from city to city in the Dominion, practically supported by taxation.

London workhouses, too, were guilty of sending "large numbers of their boys and girls over the water, without any previous industrial training or separation from a pauper life than voyage on board a ship, such that the Canadians become alarmed at the probable influx of little paupers, who must, they fear, soon become a further charge upon their comparatively scanty means!" Some had been involved, in juvenile offences, which were reported in the Canadian press under the heading of "Another of Barnardo's criminals", although they had no connection with him.[27]

The Canadian Knights of Labour had added to the opposition, regarding "with intense disfavour and jealousy, emigration of any sort as being certain to bring fresh competitors into the... labour market". They viewed the constant invasion of outsiders as a threat to the price of labour commanded by home workmen. This accorded with the warnings given by a specially informed contributor to the *East London Observer*:

> We are kept posted in the doings of the Toronto Trades and Labour Council, as Mr O.J. O'Donogue, the Secretary of the Legislative Committee of the Council, regularly sends us the *Toronto News*, containing the record of the steps taken by the Council to make known the true state of the labour market in Canada. The agitation now going forward is with the object of inducing the Dominion Government to cease its encouragement to immigration, and of late the contention has gone further than that, viz, to call for an issue of an Order in Council to prevent the landing in Canada of persons rejected as immigrants by the U.S. Authorities. The Trades Council also get together facts as to the remuneration of labour and the numbers of unemployed, and the information thus collected does not appear to us to indicate Canada as the land flowing with milk and honey, either for the artisans' class or the agricultural labourer. The latter class just now are specially ill paid, the remuneration being in some cases as low as two dollars a month. In the building trade too there is great depression, and the result is seen in the circumstance that during the last year the St. George's Society of Toronto relieved no less than 6,655 persons.[28]

The same paper had previously stressed that other "promised lands" of the Dominions were proving a chimera. Reports from Australia evidenced the incidence of unemployment there, with an allusion to current "distribution of 11,699 ration tickets and the sending of 1,586 men to government relief works". A poem, "The East Londoner's Lament", illustrated the disillusion of an East Ender, who, unemployed at home, had sought new prospects in Queensland, only to find himself with others back on the breadline:

> Hundreds, too, of slaved dead beats,
> All, all stone broke,
> Perambulate the Brisbane streets,
> Fit, fit to croak,
> Rents are high and work is not.
> Few can keep a boiling pot;

Such a miserable lot,
Is, my friend, no joke.[29]

From far-away Texas came a similar tale of woe publicised by *Justice*. An SDF Branch secretary, "beguiled into emigrating" there, found himself unemployed and destitute, so that "our Tottenham comrades actually raised and sent him nearly £20 to bring him and his starving family home". *Justice* had a point when it advised: "Far better stop at home and fight the struggle than be shipped off to starve and rot thousands of miles away!"[30]

Back home, in such dense conglomerations as Tower Hamlets, the unemployed continued to be reckoned a perpetual source of danger. Hence the urgency of recommendations for solutions and, in the process, the historical re-appraisal of the efficacy of *laisser-faire* "theology". The farm colonies, agreed upon by both Charles and William Booth and by Barnett, posited a means whereby state intervention could overcome not only the "problem of unemployment and urban degeneration, but also rural depopulation".[31] Charles Booth defined the greatest menace: Class "B", the casual labour class, whose nature and condition in a free society rendered them unemployable. A form of compulsion was needed to remove them from the centres of mischief (ie those of urban decay) and, above all, to protect the "respectable" working men from their baneful influence. The social imperialists were concerned that the majority of emigrants did not consist of the casuals. Therefore one school felt it imperative for the state to impose technical education on its young until the age of 12, which would "deodorise... this foul humanity", so "fitting our people to use the wonderful safety valve we possess in our vast colonial empire".[32] This policy was already being implemented in Dr Barnardo's experimental schools. Nevertheless, on the home front, the powerful "individualist" lobby had a staunch defender in the Charity Organisation Society which, participating in a Parliamentary Commission on Metropolitan Poor Relief, successfully urged the rejection of such state impositions proposed by Barnett and Charles Booth, on the grounds that

> it is hardly necessary for us to set forth the serious objections to extensive schemes of this kind, if undertaken by the poor law authorities or by any agency connected with the government. Apart from the practical difficulties attending them, and from

the question of expense, it is to be feared that they would lead to a widespread belief that it is the business of the government to provide work at suitable wages for all who apply to it for employment.[33]

But it was to be a losing battle, and 1888 was the turning point. By then, as Stedman Jones acutely points out, the middle classes were already prepared to consider that "unfitness or degeneration was the condition, not of isolated individuals, but of swelling and threatening aggregates. In such circumstances, the problem of degeneration and its concomitant, chronic poverty, would ultimately have to be resolved by the state."[34] Otherwise the prospect of "the Deluge" was very real in the fears of contemporary Victorians.

The sweated

Sweating and unemployment were interrelated. The former was engendered by the entrepreneurs' need to reduce expensive overheads, especially wages, rents and fuel, to meet provincial factory competition. Within London itself the margin of profitability could only be maintained by cut-throat competition. Hence the pressure exerted on labour costs, which had to be kept to a minimum, was a major factor in the battle for survival.

East London contained a plethora of small pre-industrial-revolution type industries, which demanded little space or fixed capital, together with a vast reservoir of potentially cheap labour. Tailoring and cabinet-making were an example of local staple trades, in which little capital input was required to set up as a small master and skilled work was "sub-divided within the shell of small-scale production", where specialisation of function remained sharp and the cohesive group-consciousness of, say, miners or large-scale factory workers was notoriously absent.[35] Seasonal work predominated and output was geared to the immediate disposal of goods, which meant irregular employment for the majority. A burden facing the small master was the need to retain a nucleus of skilled workers through slack periods, who might be lost to rivals when the inevitable busy season returned. This certainly applied to East End concerns such as clothing, shoemaking, furniture-making, coopering, brush-making and most forms of dockside employment. Weather, according to Mayhew, was the most important barometer of employment in London. Cold winters caused particular distress among coal porters, lightermen, and non-specialised dockers, at a time when fuel and lighting costs were at their maximum. The numbers of destitute increased, and in previous bad seasons desperate men and women broke into Whitechapel and Poplar bakeries.[36] The advent of the steamship in the 1870s, which helped overcome the problem of getting to port and docks in icy weather, was one factor in ameliorating the situation by helping to sustain continuity in dock work during the harshest winter.

The long hard winter of 1887 directed not only the mass of unemployed, but also their wives, into the labour markets, and this spread the effects of distress into other occupations normally unaffected by weather. (August and September provided a respite when many of the unskilled could be, temporarily, absorbed in the building trades or in the annual "hopping" exodus to Kent.) By 1888 the coincidence of an army of unemployed and the persistence of small-scale production encouraged ambitious artisans to set up as small masters, notably in clothing, bootmaking and furniture. The result was competitive downward-bidding for contracts and the intensification of poverty for the sweated worker. As the casualisation of both skilled and unskilled gathered pace, the spin-off was an over-supply of recruits into the sweatshops of East London.

Why the concentration here? The existence of wholesalers in the eastern borders of the city and the availability of plentiful cheap labour were the positive determinants. In the East End was found the reversal of current industrial trends where cheap manual labour could substitute for capital equipment. Workers in dying industries, such as the silk weavers of Bethnal Green, could feed quickly into local tailoring, while redundant Poplar shipwrights turned to furniture making in Shoreditch workshops. In addition a captive market of cheap female labour, notably women engaged in outwork, lessened overhead costs for the employer. After 1881 the influx of Russo-Polish Jewish immigrants brought additional recruits to the overstocked labour mart. By 1888 the problems of immigration and sweating had come to a head, thanks to the agitation of the major newspapers and political demagogues on the make. The Jews were now associated with both the cause and the perpetuation of the economic evil. The old scapegoat was available in all his vulnerability.[37] Unemployment and the populist mood from below (derived from the irrational fears and hatred festering in the minds of the local slum-dwellers) jostled the government into positive action.

In February it appointed a House of Commons Select Committee to report on emigration and immigration, paralleled by a House of Lords Committee to investigate sweating. The inference was the identification of the latter as an immigrant importation. This was emphasised in John Burnett's Report to the Board of Trade on the Sweating System in the East End following a Board memorandum on immigration.[38] It was a debate initiated by the Earl of Dunraven in the House of Lords on 28 February which resulted in the setting up of a special Committee "to inquire and report into sweating". The *East London Advertiser* was jubilant. With its self-publicised, watchful eye on local affairs, it set the tone of those "patriots" who had prejudged the issue, even before the evidence had been called:

> At the time the report of Mr Burnett appeared we expressed our opinions very fully and without any reserve. The system exists, is in full swing, and in the present state of the law will, it seems to us, continue to do so. As it is carried on, the Factory Acts are powerless, while the inspection by the local authorities is all but useless. Hence foul air, long hours of drudgery, and starvation pay are producing in our midst colonies of human beings who are infinitely worse off than were the slaves of bygone times. "The Song of the Shirt" is now succeeded by "The Song of the Coat". For it is the tailoring trade that is responsible for the most part of the introduction of the sweating system... The swarms of foreign Jews, who have invaded the East End labour market, are chiefly responsible for this system and the grave evils which are flawing from it. Of course they are numbered among its victims too: but the brunt of the hardships involved in it fall with tenfold severity upon the English men and women who cannot live on the same paltry pittance as their foreign rivals. If this foreign immigration can be checked half the battle against the sweating system will be won.[38]

The *East London Observer*, equally censorious of sweaters and the legal impediments to combatting the evil, was more cautious in attempting to advocate easy solutions:

> But how to interfere is the difficulty. The "sweating system" is a consequence, or perhaps it would be more correct to say partly the consequence, of cheap foreign labour to our poverty markets. The sweating system is mainly the result of excessive competition in the tailoring trade, to which a number of the pauper foreigners have turned their hands.[40]

Other newspapers were eager to get in on the act, even the most liberal. Following closely on the *Advertiser*, the radical *East End News*, which was then concentrating its polemics against the weaknesses inherent in the current factory inspection system, also lamented the inability of the Factory and Workshop Act to fulfil its function, and while so doing exposed the ruses that the sweaters got up to in outwitting the law. The week before, it had published the application made by the Jewish Trade Union leader Lewis Lyons to the Thames Police Court on the basis of a "list of 2,000 insanitary dwellings" which, under the appropriate act, empowered any constable with a warrant to enter and inspect the workshops installed therein. The paper complained:

> The legislature has thought fit to exempt sweating shops from the operation of the (Factory and Workshop) Act of 1878. It does not, of course, do this in so many words. But it reaches the end as effectually by a provision that the act shall not apply to workshops "in which the only persons employed are members of the same family dwelling there", or in which no children or young persons are employed, and by another clause which forbids the inspectors to enter "any room actually used as a dwelling as well as for a factory or workshop". Thus, as the *Spectator* shows, the sweater who wishes to keep the inspector at arm's length has three strings to his bow. He may say that he employs his relations, and that they all live on the premises; or he may employ only adult labour; or he may make the workshop additionally unwholesome by using it as a living room as well... The ordinary laws of health ought not to be set at defiance even if the victims are all related to the sweater by blood or marriage, or if they all pig together by night as well as work together by day...[41]

Both Committees continued, in their proceedings, to underline the assumption that immigrants engendered sweating. Burnett re-emphasised to the House of Commons caucus that, in tailoring, the epitome of sweated trades, "foreigners have been dominating the trade for the last twenty-five years" and "if the present movement continues, the ready-made clothing will be in the hands of foreigners". Top master tailors had become very wealthy. "The largest man in the trade in the East End is supposed to be very rich. He is engaged in trouser work and his name is Friedlander. His place is in Great Prescott Street; he employs eighty people there, and he gives work outside to another seventy to eighty people." Burnett noted that remuneration was highest among the largest capitalist sweaters, but "for the lower grade, it is becoming a business that will pay them less and less."[42] His repeat performance on this theme to the Lords Committee on 20 April moved the reforming anti-immigrant *Pall Mall Gazette* (30 April) to voice its concern at "the real cause of the decline of prices... the growth in number of clever-fingered foreigners, chiefly Jews and Jewesses, who do considerably more than three-fourths of the trade and seem to have agencies for importing labour to all places where wholesale tailoring thrives." Modification of the Factory Acts would kill the sweating system "resulting from foreign labour, stealthily imported, to benefit a few hungry-souled Jews".

This provided the opportunity for the patriot and imperialist author Arnold White to act as self-appointed crusader against the alien "coloniser". He took up the cry with a vengeance following the earlier outburst of Captain Colomb MP. "I object to England," he said, "with its overcrowded population being made a human ashpit for the refuse population of the world!"[43] Called as prime witness for both committees, White's evidence was a mixture of the informed and the prejudiced. On 13 April before the Lords, taking East End conditions as his model, he defined the sweater as one who "grinds the face of the poor... a man without capital, skill or speculation" who operated "mainly in the boot trade... tailoring and shirt making, and in a lesser degree, in cabinet making and upholstery". His comments on alien labour reflected the superficiality of his observations:

> The men were pertinaciously industrious and were well behaved as regarded morality, and very fond of their children but in regard to cleanliness, abominable. They knew no amusement, they had no pleasure in the past, no hope for the future. They were old men at forty, and their children, though very intelligent, were physically degenerate. The men became raw material for revolutionary propaganda.

White recommended the exclusion of *greeners* or foreign paupers over 50 (ie those, according to the American Act, who were likely to become a public charge, ignoring the fact that Jews rarely were, since they had their own voluntary aid institutions such as the Jews Temporary Shelter and the Board of Guardians), who could not speak English and "never brought any money with them". The provisions of the Factory Act should be extended to the adult male, workrooms registered and notices fixed outside the premises, so that every room thus certificated would be accessible to the factory and sanitary inspectors. He added, by the way, that he had never come across a single Englishman sweating,[44] but went on to contradict himself a week later by referring to an example of sweating as practised by Christians on Christians! He summed up his argument against immigration to the Select Committee of the House of Commons on 8 May: that the alien was cutting down the price of labour and therefore threatening the home-born Englishman.

Horror stories about sweatshops multiplied, stimulated by evidence, real or exaggerated, conveyed in proceedings in both Houses of Parliament. Earlier John Burnett had piled on the agony before the Immigration Committee:

> In Spitalfields a Polish Jew with a staff of five men and four women often worked in the slack season for coats at 9d each... In Great Prescott Street coats for which a few years ago 10s was paid, the man now received 6s 6d, 5s 6d of which the sweater said was the cost of labour. These coats were for a noted Regent Street firm... A few doors further on was an establishment where coats were now being made for 4s 6d, which six or seven years ago were paid for at the rate of 8s.[45]

A confused statement by a Mr Woolf Zeitlin, Secretary of the Jewish Branch of the Tailors Society, purported to refute the claim that current wages were dramatically reduced, suggesting that levels equated to those of 1882 and 1883, although there was less work to be found thanks to the importation of machinery which displaced hands. He concurred however with the overall picture of exploitation, where workers toiled "16, 17 or 18 hours a day" with women "nearly the same number of hours" and "children also 14 or 15 hours a day".[46] Apparently Beatrice Potter, in her investigations, had underestimated the average working day which she reckoned as 13 to 14 hours for male adults and 12 hours for women although "the day, if needful, is lengthened out at the workers' expense in order to accomplish it".[47]

By May a chorus of anti-immigrant tirades had reached a crescendo. The *East London Observer* openly demanded exclusion. "We are justified on the ground that they depreciate our home products and depress our markets; that their low state of civilisation tends to demoralise whole populations of native workers and that all efforts made by a handful of hard-working social reformers to raise the poor into a condition are rendered utterly unavailing."[48] Jewish officials and institutions, concerned with defending the good name of the community, were not slow to respond to the onslaught. At first the Chief Rabbi, Dr Hermann Adler, diffident in his approach to anti-alien propaganda, had hesitated to express firm views on Burnett's revelations. This attitude provoked an irate response from Trade Union secretary Lewis Lyons. In a letter to the *East London Observer* criticising Adler for refusing "to express his opinions, although he has had personal experience of the conditions of the sweaters' victims", Lyons warned that if "they (the Jewish Establishment) want to prevent a Jewish labour riot, they might assert themselves more than they do at the present time".[49] The heated debates, extensively reported, on the sweating system forced the Chief Rabbi to make a defensive statement, which, in effect, was supportive of the positive advantages accruing from the presence of cheap foreign labour:

> Apart from the unsanitary conditions of the workshops of the sweater... it is difficult to see how any case for legislative interference can be devised against the foreign immigrant. As was pointed out in the House of Lords and in the *Times*, a very important industry, the export trade of which alone amounts to £4,000,000, is kept in this country by low-priced labour. Much harm would be effected if this were largely displaced... who is harmed by the (sweating) system except the foreign immigrant himself? And for him, the conditions of life here are probably better on the whole than in his native country, so that there is no loss of human happiness to set against the economical gains of cheap production.[50]

A classic *laisser-faire* position, in which no mention is made of the dehumanising effect on the labourers. His omission was made good by the more perceptive reaction of Rabbi J.F. Stern of the East London Synagogue, who kept a day-to-day watch on his immigrant flock. In contradistinction to his chief, in a moving sermon based on Leviticus 25: 39-43, he denounced sweating and exploitation as an abomination. There was no mercy for the rich predators who fed on their poorer brethren:

> I assure you... that it is heartrending to listen to the tales of sorrowing toil and morbid despair which assail the ear of him who enters the homes of some of our Jewish poor. The position of the sweated labourer is a most deplorable one; he cannot economise, for his wages are already no more than will support existence; and they are only so much as they are, because if they were less the man could not live, and would no longer fulfil the function of the machine like which he is treated. He cannot increase his exertions, for his value as a member of society is measured by time, not by what he produces; and unless he could add more hours to those which the earth takes to revolve around the sun, he had no dispensable fund on which he can draw to meet the emergency.
> There is not the slightest doubt that the sin of grinding down the poor workmen... lies at the door of the rich. It is a sin born of selfishness, avarice and heartlessness... Brethren, I entreat you to do all in your power, in your various walks of life, to discourage this sin, to blot out this scourge from the face of the earth.[51]

This powerful indictment by a subordinate, publicly reported, may have prompted the Chief Rabbi to change his tune, for he managed to profess in like vein a week later: "I am bitterly grieved when I hear the names of certain manufacturers mentioned, who, either themselves or their managers, use every pretext and subterfuge in order to cut down payment for work, treating those who are in their power with insults and contempt. It is humiliating to read the statement made by the Government Inspector of Factories, that in these trades the maxim that 'all Israel are brethren' seems *not* to be adhered to." But a would-be stern rebuke ended with the banal admonition: "To you, both employers and employed, I lift up my voice with all the earnestness and deep affection. Obey the precepts of your God, keep the laws of the land!"[52]

Nevertheless, later in front of both Committees there were attempts by Jewish spokesmen to play down, or even refute, the accusation of alien paupers tied to a ruthless exploitative system. On 6 July, Mr Joseph E. Blank, secretary to the Jews Temporary Shelter, spoke of earnings relating to "full or part week's work for a machinist tailor were from £2 10s a full week to £1 or £1 5s a week averaging only two or three days, according to busy or slack season", implying that both met the needs of subsistence.[53] There were even local apologists among the workers, obviously "briefed" by their employer, who would make sure that no aberrations in work conditions could be attributed to him. Thus on 13 July, employees of Mr Mark Moses, a powerful Whitechapel master tailor, gave evidence to the Lord's Committee as follows. Miss Rachel Gashin, buttonhole maker, said she could earn a maximum of 26s a week.

> The witness then made some buttonholes before the committee, finishing four in 13½ minutes. She was paid a halfpenny per buttonhole, and that produced 9d an hour. She considered that good pay and worked as a rule from 8am to 8pm each day. The "twist" and "gimp" cost 4s in each sovereign earned... Mr Morris Marks, a machinist, formerly president of the London Tailors' Machinist Society, corroborated evidence of Mr Moses as did a Mrs Annie Session, a baster, and Mrs Jane Sessions (Christians) who said they had no complaint to make, had proper hours for meals and were paid overtime.[54]

All this information was given under the watchful eye of Mr Moses!

Disclosures of the horrors of sweating to both Houses would refute the cosy pictures or defensive arguments put forward by Moses and other Jewish Establishment interests. From the beginning of the enquiries the reports exposed the feed-in to the system by the influx of out-county unemployed. The Rev. J. Monroe, in his statement to the Lords Committee on 24 April, verified not only this but also the dependence of sweaters on the labour of local women whose husbands were either unemployed or physically incapable of working. "Accompanied by Arnold White he went through the streets of the East End early on a Sunday morning and found seventy persons who had come up from the country on Saturday to find work, and had been unable to pay for their lodging. They were mainly agricultural labourers, but some were from Tyneside, where a strike prevailed at this time." The miseries heaped on the sweated victims, of diverse ethnicity, are brought to life by a series of illuminating vignettes presented by witnesses. On that same journey the Rev. Monroe had questioned a number of working wives:

> Mrs Glaister, shirt finisher, wife of a dock labourer, 67 years of age, said she had to do shirt-making because her husband could

no longer compete with younger men in dock labour, and Elizabeth Killick, a poorly dressed woman of middle age, stated that her husband, a boiler maker, had been in the infirmary, three years paralysed, and that she received no money from his club because he had been "scratched" there seven years. She was a trousers finisher, and could make 14d a day by working from 6 o'clock in the morning till eight at night, but out of that she had to provide trimmings, soap and cotton and made only 1s a day clear. After paying 2s a week rent, she had 5s a week to provide food, fuel, light and clothes for herself and three children, the youngest three years of age and the eldest ten. Asked by Lord Aberdeen if the money she earned was sufficient to provide food, she said it was not, but she had to make it do. Asked what she got chiefly she said a herring and a cup of tea, and as for meat she did not suppose she had had a bit for six months.

Mary Hayes, trousers finisher, widow of a soldier, gave similar evidence stating that she worked from eight in the morning till ten or twelve at night, and only managed to get a bit of meat at 5d per 1b for Sundays.[55]

These were two of many examples of Christian victims in the needle trades. Equally shocking were those attributed to Jewish immigrant labour. Arnold White was quick to evidence their suffering. On 8 May he submitted a series of letters in Yiddish describing workshop conditions. One, in translation, described a room, "which is by no means an exceptional one", used for domestic outwork:

In a certain street in the Ghetto of Whitechapel is a Polish slipper maker. He, his wife, and their several children exist in one room for which they pay 3s 7d a week. The room reeks with the smell of human flesh; cinders, dirt and babies occupy the uncarpeted floor. No pet birds, flowers or animals suggest the existence of any side to life but that of anxiety, squalor and toil. This slipper maker earns threepence a pair for making slippers and he finishes six pairs in the day. His earnings are accordingly 9s a week, of which 3s 7d are absorbed by the rent. The children have no appearance of childhood; a wistful look, as though of tired age appears in even the babies' eyes. The misery of this Pole, who has recently arrived in London, is a measure of the misery he and his countrymen have wrought on the English workers in the cheap slipper trade.[56]

The last statement was a reflection of White's own prejudice. It was soon clear to the investigators that he deliberately sought out the worst examples, his paid aides even fabricating others, to make his point. More convincing was the personal account of one Myer Wilchinski (published in *Commonweal* on 26 May as "The History of a Sweater") produced as testimony before the House of Lords Committee on 7 August 1888. Although "literally fictitious but circumstantially true", the validity of his description was reinforced by the current publication in the *East London Observer* of nine articles (ending on 23 June) on "The Merchant Taylors Company and the Sweating System" by the Jewish union leader, Lewis Lyons.

Wilchinski, from the city of Kohl near Carlish in Russian Poland, had gone through the whole process of rags to riches via many years' experience as workman and master in East End sweatshops. His description of the *chazar mart* (unofficial employment market) is particularly moving, especially of the *greeners* (newcomers) seeking their first job.

> Many of them, like myself (were) willing to work at anything that would bring them the scantiest means of existence; some married and with families and all with that enquiring, beseeching look, that half starved, helpless, hopeless human beings must of necessity possess. I, looking perhaps brighter than the majority who really looked like so many unwashed corpses...

His grim description of life and labour in a Spitalfields tailor's home aptly exemplified conditions still prevalent in the 1880s in that trade and locale:

> I determined to chance my luck, and closed with a tailor who offered to teach me the trade and give me lodgings and coffee for three weeks, and six shillings a week afterwards, until I learned one branch of the trade (coatmaking), when I would be able, he said, to demand from four to eight shillings a day for my toil. He lived in one of the many dirty streets in Spitalfields, and the work he made was railway and seamen's coats — hard, heavy work, that required more brute strength than skill. He occupied two rooms on the second floor, for which he paid seven shillings a week; had a wife, and three children aged respectively seven, four, two: very intelligent almost crafty.
>
> The room we worked in was used for cooking also, and there I had to sleep on the floor. The wife helped as much as she could at the trade, beside doing all the work of the house and the children. A young woman worked the machine from eight in the morning till nine at night, for 3s a day; not very often making a full week's work. My work at first was to keep up a good fire with

coke, and soap the seams and edges; and the elbow grease I used was considerable. I had to get up in the morning about half past five, and we finished at night between ten and eleven, and turned out every week about thirty coats, which came to about £4. The master himself worked very hard indeed; and he himself told me afterwards that he had left the old country for the same reason as myself, and that a few years previously he had been a cowkeeper and dairyman, but was now a "tailor".

A shrewd operator, Wilchinski was resolved to "get on" whatever the cost, rejecting the overtures of the local marriage broker while he was "too intent on money getting" and raising himself higher in the social scale. His was a success story. To date he was operating a large workshop, and from the profits had also invested in a cigar business. But he never forgot his early years as a victim of exploitation, was evidently a generous employer and, curiously enough, a self-confessed supporter of the Nihilist movement![57]

Lyons' impressive account, built up by instalments, was more specific. He probed wide and deep into the whole process of sweating, past and present. He first presented a riveting description, derived, with acknowledgment, from articles in the *Pall Mall Gazette*, of two sweating dens in the East End. In the larger the workers had no more than 160ft^3 allotted them. The smaller, in Plumbers Row, had space for 130ft^3 per hand, which, Lyons asserted, contravened rudimentary health requirements for the individual in this setting, citing a Mr Angell, (who) in his work on "Animal Physiology" says "No human being should work in a workshop which is less than 800ft^3 and breathe less than 100ft^3 of air." In consequent articles the workings of the specialisation of function by hands via the roles of fitter, machinist, baister, presser, feller and button-maker were closely defined. Because of the failure of the Merchant Taylors Company to put their trade regulations into practice during the last 200 years, bespoke tailoring, based on the "complete tailor" who could take a garment through all the process of creation, was doomed, to be currently replaced by sweating. The degradation of women was linked to the supply of *greeners* and contributed to the malfunctioning. of the industry. Lyons, a working tailor, could speak with authority:

> The sweaters can... get these men (*greeners*) to work cheaper after a few months' training, than females. It is not a question of sex to them, but one of cheapness... unsuccessful (ie in marriage)

(women) are compelled to take a less sum for their hard work in consequence of the sweaters teaching a "greener" in a very short time, and paying them a starvation wage, (and) have no alternative but to prostitute their bodies in order to get more money so that they may exist. I have spoken to some prostitutes whom I formerly knew and worked with in sweating dens, and asked them whether it was from their own free will that they were leading an immoral life or because wages were low, and they attributed it to the latter.[58]

Young, single, female labour was considered unreliable anyway ("since they only think in short term before marriage, when they hope to stop working"), while men were forced to remain under permanent control, since whether married or single, they had to work to live. In effect the married men were driven to an unlimited application to labour in the workshops so that they might at least meet the demands for subsistence for themselves and their families. Beatrice Potter's observations in her own ephemeral employment in a Jewish coatmaker's accord with those of Lyons. In 1888 she pinpointed coatmaking as being concentrated "within an area of less than one square mile, comprising the whole of Whitechapel, a small piece of Mile End, and part of St. George's in the East." Her study of the tailoring trade embraced 901 Jewish coatmakers classified according to the numbers employed and the quality and price of the product. What emerged was that 76.1% of their shops employed less than ten hands and, of these, 541 small masters were engaged in producing the cheapest quality and, therefore, the lowest priced garments (referred to as "Stock and Common" and "Very Common, ie slop" goods).[59]

The volume of evidence accumulating in both Houses was paralleled by a torrent of anti-alien rhetoric outside in press and pulpit. It was generally conceded that sweating, and by association, the immigrant, were both unpopular and undesirable. Yet as late as 23 June, Lionel Alexander, the stern Hon. Secretary of the Jewish Board of Guardians, was bold enough to argue in defence of sweating before the Lords Committee. "In his opinion the 'sweater' was an essential personage in the production of clothing as the merchant tailor could scarcely maintain a factory independently of whether he was busy or "slack"... The sweating system had developed a class of trade in clothing and boots which did not previously flourish, which did not compete materially with the higher-paid work of the Englishman and which enabled the poorer people to obtain at a cheap rate articles which were previously out of their reach." He dared to refute the accepted view with the challenging assertion that "the sweaters' shops in the tailoring trade were better in a sanitary sense than the domestic workrooms and were seldom overcrowded".[60] Beatrice Potter produces partial support. In her judgment better sanitary conditions and general comforts of the workshop depended on the wealth and importance of the contractor:

> Those who organise and superintend the workers monopolise the best shops in the district: they will secure light (a marketable commodity to the tailor, as it saves artificial lighting), they will substitute the more efficient gas stove for the coke fire, and they are more amenable to Government inspection in regard to sanitation and space. A well-to-do Jewish contractor could spend the day with his workers, helping, encouraging, or driving them, according to his individual nature.

But these were the exceptions. Since Class C, the small workrooms employing fewer than ten hands, formed, according to Burnett, 80% of the East End trade, it was there, that the most deplorable examples of exploitation and unhygienic conditions were found. There the small master "seldom knows the distinction between a workshop and a living room; if he himself sleeps and eats in a separate room, some of his workers will take their rest on a shake down between the presser's table, the machines and scattered heaps of garments... here it is overcrowding day and night — no ventilation in the room, no change to the worker." Against this Beatrice Potter posed the necessity for a certain minimum space for a presser's table and bulky coat machine and, in the lowest class of trade, this proportion increased. She reckoned that, as a whole, in the East End tailoring industry the presence of large machines and the marketable value of light were physical impediments to the cellar occupation and huddled misery attributed to the lowest class of boot finishers.[61]

In placing the boot trades higher up in the sweating league than tailoring, she may well have been right. East End bootmakers, although some were already equipped with new US machinery, needed all the labour strength they could muster to compete against the factory giants emerging in the provinces. For, even in 1888, the hand-made trade in the metropolis was already succumbing to the rivalry of outside large-scale factories centred in Norwich, Leicester and Northampton; and, as the London producers quit, they left groups of displaced employees to compete with each other for inferior outwork.[62] Of course the ubiquitous Arnold White was quick to offer his expertise on bootmaking. Examined before the Lords Committee, he delivered an informative account of the functioning of small concerns, marred, as usual, by his emotionally charged, and therefore prejudiced, evidence against the alien worker. It is significant that although the local trade consisted of both Jewish and Gentile labour, hearings were geared mainly to testimony offered by the former. White opened initial proceedings with an overall analysis of the state of the trade. He viewed the introduction of sweating as a consequence of the use of machinery and the immense influx of foreign paupers after 1885. Such new machines had increased the ranks of the manufacturers and caused intense competition. The colonial markets were flooded with work of the most worthless kind. (He actually produced a piece of paper taken from the sole of a boot produced locally.) In the slop trade small masters sought work from so-called manufacturers who were unable to influence the price of leather or the amount of rent and had no other factor to reduce than wages. Income from the final products was divided as follows: one half to the master, and the balance split between three classes of workmen. If a master contracted for 25 dozen boots for £7 10s to be completed in a week he took £5 15s, out of which he found rent 3s 6d, gas 2s 6d and grinding of tools 12s 6d: the profit being derived being without capital or labour on his part.[63]

Again confirming Beatrice Potter's assessment, conditions attributed to boot-making proved much worse than those in tailoring. A *Shoe and Leather Record* reporter, visiting a one-room sweatshop in the East End, was horrified at the scene, even more so at the rubbish produced there which would be foisted on the more gullible, ie lower-class, public as footwear.

> Besides the six workers there were in the room, two women and two little girls. The latter appeared to be waiting for some fish that the mother was cooking for supper in the same room in the

small hours of the morning. The master showed me one pair which he had back from the shop because the bottoms were not clean enough. I have seen some rubbish in the guise of boots and shoes, but these were the worst I have ever seen. It is horrible and pitiful to think that men should wear out their lives on the manufacture of such wasteful products. Here are some of the prices. Girls kid button, strip waist 2s 4d per dozen; women's kid shoes, strip waist 3s 9d per dozen; mock kid shoes, black, black waists 2s 6d; lasting S.S. paper heels 2s 3d; children's leather lined 1s 6d per dozen.... The employer's... constant threat seems to be that if his unfortunate slaves don't come to his terms he can get others who will.[64]

His observations were confirmed by evidence given by boot workers themselves before the Sweating Committee. Most victims instructed to give testimony were, pointedly, immigrants. Their harsh and bitter existence, voiced in a barely comprehensible jargon, struck a discordant note within the dignified, ornate setting of the Lords' chamber. Samuel Wildman, a Hungarian Jew, delivered the more articulate rendering of his own miserable experience, implicit in the lot of his fellow *greeners*.

An ex-teacher, unable to gain a living because of anti-Jewish restrictions in his own country, he had arrived in London ten years before. For three months he was unemployed and the only opening he could find was as boot and shoe learner in a local workshop where he was told he could learn finishing within a month. While a beginner he worked for nothing, the hours being from 5 in the morning till midnight. He now laboured from 6am until midnight, and was paid 15s 8d per week (being allowed a cup of coffee and tea but no bread as a sort of bonus!) He had to be present in the work room for six days a week, even when there was insufficient work to justify it. The work room was four-and-a-half yards square and two or three yards high. It had two windows, two gas lights and one heating bracket, and within these cramped confines worked the master and five men. He conceded that in the best times a boot finisher could earn 28s a week, but in the worst (December and January) only 13s — if he were lucky enough to be employed at all.

His testimony was underlined by others. A recently arrived Odessan Jew, Meyer Feillick, was learning the trade from an established fellow-countryman, and in return for daily labour, which lasted from 6am until midnight, he received breakfast and dinner. Another long domiciled finisher, Solomon Rosenberg, added his own tale of woe. His working hours were normally 7am till midnight (in "busy" season 6am till 1am the following morning!) for which he received 15s a week. Out of this meagre sum his weekly commitments were 6s 6d for rent, 1s 5d for paraffin, 1s 5d for coal and 6d for school fees for his six children. The remaining 6s 2d was all he had to feed himself and his large family. It is interesting to note that Wildman, an immigrant himself, attributed the failure of all attempts to form a trade union among the boot finishers to the fact that "the men spoke different languages" and also to the "continued arrival of *greeners* (which) rendered combination impossible". This theme was repeated by Rosenberg, who confessed that he had tried unsuccessfully to form a society for the finishers, but his efforts were negated by the constant inflow of *greeners*. "He was opposed to his countrymen coming over here, spoiling the trade, and inflicting suffering upon their fellow countrymen of long standing in this country." Arnold White had set the tone with his affirmation that since 1880, wages had fallen by one third thanks to foreigners emanating from Minsk, Odessa and Russian Poland. While another immigrant made good, Charles Soloman, Secretary of the Jewish Boot and Shoe Trade Masters' Association, vied with the leading anti-alienist to pin-point the newcomers as the source of evil that had led to the flooding of the market with would-be masters, thus diminishing their capacity to resist the lowering of prices by manufacturers, who thrived on this "unhealthy competition". And as though to clinch the evidence mustered against them, William Hoffmann, special commissioner for the *Boot and Shoe and Leather Record*, assured that same Committee: "the sweating system, as far as the boot trade is concerned, is confined principally to the Jews."[65]

Such accusations did not go unchallenged. Efforts to refute them came from diverse quarters, some presumably to defend the good name of the Jewish community, others to justify the system. Mark Moses, established master tailor of Princelet Street, Spitalfields, repudiating on behalf of his local colleagues the so-called horror myths attributed to their workshops, made some telling points. He posited that the so-called "sweating dens of the East End" were far more healthy, better kept and ventilated than the underground cellar shops in the City of

London, or the living rooms of the back slums in the West End. (A questionable argument, since the numbers and density of small shops including both these types of malaccommodation was highest in Whitechapel!) Criticism of sweating had over-occupied the attention of philanthropists, "well-meaning ladies and gentlemen, possessing little or no practical acquaintance with the subject". Their desire to annihilate the middleman and replace him by either wholesale firms or workers' co-operatives was an example of uninformed, and therefore wishful, thinking. A manager would never have the overriding will to succeed implicit in personal ownership, The inevitable result would be either a reduction in wages to meet the increased liabilities or increased prices for the goods, ie a change which would be to the disadvantage of workers and consumers. The co-operative scheme had been tried and failed in a Tenter Street Building Workshop three years before. The capital had been provided by the Rev. S. Barnett of St. Jude's and Mr D.F. Schloss and, according to Moses, "proved a complete fiasco". He concurred with Schloss, who explained the failure as "principally, though perhaps not entirely, in consequence of the unwillingness of the workers to work with reasonable care and energy under a competent foreman elected by themselves". As for the influx of foreign paupers *determining* the fall in labour wages, this was demonstrably false. "They were not of much practical use in the trade... and as for journeyman tailors the tendency was the other way and he could say that the hands were paid 25% better wages than they received six or seven years ago." He contested Lewis Lyons' remarks on the weights used by the pressers and the length of hours worked. Machinists were on a maximum 13 hours a day and demanded and received extra pay for overtime. Unskilled labour, of course, had to put up with what they got. However, he certainly put Arnold White on the spot. Moses dismissed his complaints against the Jewish labourers with the contention that "the Jews at least, whose presence seemed to distract Mr White's peace of mind, certainly did not compete with the English sweaters by making that wretched class of work... There were no Jews in the shirt or suit trade, and he only knew of two in the vest trade." As for the alleged insanitary conditions of Jewish workshops, how was it that the mortality rate among Jews was *exceedingly* low? Here Moses was on insecure ground, and he knew it.[66]

Positive support for a system guaranteeing cheap products via cheap labour was also forthcoming. In reply to questioning by local MP Samuel Montagu in front of the House of Commons Select Committee on 22 June, trade expert Robert Griffin confirmed a steady expansion in the export of apparel and slops from the Port of London. (The figures he submitted showed income derived therefrom rising from £604,280 during the first three months of 1887 to £747,203 for the corresponding period in 1888.) As much to vindicate immigrant labour, Montagu pressed Griffin to agree that "cheap production has that tendency" to increase exports in the clothing trade.[67] It would appear that the moral implication of such profit derived from the harshest exploitation was irrelevant.

White's early contention "where there were no foreign paupers there was no sweating" was dismissed before the Lords Committee by Mr Jacob Flatau, member of an established firm of London and Northampton boot manufacturers. He emphasised that the system was *not* peculiar to Jewish or foreign workmen and that White's statement that wages had been reduced 30 or 40% since 1885 by Jewish houses was utterly unwarrantable. He estimated only 2,000 Jewish boot and shoe makers in London and, therefore, "to state that the wages throughout the country were affected to any appreciable extent by the competition of foreigners in London was clearly incorrect". (In 1881 the census had recorded a total of 267,000 in the boot trade.) Christian masters employed the same men as their Jewish counterparts, and Gentile hands worked in teams with a sub-division of labour in the same way as Jews. His view was confirmed by Thomas Lilley of Lilley and Skinner who reiterated that "the sweeping assertions made in respect of the Jewish houses were hardly just". He added, however, his own peculiar recommendations for combatting sweating. These had been considered by the Bootmakers Association, who had urged the operatives to co-operate with their masters to solve the problem, but "it had been found that trade unionism militated against any settlement!"[68]

There was the recurrent problem of defining what one was supposed to remedy. Sweating meant different things to different people. Lewis Lyons, who had been on the receiving end and purported to be a specialist in the field, submitted that "the word sweat derives its origin from the Anglo-Saxon *swot* and means the separation or extraction of labour or toil from others for one's own benefit. Any person who employs others to extract from them surplus labour without compensation is a sweater." The middleman sweater was one who acted as a contractor for labour for another person. Conditions became more aggravated when the middleman employed the labour himself at his own home for the purpose of extracting a double quantity of labour, either by lowering wages or working longer hours. Further, a sweater was one who sub-divided an industry into several branches, and had no apprentice system or other official training scheme connected with such an industry. Lyons scoffed at Beatrice Potter's attempts at a serious assessment: "Just fancy, a lady working in a sweater's den for three weeks, and collecting, as she said, all the details connected with the sweating system which has taken fifty years to develop!" Yet her proposal that any investigation would have to entail an inquiry into all labour employed in manufacture which had escaped the regulation of the Factory Act and trade unions, was essentially valid.[69] Clementina Black blamed the consumer for both cause and effect of the evil. In her view "as long as the public persists in buying the cheapest article on the market, so long will wages be determined, not by the just measure of the Mosaic law, but by the lowest rate at which the worker will consent to exist".[70] While the SDF journal conceived "the true definition of sweating (as) being the robbery by the monopoliser from the worker of a large portion of the produce of his toil", it was the Socialist League's *Commonweal* that appeared to penetrate deeper into the roots of the question:

> We are all much too ready to abuse the so-called sweater, the sub-contractor who grinds the faces of the very poor. But the sub-contractor is himself merely the instrument of superior forces. The surplus value produced by the "hands" under his supervision is not for him. The classes who really profit by his exertions are three in number... the landlords of town site or slum tenement whose rents are raised by the overcrowding and local congestion which makes sweating possible... the large contractor, whose command over the instrument of production enables him, by advances, discounts, rebates, and what not to squeeze his sub-contractor. And finally the investing capitalist, himself holding aloof from the contamination of actual trade, innocently shares the plunder with the contractor in the forms of dividends, interest on bank deposits, and so on. But the first

two classes sit in Parliament, and the third philanthropically goes "slumming". Hence all the social obloquy is reserved for their poor tool, the sub-contractor who does not in the least understand what it is all about.[71]

Divergences in the understanding of sweating led to diverse suggestions for its remedy. Arnold White's proposals were clear and unequivocal. The first priority was the restriction of foreign paupers, especially "elderly men ignorant of a trade, speaking no language but their own, and bringing no money with them". The Factory Acts must be extended to adult males, and all work rooms registered. As for the main target, the "pauper" alien, most journals, including *The Times* and, locally, the *East London Observer*, concurred with White. Compulsory registration had been widely mooted as a result of Burnett's report and emphasised in the attestation by W. Hoffmann, ex-foreman of a large boot factory, in front of the Lords Committee (14 April). The more sympathetic *East London Advertiser* concentrated on two remedies: "One to form a number of factories which would replace the pestiferous sweating dens; another to sweep away the middleman and bring the worker into direct contact with the principal employer."[72] A follow-up article by its correspondent "Rambler" described a large Government clothing manufactory for soldiers' uniforms in Pimlico, outlining the advantages of large-scale production:

> In a large central hall 700 women were at work. Long rows of machines, all worked by machinery, formed a number of aisles, as it were down the hall. At the time I was there a large order for soldiers' tunics was being executed and the machines were bright with crimson cloth. Flashes of scarlet gleamed in all directions and bursts of bright laughter and merry chatter arose at intervals above the continuous hum of machinery. The air was pure and fresh as any sanitary faddist could desire, although taking in the galleries, there were 1,200 people employed in the building.

On this and other evidence "the general consensus of opinion is coming round to the belief in the adoption of the factory system" under which "work would be carried on under sanitary conditions instead of the filthy dens at present".[73] This trend was already in motion. Beatrice Webb recorded a contemporary interview with the principal partner of the large H & E Wholesale Clothiers firm.

He boasted of a revolution taking place in the tailoring trade, with small tailors being wiped out, so that it was "now a trade in which capitalists invested money and worked on a wholesale scale": a generalisation which was not applicable to the East End where small workshops were still proliferating.[74]

Clementina Black suggested the compilation of a public record of good employers to "help establish that somewhat wavering sense of personal moral duty in commercial dealing which is beginning to have a recognised place in their public opinion". This would be published by a Consumers League that would also issue a proscribed list of firms who underpaid or ill-treated their employees, If such an organisation were founded, it could act as a valuable advertisement for those who subscribed to it. Lewis Lyons' prescription was far ahead of his time. He would reduce the hours of labour per day until everyone was employed, given that the basic rates of pay were universally recognised and enforced. In accord with current mores the introduction of workers' self-help factories was feasible, provided they were under the control of professionals. That such experiments were already functioning was revealed in the *East London Observer* (18 February). According to a letter from correspondent R.J.W., a "Workers Protection Society" to oust sweating was inaugurated at the Shaftesbury Memorial Hall, Poplar, where, since the previous December, a shirt-making factory had been installed with "the co-operation of a City House", which obviously exercised overall control. Some extraordinary claims were made by the writer:

The full payment received by the Society for work done is passed on to the workpeople with the nominal deduction of one penny per week for refreshments supplied daily in the workroom... It stands as a memorial of what a few merchants, acting quite disinterestedly, have been able to do in the way of defeating the selfishness that appropriates the just reward of labouring folk to the personal end and aggrandisement of a grasping master. Those who work for the Society are paid precisely at the same rate as City firms give out their work to be done. It is not a case, therefore, of undertaking labour at a reduction which would swamp the competition of the sweaters; it is a simple affair of those who do the work pocketing the proceeds of it.

Other co-operative ventures were certainly pursued throughout that year, as shown by two reports in the local press. On 3 December, at St. Paul's Hall, Goulston Street, a public meeting was called by the London Independent Co-operative Clothing Manufacturing Society for the purpose of advocating co-operation as a means of remedying the sweating system. Among the many messages of support were those from the Chief Rabbi and Mr Cunninghame Graham MP. The chairman, the Rev. Rowland Young, opened proceedings by declaring his belief in "two principles which the working classes of this country had never sufficiently appreciated: the first is self-help and the second is unity of effort." Apart from himself all the members of the Board of Management were bona fide working tailors. He proposed to raise a fund by issuing £1 shares, subscribed for by small weekly instalments, for the purpose of opening a number of shops and furnishing them with machines and materials. Income would be divided among the shareholders so that they would be their own employers, their profits accruing from their own labour. Implementation of the scheme would take some time, as "the tailors at present are dependent on themselves". He boasted, however, that although the society had only been founded in April, it already numbered 800 members.[75] The problem was one of attracting true working-class shareholders. For how many of them would dare gamble the price of an initial share? Although only £1, it would certainly be beyond the means of the majority of hands who, needing every penny to ensure day-to-day survival, could not invest in even short-term projects.

The *East London Observer* continued to display an open forum of letters to the Editor on themes pertaining to the elimination of the evil. One correspondent aptly summed up the views expressed by so many of the others:

> A stop must be put to this baneful (sweating) system once and for all; and there are three ways by which this may be done: First, by the government, for the time being, either having all clothing for its employees made in its own workshops and under its own regulations, or by insisting that effective supervision shall be exercised in factories in which persons not receiving state pay are employed. Secondly, to oppose the landing on our shores of persons who are wholly without means of subsistence and who are actually under the conduct of an individual or set of persons known or suspected to be interested in making profits out of cheap labour in certain spheres of industry in our large towns. Thirdly, to punish with severity, persons found employing their work people beyond a fixed limit of time each day and to determine, on reports furnished by leading men engaged in the

particular and several industries, the pay per hour or day to be given to the workers.[76]

The radicals approached the question from a different angle. The Socialist League's *Commonweal* (21 April) immediately refuted White's strictures on foreign immigration and his "proposal to crush out the small employer by a tax on workshops and then to stand by and see how much people would starve", as well as questioning "whether White's confident assertion that all the sweaters are foreigners is strictly true". The SDF organ joined in the battle to disabuse the public minds of White's pet remedy for the grievance, ie the exclusion of alien labour. Arguing that "the Russian Polish Jews who are sweaters are in no wise paupers" it pointed out that in most of the dens nationally "neither sweaters nor sweated are foreigners, and they would in no wise be affected by a poll tax or even the complete exclusion of foreigners". On the political level it warned that "on the pretext of preventing the exclusion of the sweating system (the Government) will see that no political refugees land on our coast whose presence might strengthen the socialist movement in England". Such fears on the part of authority were ascertained in Factory Inspector Lakeman's recent Report on Female Labour with examples specially selected from the East End. ("It is hardly to be wondered at, that revolutionary doctrines prevail in London when the fact is recalled that this squalor and wretchedness exist side by side in the metropolis with the greatest wealth and luxury.")[78]

The controversy over causation and meaning was sustained throughout the whole year. On one occasion the *Times* analysis marginally accorded with that of the SDF. The *Justice* editorial of 9 June, commenting on the former's analysis of the roots of sweating ("Competition, pitiless and incessant, determines the lower rate of wages. To extinguish the competition of the *greeners* by prohibiting immigration of foreign paupers is rather a palliative than a remedy. It would relieve the pressure for a time; but the growth of population amongst the lower classes of our own people would still tend to intensify competition and to bear down wages to a point just above starvation"), was surprised to note that "the iron law of wages receives the sanction of the *Times*: that is an advance!" But it was Herbert Burrows, later in the same journal, who gave ultimate definition to a socialist standpoint:

> They (the socialists) are the only people who dare to say out in the light of day that every landlord and every capitalist who exploits the worker is a far worse sweater than the Jew who employs half a dozen of his countrymen in a London garret...
> Wherever we look, in every country in the world where there is a monopoly of land and capital by a class, then sweating obtains; the true definition of sweating being the robbery by the monopoliser from the worker of a large portion of the product of his toil.

In the end, it was as in the beginning. The authorities debated interminably; mustering their evidence in closed Committee sessions in both Houses, eventually issuing erudite commentaries, barely masking the anxieties felt by the overseers about the dangerous state of the "lowest" classes: to the undiscriminating a mélange of the workless and the sweated poised dangerously near the residuum. Inside and outside Westminster, middle-class laymen, sympathising with or damning the "feckless" and "workshy", were united in urging practising Christians to succour the needy, while exhorting the latter, according to sound Samuel Smiles precepts, to help themselves, either by thrift or good husbandry or by joining together in co-operative ventures. It was extraordinary advice to offer to an unemployed East Ender or sweatshop worker with a large family, facing a daily struggle for bread; and the published, and yet unpublished, findings and recommendations of the two great investigatory Committees in both Houses brought no relief to either the exploited or the unemployed.

As for the recipients of all this gratuitous advice, many were responding quite differently to the urgings of their betters. On 12 May 300 journeymen bakers, Jews and Germans in united action, went on strike and paraded through the main thoroughfares of Stepney. It was a dress rehearsal for things to come. On 5 July at Bryant and May's match factory in Bow the unbelievable happened. 672 women downed tools in solidarity with a girl unjustly sacked[80] and sparked off the historic strike which, in victory, changed the face of British trade unionism. Thenceforth a host of public meetings and demonstrations, especially against sweating and unemployment, grew noticeably larger and, to the authorities, more menacing as the year progressed. The troglodytes hitherto entombed in their cellars came up for air and smelt battle. That year they had reclaimed the weapon of collective action. The following year it would be put to the test. The dockers, tailors and bootmakers would point the way to redemption among the unskilled by their great strikes fought out in the streets of East London.

Footnotes

[1]R.C.K. Ensor, *England 1870-1914* (Oxford 1936) pp. 111-12.
[2]*Justice* 14 January 1888, "The Unemployed".
[3]*Justice* 31 March 1888, "Labour Notes".
[4]*Punch* 18 February 1888.
[5]*ELA* 3 March 1888.
[6]*ELO* 28 April 1888, reporting on Vestry meeting of 25 April.
[7]*ELO* 26 May 1888.
[8]*Justice* 8 December 1888.
[9]*Out of Work*, pp. 82-3.
[10]*In Darkest England*, p. 39.
[11]*Out of Work*, p. 129.
[12]Ibid., p. 233.
[13]*East End News* 20 November 1888, "Trading Improving at Last".
[14]*In Darkest London*.
[15]*ELO* 11 February 1888, letter from R.J.W. to Editor.
[16]*ELA* 18 February 1888.
[17]*Justice* 22 September 1888, "A Saviour of Society".
[18]*ELO* 28 January 1888.
[19]See below, pp. 000.
[20]See also *ELA* 24 March 1888 and *ELO* of the same date which detail Barnett's propositions and the outcome of the debate.
[21]*The Nineteenth Century* XXIX (November 1888) "A Scheme for the Unemployed" by Samuel Barnett, pp. 754-5.
[22]*Life and Labour of the People of London*, vol. I, p. 166.
[23]*ELO* 21 April 1888.
[24]*The Echo* 6 January 1888, "East End Emigration".
[25]Dr Barnardo, *Night and Day* December 1888, pp. 145ff. For further comment on ~migration policy see below, pp. 241-3.
[26]This is discussed in Lady Gillian Wagner's *Children of the Empire* (London, 1982).
[27]*Night and Day* May 1888, p. 49.
[28]*ELO* 10 March 1888, "Canada Communicates".
[29]*ELO* 4 February 1888, "Unemployed in the Colonies". Poem reproduced from Queensland *Figaro*.
[30]*Justice* 22 September 1888.
[31]Gareth Stedman Jones, *Outcast London*, p. 304
[32]Samuel Smith, "The Industrial Training of Destitute Children", *Contemporary Review* XLVII, January 1885.
[33]C. Poor Law Relief (1888) pp. vi-vii.
[34]*Outcast London*, pp. 312-13.

[35] A scholarly analysis of sweating, in the context of London industry, is given in *Outcast London*, pp. 23-32. For seasonality of production see pp. 33-51.
[36] The bad winters of 1854/55, 1860/61, and 1866/67 produced bread riots in Tower Hamlets.
[37] See below, pp. 146-50.
[38] John Burnett, Report to the Board of Trade on the Sweating System at the East End of London, by the Labour Correspondent of the Board. P.P. 1887, vol. LXXIX. See also Board of Trade Memorandum on the Immigration of Foreigners into the United Kingdom. P.P. 1887, vol. LXXIX.
[39] *ELA* 3 March 1888, Editorial.
[40] *ELO* 3 March 1888.
[41] *East End News* 13 March 1888; and on Lyons's application see the issue of 9 March 1888. On the weaknesses of the 1878 Act see *ELA* 10 March 1888.
[42] See Report from (House of Commons) Select Committee on Emigration and Immigration (Foreigners) 1888. Minutes 533-48 and 562, 629, 653, 654, 656.
[43] *East End News* 21 February 1888. Captain Colomb was Conservative MP for Bow and Bromley, a constituency well outside the area of immigrant concentration.
[44] *Pall Mall Gazette* 14 April 1888, reporting and commenting on White's evidence to the Lord's Committee on 13 April. See also White's follow-up evidence to the same committee on Friday 20 April, as reported in the *ELO* 28 April 1888, "The Sweating System".
[45] Summarised in *ELO* 5 May 1888.
[46] Report from Select Committee on Emigration and Immigration, Minutes 2873, 2962, 2963,2965.
[47] Beatrice Potter (later Webb), "The Tailoring Trade", ch. 3 in C. Booth, *Life and Labour*..., pp. 209-40.
[48] *ELO* 19 May 1888.
[49] *ELO* 10 March 1888.
[50] *Jewish Chronicle* (hereafter *JC*) 2 March 1888, editorial.
[51] Sermon delivered on Saturday 5 May, reported in *ELO* 12 May 1888.
[52] *JC* 18 May 1888. On Adler's sermon at the Great Synagogue, Sabbath 12 May.
[53] Report from Select Committee on Emigration and Immigration (Foreigners), Friday 6 July 1888. On incomes of foreigners.
[54] *JC* 20 July, reporting on the meeting of the Lords Committee on 13 July.
[55] *ELO* 28 April 1888, "The Sweating System — Further Shocking Disclosures".
[56] Report from Select Committee on Emigration and Immigration (Foreigners), 8 May 1888, Minutes 1376, 1380, 1381.
[57] House of Lords Select Committee... First report 7 August 1888 (Sessional Papers, 1888 XX) pp. 391-406. See also Lloyd P. Gartner, "The History of a Sweater", *East London Papers* 4, no. 2 (October 1961). Wilchinski's evidence is reported by radical Henry Samuels in

The *Commonweal* 26 May and 2 June 1888.

[58]*ELO* 16 June 1888, "The Merchant Taylor's Company and the Sweating System" by Lewis Lyons. For further comments on the relationship between unemployment, sweating and prostitution see below, pp. 122-4.

[59]"The Tailoring Trade", pp. 218-19.

[60]See *JC* 22 June, and *ELO* 23 June 1888, for complementary reports on Lionel Alexander's evidence.

[61]"The Tailoring Trade", p. 221. White concurred that "sweating obtained most in the boot trade".

[62]18 August 1888.

[63]*ELA* 21 April 1888, recounting White's evidence of 14 April.

[64]Cited in *Commonweal* 7 April 1888.

[65]A comprehensive reporting of the Lords Committee evidence was given in *ELA* 21 April, *ELO* of the same date and in the *Pall Mall Gazette* dated 14 and 18 April. For Hoffmann's report see *ELO* 28 April.

[66]Mark Moses' evidence in front of Lords Committee, 13 July 1888. See also *JC* 20 July 1888 for its informed commentary on this evidence.

[67]Report from Select Committee, etc., House of Commons, Friday 22 June, Minutes 2090-2094.

[68]*JC* 20 July 1888.

[69]*Justice* 20 October 1888.

[70]*JC* 10 August 1888, commenting on letter from Clementina Black on the "Moral Duty of Buyers".

[71]*Commonweal* 19 May 1888, "The Meaning of the Sweater".

[72]*ELA* 28 April 1888, "The Sweating System".

[73]*ELA* 19 May 1888.

[74]Beatrice Webb (née Potter), *My Apprenticeship*, pp. 269-70.

[75]*ELA* 8 December 1888.

[76]*ELO* 12 May 1888.

[77]*Justice* 21 July 1888.

[78]*ELA* 7 April 1888, summarising Lakeman's report.

[79]*Justice* 28 July 1888.

[80]See below, pp. 284-8.

Chapter 4
Paupers and "Bastilles"

> They leave all hope behind, who enter there;
> One certitude while sane they cannot leave;
> One anodyne for torture and despair;
> The certitude of Death...
> JAMES THOMSON, *THE CITY OF DREADFUL NIGHT*

Over the sweated and unemployed, the casuals, the old, the lame, the blind and the indolent hung the shadow of the "Bastille" — the workhouse. In the fight for survival, for most of the labouring poor, it symbolised the ultimate humiliation for genuine workless and pauper alike. For the "armies of despair" concentrated in Tower Hamlets it threatened a terrifying finale.

William Booth, referring to Charles Booth's findings, hailed his study as "the only one which even attempts to enumerate the destitute". Applying Charles Booth's diagnosis, the General calculated that East London "proper" (comprising Tower Hamlets plus Shoreditch, Bethnal Green and Hackney) had 17,000 inmates of workhouses, asylums and hospitals, the rate of destitution being "double the average for the rest of the country". In the context of a national army living on the margin and estimated at 3 million, 331,000 were located in the East End boroughs.[1] On 13 November 1888, the *East End News* confirmed that the total number of paupers in London had risen to 108,638, compared with 104,431 the year before. It was not surprising that the workhouse population in Tower Hamlets reflected this trend.

In accord with the spirit of the 1834 Poor Law Act, the workhouse constituted a deterrent. Both Charles Booth and the Warden of Toynbee Hall subscribed to this. The former assented to those rules applied to "families who are below limits of current deficiency in their accounts", which were to "move them on to the poor house, where they would live as a family no longer. The socialistic side of life as it is includes the poor house and the prison, and the whole system, as I conceive it, would provide within itself motives in favour of providence, and a sufficient pressure to stimulate industry." Charles Booth had a curious interpretation of the meaning of socialism.[2] Samuel Barnett, according to his wife, concurred with this form of treatment. "My husband thought that the pauper spirit which pursued the masses of the indigent was a national evil which would become worse, and that like wise physicians, we must bear to inflict suffering if it were necessary to effect a cure." Barnett was therefore all for the abolition of out-relief. "The weekly dole, or 'O.R.' (outdoor relief) administered by a Relieving Officer bound to suspect every assertion, brings out the greed of the applicant, destroys his self respect, checks his energies and has a distinct effect in keeping down wages."[3] The mentality and terminology behind such a prescription as applied to an "ailing" economy is, not surprisingly, still with us.

The destitute were, to the respectable, a nuisance bordering on the criminal. When they were not lounging under the railway arches of the LNER, or scrabbling and scratching on the grass edges of Itchy Park and other local churchyards, they were stretched out, in their scores, at night, in the open air "doss" at Trafalgar Square. Here there would be no respite. Margaret Harkness, as observant as ever, conveyed the message:

> Orders came to clear the square of vagrants. It was a nuisance for the public to see so much misery. The outcasts must hide away in prisons or workhouses. So much scum was dangerous.
> "Pass on, pass on!" said the policeman to vagrants, who had been foolish enough to think that the square belonged to the public.[4]

For the affluent West Enders, the residuum encamped on their doorstep spelt danger. But to shut their eyes to the source of that threat, the deprived East Enders, was an act of criminal stupidity. So warned the perceptive Harkness, through her mouthpiece, the Whitechapel parish doctor:

> The whole of the East End is starving. The West End is bad, or mad, not to see that if things go on like this we must have a revolution. One fine day the people about here will go desperate, and they will walk westwards, cutting throats and hurling brickbats, until they are shot down by the military. I know perfectly well that my ideas would be called exaggerated if I put them in print — people prefer to read the pretty stories about the East End made up by Walter Besant.[5]

She also caught the mood of the Salvationists' antipathy towards the institutionalised barracks set up to keep the poor out of sight. (For William Booth there was no undeserving poor: to be poor, was, by definition, to be deserving.) The atmosphere of the workhouse was not only stifling for the individual soul, but also robbed him of his last shred of human dignity. The Guardians' plea that "pauper souls were well provided for by the parish" was rejected by Army folk. Captain Lobo expressed the frustration of attempts to bring the message in from outside:

> General Booth has stormed many places, but he has not gained admittance for his red vests and poke bonnets into the metropolitan workhouses. These places remain closed to him. The Salvationists hold meetings and sing hymns at the gates, and they seem to think the time is coming when their drums will be heard even in the Bastille. But at present workhouse religion is carried on to order, and pauper souls are as strictly watched as pauper bodies. Paupers pass from the Bastille into the infirmary when too old for work, and before they go there the routine of their lives makes them into automatons. At last death snaps the chain of Poor Law disciplines and they are buried in coffins made on the premises. Little wonder, then, that poor men and women have a wholesome dread of the parish.[6]

Naturally the socialists regarded the whole concept of the Poor Law as anathema. When the Ripper struck, local street walkers fled to the workhouses to escape the terror. This prompted *Justice* to put forward a novel means of undermining the system. "If all the unemployed and other unfortunates could be induced to follow their example a complete breakdown of the present poor law system would ensue, and the well-to-do classes would see the necessity, for their own sakes, of providing the opportunity of useful work for those whose only crime is poverty. Everyone should duly note, too, that only a homicidal maniac could induce these poor wretches to prefer 'the bastilles of starvation' to the less dubious horrors of selling their bodies to any male bidder on the streets."[7]

How far was popular fear and hatred of the workhouse a myth or a reality? This can be assessed from at least two sources: one from outside investigators — philanthropists, social observers, novelists and reports from government sponsored commissions; the other within, by careful scrutiny of records of clerks and committee officers for the local Board of Guardians. The latter come down to us parish by parish and therefore disclose in totality the monthly "state of pauperism" in Tower Hamlets.

The tragedy is the absence of any written text from the paupers themselves, who lacked either the ability or the desire to write. However, sharp vignettes of workhouse life are revealed to us in records of odd misdemeanours and complaints concerning the inmates. Sometimes the inarticulate are given a surrogate voice by an objective or sympathetic chronicler. The quality of their existence, alas, can mainly be gleaned only through the interpretations of their literate "superiors".

Quantitative information is more forthcoming. Throughout 1888 the East End had, in accordance with tradition, an army of paupers incarcerated behind the workhouse gates. Census of metropolitan paupers reveals a steady rise in inmates. From the end of the second week of June 1885 to the same date in 1888 indoor numbers had risen from 51,438 to 55,187, while those registered as outdoor relief had risen from 33,588 to 37,315. By October numbers had again expanded to 58,556 and 37,799 respectively. Sample statistics of paupers maintained by indoor and outdoor relief during the periods of cold or inclement weather suggest a consistent rise in indoor numbers compared with the same date in the previous year, in three local major Union workhouses.[9] The exception was Whitechapel, whose administrators' rigid adherence to the spirit and letter of the Poor Law was, on public record, an example to be followed.

Pauper Numbers in 1888

Week Ending	Whitechapel Guardians	Poplar Guardians	Mile End Guardians	St George's Guardians
25 Feb		In 2,250/1928* O.R. 1,898/2,023* Two weeks previously when indoor numbers were at 2,187, the committee discussed need for extension of workhouse		
1 March			In 1,478/1,407* O.R. 529/513*	

2 March			*In* 1,387/1,265*
6 March	*In* 1,651/1,406*		
20 Oct	*In* 1,482/1530*	*In* 2,145 O.R. 1,795 compared with total 3,836 the previous year	
25 Oct			*In* 1,279/1,202* See (a)
1 Nov		*In* 1,327/1,272*	
3 Nov	*In* 1,500/1,564*	*In* 2,170 O.R. 1,724 compared with total 3,939 the previous year	
9 Nov			*In* 1,354/1,193*
17 Nov	*In* 1,503/1,551*		
23 Nov			*In* 1,165/1,003*
29 Nov		*In* 1,340 O.R. 502 compared with total 1,824 the previous year	
30 Nov		*In* 2,192 O.R. 1,764 compared with the total 3,964 the previous year See (b)	
1 Dec	1,517/1,577*	*In* 2,228 O.R. 1,743/1,904	
6 Dec			*In* 1,353/1,259* See (c)

In = Inmates
O.R. = Outdoor Relief
* Second figure for numbers on same date in 1887
(a) The committee complained that since there was no casual ward accommodation in Stepney, Poplar and Bethnal Green, St. George's ward was overflowing with casuals such that fresh intakes had to be sent to the workhouse where beds were set up for them.
(b) But increase of indoor paupers meant overcrowding and the committee called for the clerk to search for a building to accommodate the overflow. Also a suggestion was put for Poplar to provide a casual ward in a site on North Street to relieve St. George's Union since Stepney, Poplar and Bethnal Green lacked one.
(c) Again there is a protest by Guardians who objected to taking on the "overflow casuals of the Metropolis". Also, a Mr Crowder, referring to the master's report on the overcrowded state of the house, stated "that the present increase of pauperism is altogether abnormal, and *nothing like it has taken place during the last 12 years of his experience.*" He suggested that the master and clerk be instructed "...to look round the parish and see if there are any buildings that can be used in the case of emergency for temporary accommodation".[10]

Figures and categories are no guide to the flesh and blood tragedies endured within the confines of the "House" and its ancillary — the casual ward. The latter was open to penniless and homeless men and women on the tramp seeking a night's "kip" in the "spike". Respectable workless in desperation, washed-out drunks, criminals on the run and vagabonds lined up for their last hope of shelter, vocalising their misery with a rendering, in unison, of the popular ballad "Starving in the Queen's Highway" and ending with that *cri de coeur*

> What will become of us
> If things go on this way?
> If honest working men
> Are starving day by day.

Walter Besant confirmed that next to incarceration in the workhouse itself, the casual ward was "a place where *no one will go* if he can possibly avoid it".[11]

Harkness describes the degrading questioning by the master of casuals seeking admission. In *Out of Work*, Jo's humiliation is complete when he is forced to strip naked and wash himself in a common bath. But the worst was yet to come:

He was then taken into a cell that measured 8ft by 4ft, at the end of which was a small dark hole called the stone pit. The cell was lighted by a jet of gas, and the first thing he saw there was an inscription, written in uncouth letters on the white-washed wall opposite the entrance: "I've served my Queen and my country for 15 years, and this is what I've come to."

It was a miserable scenario — alone, freezing and hungry in a cold cell that

> had no furniture whatsoever, except the mattress and the rug on which he was sitting. An icy wind swept through the stone pit, so he went to see if a door would shut off the draught. But no door was there, only a large iron window, with bars across, through which flints must be thrown when broken, into a yard beneath.

In the cell lay large blocks of granite and a hammer in a stone pit. Breaking stones or picking oakum was compulsory for all casuals in lieu of payment for food and shelter. There was no seat and the floor of the cell dipped in the middle, so that it was almost impossible to stand upright. The hammer was thought sufficient by itself to enable the breaker to crush the flint. There was no need, in Poor Law reckoning (it would be deemed wasteful expenditure), to employ protective devices such as eye shields or strong gloves.

The casual was locked up for the night with the regulation supper — a tin containing "½lb of gruel and 8ozs of bread" (in Jo's case considerably less: "the whole provision could have been put into a tea cup!"). In the morning, when he ought to have been outdoors seeking work, he was obliged to perform the standard task of stone-breaking or picking oakum, a half ton of the former or four pounds of the latter, which required the whole day to finish it, if he could. If unable, he was forcibly detained as a punishment for another day and night, with corresponding increase in the labour load imposed on him. This was normal practice, in line with Poor Law regulations. Jo, being less fortunate — the exercise required a knack and he was unable to crack the granite — was held in for three days and two nights, and was eventually released only by order of the master when a piece of granite flew into his eye. The meals were hardly fit to sustain him, with breakfast the same as supper, and dinner containing the exact 8ozs of bread and ½oz of cheese. Should he, in desperation, be forced to return, the master forewarned "'Don't come back within the month. If you do, you'll be kept in twice the time'... All the time he lived afterwards, Jo never forgot his sensations when the casual wards closed after him..." The ordeal, as intended, was sufficient deterrent to persuade the genuine unemployed and homeless to keep well away. Walter Besant bitterly condemned the mentality behind it. "With refuges for the destitute where they are starved and made to work on insufficient food, with prisons for the criminal where manhood is crushed and strength is destroyed by feeding men on gruel, we support bravely the character of a country obedient to the laws of God and marching in the footsteps of Christ."[12]

From the evidence handed down to us, there is no doubt of the fears inculcated in the minds of East Enders by the threat of incarceration as a pauper in the "House". Yet in comparing attitudes and conditions within the various Unions we must be cautious about generalising. Certainly they were all set up for the rigorous application of the Poor Law. Dependent on the personality of the Master and the sentiments of the Board committees, rules would be modified or set aside where human consideration for an individual pauper was concerned. A close scrutiny of the minute books of at least three Unions in the borough[13] discloses what may appear to be extraordinary acts of compassion to that end. This does not detract from the overall policy of each Board which was to maintain the principles set down by the law. Ultimately the spirit of deterrence rather than comfort pervaded the grim walls of the workhouse.

The report of the Whitechapel Guardians for the half year ended Lady Day 1888 boasted of "its establishment, which has been known as the best managed of its kind". Indeed it was Whitechapel that had pioneered methods of reducing expenditure on outdoor relief. Since the experience of the terrible winter of 1869-70, the Guardians saw fit to aim at reforming the system "which was felt to be fostering pauperism, and encouraging idleness, improvidence and imposture, while the 'relief' in no sense helped the poor". The thinking behind their need to overhaul procedures was strictly in accordance with the spirit of the Poor Law. The greatest threats to the true "professionals" were the individual acts of charity, dictated by a misguided concern for the poor, especially the undeserving.

> It was seen that voluntary charity largely consisted of indiscriminate alms-giving, that it accepted no definite obligations as distinct from the function of poor-law relief, that the poor law was relied upon to supplement private benevolence, that the alms-givers too frequently were the advocates of the poor in their demands upon the public rates and that both poor law and charity were engaged in the relief of distress, much of which a thoughtless benevolence and a lax relief administration had created. Looking forward to the ultimate possibility of laying down a broad distinction between "legal relief" and "charitable aid", and of interpreting the former as relief in the workhouse or other institution for the actually destitute and the latter as personal sympathy and helpful charity, they began by gradually restricting out relief in "out of work" cases, until they were able to entirely suspend the outdoor relief regulation order and to supply strictly the principle of the prohibiting order.

This ruthless adherence to the rule book worked.

> In this process of restriction it was found that about one in ten of those who were offered indoor, in place of outdoor, relief entered the workhouse and these, in turn, gradually withdrew themselves, so that eventually the indoor pauperism resumed its normal condition.[14]

The report certainly confirmed that the new departure had not only resulted in a diminution of indoor pauperism but also in the more dramatic decline in outdoor relief. Mr E.H. Pickergill, in a lecture at St. Jude's School on 17 January 1888 involving comparisons of numbers receiving outdoor relief in the various East End parishes during September 1886, noted Whitechapel as bottom of the list with only 12 successful applicants. (The others in ascending order were St. George's 30, Stepney 33, Mile End 192, Shoreditch 595 and Bethnal Green 895.) The Whitechapel Clerk to the Guardians boasted the decline in a paper delivered in June. He emphasised that, thanks to changed policy, those receiving outdoor relief had been reduced from 5,339 costing £168 17s 4d per week in 1870 to only 63 in 1888 at a total cost of £2 10s 11d. In his view the lesson learned was that "while a lax system of out-door relief obtained, there would always be people ready to drop their self respect, and to accept the doles of pauperism" and that the Whitechapel system certainly proved conducive to deterring outdoor relief "without an appreciable increase in the number of indoor paupers".[15] The clerk, William

Vallance, was no easy dispenser of compassion or charity. A master administrator, he kept a sharp eye on the cost-effectiveness of policy where the welfare of inmates were almost subordinated to the demands of the balance sheet. It is no wonder that under his authority the Whitechapel Union remained a staunch bastion of Gradgrindism.[16]

Early that year the regime appeared fortified by the appointment of a new Master, Mr Badcock, at the Union workhouse in South Grove.[17] Harkness had obviously met him, and gives a sharp characterisation of the man against the background of his job. She reveals some manifest contradictions in posture: as a humane spirit often battling against the dehumanising implications of a regime he is obliged to enforce.

> He was an orthodox Poor Law servant, but he found it difficult to keep up the role of a disciplinarian, for nature had made him underhearted; and although his attempts at severity had hardened into a sort of second nature, he was constantly trespassing against Poor Law discipline... for instance... he was counting his cabbages in order to see if he could give the old people "a feed" the following Sunday, and thinking he would root up sundry currant bushes to make room for more vegetables... But when he opened his mouth to speak, behold! a eulogy of the Poor Law came out of it, and he said that "discipline is discipline" which sentence, of course, needs no interpretation. He was a man of about forty, tall, strongly built, with a pleasant voice, and possessed of a *sine qua non* of his office, invincible courage, although he had nothing more dangerous to deal with than paupers and lunatics.[18]

The atmosphere of the place, a model of its kind, is conveyed to the outsider by its immediate environs, recalling, by its cold precision, the clinical inhumanity of a Nazi labour camp:

> Ringing the workhouse bell, they enter into the forecourt of neat flower beds, closely shaven grass plots, smooth paths, and trees which had been pruned until their branches had reached the legitimate amount of foliage. The Bastille stretched further than the eye could see, and seemed a standing rebuke to its poverty-stricken surroundings, for it was clean... not a spot on it, not a stain, nothing to show a trace of sympathy for the misery and sin of the people who lived in the neighbourhood.[19]

As the prototype workhouse it epitomised the Poor Law incarnate in stone and brick. Official dietary tables to be introduced on 1 April laid down strict measurement of food according to age.

No. 1. Full diet (Men and Women).

Breakfast 5ozs bread, ½oz butter, 1 pint of tea.
Dinner 4ozs cooked meat, 8ozs potatoes, 2ozs bread.
Supper 5ozs bread, ½oz butter, 1 pint tea.

Four types of diets with children under seven receiving half the appropriate allowances except the lowest.

Sugar, arrowroot, sago, milk, wine, spirits, beer and porter are in all cases to be treated as extras to be expressly ordered when required.[20]

Harkness, in more expressive terms, noted that the men were not allowed to smoke inside, while

> the young women never taste tea, and the old ones may not indulge in a cup during the long afternoons, only at half past six o'clock morning and night, when they receive a small hunch of bread with butter scraped over the surface, and a mug of neat beverage which is so dear to their hearts as well as their stomachs. The young people never go out, never see a visitor, and the old ones only get one holiday in the month. Then the aged paupers may be seen skipping like lambkins outside the doors of the Bastille while they jabber to their friends and relatives. A little gruel morning and night, meat twice a week, that is the food of the grown-up people, seasoned with hard work and prison-discipline. Doubtless this Bastille offers no premium to idle and improvident habits, but what shall we say of the woman, or man, maimed by misfortune, who must come there or die in the street?[21]

A harsh appraisal indeed, but one derived from on-the-spot observation. What evidence is there to modify or question opinions which often smacked of preconceived notions? It is to the minute books that we must turn and, from the yellowing pages filled with committee reports and income and expenditure columns, attempt to extrapolate the realities underlying the human dramas played out behind the closed union walls.

Strict accountability, with a close eye on economy, was paramount. The Samuel Smiles concept of "self-help" was intrinsic to the day-to-day running of the institution. Earn what you eat, payment for services rendered were obligations imposed on both pauper inmates and outsiders, admitted for medical treatment in the infirmary. The cold hand of utilitarianism was supremely evident: in reclaiming monies from the local labourer whose child had been treated in the infirmary (such admissions were nearly always prompted by dire necessity, as the last resort for a desperate parent or partner!); in pressing demands for maintenance of inmates from relatives; in extorting fees for disposing of a dead infant, where an impoverished parent (and they were a majority) had been forced to beg parish aid to ensure a regular Christian burial! For all such "relief", the clerk solemnly informs us in his splendid copper-plate hand, "being now declared to be by way of a loan".

In most dealings the cash nexus was absolute. Maintenance orders were firmly demanded and served continuously throughout the year. Notices were scrupulously kept and action monitored by committees. One example. of a comprehensive list of demands was that recorded in the Whitechapel Union minutes of 4 February when orders were served against:

> Hyman Gerenraip of 82 Brick Lane for 2s 5d in respect of medical relief for himself.
>
> Lazarus Yuntag of 28 King Edward Street, for 4s 0d and Myer Rosenthal of 2 Montague Court, for 4s 0d both for medical relief.
>
> Patrick Kearney of 84 Bakers Row for cost of maintenance of wife in infirmary.
>
> Sons of Elizabeth Young for the sum of 2s 5d per week each for maintenance of mother in the workhouse.
>
> Charles Worster of 13 Union Street, High Street, Stratford for the sum of 5s 0d in respect of maintenance of his two children in the Fever Hospital.
>
> Two sons for the payment of 3s 5d weekly each for the maintenance of mother Sarah Langleben in the infirmary.
>
> Father, Israel Morris of 3 Montague Court, 2s 5d for medical relief granted him for his child.
>
> McCarthy. Collector to require payment by John McCarthy of 9 North Wall, Dublin, of the sum of 5s 0d per week in respect of the maintenance of his mother in the infirmary.
>
> Ginger. George Ginger of 21 Thrawl Street. 5s 0d in respect of order granted him for the burial of his child; such relief now being declared to be by way of a loan.
>
> Newman of 160 Lolesworth Buildings. Payment of John (senior) of 1s 0d a week and John (junior) 1s 5d per week respectively for

maintenance of Elizabeth, wife of former, in the infirmary.

Brand. Henry. 7s 0d a week for maintenance of his wife in the infirmary. (149 Katherine Buildings).

Moore, Janice, 88 Sidney Street. 5s 0d for maintenance of child in Fever Hospital.

Bellhouse. James, 18 Bradbury Street to pay for cost of father in infirmary.

Cunningham. James, 2 Mary Street to pay 10s in respect of order given him for burial of his child...

There is no record of legal action taken against non-payment of orders. Yet the burden on the recipients must have been heavy. From the names and addresses of the debtors we may conclude that they undoubtedly belonged to the class of labouring poor living on the margin, and the costs incurred would have been difficult to meet.

The Local Government Board, acting as arbiter in the disposal of public funds, was committed to the policy of rigorous economy in their use. Extra items of expenditure had to be agreed by it. With the appointment of the new Master and his wife as Matron there arose the question of their child being permitted to reside with them. This was submitted to the Local Government Board who agreed that the boy could, until the age of seven, at an expenditure set against the Guardians' funds. In turn the clerk forwarded the statement below of victuals, itemised with costs, required to feed the boy weekly:[22]

Bread	3½lbs	@	8/4 cwt	3
Meat	3½lbs	@	8/2 stone	2.0½
Butter	¼lb	@	1/4 lb	4
Cheese	½lb	@	7d lb	3½
Sugar	½lb	@	16/9 cwt	1
Loaf	¼lb	@	2d lb	½
Tea	1½ozs	@	1/8 lb	2
Coffee	2ozs	@	1/5 lb	2
Milk	3½ pints	@	1/4 per barn gln	3½
Potatoes	2½lbs	@	75s per ton	1
Other vegetables to the value of				3
Total				4s 0d

Droll as the procedure might seem, it was otherwise revealing. The quantity and quality of food allocated to the Master's son was noticeably superior to that allowed for in the No. 1 diet for adult paupers!

Under successive amendments to the 1662 Act of Settlement and Removal anyone not born in the parish and becoming a charge on the rates was to be returned to his place of birth, where the local Guardians must then assume future responsibility for his relief. Pregnant women, who were potentially expensive and, therefore, the least desirable to maintain, were major casualties in this cruel scheme. The Whitechapel Union had the reputation of rapidly disposing of unwanted paupers under the Settlement Laws. On 21 February the clerk was ordered tp "take all necessary enquiries for obtaining evidence of settlement, elsewhere than in the Whitechapel Union and their removability". A list of twenty followed, and removal orders were ruthlessly carried out, throughout the year. The success of such operations was indicated by the diminution in numbers of settlement cases remaining in the later months.[23] The horrors associated with the forceful transportation of a human being from his or her lifelong habitat need not be left to the imagination. Some old, infirm labourer, perhaps a widower, who has lived and worked in the East End most of his years and in desperation is seeking parish aid, is suddenly forced to take the long journey back to his birthplace which he had quit almost a lifetime before.

What was more appalling was the lack of sensitivity displayed by officials in the disposal of child inmates legally under care. Barnardo estimated that, of a thousand boys unemployed on the streets and living in lodging houses, two-thirds were brought up in a workhouse.[24] The burden within could be relieved in certain ways. Emigration was one.[25] On 6 March the Union committee ordered that "the clerk do enquire and report as to the eligibility for the emigration to Canada and as to their consent or otherwise of:

Rose Staples	10	Orphan
Vincent Staples	14	Orphan
Elizabeth Buckle	11	Deserted
Robert Buckle	9	Deserted
Mary Clifford	9	Deserted
Sarah Walton	13	Deserted
Frederick Walton	11	Deserted

(It would be interesting to know how an immature child could give thought and ultimate consent to such a change, which is known, by adults, to impose such emotional and even physical strain!) By 17 April, in the soulless language of bureaucracy, the despatch of the innocents was officially underwritten:

> The clerk submitted and read the following "Certificate of Consent" pursuant to Sec. 4. of the 13th and 14th Vic., cap. 101.
>
> ### Whitechapel Union
>
> I, the undersigned, being one of the Magistrates of the Police Courts of the Metropolis sitting at the Thames Police Court do hereby certify that I have this day personally examined (as listed above except Mary Clifford) at present maintained at the Forest Gate District School chargeable to the Whitechapel Union etc... and that they have severally consented to emigrate to Canada. As witness my hand on the 6th day of April 1888.
> *Sgd. Franklin Lushington*

Whereupon it was resolved

> That the six orphan and deserted children... having consented to emigrate to Canada, the necessary steps be taken to effect the emigration and that a sum not exceeding eleven pounds be expended for each child and charged upon the Common Fund of the Union.[26]

This pathetic farce was supposed, in theory, to secure the workhouse child far greater protection than the young destitute or vagrant, who could be emigrated without the formality of consent. In practice it meant the same: that for the outlay of a few pounds now, the Guardians were relieving themselves of a far larger, and longer, expense in the future. Yet, as one detects elsewhere, there is some evidence of humane consideration for the child even in acts of expediency. Replying to a circular letter from the Paddington Board of Guardians, the clerk of the Whitechapel Union notified them that his board had already "addressed the Local Government Board in advocacy of legislation to secure the withdrawal of children from the custody and control of vicious and negligent parents and the endowment of Guardians with powers to emigrate such children, or otherwise to deal with them, as in the case of children deserted by their parents". For, in the end, the necessity to offload costs overcame the dictates of humanity.[27] The Whitechapel Union reinforced the message in a resolution sent to the Local Government Board, with a copy to the Home Secretary during the debate on the Industrial Schools Bill currently before Parliament.

> That Guardians should be empowered to make application to Justices for an order to commit either to their own guardianship with authority to emigrate, board out or otherwise dispose of any child who may have been — continuously or otherwise — chargeable to the poor rate for a period of one year, who may have been deserted by its natural parent or parents during such period, or to send such child to a certified Industrial School.[28]

Other avenues for "disposal" were recruitment into either the army or the navy. Vallance's own personal commitment to the training ship Exmouth meant stronger encouragement for recruitment. In the minutes of 26 July we read of a circular letter from the Clerk to the Managers of the Metropolitan Asylum District intimating that there were a large number of vacancies on board the Exmouth. The locally controlled Forest Gate School managers were, naturally, not slow to respond. On 21 August a list of volunteers was forwarded to the board.

Walter Woolcott	12	Child of widow
Alfred Simpson	14	Orphan
William Collins	13	Child of widow
Joseph Bray	14	Orphan
Charles Pitt	14	Deserted by father
Alfred Bean	14	Orphan
Alfred Skates	13	Orphan

The Guardians resolved "that subject to the required consent by parents, if living, the necessary steps be forthwith taken for the transfer of the above to the training ship Exmouth". We can only hazard a guess as to what pressure or other influences were brought to bear on an immature lad, isolated within an authoritarian institution, to "encourage" him to volunteer! The other outlet for youngsters eager to quit was the army band. On 7 August the Board approved and adopted a plea of consent for two fourteen-year-olds — George Rossenbach, to be enlisted into a band of the regular army, and Alfred Wade, to be sent for training in the House Boy Brigade. More poignant was the record in the minutes of 18 September permitting Alfred Scales, an orphan, aged only thirteen, to enlist.

The policy of "boarding-out" to foster parents in a country district, to enable a child to be nurtured in a healthier environment, was a more positive step. It was fraught with difficulties, not least those arising from a child being forcibly removed from his or her "roots", however insalubrious. As a safeguard, inspectors were appointed under the auspices of local committees (generally chaired by a parson) and answerable to the Guardians who had boarded out the child. On 2 October the Whitechapel Board was presented with the case of a boy reported uncontrollable, and evidently a juvenile delinquent:

> Alfred Thomas, aged 9, boarded out to foster parents, aged people. Convicted stealing eggs from a farmer (6 months probation); nearly convicted for breaking a railway lamp (foster parent paid 3s 6d for damage); "uses bad language and untruthful" and constantly truanting.
>
> The local committee decided (to) tell the lad that the next charge of stealing, of lying, of swearing, or of playing truant, will make him be removed from his "father" and "mother" to strangers, and if he still goes on in the same way after that he will have to go back to the Workhouse School where he must stay the rest of his time. By this means we shall put the utmost pressure upon the foster parents to control the lad; and upon the lad himself to cure his bad habits and where he has contracted them. Removal always does a certain harm and, though sometimes necessary, we are not always sure of getting any good by it.
>
> Resolved (by Whitechapel Guardians) that Alfred Thomas be removed from his present foster-parents; that the Kings Norton Boarding Out Committee be invited to find a more suitable "home" for the child, and that failing this, the child be withdrawn from the care of the committee.

We hear no more of him that year. Judging by the lengthy and detailed reference to his case, he may have been an exception. Elsewhere, from Ampthill, came an inspectorial report by a Miss Mason on two girl boarders which was much more favourable. One is not surprised, considering the conditions afforded them by their foster-parents:

1. Emily Smith — aged about 14, nine years with a Mrs Letting, Oliver Street, Ampthill, couple with children of their own. Foster father a gardener to a neighbouring gentleman. Their home is their own; it has two good bedrooms and two sitting rooms and a good garden. They keep pigs. Emily has a good room and bed to herself and an excellent stock of clothing. She was on trial for service at the schoolmaster's house. She looked very well and neat and tidy. Her mistress seemed scarcely able to praise her enough.

2. Clara Smith. Aged nine with old widow. Also good report although widow "has been in the almshouses for about a year. Takes Clara with her to see her daughter in London".[29]

We learn, from innumerable tales, how workhouse children craved affection, rarely received, longing to be accepted as normal to erase the stigma of the parish; that for such a child love and security were more important than cleanliness. The overall failure rate of those with foster parents was assessed as below 10%, which suggests that most of the pauper nippers of Whitechapel boarded out must have derived due benefits from a surrogate family.[30]

Domestic service was a Victorian industry drawing heavily upon Board of Guardians "recruits". It was one of the few avenues of employment open to workhouse girls, and it was stocked by them, since they were trained, almost exclusively, in house duties. There is a mass of authentic accounts of the exploitation of servants by masters or mistresses, and the legend prevailed that there was nothing worse than that of a maid-of-all-work in a single-servant family. It is not surprising that the glitter and profit of street-walking in the short term was, to many young East Enders, a far better proposition than the long-term miseries of a house scrubber.

The Whitechapel Guardians were evidently quite active in placing their girls into service. On 3 April they ordered that two girls from Harrow Cottage, chargeable to the Union, be dealt with as follows:

Mary A. Peters be placed in the domestic service of Mrs. Charles Lang, Lincoln House, Acton.

Emily Heane be placed in the domestic service of Herman Grosschalk, Holland House, Arkwright Road, Hampstead.

On 7 August two others from the same establishment Rose Lyon (14) and Kate Reeves (15) — followed. What is novel in the same minutes is the placing of a Jewish girl, Esther Schwarz, aged 15 (maintained in the Jewish Orphans Asylum, West Norwood, but chargeable to the Union), into the service of a Miss Simmonds, dressmaker of 78 Brondesbury Villas "and that the sum of £4 be paid and allowed for outfit". This is one of three cases involving Jewish youngsters that year and unusual in the sense that these were generally catered for by the Jewish Board of Guardians, who regarded themselves as being solely responsible for the welfare of their own community.

London's northwest was, as it still is, an area of affluence where servants were always in demand. Boarding-out children of good character were often directed there after reaching the official school leaving age. The minutes of 18 September recall a letter read from the Rev. J. Bamber "submitting proposals to place Caroline Canty, a poor child, boarded out under the care of that committee chargeable to this Union, in the domestic service of Mr André, 84 Mansfield Road, Haverstock Hill". The board agreed and recommended that "an outfit to the value of £3 be provided for Caroline". The hard-headed dispensers of the Poor Law were not without heart. A final report that year suggests that there was a reservoir of concern for individuals whom the Guardians chose to treat as deserving poor. The case of Mary Cathcart of 92 Pelham Street (located in the heart of the worst Spitalfields slum) illustrates this point. A Mr K. Maclean wrote to the clerk:

> I am anxious to call to your attention the case of Mary Cathcart, aged about 23 for whom I am most desirous of obtaining some months training in a home suitable to her case. She is a girl who cannot earn her own living without the above care on account of being decidedly "dull" but as she is strong and able-bodied, I believe would anyhow be able to help in her own support were she carefully trained.
>
> I have obtained the promise of a vacancy now ready for her acceptance in just such a home as will suit her.
>
> Her mother is a woman who will and does work to keep herself out of the House as long as her health will allow but last winter I induced her to enter Bakers Row Infirmary for a few weeks on the attention of the Whitechapel House Committee. Mrs Cathcart was then too ill to be anywhere but in bed.

> I feel it to be a last chance of keeping them independent through the winter, as the mother can support herself, but what she earns means starvation for the two — her health then gives way — and I see nothing for them both but the House this winter, if the girl does not learn to earn something for herself.

The clerk then read the relieving officer's report which concurred with the substance of the letter and also revealed the nature of the jobs that mother and daughter were forced to undertake to keep themselves alive.

> They are both respectable and industrious but poor and delicate. I assisted them last winter from a private source — they were obliged however to come into the infirmary, and the C.O.S. has also helped them by paying their rent and in other ways have been very kind to them. They used to get a living at a Pickle Warehouse, also at Orange Peeling but that is a precarious mode of getting a living now.

It was resolved by the Guardians that "subject to the approval of the Local Government Officer this Board do consent to defray the cost of maintenance of Mary Cathcart in the Home for Day Servants, 45 Aubert Park, Highbury, during a period not exceeding six months at a cost of 7s per week".[31]

Other humane acts are detected. There appeared to be a liberality in the granting of new civilian outfits for orphans discharged from the workhouse;[32] and there are instances of a sympathetic response to the needs of the blind. One such example resulted from a "request from the Secretary of the Whitechapel Committee of the Charity Organisation Society dated 14 June re a Louisa Bacon, aged 34 of 29 Bakers Row, blind, for the Guardians to help towards the cost of the poor woman learning a trade at the Berners Street Institution for the Blind", when the Board "agreed to undertake the cost of the instruction... to the extent of 4s weekly.[33] A seemingly graceful touch on 1 May was the authorisation for the Steward of the Infirmary "to expend a sum not exceeding £2 on the purchase of plants for the Garden Beds of the Infirmary", albeit, in Harkness's reckoning, to augment the regimental uniformity of their lay-out so deplored by her.

It was under the firm hand of William Vallance, the clerk, that the Whitechapel Union was given guidance and direction. It was he who, in Barnett's attempt to obtain national support for his

Agricultural Colonies scheme[34] undertook the laborious task of mobilising an all-Guardians conference. A stickler for legality, with cost-efficiency as the maxim, his reign that year was marked by an ambivalence in tone. There was a large turnover in staff; resulting one suspects from his strict enforcements of pay limits and conditions of service. Even with vacant capacity in the wards, he refused requests from other institutions to house a temporary overflow (such as Shoreditch and St. Marylebone — the latter under structural alteration) with the plea that such action was against "the existent contract with the Guardians of Mile End Old Town".[35]

Complaints — and there was an official complaints procedure — were passed on, and advised upon, by Vallance to the committee. One case, outlined in detail would suggest that, because of the lack of objective judicial safeguards, harsh injustices could be perpetrated against inmates. It would take a brave pauper indeed to make an official protest, considering that probably for the rest of his life he would remain defenceless against the power of Union authority. However on 15 May Vallance read out a letter sent to the Local Government Board by an inmate:

Dear Sir,
19th April 1888

Just a few lines to let you know how things are carried on at South Grove Workhouse. On last Wednesday a man by name John Pitkin, the master, the labour master and the asstistant stoker got the man down and took his things away from him in the dining hall. The man was 73 years old and has had heart disease 34 years and he had a struggle with them in there. Mary Ann Brockingtan on the 12th April, the matron, the labour mistress, the labour master and the portress got the woman down in the yard to search her. The poor woman is subject to fits. Her shrieks and cries brought the people's attention from South Grove Model Dwelling Houses. They were all outside looking at them to see their cruelty towards her. It drew the attention of the police from the top of the house to see how they were serving her. She wanted to see the Guardians on Monday but they would not let her. They also bring the dirty flock beds from the infirmary without being disinfected. Well we may have the scarlet fever in the House. There is nothing carried on right in the place any way. I think the Local Board ought to know how we are treated in the house. We are being treated worse than dogs.

(Sgd) Pr Jas Marsh.

The reply from the Master to Vallance, who requested his observations on the complaint, although plausible in his own defence (he had all the evidence of his officials mustered on his side), neither proves nor disproves the accusation. It certainly confirms the petty restrictions imposed on those who had little enough comforts to sustain them in adversity. The minutes record that "T. Badcock, Master" writes:

> I beg to report as follows with reference to the man Pitkin. He was suspected of having tobacco and matches upon him and upon being requested by the Labour master to turn out his pockets he refused. Then he was brought to me and after a little persuasion he gave me what he had. No force was used to get it. The Stoker was not present.
> Mary Brockington was found to have taken a portion of her dinner out of the dining hall. She was discovered by the Matron and myself and upon being told to give it up or go back and eat it in the dining hall she refused. I then sent for the labour mistress who took it from her, the Matron and myself being present. The labour master was not present nor any police. Mary Brockington afterwards apologised to the Matron and labour mistress. She has never requested to see the committee. Had she done so of course she would have been allowed.
> As regards the flocks from the infirmary they are all fumigated.
> The writer of the letter, James Marsh, was an inmate of the workhouse but could not possibly have seen any of the occurrences he mentions as there is no access to the female side of the house for the male paupers!
> Trusting this will be a satisfactory explanation,
>
> I am & c, T.B. Master.

There is no further reference to the matter. Nor were there any more reports of pauper complaints for the rest of the year. We can only guess what life held for the complainant thenceforth. At least homage is due either to a pathetic story-teller or to a man who still retained a vestige of respect for individual human dignity. In the workhouse such an act demanded a sort of reckless courage.

Yet we have an instance where the policy of rigid adherence to procedures within the limits of the Poor Law is curiously abandoned: one where Vallance interceded on behalf of a mother who claimed that her boy had been severely beaten by the headmaster of the Jews Orphan Asylum. Here we see Vallance in the role of a just and humane administrator. The case was unusual in that it evinced a pro-Jewish attitude at a time when animosity towards the "alien" (ie Jewish immigrant) was at its height. Details of the story of the confrontation between the Whitechapel Board and the Jews Asylum are etched out for us in the minuted correspondence. The complainant mother of Joseph Abrahams, aged 13, chargeable to the Whitechapel Union, unfolded her tale to Vallance.

On 4 September she visited her boy at the orphanage and found him ill, suffering as a result of a birching "received the previous day... badly marked and the wounds bleeding". The child had been under treatment for "incontinence" at the Hospital for Urinary Diseases for a considerable time until the previous December. The mother stated that "although she had hoped that the boy had been cured she was convinced that the act of wetting the bed was an involuntary one". The sick lad informed her that he had received 32 strokes with the birch, pleading that he "could not help wetting the bed", presumably the "crime" for which he was punished while the headmaster claimed that the act was "a wilful and voluntary one, that the medical officer was of the same opinion" and that the punishment, authorised by the committee, was "very slight"! The mother declared further, in the clerk's presence, as well as the headmaster's, that "upon the occasion of the death of her husband in the lunatic asylum, she went to see her children with an order from the Guardians and that the headmaster not only refused to allow her to see her children but tore the order to pieces, saying "I am Master here!"

Such arrogance moved Vallance to prompt action. On scrutinising the punishment book he duly commented that "during the present year 64 boys were recorded as having been punished — largely by caning and birching. There was also one entry of several boys having been punished, no names being inserted. There was no record of the number of strokes in the case of birching. The case of Joseph Abrahams was not entered, but it was stated by the headmaster that it would be!" An undertaking given by a Mr Stephany, official of the orphanage, to bring about a searching enquiry was accepted, with the promise that its findings be submitted for further consideration by the Guardians. The Jewish authorities, quick to respond to any public criticism involving any aspect of communal behaviour, especially where the treatment of children was concerned, reacted accordingly. A letter was soon received from Mr Henry Behrends, President of the Jews Hospital, dated 25 September, which confirmed "that the punishment was severe, without however amounting to cruelty (the Guardians had defined the act as a cruel beating) and the evidence is so conflicting that it is difficult to arrive at the exact truth... They (the committee) are of opinion, however, that the number of strokes of the birch did not exceed twelve... The committee had given strict instructions to the headmaster in future never to exceed six strokes either with the cane or birch." Hardly a satisfactory answer for the shrewd clerk, who was quick to chide the Jewish Asylum officials for their obvious insensitivity in not considering that the boy had, in effect, been punished for an involuntary illness:

> Mr Vallance accepts the opinion that the resolution of the House Committee of the Jews Orphan Asylum... will preclude the possibility of the recurrence of a similar event... (but) at the same time, it would have been more satisfactory to the Guardians if the house committee had considered the primary question whether the child had been guilty of an offence worthy of punishment at all, and whether he was not, in fact, severely punished for an involuntary act arising from physical weakness.[36]

The same Vallance would lend his support to the resolution "that the sum of 10 guineas be paid as a subscription for one year towards the funds of the Jewish Home (Stepney) subject to the approval of the Local Government Board". His authority was sacrosanct; and, in recognition, there was no opposition to the proposal of his Union Assessment Committee (also ratified by the Local Government Board) that he be awarded the princely sum of £120 for his services to the committee during the year ended April 1888.[37] Furthermore in the 24 July minutes, we read of a resolution to award a gratuity of £150 to the same for extra services, including the "weekly review of paupers admitted to the workhouse and infirmary and periodically remaining therein, in order to secure consideration by the Guardians of circumstances attending chargeability, the enforcement of obligations on relations and the practicability of means for dispauperisation". Such was his reputation that even this additional payment was ratified by that economy-conscious body, the Local Government Board. They recognised a Master in the practice of cost-efficiency and duly rewarded him in cash terms![38]

The Guardians made other, superlative, claims for his performance. His successful economy within the workhouse was deemed to encourage thrift and responsibility among the poor outside!

> There is also reason to believe that the policy which has been pursued has resulted in an improvement in the condition of the poor. Rents are said to be better paid, and more money to be deposited in savings and penny banks than formerly, while publicans and pawnbrokers are equally lamenting the badness of trade. The poor are certainly more self-respecting than they were...[39]

It could be that the régime imposed by Vallance and the master was certain to deter even the most desperate of the "respectable" poor. It is, again, Harkness's pointed revelation of the loss of the individual's freedom and dignity that defies the rosy projection conceived by Union officials:

> The workshops lay close together and in each of them men were redeeming the time by making something for the use of the workhouse. Tailors squatted on tables, bootmakers cobbled and patched, men plaited mats; each pauper had his task, and each knew that the morrow would bring the same work, that as surely as the sun rises and sets, his task would be the same tomorrow as it was at the moment. 6 o'clock would set him free for tea, but after that he would be handed over to an instructor until bed time.
> The Whitechapel Union allows no man to remain idle from the time he gets up until he goes to bed again. A sodden look has settled on the faces of the older men and they apparently thought little of what they were doing... not a voice was to be heard in the workshops, the men did not whistle or sing; they looked like schoolboys in disgrace rather than free-born English citizens.[40]

Poplar Union, on close scrutiny, reveals a larger institution, since it embraced a wider and more populated catchment area, and yet its image is of a more humane body, in which the needs of individuals were more liberally catered for. There was an overall increase in the number of paupers compared with the previous year. A joint relieving officers' memorandum in January requested "clerical assistance to enable us to daily perform... Owing to the greatly increased number of applicants it is a matter of utter impossibility for us to visit and make due enquiries into cases with the present staff.[41] An LGB inspector, concerned with the pressure of intake, reported the administration "in good order and satisfactory as the present overcrowded state of the house will allow". This occasioned the central authority at Whitehall to instruct Poplar to produce contingency plans to meet the overflow, which prompted the Union to consider commissioning architects for that purpose. Expansion was mooted "to the extent of 296 beds". The LGB in turn proposed that "the best mode of enlarging the workhouse would be to build a new block on the male side and to enlarge the existing small block on the female side".[42] It was not to be. By October it was decided to postpone action until the new London County Council had been formed and its functions defined, although deferment was as much due to the opposition of Bromley Ratepayers Protection Association protesting against the public expenditure involved, as to a firm request by the Trustees of Poplar Union to abjure any further outlay.[43]

Poplar's application of the Poor Law does appear, by its own record, milder, and yet it still maintained certain less humane features in accord with the norm elsewhere. There was participation in child emigration schemes, and a continual supply of boy "volunteers", chargeable to Poplar, from the Forest Gate School into army bands and the House Boy Brigade, as well as into the Exmouth naval training ship. There is one entry, poignant in its inference: "Deserted lad joins army band. Consent was given to Joseph Humphries aged 14, a deserted child being permitted to join a band of a regiment in the army." In their reckoning, it was better for the boy to be in the ordered security of a military collective where he would find a substitute family. It also meant less expenditure on the parish.[44]

Complaints against staff by inmates were formally accepted and recorded, but judgment was rarely found against officials. It was reported (minutes of 15 May) that an inmate, Joseph Cleaver, made an accusation against Assistant Matron Brown that "in consequence of violent language addressed by the officer... to his wife, who was also an inmate of the workhouse, she had fallen in a fit in the needleroom". An investigating committee of Board members found "that no more than ordinary language(?) was used by the Assistant Matron, and that no fit had occurred... Cleaver had no cause for complaint." A somewhat different outcome resulted from a later incident in which a pauper reported a theft of clothing while he was lying ill in the sick ward.

Complaint — stealing from inmate
Joseph Watkins — inmate — complained that upon discharge from the sick asylum in January last he was refused to be allowed to have his clothes and when his bundle was brought to him on the 21st ultimo he found that several articles had been abstracted therefrom.

The final report declared that the asylum "managers had carefully enquired into the matter and have no reason to think that the bundle had been tampered with in their possession". However, "it was ordered that he be supplied with the necessary (missing) clothing". It was an unspoken recognition that the act of pauper stealing from pauper was as common as that played out behind prison walls.[45] Yet the Poplar régime could not have been as oppressively authoritarian as elsewhere. One notes the cool reaction to a rather cheeky request from one of the inmates. In the minutes of 29 June we read of a pauper, James Mathias, "stating that he had been elected to an annuity from the Masters' Boot and Shoe Makers Institution" and, therefore, asking "to be appointed to execute the boot repairing at the workhouse". Although he received short shrift, the atmosphere of the house must have been conducive to such requests for them to take place at all. Although reluctant to find their own officers guilty of offences, they were quick to take up the cudgels for outside complainants. For example, a report declaring ill-usage of one of its own paupers on entry was sharply dismissed on the joint evidence of the officials concerned, who declared that the applicant "was... worse for drink and refused to conform to regulations", while a letter of complaint by a Mrs Johnson to Poplar Union, suggesting that the porter of the Stepney Union had been abusive, was quickly passed on with a plea for action by their neighbour. (The Clerk of Stepney, in his reply, agreed that maltreatment had actually taken place.)[46]

There were always some contradictions in practices carried out by anybody compelled to operate within the rules. On the one hand we have a case, later in the year, of a heartless action involving a deaf and dumb girl, M.A. Sudgrove, under Poplar's charge, ensconced in a Brighton institution. In a moving letter the latter's director pleads for the retention of the girl until she finds a suitable job:

The Clerk of the Guardians, Poplar.
Sir,

re M.A. Sudgrove.

I am glad to say the girl is in excellent health and that I can give a very good report of her. She is willing, obedient, attentive and industrious — the workmistress says she is very good at house and laundry work, and that she can sew and knit fairly well. I think she is about nineteen, but deaf and dumb always appear at least two or three years younger when compared to others their own age. They do not succeed well as household servants as their affliction prevents them hearing bells or giving messages tho' they scrub and clean very well. If M.A. Sudgrove could be placed under the watchful care of someone who could take an interest in her I feel she would give satisfaction. She is very much liked by all who have to do with her. She can remain here till some employment is found for her.

I remain, sir,

Yours truly,

William Sleight.

The Poplar Guardians refused the last suggestion and ordered that "M.A. Sudgrove do now return to the workhouse", most likely on the premise that it cost less to maintain her there. In contradistinction to this, they had earlier acquiesced in the case of another deaf-mute, Frederick White aged 17, in their care, under the following circumstances. He was offered a three-year apprenticeship as a bespoke tailor and the details proposed give us an insight into the current terms for entry into the trade.

Wages 1s weekly plus board, lodging and washing first year; 3s second year *et al*; 6s third year *et al*.
Name and address of clergyman or Minister of Church or Chapel to attend:

The Rev. C. Rhind,
St. Saviour's,
Oxford St., W.
The boy will sleep with another apprentice. Hours of work from 7am to 7pm. Apparently a comfortable home for the boy.
   Premium required £15.

(Sgd.) E.B. Nichols.
R.O., West District.[47]

The Guardians resolved to effect the binding and that a premium of £15 and clothing be granted the lad! Yet on two other occasions when a committee member, concerned with keeping out the unemployed and "honest" poor, put the resolution to legalise the extension of outdoor relief it was overwhelmingly defeated by the Board. The tone of the rejection was set by the chairman, the Rev. A.G. How, who warned that "greater possible judgment should be exercised in granting out relief; otherwise it would tend to destroy the strongest incentive among the poor to temperance, thrift, providence and decent living.[48] In the final count the basic obligations under the Poor Law would be adhered to.

In the case of Poplar, evidence does suggest modifications in policy arising out of a more amenable response to the needs of individual or groups of paupers. There is an extraordinary report in the *East London Observer* on the board's proceedings of 3 February when an irate member, Mr Dean, "called attention to the increase of consumption of stout in the workhouse, which, for the week ending 7 January, amounted to 791 pints against 161. pints for the corresponding period". The medical officer responsible for this ascribed the dramatic rise in stout-drinking to "the prevalence of illness".[49] (Such a situation would never have arisen under that severe puritan accountant who "ruled" Whitechapel.) Another incident involving a curious change in rates of consumption was provoked by another member, Mr Agar, who was agitated about "the fact that with an increase in the number of inmates... there was a decrease in the consumption of bread" and a subsequent increase in the consumption of (the more expensive) meat. How could this happen? "The clerk explained that this was due to a change in the character of the inmates who of late years have included a larger portion of sick and infirm."[50]

Other apprentice schemes were, on record, generously supported. A report from the Relieving Officer of Bromley District recommending the apprenticeship of a boy, William Harrison, to local hairdresser John Elie of 23 Bow Common Lane, was agreed in a resolution passed "to effect a binding", adding "that an outfit be supplied". (The indentures were duly executed binding the boy to his master for five years.) Three further cases that year included aid to another deaf-mute, a girl, who was bound apprentice to a dressmaker, as well as assistance to a number of girls entering domestic service.[51] Other acts showed particular concern for inmates. As a result of injury to an infirm woman who had fallen out of bed at night, the committee appointed an additional day-and-night attendant and ordered that rooms be strengthened by padding to prevent future accidents; and, in the case of room temperatures falling as low as 43°F, the Master was authorised to place a hot-water coil under the floor of each padded room in the female lunatic ward.[52] In June inmate Julia Callaghan was allowed to visit her children at Lawn House, Margate, the cost of her return railway fare being met by the Union; in August an O.R. pauper Eliza Saunders was permitted to visit her son at Leavesden with all expenses paid. One notes further, in September, the incident of young William Adams, inmate of St. Mary's Orphanage, North Hyde, and chargeable to Poplar, being granted travel money to visit his sister at Southend. There were other acts revealing more than a modicum of concern. In May, with summer approaching, the committee resolved that "the Master be authorised to spend a sum not exceeding £2 on plants for the yards and window sills of the infirm wards"; and during the next meeting a change of diet was ordered, with a lighter fare of bacon and cabbage to replace the stodgy mish-mash hitherto on offer at all seasons.[53] Concurrently seven children were fostered out to country folk under the superintendence of the Corsham and Atworth Boarding Out Committee with all costs met by the Union. In the only recorded case of aid for an emigrant to New York, Jane Sullivan, a full grant of £3 was voted to assist her, which was rescinded by the LGB who only sanctioned the sum of 16s 6d towards travelling expenses and no help towards an outfit.[54] One suspects that it was not the first time that the Poplar Guardians had gone beyond the limits set by the Poor Law to help their charges, albeit friendless and without power, as individuals!

The St. George's Union emerges as the least edifying of all three institutions. The "House" at Princes Street, Old Gravel Lane loomed threateningly over the congested network of grimy, narrow alleyways and culs-de-sac that lay astride the Wapping waterfront. It was a magnet for the destitute casuals crowding the docks and needing shelter. This led to the almost insoluble problem of overcrowding in the casual wards as well as increased numbers involved in the complexities of settlement.

The district suffered from a dual handicap. Though small in size, it was the second largest in Tower Hamlets in terms of poverty. Its ratepayers consisted of the less affluent echelon of publicans, shop and store keepers, pawnbrokers and the like. Limited income meant pressure to adhere to strict economy, which in turn defined conditions within the workhouse. Overcrowding by casuals was the norm. Before the previous Christmas, 34 destitutes "applied for admission over the numbers the wards are certified to hold", so that the Guardians ordered the Master to discharge them "at his discretion". On 11 May the clerk read a letter from a relieving officer complaining that the police at King David's Lane were sending all wayfarers they found in the streets for admission to St. George's Workhouse, which led to a letter of protest being sent to the Commissioner of Police. A dramatic increase in casuals, averaging 25 per night, was duly reported in the *East London Observer*.[55] Later that month local R.O., Mr. Merritt, notified the Board that "persons were in the habit of applying for relief up to as late as 3.00 in the morning" and was thereby instructed to refuse orders of admission to able-bodied paupers after 12 o'clock midnight unless brought by a police constable. By June the Master was forced to admit the overflow from the casual ward into the main workhouse, where, he lamented, "they got a better diet and less oakum to pick"! The *East London Observer* noted that the knowledge of this seemed to have attracted the casuals in such great numbers that the Guardians decided to provide temporary accommodation in another portion of the building to meet the emergency.[46] The invasion continued, and by September a large increase of tramps and casuals in the wards persisted, partly, according to the committee, since "they were more comfortable and better treated than in other institutes" and because neither Bethnal Green nor Stepney had provision for them. That the House was located in the heart of dockland, where competition for work was desperate, seems to have escaped their calculations. That accommodation was in short supply was an understatement. In consequence of an overcrowded infirmary, convalescents, including outsiders, were transferred to the workhouse — a traumatic experience for the non-inmate, and certainly no inducement for a rapid recovery.

With the Guardians over-obsessed with economy, the drive to cut costs was paramount. A brief scrutiny of the return of stimulants consumed over annual periods shows, in contrast to Poplar, a sharp drop in expenditure. This drew praise from the committee, who resolved that "best thanks be rendered Dr Steer for care in ordering stimulants" (ie for reducing orders so dramatically over the last three years), and, as a good example for others to follow, "a copy of the return be forwarded to each Board of Guardians in the metropolis".[57] Further acts bordered on parsimony, one at the expense of pauper children under their care. On 17 February there was a report concerning the current milk allocation to pupils at Plashet Schools for the purpose of reducing the quantity used, as a saving.

All Children have ½ pint pure milk for breakfast and ¼ pint for supper. To make one gallon of milk cocoa the qualities and price are as follows:

3 pints milk, farm prices 1s 3d per gallon	5½
4ozs of cocoa	2½
4ozs of sugar	½
	8½d

Water added.

3 pints milk, contract price 8½d per imperial gallon	3¼
4ozs cocoa	2½
4ozs sugar	½
	6¼d

Water added.

Therefore cocoa made with contract milk is cheaper than all contract milk by 2¼d; cocoa made with farm milk is cheaper than all farm milk by 6½d and cocoa made with contract milk is cheaper than all farm milk by 8¾d per gallon.

The Medical Officer *prefers* a milk diet to cocoa but would change the diet now and then, as, by so doing, he thinks it would benefit the children.

By substituting cocoa for milk the cost of children maintenance would be considerably less, say about £200 if farm milk is used.

The Committee so recommended that cocoa and milk be substituted "for all milk for all children over seven years of age forthwith". The LGB promptly agreed! Where economy was sacrosanct, the welfare of the charges proved of secondary consideration.[58]

Other measures showed the persistence of this attitude. The sale of Plashet schools and grounds was discussed over the problem of providing alternative accommodation for the displaced children. Although LGB regarded this as inadvisable (on the premise that new provisions or schooling locally might cost the parish £30,000), this did not deter the schools committee from pressing on with the recommendation that "9 acres of the land at Plashet be sold and the office of assistant schoolmistress, tailor, scullery maid, hall woman, boys' attendant, cowman, gardener, and barber be abolished".[59] The Union was adamant in its opposition to an extension of outdoor relief; and, in form, a report back by delegate A.G. Crowder from the conference on Barnett's "Agricultural Training Homes" opposed the scheme, objecting to "spending the money of ratepayers in order to provide a certain class of adult paupers an apprenticeship without conforming to rules which are suggestive of the workhouse". The Board was quick to seize on any monies received by inmates. When a legacy of £50 was left to a pauper, F.E. Barnett, it was promptly "resolved to take steps to recover the amount due to the Guardians".[60] Settlement cases were rapidly dealt with and out-county paupers ruthlessly despatched to the parishes concerned.[61] "There was, however, no curbing of expenditure on payments to informers for information leading to the apprehension of parental deserters, where the abandoned children became chargeable to the parish. The St. George's Union was not slow in off-loading such children via emigration.

On 6 July it reported that seven deserted children, aged from 10 to 13 years, emigrated to Canada under the authorisation of the LGB. One notes that the cost per child was as high as £12, but in Poor Law reckoning the long-term savings on such action were incalculable.

Such economies, however, did not make for efficiency. There were strange lapses in the Master's handling of accounts. On 27 April the clerk reported "the wood book had not been made up since the 9th instant; the Master on being called in stated the labour master had failed to bring his book to the office but, for the future, he would see the book was regularly made up... The clerk also reported the Coffin, Wood, Bakery and Houseless Poor Accounts were inaccurately kept." Later that year the Local Medical Officer of Health, on inspecting the wards in the infirmary, declared them "in a very bad condition, some of them being infected with vermin".[62] There was a log of complaints by inmates accusing officials either of harsh treatment or of favouritism.[63] One serious accusation came from outside. It was brought by Dr Frederick Treves of the London Hospital and charged the Board with interring two dead paupers in unconsecrated ground "in contravention of the statutes".[64] Although the officer concerned countered by stating that he had already "explained everything to the satisfaction of Mr Hawkins, Inspector of Anatomy", the whole affair showed the Board's lack of sensitivity towards its charges.

Under the policy of self-help applied by all Unions, one activity roused a furore locally: namely, their involvement in wood-chopping where pauper labour could be income-producing. Wood was the main fuel in an area where the price of coal or even coke could be prohibitive, and the preparation and sale of bundles had, for generations, provided a livelihood for those living on the margin. In February the Master of Stepney Workhouse was faced with a strike among paupers engaged in turning the wheel on the wood saw. The cause was not reported.[65] Objections from outside peaked during the winter months to the extent that the LGB was forced to intervene. It advised that "manufacture of firewood on a large scale by pauper labour should not be carried out in any metropolitan workhouse, and that in the employment of inmates, machinery should be avoided, resort being made to pure manual labour. It was also essential that the full market value of the firewood should be demanded in order that the independent producer should not be subjected to unfair competition."[66] All three other Unions were targets of complaints, especially St. George's. A letter from the Firewood Cutters Protection Association was concerned that the latter's "practice in supplying firewood has tended to reduce the wages of firewood cutters employed by the independent(s)... and that if the practice be not discontinued the result will be that a large number of persons will be thrown on the parish for relief. Whitechapel, true to form, argued that, however anxious they were to avoid unfair competition, they were not prepared to admit "that the fact of a man being employed in the workhouse deprives him of the right to contribute to the labour of the country the produce of which he is a consumer". Poplar and St. George's concurred with the LGB ruling that the full market value, equal in size to those manufactured outside, would be enforced so as to obviate unfair competition. It was imperative that the free market in goods remain inviolate.

Mile End Union, situated in a more salubrious part, adhered, in prac- tice, to the strictest application of the Poor Law. Evidence of maltreatment of old inmates was brought to light by the lively remonstrances of the reformist Guardian Mr T. Richardson. On 17 May he alleged that:

> an old man named Young, aged 74, on the previous Monday had been ordered to the labour house at South Grove, although seriously ill; had died on the following Wednesday after waiting for medical attendance for some hours, and had been buried in a roughly made "box", the bottom of which was not even painted black![67]

The following month he publicised a second case of an old woman, over seventy years of age, who had been compelled to work at "rolling" in the laundry from half past six in the morning till half past four in the evening with only one hour's interval. It was his tenacity in following through the evidence that compelled the House committee "not to allow any inmates over 50 years of age to be sent to the labour establishment at South Grove; and to provide, in future, for the proper "dressing" and burial of deceased inmates".[68] Yet it was the same Richardson, as one of the caucus of militant teetotallers led by Frederick Charrington, who tried to stop the supply of beer traditionally allocated to paupers as part of their Christmas dinner, this time with less success (although the allowance was reduced from 1½ to 1 pint as a compromise).

With winter approaching, the editor of the *East London Advertiser* summed up the grim prospects facing the local poor. In somewhat emotional vein, he berated the soulless Gradgrindism which determined official policies, and warned of the social consequences of their thinking.

> What will the winter bring? Already there are signs of grim poverty and dire distress. The workhouses of Poplar and St. George's are full, while the other East End pauper institutions are beginning to feel the effects of the approaching winter...
> East London, swarming as it is with a population who live from hand to mouth, is always first to feel the shoe's pinch, and it is here that may be expected that the sound of woe will be heard most. That the guardians of the poor will, in their official capacity, be tried to the uttermost, is certain; and in order that when the time arrives to act nothing shall be done in a panic, the complex and difficult question of relief should be considered while there is time for careful deliberation and anxious thought. There must be no more Mansion House Funds indiscriminately distributed with a careless hand, as these only serve to attract from afar those who prefer to eat the bread of idleness. Yet the arm of philanthropy must not be shortened because of fraud and deceit on the part of some of the recipients... it would rather be better to help nine rogues and one honest but unfortunate man than help none, and so let the deserving feel the pangs of rejection when he deigns to ask for help. Think of the children! They have done no wrong, yet they suffer... "With eyes too tired of weeping and hearts too sad for play" their pitiful faces are a shameful reproach to the civilisation of the 19th century, whose greatest men are political economists with only facts and figures, themes of supply and demand, price and average, to keep men's lives pure and their ambitions above mere self. Whatever the remedy — if there exists a sovereign remedy — for the curse of poverty it is hard to find... we can extend to the weary and wan — to the outcast and the homeless — kind words and a real, loving sympathy. This costs nothing, yet is efficacious in raising a drooping spirit. The winter is coming; let us face it in that spirit, and there will be no talk of rise and revolution.[69]

Christmas 1888, did, however, record a local response to that traditional "time of year when even Bumbledom relaxes some of its sternness and dignity". It was also the time for the annual visitation by *very important persons*, when the Yuletide spirit must be seen to brighten up the life of the meanest inhabitant; the one day of good cheer when "he is given a taste of the good things going". It was the only occasion too, at which "the late Mr F.J. Wood, Chairman of the Mile End Guardians, used to make it an unvarying practice... to taste the food provided for the inmates, but though several of the Guardians were present, it is a matter of uncertainty whether the thoughtful kind and useful practice was followed!" Even the doyens of the Poor Law in Whitechapel relaxed their strict adherence to the balance sheet. On Christmas Day each pauper received "½ lb of port, 1lb potatoes, ½lb plum pudding, a pint of porter, 5ozs of bread, 1oz butter, a pot of tea and ½lb plain cake, whilst tobacco, snuff, oranges etc. were distributed". Similar delicacies and jollification were found in the "Poplar and Stepney Unions, where the workhouses were in a crowded state much in excess of the numbers last year".[70]

Within their own terms, the workhouses kept the weakest and desperate alive. Whitechapel perfected a system which eroded the self-confidence of the chirpy East Ender for whom a roving freedom was the very essence of his being. Outside the gates he, at least, had some choice in how to keep going — be it to steal, con or sell his labour cheaply in the marketplace. Except for the misfit or unemployable, the "House" was the ultimate in social degradation, since it threatened the horror of a pauper's grave.

Among the glib parrotings of those Guardians and their bureaucrats who purported to carry out Poor Law duties to the letter may be detected the repository of a Christian conscience, exerting itself according to the precept "I am my brother's keeper!" But the workhouse remained the workhouse. The image of a dull, soulless monotony imposed by a harsh authority perpetuated the legend. On 27 March 1929 the LGA, which spelt *finis* to both the 1834 Act and the Workhouse, received Royal Assent. Even today the wounds they inflicted remain embedded in local memory. Under the comparative benevolence of the welfare state there are still some old folk, raised in the shadow of the "Union", who, though in need of extra cash to make ends meet, would rather "do without" than apply for any benefit, which, in their mythology, is equated with the hated parish relief.

Footnotes

[1]*In Darkest England*, pp. 21-3.
[2]*Life and Labour...*, vol. 1, p. 168.
[3]*Canon Barnett*, vol. 1, p. 202.
[4]John Law, *Out of Work*, p. 177.
[5]John Law, *In Darkest London*, pp. 189-90.
[6]Ibid., p. 200.
[7]*Justice* 20 October 1888, "The Workhouse as Sanctuary".
[8]See *East End News* 26 June and 28 November for metropolitan figures.
[9]The Union was the official title of the Board of Guardians who locally administered the Poor Law and the parish workhouse.
[10]*ELA* 15 December 1888. The same paper reported detailed statistics of pauperism regularly throughout the whole year.
[11]Walter Besant, *East London* (London 1903) p. 249.
[12]Ibid., p. 250.
[13]Whitechapel Workhouses at South Grove E3 and at Bakers Row, Thomas St. E1; Poplar Workhouse, 86 Poplar High St. E14; St. George's-in-the-East Workhouse, Raines Street, Wapping E1.
[14]*ELA* 8 September 1888, "Poor Law Administration in Whitechapel".
[15]*ELO* 30 June 1888, "Poor Law Lessons".
[16]William Vallance, born in Woolwich in 1834, was Clerk to the Whitechapel Board of Guardians from 1868 to 1902. He became a nationally acknowledged authority on all questions referring to the Poor Law, and during a long career was often consulted by government departments, He was founder of the Poor Law Officers Association and was also founder and chairman of the Exmouth, a training ship for pauper cadets. To commemorate his work in his lifetime, Vallance Road (formerly Bakers Row) was named after him in 1896.
[17]Whitechapel Union Minute Book No. 70 (1888). Minutes of 24 January record his appointment with effect from 17 January. The *ELO* of 21 January reports that he and his wife were recipients of many tangible marks of esteem from their previous inmates at Christchurch Union, where he was apparently a popular Master.
[18]*In Darkest London*, p. 198.
[19]Ibid., p. 196.
[20]Whitechapel Union Minute Book 24 January.
[21]*In Darkest London*, p. 197.
[22]Whitechapel Union Minutes of 21 February.
[23]Ibid., 6 March records 35 removeable cases with 3 examined "touching the legality of their remaining in". On 20 March there were 21 settlement cases. On 9 August there were only 9 removals and two legally acceptable from outside Unions. By 27 November there were only 4 removal cases.
[24]Barnardo, *Night and Day* March 1888, p. 8.
[25]See above, Chapter 3, pp. 56-7.
[26]Minutes of 6 March and 17 April.
[27]Ibid. 1 May. The Paddington note referred to the deplorable results attending the vagrancy of children under 15 years of age, and urging the

necessity of such legislation as would assume the Guardians' control.
[28] Minute on Industrial Schools Bill, 13 November.
[29] Minutes of 11 December: Ampthill Boarding Out Reports from Inspector.
[30] See Norman Longmate, *The Workhouse* (London, 1974) pp. 189-91.
[31] Minutes of 2 October: Case of Mary Cathcart of 82 Pelham Street.
[32] For example see Minutes of 7 February, 1 May and 24 December.
[33] Though later, on 18 September, the Medical Officer refused to recommend a request by the same society to send a blind man to a seaside convalescent establishment since "no permanent benefit could result from sending him there".
[34] See above, pp. 54-5.
[35] Minutes of 4 September and 18 September.
[36] Ibid. 18 September and 2 October. Upon Abrahams' discharge from the Norwood Asylum the Guardians provided him with an outfit to the value of £4 (see Minute dated 30 October).
[37] Ibid., 1 May.
[38] Ratification of the award by the Local Government Board is reported in Minutes of 18 September.
[39] Report of Whitechapel Board of Guardians for half year ending Lady Day 1888.
[40] John Law, *In Darkest London*, pp. 199-200.
[41] Poplar Union Minute Book 13 January 1888.
[42] For extension proposals see ibid. 27 January, 9 March and 20 April. On 1 June, Poplar had to reject a request from the Clerk of the St. George's Union to accommodate some of its permanent paupers with the plea "that there is no spare accommodation in this workhouse".
[43] See ibid. 5 October.
[44] A clutch of recruits to both army and the Exmouth is recorded in ibid. 10 August. Two more boys are registered as enlisting in a regimental band (21 September) and two others on the Exmouth (2 November).
[45] Ibid. 1 June and 15 June.
[46] Both cases were reported in ibid. 24 August and 7 September.
[47] See ibid. 15 February and 29 June.
[48] See *ELO* 9 June for first resolution and *ELA* 13 October for second. The first proposer pointed out "that if the Local Government Bill passes next March 1st, the Guardians will receive a contribution of 9d per head per day for indoor, and nothing for out-door poor. This would be a premium to make as many indoor paupers as possible", no doubt he cared for keeping the genuine poor out where they could at least preserve a modicum of freedom and personal dignity.
[49] *ELO* 4 February.
[50] *ELO* 26 May.
[51] See Poplar Union Minutes of 7 and 24 September.
[52] Ibid. 23 March.
[53] Ibid. 18 May and 1 June.
[54] Ibid. 15 and 29 June.
[55] *ELO* 28 April.
[56] St. George's Union Minutes of 8 June. Also see *ELO* 16 June and *ELA*

8 Septamber.

[57] Minutes of 3 February show that the total cost of intoxicants consumed after 1885 fell from £179 9s 6¾d to £57 3s 4½d in three years.

[58] Ibid. 17 February and 16 March.

[59] Ibid. 6 July.

[60] Ibid. 22 June.

[61] They needed to be. Settlement cases (out) rose from 27 reported on 23 December 1887 to a maximum of 75 on 13 April 1888, diminishing in the summer period but rising again during the last two months of 1888. Work in the docks was attracting desperate labourers from as far afield as Bodmin and Nottingham.

[62] *ELA* 6 October.

[63] Minutes of 2 March, 13 April, 22 June and 6 July register a variety of complaints. See *ELA* 10 March for complaints against admission porters.

[64] Frederick Treves discovered and was current "host" to the Elephant Man.

[65] *ELA* 11 February.

[66] *ELA* 2 November. For further reports on wood-chopping as it affected other unions, see *ELA* 13, 23, 27 November and 1 December.

[67] *ELA* 19 May, "An Alleged Scandal".

[68] *ELA* 16 June, "The Treatment of Inmates".

[69] *ELA* 3 November, "The Coming Winter".

[70] *ELA* 29 December, "At the Workhouses".

Chapter 5
Women and Children

> Is it well that while we range with science glorying in the time,
> City children soak and blacken soul and sense in city slime?
> There among the gloomy alleys progress halts in palsied feet,
> Crime and hunger cast our maidens by the thousands on the street.
> There the master scrimps his haggard semptress of her daily bread,
> There a single sordid attic holds the living and the dead!
>
> Introduction to *Toilers in London, or Iniquities Concerning Female Labour in the Metropolia*, being the second part of *Tempted London*, by the *British Weekly*, edited by Margaret Harkness (1889)

In the predatory climate engendered by *laisser-faire*, among those fighting to survive in this "jungle of empire", where "preying upon the weak and being preyed upon by the strong" was the norm, women were the most vulnerable. For those East Enders categorised by Charles Booth as on or below the poverty line, it could be an unrewarding struggle for bare existence.

In 1888 it was particularly so. The "crime" of being born female meant that women were at the bottom of the pecking order. Again, we turn to Harkness for an insight into city occupations involving local girls. It was the result of a six-month research project on hours and wages and disclosed a record of unmitigated exploitation.

> So far I have found that there are at least 200 trades at which girls work in the city... namely, brush-makers, button-makers, cigarette-makers, electric light fitters, fur workers, india rubber stamp machinists, magic lantern slide makers, perfumers, portmanteau makers, spectacle makers, surgical instrument makers, tie makers etc. These girls can be roughly divided into two classes: those who earn from 5s to 14s, and those who earn from 4s to 8s a week. Taking slack time into consideration, it is, I think, safe to say that 10s is the average weekly wage of the first class and 4s 6d that of the second class. Their weekly wage often falls below this, and sometimes rises above it. The hours are almost invariably from 8am to 7pm with one hour for dinner and a half holiday on Saturday. I know few cases in which such girls work less; a good many in which overtime reaches to 10 or

11 at night; a few in which overtime means all night. There is little to choose between the two classes. The second are allowed by their employers to wear old clothes and boots, the first must make "a genteel appearance"... how the girls have to stint on underclothing and food in order to make what their employers call "a genteel appearance"!

Many a family is at the present kept by the labour of one or two such girls, who can at the most earn a few shillings. "The youth of a nation are the trustees of posterity." What sort of daughters are these girls with their pinched faces and stunted bodies likely to give England?[1]

This was repeated in her current novel, in which she focused in on a group of local girls seeking work outside a factory. Here her concern was somewhat marred by a middle-class sniff of distaste for their "vulgar" posturings:

A more miserable set of girls it would be difficult to find anywhere. They had only just escaped from the Board School, but many had faces wise with wickedness, and eyes out of which all traces of maidenhood had vanished; the "universal adjective" fell from their lips as a term of endearment, whilst the foulest names were given to girls they did not like, also blows and kicks by way of emphasis.

They were offered work at 5d a day, "enough to buy bread with". As new recruits to the vast reservoir of local labour, they had no alternative but to accept. "It's no good to talk to the girls about combination, they're so downtrodden and mean-spirited... They (the capitalists) use the girls to cut the throats of the men... It's work, work, work, with them from the time they get up till they go to bed, except on Sundays." Yet mutual aid, the poor helping the poor in adversity, was never absent. "They're good to one another, they are. You'd be surprised to see what they'll do to help a girl that's ill, and how they'll put themselves about to buy crape when a girl is dead and has to be buried." The suffering of a lifetime could be compensated by the prospect of a "correct" burial. As we have seen, for the poor the ultimate horror went beyond dying, to the more fearful threat of a pauper's grave. Harkness recalls an old woman who only accepted alms to ensure that her dying daughter "met the Almighty like a lady. I've got her a muslin dress, in which she made her first communion, to lay her out in. I'd like to think as she'd stand before the Almighty in a pair of white silk stockings!"[2]

The degradation of women was inherent in an oppressive, patriarchal society. Their pauperisation locally is constantly brought home to us by a mass of evidence from diverse sources. Much of it stemmed from male unemployment, when men were involuntarily ousted from their traditional role as breadwinner. This could account for even the most respectable unemployed East Enders, condemned to frustration and loss of self respect, resorting to outbursts of violence against their working wives who bore the triple burden of mother, housekeeper and sole wage earner.

Sometimes the responsibility was shared by the eldest daughter. Dr Barnardo tells of a Mrs G., mother of a one-parent family of six children crowded into two rooms in Bow Common:

> The eldest daughter, 17, is the only wage earner among the children who plies the precarious trade of making knickerbockers for a large firm. She is paid at the rate of one penny for each pair, supplying her own needles and thread! By dint of the hardest work the eldest daughter can earn 6s, or 6s 3d in the week.
>
> The mother "finishes" the knickerbockers which the daughter makes, and she gains thus a second penny per pair, also supplying her own needles and thread. Her wage limit is accordingly about the same as her daughter's.
>
> Co-jointly their best earnings are 12s 6d a week of which 5s 6d goes on rent, 7s to feed and keep warm two adults and five children... She would have been sorely troubled to be called one of the destitute poor. Her only complaint is that the work isn't constant. "We often, in some seasons, have to go for days without work at all. That's the hardest to bear. And even when work can be got, we often lose two, three or even four hours when we go to fetch it. Sometimes I have to stand two hours after a long walk down, and with the walk back before me, waiting with a crowd of others to get my bundle."[3]

Barnardo estimated that there were hundreds of such families living practically within a stone's throw of the *Edinburgh Castle*.

In some cases the only provider for a large family could be an elder son. This was exemplified in the report of young Tom Gott to Dr Barnardo of his mother who, although dying of cancer, had discharged herself from hospital to be among her family to the end.

> "She had toomers (tumours). She wor in the London 'Ospital nine weeks to be operated on. She kem out last Tuesday 'cos

things was so bad at 'ome, and she didn't want to die in the 'orspital. She said she wanted all on us to see her die at 'ome."

The only source of income for the whole family is derived from one of the boys, aged twenty, who as a lighterman's labourer earns fifteen shillings a week. The mother comes back to die in one rented room and she is many weeks behind in the rent.

Barnardo appealed to the conscience of a well-fed audience for alms to salvage as much of the human wreckage as he could:

> What do we know of starvation? What do we know of the cupboard without a crust, of the grate without a fire? Of the bed which is only a pile of dirty flock in the corner of the room, and the ever-haunting sense of destitution looming near for herself and her unemployed children so soon to be left orphans?[4]

There is overwhelming evidence of the many forms of oppression suffered by women through their conditioned subservience to the needs of the family. At the House of Lords Committee sitting of 24 April we read of statements of wives who had to support disabled, unemployed husbands. Elizabeth Killick, a trouser-finisher of 22 years experience with three children, the eldest being ten, could not earn more than 1s 2d a day, which, after paying for trimmings, meant 1s. "She was up at 6 o'clock in the morning and never finished till 8pm. She paid 2s a week rent. Her husband was in an infirmary paralysed all over one side, and had not earned any wages for three years." Questioned by Lord Aberdeen on whether she earned sufficient to provide herself and her family with food, she replied that it was not but she had to make do with it. Her daily subsistence was "a herring and a cup of tea", and as for meat, "I suppose I have a bit of meat about once in six months." In toto she had 5s a week to live on, out of which "I have to pay for fire, lighting, food and clothes". Similar hardship was experienced by trouser-finisher Mary Hayes, shirt-maker Mrs Casey, shirt-machinists Mrs Liddell and Mrs Hutton and shirt-finisher Mrs Glaister: the whole a terrible indictment of exploitation of half-starved wage-slaves.[5] Premature death from starvation was not uncommon. Rather that than the ignominy of parish aid. One of many examples recorded that year was the death of Sophia Hill, aged 43, mantle-maker, of Poplar:

> On 31st July she returned home late feeling very unwell. He (her husband, a surgeon's assistant) noticed her getting weaker from

want of food for some time past, as he had been unable to procure sufficient to sustain them. He earned nothing and his wife's earnings were not more than 6s a week. On the Wednesday morning she got worse, but refused to allow him to fetch the relieving officer. He had no money, but he called in Dr Harvey, who prescribed brandy and left the money to pay for it. No hopes were given of her recovery and at 7.30pm she died.[6]

At the inquest it was revealed by her daughter that her unemployed father used his wife's wages to get drunk and, thenceforth, beat her; for which he received a public admonition from the coroner who "trusted that this would be a warning to him for the rest of his life". Another case of a woman being worked to death, nominally fictitious but almost certainly based on fact, is that of a dying mangle-mother (condemned to an onerous occupation widespread in the East End) described by Margaret Harkness.

> The woman had supported the whole family for months with a mangle, and on the borderland of death, unconscious, she still swung her arm round and round while she said, "My God, I can't keep on."
> The husband was left with the children. "It's bitterer than death for me to watch her like this. I'd better have died than the missus. I can't get work, and now we'll all have to go into a workhouse."[7]

The same author, in a serious article in *Justice* (25 August), outlined the conditions of women in local home industries. It was prompted by the action of the Match Girl Strike as a result of which the homeworkers were, thrown out of employment. ("The match box girls realise this, and on the 14th ult. after they had received their wages in Mr Charrington's hall on Mile End Waste, not a few wanted to make a collection for the "ins-and-outs" workers, ie the makers of the trays and covers of match boxes.") The homeworkers' miserable income was further threatened by the incidence of widespread unemployment when "many men who are out of work now take to these small occupations, and the wives of clerks and tradesmen, who are being crushed beneath the wheels of the juggernaut of competition, now undersell the women who a few years ago controlled the whole of the home industry market".

An impressionist view, fictitiously representing an outdoor match worker, is fleshed out by Harkness:

> Half the room was filled by a large, low bedstead, and there lay the lame girl asleep, with her crutches resting against the bundle of rags that served for a pillow. A dirty blanket covered her feet, and across her breast was the little coloured triangular shawl that the factory girl buys so cheap, and which she rejoices to wear with a smart coloured feather.
> "She's had no tea", the mother said, apologetically. "I fetch the loaves from a tea shop where they taste samples, but today these match boxes came in to be done, and I've had no time to go after 'em... But for her four shillings we'd all been in the Bastille long before this... She's a good girl, and she gives me all the money, but she's not strong. You see she was born on the workhouse doorstep, for they wouldn't take me in until I was ill, and then I fainted at the door of the Bastille..."
> Meanwhile the woman's hands were busy with the match boxes. Strips of magenta paper and thin pieces of wood came together with the help of a paste brush. They were then thrown on the ground to dry, forming pyramids of trays and lids which would presently be made into matchboxes, tied up with string and sent back to factories which give 2¼d per gross for match boxes. Two little children stood on the floor amidst the trays and lids and an older boy chopped wood in a corner of the room with a look on his face of hungry impatience. The babies, who had on apologies for petticoats, were quarrelling over a jam-pot full of water, and seemed hungry enough to devour their own naked toes if their mother did not make haste to finish the matchboxes. The room had no furniture but the table, the bed and a few old hampers; a heap of coke was near the fireplace with which to dry the woman's work, also some cabbage leaves and onion stalks. This refuse, the children would eat later on, if nothing was forthcoming. It had been thrown in as fuel by the vendor of the coke, and a dog would scarcely have swallowed it. But in these days animals are better off than slum children.
>
> (The owner of that alley has been heard to say, "My dog turns tail when I go in; it's so disgusting.")[8]

In her article in *Justice* she attributes the worst conditions to those women employed as fur pullers. Since, to date, such labour could not be performed by machinery, the out-workers received 1s 1d per five dozen rabbit skins. An outsider, visiting their homes, would soon recognise that the boasting of those merchants, who congratulated themselves on marketing cheap fur cloaks or hats, was a cruel mockery. "The fur puller sits...

scraping the skins of rabbits with the fluff in her hair, nose and mouth, choked and half blinded. I hear that the Brompton Hospital for Consumption is the home of these women when they are 'past working'!" Another class of female labour, terribly exploited, was the canvas workers

> who make break covers, blinds for shops, tents, coal sacks, etc., (and) may be seen in the East End, staggering home with heavy loads on their heads or their hips, which in the course of years make their bodies bent or crooked. The pay is 2s for twelve sacks, 5s 6d for ten hammocks, etc. One woman near Aldgate, who makes sacks for the navy receives 4s for ten large sacks, each of which has eight holes in it; 4 splices and 2 patches, each of which must be sewn, roped and marked with a broad arrow for government. She works from 5am to 8pm standing; and some idea of what canvas work is like can be had from the fact that she has sprained both her wrists over it.

Other local domestic industries engaging women "at a starvation rate of payment".[9] are listed; and Harkness, somewhat naively, concludes: "I am sure if the public knew what the hours of work are for those unfortunate women, and their pay, people would shudder to think of the price in blood and flesh that is paid by the workers in order that the rich may congratulate themselves on bargains."

As if exploitation were not enough, there were further indignities to be suffered. Wife-beating was common practice, an intrinsic part of the East End's unsavoury image. Why this infliction on the "woman of the lower Ghetto classes (who) is as much the slave of her husband as is the Indian squaw..."? Jack London's perceptive reply to his own question was just as pertinent fifteen years earlier:

> The men are economically dependent on their masters, and the women are economically dependent on the men. The result is, the woman gets the beating the man should give to his master, and she can do nothing. There are the kiddies, and he is the breadwinner, and she dare not send him to jail and leave herself and the children to starve. Evidence to convict can rarely be obtained when such cases come into the courts; as a rule the trampled wife and mother is weeping and hysterically beseeching the magistrate to let her husband off for the kiddies' sake.[10]

For others Harkness had already voiced the reality. Her wives of the casuals in Charlotte's Buildings "added to the family income by charing, tailoring and sack-making, besides doing all the housework." They were little better than beasts of burden... for East End husbands have but a low opinion of the weaker sex.

> "I'm yer husband, aint I?" is their invariable answer to any complaint, which means, "I can knock you over if I like."[11]

Saturday was the hardest day. The rule, for women, was to rise at dawn and return to bed in the early hours of next morning, a routine without respite. "They must clean their 'place' to get the children's clothes ready for Sunday, scrub, cook and bake, whilst boys and girls hung about and husbands did nothing. Little wonder that public-houses enticed them on their way back from the market. A glass of something took their thoughts off troubles, drove away headaches, and lifted the cloak of monotonous toil for a few minutes. Alas! One glass was never enough. They began with beer and ended with spirits." Perhaps the booze enabled them just to keep going. On top of all else, if her man was jobless there was the humiliating trip to "uncle" — the pawnbroker — to make the recurring weekly pledge of dad's Sunday suit, boots or family trinkets (in the last resort even the bed linen and blankets), to be redeemed only if any money came in. The more respectable, ashamed to be caught entering, could be seen hovering furtively round the gilded facade, above which swayed the telling three brass balls.

Since wife-bashing was the score, women "baiting" was the favourite slum game. Again our chronicler records a crowd gathering to bait a woman who, half naked, from a window bawls

> "If you bait me... I'll come down, I will. I'd like to know what you mean you *********** shouting at me. I'm as good as you are and better!"

She notes, too, a "slummer" refuge in Angel Alley, where Salvation Army lassies have set aside a room in their lodgings to shelter children deserted by their parents, or a woman whose husband after a drinking bout had beaten her and turned her out into the street. A low bedstead and a chair provides the only furniture.[12] Violence begat violence, even among the women themselves. It was not uncommon, day or night, to come across two drunken besoms, naked to the waist, clawing and beating each other, egged on by a howling mob revelling in a knockabout piece of street theatre. Yet such incidents were rare compared with those daily assaults by men on women whose range of unpleasant aberrations will be listed below.[13]

Prostitution, for both young and old, offered one way out, although relief proved ephemeral. Beatrice Potter made a realistic appraisal of the temptations facing work girls. "Miserable wages, long hours and a vibrated atmosphere tainted no less by foul words and coarse language than by fetid air are apparently the lot of the sweater's girl... you cannot accuse them of immorality, for they have no consciousness of sin." After the dreary monotony of the sweatshop "they rush into any form of excitement in the evening to distract their minds from their miserable fate to gather in the multitudinous excitements of the East End street; while their feelings unburden themselves in the pleasures of promiscuous love-making."[14] For the "respectable" working-class women, *selling* their bodies was something else. Harkness tells of a family whose only income is derived from their daughter's wages of sin. Once a clean-living girl, she had become one of the "unfortunates" through dire necessity. ("Virtue is easy enough when a woman has plenty to eat, and a character to keep, but it's quite different when a girl is starving!") Mother pleads, "'I've tried my best to get charing but work is slack'... Father, out of work, but dare not go into the Bastille, for employers never take on a pauper when other men are forthcoming... The man, on his face a look of anguish, explains 'It's ten shillings a week, labour mistress!'" Except for the daughter being "on the game", the home would have long since broken up.[15]

William Booth estimated that prostitutes constituted "a large standing army whose numbers no one can calculate... The ordinary figure given for London is from 60,000 to 80,000. This may be true if it is meant to include all habitually unchaste women... There is no doubt that it is a fact that there is no industrial career in which for a short time a beautiful girl can make as much money with as little trouble as the profession of a courtesan... the only career in which the maximum income is paid to the newest apprentice!"[16] Many an East End lass got the message. The streets provided a world free from the immediacy of want and drudgery as well as the prospects of wealth and comfort. At the least they could expect to make more in one night than in a whole week at the sweatshop. The girl who recognised her own physical talents could exploit them to the full by way of the glittering thoroughfares of the West End. But the liberation of the streets was an illusion. The cost would soon be exacted, for the penalties of disease and degradation were inescapable.

Voluntary involvement was one mode of recruitment, forcible conscription another. "Many are orphans or children of depraved mothers, whose idea of a daughter is to make money out of her prostitution" (William Booth). *Justice* revealed that child prostitution was currently rife, the victims "bartered for gold, the agents alone being punished, when the police choose to discover them, whilst the names of their purchasers are suppressed". There was perpetual demand for the "services" of poor women and children by wealthy young bloods from the West End. It was a buyer's market. *Justice* fulminated against the hypocrisy of those "bourgeois" pontificators who praised the young men of their class for their so-called self-imposed chastity in opting for late marriages.

> The young men of the middle and upper classes are commended by our social reformers, political economists and Malthusians, for being more prudent and provident than those of the working class because they marry late in life: these expounders and eulogisers of the present system of society conveniently ignore that these prudent and provident young men usually gratify their passions by ruining the daughters of the working class, which economic conditions offer as a vicarious sacrifice for the ladies of the wealthy classes to whom these popinjays of society ultimately unite themselves.[17]

The East End offered diverse attractions, according to taste, for sexual adventurers from the West. Employers, with an eye on the main chance, were on the look-out for attractive young girls, desperate for work. William Booth noted how such predators "hunted from pillar to post... a young, penniless girl, confronted always by the alternatives — *Starve or Sin*. And when once the poor girl has consented to buy the right to earn her living by the sacrifice of her virtue, then she is treated as a slave, and an outcast by the very men who have ruined her."[18]

On being seduced, the girl was often so appalled by the shame and horror of her deed, that she had no alternative but to acquiesce in her future role as "unfortunate". She would then tie herself to a procureur (ponce) with terrifying results. Tales of cruel treatment by their "bullies" were legion, while the victims "always hoping for the dignity of wifehood from them" on the premise that "they were never somebody until they are married and will link themselves to any creature no matter how debased, in the hope of being married by him". It was a sad illusion. The Salvationists understood and comforted where they could. General Booth was well aware of the score:

> This life induced insanity, rheumatism, consumption, and all forms of syphilis. Rheumatism and gout are the commonest of these evils. Some were quite crippled by both — young though they were. Consumption sows its seeds broadcast... We have found girls in Piccadilly at midnight who are continually prostrated by haemorrhage yet who have no other way of life open.
>
> In hospitals it is a known fact that these girls are not treated at all like other cases; they inspire disgust, and are most frequently discharged before being really cured.
>
> Scorned by their relations, and ashamed to make their case known even to those who would help them, unable longer to struggle out on the streets to earn the bread of shame, there are girls lying in many a dark hole in this big city positively rotting away and maintained by their old companions on the streets.
>
> Many are totally friendless, utterly cast out and left to perish by relatives and friends.[19]

Harkness, too, voiced her passionate concern for these outcasts. "Of all the
victims of our present competition system I pity these girls most. They are so fragile. Honest work is made for them almost impossible, and if they slip, no one gives them a second chance, they are kicked and spat upon by the public." She posed the dilemma facing those who strove to maintain their virtue and warned of the dangers accruing to a country which treated its working women as expendable. It needed a homicidal maniac to reinforce her point and, at least, shake the complacency of her comfortable readers.[20]

One illustrative and emotive portrait of an East End prostitute and her reaction towards two possible clients, identified as middle-class outsiders, is skilfully etched by John

Mackay. The young men, Auban and Trupp, enter "The Chimney Sweep", a gin palace of the lowest order in Church Lane, the thoroughfare bordering Brick Lane.

> Here misery was in search of its frightful happiness by drowning its hunger in drink. It was a genuine East End crowd; men and women, the latter almost as numerous as the former; some with infants on their withered breasts, but most of them old or at any rate appearing old. Through the grown people ragged children were forcing their way. Almost all were drunk, in the first stages of the Saturday drunk from which they sober up in sleep on Sunday.
> On the bench, opposite to Auban, sat a young, completely neglected girl. Out of her large dark eyes shot forth bolts of wrath at Trupp. Why? From hatred against the foreigner whom she had recognised in him?... For his cool defence?
> Auban studied her. Her debased features, in which contempt mingled with meanness and hatred, were still beautiful, notwithstanding her right cheek was scratched bloody and her hair fell over her forehead in wild disorder. Her teeth were faultless. Her disorderly dress, the dirty linen sacque, was torn open, as if with brazen intention, and revealed to view the still childlike white breasts. "Why should I be disturbed about you?" all her movements seemed to say.
> (Later) the young girl had come up to Trupp and placed herself breast to breast against him. She looked at him with her large eyes sparkling with morbid desire. But she did not say a word. Trupp turned aside from her towards the door.
> "You are a fool!" she then said with an indescribable expression. Auban saw her return to her place and cover her face with her hands.[21]

For she knew, only too well, what the future held: a short life and a miserable one for all sisters fallen from grace.

What could one expect, argued Beatrice Webb, when even those employed on legitimate work "could chaff each other about having babies by their father and brother... a gruesome example of the effect of debased social environment on personal character and family life?... The violation of little children was another not infrequent result... sexual promiscuity, and even sexual perversion, are almost unavoidable among men and women of average character and intelligence crowded into one-room tenements of slum areas, and it is the realisation of the moral deterioration involved, more than any physical discomfort, that lends the note of exasperated bitterness characteristic of the working-class representative of these chronically destitute urban districts."[22]

Women living on the margin and forced to work, sometimes the only breadwinner in either a one-parent family or one in which the husband was unemployed, spelt child neglect. Malnutrition was widespread, which in turn contributed to the incidence of high truancy in local Board Schools. Harkness estimated that School Board visitors had currently taken out 3,000 summonses for non-attendance cases within twelve months at the Thames Police Court.[23] It was stressed that, in the absence of the working mother, it was a necessity for these youngsters to go foraging in the streets and that juvenile crime was inevitable. Of those attending, Barnardo, who had undertaken a personal survey throughout the area, found that 7% of East End schoolchildren arrived at school without morning breakfast and that 13% never had sufficient food. (There was no counter-evidence that this was an exaggeration. In fact he might have *underestimated* the numbers.) To help feed them he was offering "600 hot breakfasts daily and 400 hot dinners four times a week" at his own free day schools. At the close of his report he appended a maudlin poem, "Hungry Scholars", a ploy he often employed to enhance his plea for aid:

> Do you hear the tear-filled voice?
> "Please I've forgot the date."
> "Then you'll stay and copy this history page
> For half an hour on your slate."
> Poor child, poor child, the fast tears fall;
> For that morning mother had said,
> As she sent her breakfastless off to school,
> "In the afternoon we'll get bread."

It never failed to bring in the (middle-class) contributions!

Paradoxically, in one area parental depravity — or, more likely, despair — could offer hope for the future of a child. Baby-selling was not uncommon. Salvation Army lassies on the look-out by the gin shops could pick up a baby from its mother in exchange for a few pence. One lass explained: "The people about here often ask us to buy their babies; sometimes they offer them to us for nothing. They know that we have a home for children at Clapton; so they think that will make their boys and girls into soldiers. They say, 'You can bring them up to earn a decent living. We have nothing for them to eat, and with us they must see a deal of wickedness. Take them to your home, and give them a proper start.'" Criminal neglect, even a profitable commerce in infanticide, was another probability.[25] Everywhere in the crowded thoroughfares and street markets would be seen bands of homeless children, orphaned or cast out, pathetic recruits from the gutter in the battle for survival.

Undoubtedly the majority enjoyed the rudiments of family security whatever the grade of poverty. Parental love decreed this. Harkness rejected the "theory current that East End mothers do not love as West End mothers love. Let those who believe it go down Whitechapel and there they will find love intensified because love *is* dumb."[26] Yet the incidence of homeless and abandoned children was horrific. A number of examples were reported that year. On 17 March the *East London Advertiser* noted that a small child had been deposited on the doorsteps of the porter's lodge of the Mile End Workhouse. In a letter of appeal at the beginning of the year, the old campaigner Barnardo warned that "more homeless children are now to be seen wandering about or asleep at night in our streets, *than ever before*. Each day crowds of starving little ones besiege our gates."[27] On 3 March the *East London Advertiser* outlined the case of a baby, left in a house and found burned to death one of many resulting from the same circumstances: mother at work, the baby left with a sister, who was herself a child.

A Child Burned to Death (24 February 1888)
Catherine Delany, the mother, stated that she had to go out to work, and the deceased (aged 2 years) was left in charge of her sister aged 12 years... Nora Delany, the little girl referred to, said that on Friday she was at home looking after the baby. The fire nearly went out, and she had no money, so she had to go and look round the streets for bits of wood and coal. There was none about home, so she went as far as Billingsgate and on her return found her sister burned.

At the inquest the young witness declared that she had never left the baby alone before — an unlikely plea — which was accepted, and a verdict of accidental death was returned. At least the surviving youngster had bread and a roof over her head. At Thames Police Court a 12-year-old boy faced the stern ministrations of the local magistrate, Mr Saunders.

Who's to Blame?

Charles Nelson, aged 12 years, was charged with sleeping in the open air without any visible means of subsistence. At a quarter to 5 o'clock on Tuesday am. (13 March) Constable 180H was on duty in Stacks Place, Limehouse Causeway, when he found the prisoner huddled up asleep in a cart, and on awakening him and asking him what he was doing there at that time in the morning, he said he had no mother, and his father would not give him any food, and he turned him out of doors. The constable saw his father, who said he could not do anything with the boy, who stole 6s at Christmas time. The father, who was in court, said that his boy would not go to school, and he had done his best to clothe him and keep him respectable. Mr Saunders sent the prisoner to the workhouse for a week and directed the constable to communicate with Mr Hiscock, the Industrial School Board Officer, with a view to get him into the school.[28]

The reporter added that there were three indictments for purse-stealing that same week against truanting urchins in Whitechapel — at Duncan and Charlotte Streets.

As expected, the most desperate cases ended up at Barnardo's. It is worth recording in full that of Robert F, aged 15, admitted that year — one, as the Doctor claimed, of "thousands yet unreached".

> Robert never had a home; he was actually born in a common lodging house, the son of a tramp, brought up as a tramp, and he continued as a tramp up to the time I reclaimed him for society. His father and mother both died in common lodging houses, the former *actually of starvation*. The lad, thus left orphaned and friendless, wandered aimlessly over the country, selling matches, carrying parcels and begging, sleeping nightly beneath the open sky, in fields, under hedges, or where he could find a resting place. He was never at school in his life; he could not write, and can read only a very little.
>
> He came to me shoeless, clad in filthy torn rags, well-nigh starving; in fact, faint from prolonged want of food. His last meal had been a piece of bread picked up in the street on the morning of the previous day... Robert is only one out of hundreds sealed with the same terrible imprint of starvation and suffering — suffering not felt for a day or a week or a month, or even during one specially bad season, but patiently endured for the whole term of their natural lives.

Yet, with all the danger and uncertainty of a life of vagabondage, Barnardo was puzzled by the curious phenomenon of pauper children preferring the freedom of the streets to the comparative security of his own institution. After a grand supper for thousands of waifs collected during the cold night of 5 January, a mere 200 volunteered to be selected for permanent admission into his home, while the rest, a host "of gaunt, half-famished looking lads marched cheerfully away from the relief offered them, although they returned only to the lodging houses, or had actually to roam about the streets all night". Part of the answer was on hand. A benefactor from South Australia had stationed people at the exit offering a new sixpence to each youngster leaving the hall. "To them, as to Esau of old, the (immediate) 'mess of pottage' appeared better than the inheritance," The rest he attributed to the current attitude of authority who treated the problem of the homeless ones "too much... in the spirit of a government department, and too little in the spirit of the Christian faith". Officials dealt with the waif children as "cases". Christians were just feeling their way to considering them as "persons". It would need a far more mature and discriminating mind than that of an unredeemed street waif to be convinced of the difference.[30]

What was to be done with the bands of parentless children adrift in the streets? We have already noted how those, under the *legal* control of the Guardians, could be dealt with.[31] There was unanimity in support of an application by local Unions to the LGB and Home Secretary, to be empowered, through a magistrate's order, to detain children "deserted by their parents at an early age". (Those already in their establishment for 12 months to be further detained and sent to an industrial school or otherwise according to their discretion, with a further addendum that the Guardians should become their "natural" guardians until the age of 16.) At the Forest Gate Schools made up of pauper children conscripted from the Whitechapel and Poplar Unions, the primary task, according to the ubiquitous Vallance, who was also Clerk to the Schools Board of Management, was "to make the lads practical seamen". In April he was pleased to inform his Board that to, date, 2,028 youngsters had been discharged into sea service "the majority of lads (having) entered the navy only", wherein, he had previously been proud to report, "three of them had already acquired the Egyptian Star!" All were offered instruction in the shoemaking, tailoring, carpentry and engineering shops but, for the majority, training was geared to naval service.[32]

Barnardo had definite opinions on the school system. He viewed it as a contributory factor to the incidence of truanting and the proliferation of young unemployed loafers. He perceived one remedy in altering the curriculum towards an emphasis on industrial training which "fascinates nine boys out of ten". This would "teach the use of hands which will train the eye and create a love for toil, systematically and thoroughly supplied during the day to every boy and girl educated by the state, and by a system of night industrial classes to all the children of the Board Schools, as the only way by which to cut off the streams of pauperism from above". Although this could never offer a panacea for unemployment, it was certainly more realistic than current practice in local schools where the overriding concern was the acquisition of the Three Rs. And, unlike Vallance, who concentrated on turning his pauper charges into servicemen, Barnardo was proud to report that, among his old boys, as a result of technical training at the homes, there was a greater diversity of occupations, ranging from soldier, policeman and sailor to clerk, telegraph boy and mechanic.[33] Nevertheless Barnardo was putting forward a remedy which treated the symptoms rather than effecting a cure. In a malfunctioning economy where unemployment was inbuilt into the system, it would merely result in a greater supply of trained technicians thrown on to a surfeit labour market.

With all these recommendations from worthy institutions purporting to aid the poor, the end of the year found little alleviation in the desperate condition of local pauper and homeless children. On the contrary, numbers had risen dramatically while philanthropists and charitable groups performed their seasonal acts of providence and strove heroically to relieve the hungry. But it was *Justice* which voiced the reality when delivering its sombre message at Christmas:

> The great and increasing number of appeals at the close of the year to provide poor children with dinners tells a terrible tale of the condition of thousands of our future men and women for whom "Santa Claus" has no blessings and the season no delights... but if children need food at one time they need it always... We see some children pampered in a hothouse of wealth and luxury, whilst others have to face the chill blast of a winter's wind with little in their stomachs and scarcely a bit of clothing on their backs.

Footnotes

[1] *Justice* 3 March 1888, "Girl Labour in the City".
[2] *In Darkest London*, pp. 103-9.
[3] *Night and Day*, March 1888, pp. 20-1.
[4] Ibid., pp. 6-7.
[5] *East End News* 28 April 1888.
[6] *ELA* 18 August 1888.
[7] *In Darkest London*, p. 247.
[8] Ibid., pp. 128-9.
[9] *Justice* 25 August 1888, "Home Industries" by Margaret Harkness. She continues to list women and girls employed in umbrella making and the dying weaving trade, outlining in detail the meagre pay for piece work, hardly sufficient to avoid starvation.
[10] Jack London, *People of the Abyss* (London 1903) p. 134.
[11] *A City Girl*, pp. 13-14.
[12] *In Darkest London*, pp. 245, 246, 249.
[13] See below, pp. 203ff
[14] *ELA* 1 September 1888, "A Work Girl's Existence".
[15] *In Darkest London*, pp. 133-5. Lewis Lyons, trade union leader reported in *ELO* 16 January 1888, confirms the incidence of prostitution among tailoresses. "I have spoken to some prostitutes, whom I formerly knew and worked in sweaters' dens, and asked them whether it was from their own free will that they were leading an immoral life, or because wages were low, and they attributed it to the latter."
[16] *In Darkest England*, pp. 50-6, 223.
[17] *Justice* 28 January 1888.
[18] *In Darkest England*, p. 13.
[19] Ibid., pp. 54-5.
[20] Ibid., pp. 55-6, and see *Justice* 3 March 1888.
[21] *The Anarchists*, pp. 167-8.
[22] *My Apprenticeship*, p. 231n.
[23] *In Darkest London*, p. 187.
[24] *Night and Day*, May 1888, p. 60.
[25] See below, pp. 201-3.
[26] *A City Girl*, p. 151.
[27] Dr Barnardo, *Three Texts*, 1888.
[28] *ELA* 17 March 1888.
[29] *Night and Day*, December 1888, p. 139.
[30] In 1888 it would seem that only National Refuges offered a compassionate sense of hospitality to homeless children. As the Rev. A.O. Charles, director of the Tottenham Home for Little Boys (established in 1864) pointed out, with the exception of these refuges "there was no institution save the workhouse, in which little boys under 10 years of age, orphaned or destitute and unconvicted of crime, could be received".
[31] See above, pp. 94-8.
[32] See *ELO* 7 April 1888, "The Training of Pauper Children", and *ELA*

1 September 1888, which gives a comprehensive account of "The Industrial Training of Pauper Children" at the Forest Gate Schools.
[33]*Night and Day*, March 1888, pp. 8-9.
[34]*Justice* 15 December 1888.

Chapter 6
The Ghetto

By 1888 Jewish settlement in Tower Hamlets had consolidated itself around a solid base in Spitalfields, with large tentacles stretching southwards to the St. George's area and eastward to Mile End and Bow. In 1887 Charles Booth had recorded numbers amounting to 28,790 in Whitechapel, 5,880 in St. George's and 7,750 in Mile End, which, together with those settled in Bethnal Green, totalled approximately 45,000. But this may well have been an overestimate.[1] The causes and course of post-1881 Jewish immigration have been analysed in detail elsewhere.[2] What was pertinent to the authorities was that 1886 had registered a high peak both in emigration — 396,494 (of whom 281,487 were of British or Irish origins) — and immigration — 119,013 — an increase of 10,134 on the year before, "of whom those of British and Irish origins only numbered 85,475".[3] With the increase of non-English-speaking foreigners there was cause for concern on the part of local and national authorities; manifestly so in the East End of London, where the influx appeared dramatic.

For a colourful, and bizarre, change had already affected large sections of the western parishes sited nearer the city, and was rapidly spreading eastward, along and between the two main thoroughfares, the Whitechapel and Commercial Roads, from their conjunction at Gardiners Corner. Charles Booth confirmed by that year:

> The newcomers have gradually replaced the English population in whole districts which were formerly outside the Jewish quarter. Formerly in Whitechapel, Commercial Street roughly divided the Jewish haunts of Petticoat Lane and Goulston Street from the rougher English quarter lying in the East. Now the Jews have flowed across that line; Hanbury Street, Fashion Street, Pelham Street, Booth Street, Old Montague Street, and many streets and lanes and alleys have fallen before them; they fill whole blocks of model dwellings; they have introduced new trades as well as new habits and they live and crowd together and work and meet their fate independent of the great stream of London life surging around them.[4]

Among the grimy, dilapidated, leprous-walled one- or two-storeyed terraced cottages, broken here and there across Spitalfields to the river by the newly imposed high-rise, red-bricked tenements looming over them, the Jews moved in to extend their peculiar sub-culture amid a hostile milieu. From Quaker and Buxton Streets by the great brewery, down to the narrow infiltrates along Batty and that misnomer, Christian Street, astride the Commercial Road, on towards the Anglo-Irish world of dockland, the Jewish "colonists" were expanding their settlements.

Occupations, mainly operating in home-based workshops, were within a limited range and vulnerable to trade fluctuations. The Jewish Board of Guardians, who monitored the state of local labour, presents us with a list of major occupations for 1882 and 1892.[5] Those of 1888 could be approximated as somewhere in between. What does emerge is a concentration in the tailoring, boot and shoe and cabinet making concerns, findings which accord with those of Charles Booth.[6] His acolytes already noted the social and occupational divisions within the community. The old-established Dutch Jews, anglicised and often indistinguishable from their Gentile Cockney neighbours, were concentrated in Spitalfields and principally employed in cigar-making. A group of German origin, a melange of old settlers and newcomers, were engaged in a variety of trades: "bread bakers, sugar refiners, shoemakers, tailors (more of these than anything else) and dealers in clothes, furniture makers and dealers in furniture, street sellers and general dealers, small employers, shopkeepers, importers and wholesale dealers... an ambitious and industrious set (who on the whole) prosper." It was difficult for Booth sometimes to discriminate between these and the new "Polish" immigrants. That, in his view, depended on "the degree of poverty and ignorance rather than any question of origin", and he thus revealed the limitations of his own knowledge and understanding of the Jewish social scene. He confirmed, however, that the "Russian Poles" were "recognised as a separate and now very large section of the East End population", with their own distinctive sub-culture.

For they formed their own self-contained street communities, a precarious livelihood eked out in small domestic workshops, their ethnic unity perpetuated within their *stieblech* — small, house-based synagogues catering for the spiritual and social needs of the *landsleit* (families emanating from the same village or town in Russia or Russian Poland). Their identification with the sweated tailoring trade projected them on the national scene. Here, in quantitative terms, a reasonably objective assessment of the contemporary motif is proffered by Charles Booth from his case studies in "The Tailoring Trade". A qualitative account found to be literally fictitious but circumstantially true, was presented by Russian immigrant Myer Wilchinski to the House of Lords Committee (8 August 1888).[7] Both reveal the life of the "greener"as one of grinding poverty and unremitting labour. Within the job market the immigrant found himself faced with a number of harsh realities. How many Gentile employers in non-immigrant trades would be prepared to employ alien Jews, who were generally unpopular in a period of economic stress and job competition? Each was forced back on his own. "Britons first" was the normal response of masters and trade unionists. Where could the "greeners" turn for work, but to the insatiable demands of a self-generating, cut-throat industry locally already dominated by his own kith and kin? At least there he could find some promise (albeit illusory) of job security; and safety among his fellow Yiddish-speaking expatriates, sharing a common religious and cultural experience, and, above all, the bond of past persecution and imminent want.

Workshop conditions were, to say the least, socially and medically hazardous. Hands slept on the floor or on benches in the workrooms, particularly the new arrivals with no fixed abode, and breathed in an atmosphere already foetid with sweat of congested day-labourers and the steam of the press irons. Alternative job opportunities were strictly limited. The market was periodically choked with high static and frictional unemployment. Every year the inevitable gap between "busy" and "slack" seasons brought the threat of homelessness and hunger. For the ordinary Jewish worker this spelt out a precarious living, always poised on the margin of subsistence. The oft-heard Yiddish lament *"Schwer und bitter is dos Leben"* (hard and bitter is life) manifested the harsh burdens inflicted on the children of the ghetto. The difficulties of adjustment to this new land, the tensions inherent in insecure employment, the financial and legal problems to overcome before he could bring over his family from the *heim* forced him into an unlimited application to work.

Poverty was endemic in that time and place. By 1888 Booth had estimated that of the 40,000 Jews settled in the East End, 15,000 were "quite poor", 15,000 "moderately" so and the remaining 10,000 "comfortably" or "well" off. (From the 20,527 dependent on the dress trade 1,807 were classed as very poor, 11,166 as poor.) The inner structure of local boot and shoe domestic workshops was similar to that of clothing, although even worse conditions prevailed as the industry moved to full-scale factory production in the provinces (especially Northampton). Thus the East End Jewish piece worker was already faced with a declining system of production, whereby the most deleterious competitive and sweated conditions militated against their well being.

The extent of Jewish pauperism, specially focused on East London, had already been highlighted during the previous year in the *Spectator* (23 April 1887). In a leading article it ventured to offer the following categorical evidence:

> Figures (from the Jewish Board of Guardians) show that, last year, every third Jew in London was actually in receipt of poor relief, every second Jew belonged to the regular pauper class, and every second Jewish funeral which took place in the metropolitan area was a pauper funeral... (The) death rate of the Hebrews is higher, much higher, than that of the general body of Englishmen... In the period during which the pauperism of the country at large has diminished by 30%, Jewish paupers have increased 150% and their cost to the Jewish community has increased more than ten fold... The United Synagogues admit 44% pauper funerals; painful statistics as to the death of young children of the total deaths registered by the Metropolitan Synagogues, were 81% of children under 10, while the proportion in the rest of the country at large is only 43.5%.

It concluded:

> The figures we have quoted are those accepted by the Jews themselves.

This was apparently true. In the following issue of the *Jewish Chronicle* (29 April 1887), the commentator in "Notes of the Week" on the *Spectator's* findings agreed that "altogether the article is a very able and impartial resume of the most potent facts of Jewish pauperism".

The nature and extent of Jewish poverty was central to the enquiries undertaken by the House of Commons Select

Committee on Emigration and Immigration (Foreigners) in 1888. Mr Lindsay, Principal of the Long Room of Custom House, which monitored all foreign vessels arriving at the port, declared that 800 "aliens" had disembarked during the previous fortnight (ie before 4 May). He inferred that most of them were destitute and that the steam companies transported them cheaply to London. ("They bring them for 15s — and feed them"!)[8] Dr Asher, Secretary to the Council of the United Synagogues, confirmed the expansion of the numbers of poor Jews with the incidence of increased immigration after 1882. He based his estimate on the death rate of those buried in Jewish charity funerals:

1883	110 over 10 years of age buried in charity funeral gives	5,500 poor Jews
1884	126	6,300 poor Jews
1885	134	6,700 poor Jews
1886	143	7,100 poor Jews
1887	150	7,500 poor Jews

Apparently, by the same token the number of "poor" in 1881 (6,200), which coincided with those associated with the first great exodus from Russia, was greater than that of 1883. Dr Asher was quick to point out that there was no indiscriminate charity practised by his authority. In positing the gradual decrease of applicants for free Passover "bread", he argued that the actual pauper numbers could be considered reduced between 1880 and 1887, on the assumption that "perhaps people provided it for themselves; it is only a matter of saving 1d or 1½d a week, which we think they ought to do."[9] Yet the records of the Jewish Board of Guardians suggest the reverse. Of those applying for aid, the annual totals show a steady rise, peaking first in 1886 (the year of major recession) and again in 1888.[10]

Year	1881	1882	1883	1884	1885	1886	1887	1888
Total number of cases	2,629	2,953	2,882	3,054	3,408	4,139	3,313	3,513
Resident Foreigners:								
7 yrs & over	1,088	1,007	1,143	1,172	1,113	1,426	1,348	1,331
Under 7 yrs	1,974	1,503	1,273	1,456	1,871	2,222	1,514	1,753

Given the fluctuations within the enclosed labour market and the seasonal exigencies of their trades, most of the immigrants seemed condemned to unremitting poverty. Giving evidence to the Commons Select Committee on their standard of living, a tailor, Woolf Zeitlin, conceded that "in fact everyone who comes here comes rather poor; a man who has only two or three or four pounds of course is a poor man, it will not last him very long... In better times a man can spend about 10s a week altogether on food and lodging... in worse times he might live on 4s or 5s altogether."[11] Although survival was often dependent on one's neighbours — "the poor helping the poor" — cases of hungry and homeless Jews were not infrequent, and together with those of children starving to death, often provided a non-sensational news item in the local or Jewish press.

On 10 June 1887, the *Jewish Chronicle* reported the death of "Mary Spiller, aged 5 months, late of Greenfield Street, Mile End. The father applied for an order from the Jewish Board of Guardians, but there was some delay, and by the time he received the order the child was dead. The parents had only just arrived from Russia... Coroner's verdict 'The cause of death was exhaustion from want of proper food and attention.' (He) advised the father to apply to the Poor Law authorities." A year later in the *East London Advertiser* Lewis Lyons exposed the plight of "a poor young Jew, who had a wife and two children to support... employed at the tailoring factory of Mr K. in Bethnal Green, East London, where he earned 1s a day working... from early in the morning till late at night. Last Saturday week his brother, noticing a great melancholy on his face, asked the reason and received the reply, 'Why, look at my clothes, my boots; see the horrid state of my poor family!' His brother offered him a few shillings to buy boots, but the unfortunate man refused to accept unearned money. Last Tuesday the man became mad, and is now in the hospital. In consequence of that the Christian manufacturer ordered a bill to be placed in the workshop... calling on the workpeople to contribute towards a subscription for the family of the victim, himself giving the capital donation of two shillings and sixpence. The employees could hardly afford to give more than one or two pence (each)."[12] Insanitary conditions which resulted in a child's death prompted an article "How the Poor Live" in the *Chronicle* (14 September 1888). "Dr Macdonald held an inquest, Friday 7th September, in the 'Paul's Head' pub, Spitalfields, on the body of Jacob Mecklenburg aged 4 months, the son of a costermonger living in Butler Street... found dead in bed. It was stated that the parents and their 7 children lived together in one room about 12 feet square for which they paid 4s 6d rent. Dr Hume deposed that the child had suffocated, probably by overlaying."

By 1887 the problem of the growing number of destitute Jews prompted the setting up of a committee under a local politician, Harry S. Samuel, to establish a labour yard where, strictly in accord with current Poor Law precepts, destitute paupers could be employed on manual labour in return for relief. The committee recommended the acquisition of premises in "Tenter Street, lately occupied by the Jews Infant School". The details of the exercise were outlined on the basis of solid accounting, whereby an ultimate cash profit must be obtained.

> The men to do sawing and chopping, the women in a separate room the binding of the bundles. Estimates total fixed overheads and costs £170 per annum outgoing.
>
> The initial expenses for implements etc will amount to £30. Premises will easily hold 80 workers but assuming the average to be even as low as 10, the profit on their labour would be as follows — 1 fathom of best yellow deal ends, £5 5s; binders, 3s 2d. Total: £5 8s 0d.
>
> Estimates that taking the average earnings of each man at 1s 4½d per day, 10 workers would earn £178 15s per annum from which deduct expenses in the shape of rent and management, £170, leaving £8 15s profit.
>
> The committee, in conclusion, desire to emphasise this point, that whereas in some cases the labour test may deter people from applying to the board for relief, they hope that in the majority of cases it may be looked upon with satisfaction as a means of obtaining money by honest employment, instead of depending on charity.[13]

The committee had obviously entertained false hopes in mopping up the Jewish residuum, since the work test did prove an effective deterrent. (To the Jew it smacked too much, perhaps, of the hated workhouse.) For the numbers of destitute appeared to increase to such an extent that early the following year the Jewish authorities "proposed to establish in the East End a night shelter for homeless and starving Jews and a meeting in aid of the scheme was held on Sunday 19 February at the Princes Street Synagogue".[14] The danger was that they might become a burden on the rates, and there were enough false rumours around. The accusation that foreign Jews were crowding the workhouses was currently evoked by the anti-alienist, Arnold White, and could be easily refuted. The *Jewish Chronicle* quoted a letter from W. Vallance, clerk of the Whitechapel Guardians, rejecting White's contention that 340 "foreigners" were in his workhouse. "The superintendent of the casual wards tells me that he does not think that during the whole time that he has been in his present office a dozen Jews have been admitted to the wards, that is, in nearly 17 years, and it is certainly more than twelve months since the last Jew was received."[15]

On the traditional basis that the Jewish community *itself* should be responsible for its itinerant poor, the Board of Guardians was the major sponsor of charitable aid, provided that it was concerned with "the application of rational principle", that is, "to teach man that he has any right to money without work runs the risk of lowering his moral tone. This risk is avoided by the Board of Guardians to the greatest possible degree."[16]

Indeed! In 1888, out of 3,513 applicants, its records show that 1,919 received some form of monetary grant, including 421 for trade purposes and 616 loans. It did not dispense charity indiscriminately, although it is fair to add that, with the limitations of funds attained by voluntary subscriptions from the more affluent, and in the climate of the times, the Jewish Board did what it deemed possible. By November that year, commenting on the Board's president lamenting the pending exhaustion of funds ("we are worse off than at this time last year by considerably over £1,000!"), the editor of the *Jewish Chronicle* pronounced:

> The president"s appeal is a stern rebuke to the communal conscience. Here is the chief charitable organisation of the community left to face the winter without a shilling in its treasury, and like one of its own clients forced to sue cap in hand for the means of bare subsistence... The virtual indifference to the claims of the Board which is thus manifested reflects little credit on the community.
>
> In view of the empty state of the Board's exchequer it is disquieting to be told on the authority of Mr Cohen that "pressure and want especially in the East End of London, have become more acute than ever, and that the misery has reached a

point which, in the interest quite as much of the rich, as of the poor, unquestionably calls for relief."[17]

In other words, it was as much a pointed warning of the dangers accruing to the whole community from a restive Jewish labour force (as currently reflected in the anti-establishment polemics of the local Yiddish radical press), as a plea for help as a compassionate imperative.

Nevertheless charity was a growth industry amongst the East End Jews, and available from alternative sources. On 6 January, at a meeting of the Spitalfields or Jewish United Benevolent Society in the "Boar's Head Tavern", its president spoke "of the large amount of good accomplished by the Society since its commencement, in relieving distress by gifts of money and necessary articles, after a strict and searching enquiry", and promised "during the coming year, a source of even a greater amount of good to the poor people residing in the district".[18] Through the activities of Jewish middle-class volunteers engaged in the East End Visitation of the Poor group under his aegis, the Chief Rabbi kept a watchful eye on the ghetto. A subcommittee was appointed, consisting of "Revs. Dr H. Adler and Morris Joseph, N.S. Joseph and Claude Montefiore, to confer with the visitors on the subject of the issue of leaflets on cleanliness, thrift etc. to the poor". It would appear that these interlopers were not always popular. Their haughty and patronising manner also evoked the suspicion that they were acting as snoopers. This was validated by the report of a Rev. D. Fay at the Chief Rabbi's office:

> Several Jewish boys attending the Jews Free School had been (seen) hawking matches in the city, principally in the vicinity of the railway stations upon Sabbaths. The visitors promised that as far as they could, they would endeavour to obtain the names and addresses of these boys, and there was no doubt that the authorities of the Free School would assist in putting down the evil.[19]

Charity was dispensed in diverse forms. One, attributable mainly to synagogues, was a reduced marriage fee to poor brides. At Princes Street Synagogue, off Brick Lane, four brides were granted the Israelite Marriage Portion Society's endowment of 10 guineas and free marriage fees.[20] Such generosity was not to the taste of the local Anglo-Jewish Rabbi, J.F. Stern, who had railed publicly against young and improvident marriages before the Chief Rabbi and his Visitation committee. In his experience "the weddings of many of the poor who availed themselves of the reduced fees at which the ceremony was performed were conspicuous for great extravagance in dress etc... Among the poorest there were several of those who had expended a comparatively large amount upon wedding festivities had the audacity to come the next day for relief!"[21] Charity funerals, as Dr Asher had reported, were undertaken by the United Synagogue which dealt with the interment of all Jews in the East End with the exception of the Portuguese. Numbers continued to rise throughout the eighties — although, Asher added, applicants "did not by any means represent paupers. They were poor people who, in many cases, had never accepted any charity other than the funerals of their relatives." Applications for Passover "bread" gauged the extent of need more accurately, according to the United Synagogues, as "they were more searching than is the case for funerals". This appeared evident as the quantities distributed from 1880 (at 20lb for a family of five) fell from 54,552lbs that year to 39,847lbs in 1888. By the latter year, the secretary concluded that while 7,500 persons over 10 years of age of the Russian and Polish community applied for charity funerals, 6,000 were recipients of Passover bread.[22] The rate of infant deaths among the Jewish poor was duly a cause for concern among the donors, particularly at the costs incurred.

Deferring, therefore, to current holy writ demanding payment for services whatever one's means, it fell on millionaire Lord Rothschild, as President of the Board of the Federation of Chevras, to underline the message:

> The delegates were practically agreed that in order to avoid as far as possible in the future the necessity for "charity" funerals in the case of children, parents should make provision for the interment of their deceased children by contributing a small weekly amount to a *Chevra*, in the same way as they do for themselves.[23]

A like sentiment was expressed at the AGM of Sandys Road Synagogue, Spitalfields, four months later. The members discussed a scheme whereby the Prudential Assurance Company offered special facilities for funeral insurance to worshippers. It achieved considerable support, and one speaker enthused over a "scheme within the reach of all and (which) would entirely obviate the necessity for begging for paupers' funerals".[24]

One means of subverting charity was to "encourage" impoverished parents to enter their daughters into domestic service.[25] On 17 November at the New West End Synagogue, the Rev. S. Singer in his sermon remarked "on the almost insuperable aversion to domestic service amongst the Jewish poor". (Unlike him, they had learned only too well of the terrible exploitation suffered by their children in service!) He surmised that "domestic service under a humane Jewish mistress would go a long way towards obviating most of these disadvantages and dangers of working in overmanned and underpaid trades which expose them to insecurity and the prospect of beggary and living in squalid miserable abodes... to be exposed to perils to body and soul". Since a quarter of poor Christian children took up domestic labour, impoverished Jews should be encouraged to do the same, on the extraordinary premise that "until they had succeeded in enabling Jews and Jewesses to take their place in every station, and to share in every employment opened to non-Israelites, they would not have completed the work of their social emancipation, and they would but perpetrate a spirit of separateness which had nothing of religion in it, and was full of present mischief and future peril".[26]

Thus another, non-charitable, aid to girls was the "Jewish Association for Protection of Girls, Women and Children" set up in 1885, which actually lasted until 1946. It was originally conceived as a lodging house in the Mile End Road for friendless but "respectable" foreign girls who were expected to pay for their keep under the stern eye of a matron appointed to keep a register of jobs for them. In 1888 the inmates were moved to Rosaline House, Tenter Street in Aldgate. The new premises could then cater for 20 girls, including some English-born who needed temporary accommodation.[27]

At the end of the year the urgency of the problem of widespread poverty overcame the clamour of those proposing that the poor pay their way. On 19 December an East End soup kitchen was opened by the Chief Rabbi. The ubiquitous Samuel Montagu was there with his usual pontifications. ("It was accepted that there should *always* be poor in the land", etc —

otherwise how else could the rich purge themselves of their guilt but by offering *tsedokah*?) The poor at the kitchen were greeted in true oriental fashion with bread and salt, and in addition with nice hot soup. The less insensitive Rev. D.M. Gaster put it succinctly: "The oriental fashion has been reversed in the kitchen. It was not the people going out to greet their sovereign with bread and salt, but rather the homage due to the majesty of poverty. The wealthy came forward towards the indigent and showed that they acknowledged that the bond of brotherhood did not cease to exist." A mass of the hungry needed to be fed, but economies had to be preserved. Thus "six large iron steam jacketed pans have been fixed... each one of the capacity of 70 gallons. All the cooking will be by steam, which is driven by a vehicle engine. It is anticipated that the total cost for cooking and lighting will be below ten shillings a week, and the expenditure for the new pans, which amounts to £125, will be realised in the course of three seasons by the reduction in the cost of cooking."[28] For, among the affluent donors, the spirit of obligatory aid to fellow Jews (*tsedokah*) was tempered with such utilitarian sentiments as those voiced by Charles Booth. "Although Jewish charity does not lead to the demoralisation of individual recipients (there are) grave objections to the form of relief administered. Money lent or given for trade purposes fosters the artificial multiplication of small masters, and is one of the direct causes of the sweating system; efficient assistance to the mechanic out of work enables him to exist on reduced or irregular earnings, and thereby lowers the general conditions of his class." Booth echoed "sorrowfully the words of Louise Michel, '*La Philanthropie, c'est un mensonge!*'"[29]

That there was a problem of homelessness among immigrants was, indeed, evident. The Yiddish radical poet and journalist Morris Winchevsky four years before had already revealed, in prose and verse, poignant scenes of young, workless men with no fixed abode, roaming the streets at night.[30] Woolf Zeitlin, Secretary of the Jewish Branch of the Tailor's Society, informed the Select Committee on Emigration and Immigration of lodging costs (2s a week for men and 3s for women) which were still beyond the means of those unemployed.[31] Arnold White had currently tried to exploit the issue by associating it with criminal activities. He quoted a report in the *Daily Chronicle* of 15 June:

West Ham: Russian pauper immigrants, Turgis Meskekelewsche, 29, and Mikas Fasukinos, 28, natives of Lithuania, were charged with being found on enclosed premises of 22 Gray Street, Silvertown, supposed for an unlawful purpose. The evidence was interpreted by Warrant Officer Rabinowitz 141 K, and it seems that the house in question is an empty one, and they were found there about midnight. They had previously been turned out of another house some days ago. Rabinowitz said they had nowhere to go, and had nothing to eat. They complained that some boys threw stones at them. They had been in England three weeks.
(Magistrate) *Mr Baggallay*: Then they have been utterly destitute all the time, and unable to speak English?
Rabinowitz: A great many of these Russians have come over to England lately; there is one in the workhouse now, and though communicated with, the Russian consul will not do anything.
Mr Baggallay: Well, I can only discharge them. If they are destitute they must go to a relieving officer.[32]

Newly arrived immigrants without family or contacts certainly faced temporary homelessness. But not for long, for there were agencies set up by the local community for newcomers from the *heim* (homeland). As for the incidence of stone-throwing, these attacks by local hooligans were experienced daily by Jews. A good target were those identified by their traditional garb.

The main immigrant settlement was concentrated in an area already plagued by overcrowding.[33] On 1 February a deputation to Lord Sainsbury complained that "in favoured districts of London the population is 50 to the acre; in Whitechapel it is 176 to the acre; and in the Bell Lane district it is 600 to the acre, which necessitates the one-room system involving a great deal of immorality." It was followed later in the year by a large deputation to the Metropolitan Board of Works of concerned dignitaries, including the Chief Rabbi and the Bishop of Bedford, the latter reiterating that the ghetto area was dangerously overpopulated.[34] There was little response from the public authorities for their pleas for demolition and rehousing under the Artisans Dwellings Act. It was such private operations financed by the Model Dwellings Trusts, initiated by the Rev. Samuel Barnett and Lord Rothschild, that were changing the face of Whitechapel. Rothschild Buildings were opened on 2 April 1887, certainly a model of their kind. "Their function was to provide the maximum number of sanitary dwellings as cheaply as possible. Ruthless utilitarianism pared away all that was absolutely necessary to attain that end."[35] A year before, Barnett had jubilantly proclaimed the completion of Brunswick Buildings in Wentworth Street, to be followed by College Dwellings, adjoining Toynbee Hall and replacing the infamous Crown Court. But these grim, lofty, barrack-like edifices, looming over the residual Wentworth and Flower and Dean Street rookeries, were, to date, a minor incursion into an overwhelming mass of decaying one- to three-storeyed lodging houses that surrounded them. Nevertheless the erosion proceeded apace. In November, the Secretary of the 4% Dwellings Company announced that "a number of new tenements have been added to the Charlotte de Rothschild Dwellings, Thrawl Street, Commercial Street. These tenements consist of 3 rooms and other conveniences and are let at the low rate of 4s 6d per week. Commodious and light workshops are let at 4s a week."[36] After September the impact of the Whitechapel murders was to focus the issue of the local slums nationally, and thereby force the public authorities to participate actively in their demolition.

Overcrowding and decaying housing spelt fire and health hazards. Workshops were particularly vulnerable. The heat or flames from the press irons of a tired or negligent presser, or from the gas jets, could easily set fire to the cloth or fur waste, which in turn would ignite the rotting floor and dry wood structures. Fires were not an uncommon event in the ghetto streets, the worst that year occurring on 18 October. A five-floor warehouse tenanted by Messrs Koenigsberger, furriers, at 25 Commercial Street, employing 200 people, burst into flames at 10 at night while the hands were still working. Fortunately all escaped except one who, as there was no fire escape, jumped from the first floor and sustained serious injuries. Earlier that day, at 96 Leman Street, a grocery and general store run by a Polish Jew, M. Landau, a fire broke out in the basement and quickly spread upwards. Prompt action by police and firemen led to the successful evacuation from the top floor of Landau, his wife and nine children and an old female servant. Two days later a dwelling house at the corner of Back Church Lane and Commercial Road caught fire, but with a less successful outcome. "There were three women on the upper floor frantically crying for help at the windows but the flames spread rapidly. Two jumped out of the windows and were uninjured, but the third fell on the paving with great force and was terribly hurt. The poor woman, Rebecca Sapotski, died in London Hospital."[37]

Bad housing leads to bad health. It is difficult to quantify precisely the comparative degree of illness between immigrants and their surrounding neighbours. Professor Gartner has drawn the general conclusion for the period 1870-1914 that "the immigrant children were better and healthier than the English of their class". Was the *Spectator's* assertion derived from evidence agreed to by the Jewish authorities, that a greater mortality rate was recorded among immigrant children in 1886, an aberration that still needs to be explained?[38] Yet whatever improvements might be made in future, "the basic conditions of slum life and work contributed an irreducible share to the deterioration of health".[39] Arnold White was quick to demonstrate that the pressures of medical relief were greater among Jewish "paupers", citing the Mile End Old Town's Clerk to the Governors' report of 7 May, which enumerated "seven foreigners in receipt of outdoor relief, but, as an average, medical attention is given to about 50 families during the year".[40] There was some back-up to this in the monthly returns of the London Hospital, whose records for October disclose that, of the 87 Hebrew patients treated, 50 were discharged, 6 died and 31 were retained as in-patients. In addition to the other commonplace illnesses they were prone to, sweatshop conditions particularly laid them open to tuberculosis — a killer disease among tailors and bootmakers.[41]

1888 was the year that the "problem" of foreign immigration finally broke surface, and the old scapegoat, the Jew, was available in all his vulnerability. With high local unemployment and housing shortage constituting a major pressure gauge, it provided a peak opportunity for both the political demagogue flying the anti-alien kite and the new-style social investigator. The path had been well prepared.

The *Pall Mall Gazette*, a popular sensational paper, was, as early as February 1886, already referring to "A *Judenhetz* brewing in East London" and warning its readers that "the foreign Jews of no nationality whatever are becoming a pest and a menace to the poor native born East Ender".[42] Within a year the growing agitation was such that on 10 March 1887 Captain Colomb, Conservative MP for Bow and Bromley, in an abrasive speech in the House of Commons, set the tone for a generation of restrictionists:

> What great states of the world other than Great Britain permit the immigration of destitute aliens without restriction; and whether Her Majesty's Government is prevented by any treaty obligations from making such regulations as shall put a stop to the free importation of destitute aliens into the United Kingdom.

In July, Arnold White, writing en route for South Africa in the mail steamer Athenian, launched a broadside through *The Times* under the stirring title "England for the English": "Will you permit me to fire a parting shot at the pauper foreigner? He is successfully colonising Great Britain under the nose of HM Government."[43] On his return in November he resumed his attack: "The time for inquiry is over. The hour for action has arrived." The problem posed was "whether our own kith shall be sacrificed for an obsolete shibboleth and the bloodthirsty operation of an artificial competition".[44] His position was reinforced by the previous intervention and political support of the St. George's-in-the-East MP and Cabinet Minister Charles Ritchie, who in a personal letter to the Prime Minister warned that immigration was becoming the most urgent problem that "the Government would have to face the moment Parliament meets".[45] The Lipski case, in which a sordid murder of a pregnant Jewess was supposedly committed by a young Polish immigrant Jew, Israel Lipski, only recently concluded by his hanging in August, dramatically focused the issue.[46]

By the beginning of 1888 the Government appeared to be easily persuaded. At the very time when they were acquiescing in the anti-alienists' demands, and during the whole course of the dual commissions of inquiry, "robbed, outraged, in fear of death and physical torture the chosen people swarmed across the Russian frontier" to escape from a new series of ferocious decrees promulgated against them. On 10 February the appointment of a Select Committee of Inquiry on Immigration had been agreed upon by the British Government. The day before, the *Jewish Chronicle* had revealed a despatch dated 19 January from Mr G.R. Perry, British Consul General for the Black Sea area, informing Lord Salisbury that the Russian General Roop "acting, I conclude, upon instructions from St. Petersburg, issued orders that all foreign Jews residing in His

Excellency's districts, viz the Governments of Kherson, Tauoda, Bessarabia and Ekaterinislov, should be requested to leave the country as soon as possible... The law respecting the domicilation of Foreign Jews was issued in 1857, but until the present time it seems never to have been enforced!" He appended reports on the expulsion of Jews from the Caucasus by D.B. Peacock, British Vice-Consul, Batum, dated 6 January. Further expulsion orders were detailed by the Odessa correspondent of the *Daily News* in April, when "by order of the Governor-General, the foreign Jews in Kherson, who numbered about 4,000, have received notices to cross the frontier". *The Times'* correspondent (St. Petersburg, 26 April) revealed widespread Finnish opposition to the Russian government's orders to expel their Jews; on 24 July a *Daily News'* telegram noted that the decree ordering the Jews to quit Finland within 30 days "is carried out with such rigour that house owners are liable to heavy fines and imprisonment if they allow a tenant of the Jewish faith to remain in occupation of their residences after the expiration of the 30 days. Thousands of people, many of whom had been established in business for more than 20 years are being ruined." On 10 August the *Jewish Chronicle*, quoting from correspondence from St. Petersburg, confirmed that mass expulsions from Southern Russia ("the outcome of Count Ignatieff's aim to make life in Russia impossible for the Jews"), affected 100,000-200,000 of the miserable victims.[447]

Ostensibly impervious to the vicissitudes suffered by those who remained behind, the British government appeared to be bent on directing national attention (and prejudices) towards the minority that in recent years had managed to find refuge here. It is manifest from the proceedings of the House of Commons Select Committee on Emigration and Immigration (Foreigners) and the House of Lords Select Committee on Sweating set up early that year that the object of both exercises was a critical scrutiny of the immigrant Jews, with the underlying assumption of the possibility of their exclusion, should the evidence prove that they constituted a social threat to the nation.

From the evidence of those selected for interview by the Commons Committee (the proceedings lasted from 26 March to 27 July), anti-alien prejudices predominated; naturally enough, since these sentiments had permeated both the local and national press who had argued, forcibly, for the enquiry. In

January the pack was in full cry. On 14 January the *East London Observer* noted that the St. George's-in-the-East Vestry had responded to the plea by the St. Olave's District Board urging them "to bring pressure to bear upon the Government... to prevent the wholesale immigration of destitute persons into this country" by moving its adoption and appending a request that "it must be dealt with by the legislature, in order to prevent this country becoming the dust heap of every continental nation". This was in accord with Captain Colomb's statement to a *Globe* reporter: "I object to England with its overcrowded population and small area, being made a human ashpit for the refuse population of the world." One month later Mile End Vestry followed suit, while its neighbouring MP put final pressure on the government to take action. This was clinched by a deputation to Lord Salisbury on 2 February which included the local anti-immigrant Rev. R.C. Billing and xenophobe Arnold White. Both argued for exclusion. The former painted a sordid picture of "half-starved miserable Jewish children in the streets, picking up the garbage from the gutters and bearing all the traces of disease; your hearts would pity them and you would ask 'what could be the progeny of such children?' It would be a real kindness to prevent them from coming here." The latter warned of the menace of unchaste Hebrew women swelling the ranks of the prostitutes. Seizing on the disunity of the spokesmen themselves, came Salisbury's deft reply: "Almost every speaker has found it necessary to say that he does not agree with all the resolutions which he has come here to advocate", and he went on to argue that the immigrants were "not physically incapable of supporting themselves, they come here to get out of persecution... It is for your consideration whether they really bear any large proportion to the addition, which is constantly taking place to the population of London, either from natural causes, or from the migration from other parts of the country."[49] None the less "alien immigration as a political, if not as a partisan, issue had arrived",[50] and no contemporary government dared ignore it. Thus Captain Colomb's call in the House of Commons for a Select Committee bore fruit on 13 February. "To politicians of every shade of opinion... the appointment of such a Committee cannot fail to be a source of satisfaction," trumpeted the editor of the *East London Observer*.[51]

The Commons Committee was to carry out its deliberations

for nearly fifteen months, although the major evidence was collected by oral interviews during the spring and summer months of 1888. A parallel inquiry into sweating was set up in the House of Lords and ran concurrently with that of the Commons. The main object of their attention was, in effect, the East End immigrant Jew. An army of antagonists was mobilised against him. In the forefront was Arnold White armed with a mass of evidence he had compiled over years of anti-alien campaigning. Others included trade unionists, particularly from the bootmaking and tailoring trades, clergymen, doctors and sanitary inspectors. Called in defence of their foreign co-religionists were a handful of those deemed responsible members of the Anglo-Jewish establishment.

In both Houses the major attack on the immigrants was mounted by White who, to dramatise the issue, used the ploy of hiring a selection of 50 so-called degenerate "greeners" for inspection by the Lord's Committee. Even the pro-immigrant *Commonweal* fell for the deception, noting that those paraded at the interview "were distinguishable by their poverty-stricken and dirty aspect, their tattered clothes, and worn, wan looks".[52] The whole exercise was proved a fake. The group had been hired through an agent, Levy, paid to produce the most miserable-looking examples of recent arrivals. It was soon revealed that he had, in effect, promised some local Jews, settled for a longer period, that if they presented themselves as ill-clad and starving "greeners" they would be aided by a funding committee either to return to their homeland or to be shipped further on to the real promised land — the United States. Arnold White failed to repudiate Levy, and persisted, under interrogation, to press his campaign against the alien in front of the Commons Committee.

His replies, under close questioning by the Jewish member, Lord Rothschild, soon contradicted his plea that his stance was strictly anti-alien and not anti-Jewish. "I absolutely refuse to regard this as a Jewish question and that I have not gone into the religion of these people." At which Rothschild interceded, "Then why did you mention the word 'Christian' after one of them?" White, quickly brushing this aside by placing the blame on his agent, went on blandly to remark:

> There is, however, a very serious side to this question of wholesale emigration of Russian Jews to England, which the

authorities and parochial boards in London might well consider. The poor Russian Jew laughs at what he hears of English poverty and scanty fare. He has a false notion that the English artisan is generally overfed, and easily discontented, and that the Jew can live easily where an Englishman would starve![54]

A later dialogue with Samuel Montagu (another Jewish Committee member) finally debunked White's plea that he was free of anti-Jewish prejudice. Since White had overtly accused the aliens of "dirty habits", Montagu asked: "Are you aware that a section of Jews bathe every Friday and that married women bathe about once a month as a religious preparation for the Sabbath?" White replied, "I am not aware of that; and I do not believe it", and went on to reject the fact that, according to Montagu and the local authority, there were "five Jewish bathing establishments within a half a mile of Aldgate which are entirely attended and supported by Jews and Jewesses". White preferred to defer to the populist myth that such relative cleanliness "does not make much impression upon the population!" Further questioning by Montagu, Bradlaugh and the foremost anti-alienist, Captain Colomb, confirmed some of the causes which brought the immigrants to Britain, as well as the underlying bigotry of those, like White, who opposed their entry.[55]

Interviewees included representatives of those trades associated with the newcomers, so that the impact of their coming on the welfare of host workers could be gauged. Among them was Charles Freak, Secretary of the Shoemaker Society, an occupation traditionally sited in the Bethnal Green-Whitechapel area. He repeated the usual accusations: "These Jew foreigners work in our trade at this common work 16 or 18 hours a day, and the consequence is that they make a lot of cheap and nasty stuff that destroys the market and injures us." He accused them of blacklegging in disputes, when "they take the work out at any price", thus frustrating English workmen in their striving to attain higher wages, His claim that "their low, specialised type of work prevents them from moving into any other locality... because the system is not adopted in other towns" reflected the general decline in London of the small domestic-based concerns, as factorisation, with subsequent economies of scale, was already producing bulk manufactures in the provinces.[56]

Not only were the immigrants open to the hostility of British workmen, they also had to endure the harsh criticism of fellow Jews long settled in the area. During the earliest sessions Henry de Jonge, an English Jew of Dutch descent, although acting professionally for the aliens (and, presumably, paid by them) as Yiddish interpreter and legal adviser, chose to repeat current populist complaints levelled against them. He claimed that they had displaced English-born tradesmen who now "only gained a precarious living compared with what they were in the habit of getting", and that they were "driving out the English from Wentworth Street to Mile End", estimating that they were "arriving at a rate of a couple of hundreds every week". This aroused the antagonism of English workmen, which was fuelled by the growing numbers of unemployed and the overcrowding apparently caused by the foreign influx. "Wages in tailoring, shoemaking and cabinet making, which had once stood at £2 a week had now dropped by half to £1 and £1 5s." *Greeners* who were exploited by their masters lowered labour costs and thus "influenced the general standard of living which must ultimately be depressed". This self-proclaimed radical (he revealed that he was a member of the United Radical Club in Kay Street, Hackney Road, "the largest in England with 1,800 members of whom 350 to 400, if not more, were in the boot and shoe trade"), suggested that, though the aliens had good moral habits and were otherwise thrifty, the only vice they were addicted to was gambling, "carried out in dens whose fronts were Jewish restaurants". Groups of card players met illicitly. "In many instances I have known them to play for £30 or £40 a Saturday evening." The last gambit was probably valid. The rest, under closer scrutiny, more prejudiced than real.[57]

A fellow Jewish artisan, Woolf Zeitlin, Secretary of the Jewish Branch of the Tailors Society, called in to provide back-up information to de Jonge, proffered a more objective account. Himself a refugee from the earlier pogroms of 1881, he argued that there had been no substantial increase in annual numbers since the great influx of 1882-1883. He stressed that, together with many returning to their homeland, transmigration was continuously taking place. ("There are times when the numbers would be increasing and... decreasing, because they are continually going abroad or going back to their own country" — Minute 2852.) Having suggested that his compatriots were only concerned in producing third-class, ie slop trade, work, he repeated the non-Jewish tailors' complaint that "the Jewish middlemen take out work and make it in their own homes, so that they can have large quantities of work, and that does not leave anything for the English tailors to do". Since English men and women could not live on such wages acceptable to the foreigners, there was animosity between them. Replying to Captain Colomb's leading questions, Zeitlin agreed that the sweating system was chiefly confined to foreigners in the East End, but it was their middlemen who sustained the system of competitive cheap labour which threatened the livelihood of West End craftsmen. However, in contradiction, he later repeated that some unfair competition took place in the production of first- and second-class garments, but "immigrants were *only* engaged in third-class work!"[58] In front of the Lords' Sweating Committee other home-born Jews supplied further evidence against their alien brethren. "Solomon Green, fishmonger, attributed ruin and starvation in this country to costermongering, due to the large influx of foreign paupers who are doing well while English people who had lived comfortably were going down", while Edward Simmons, engaged in the dress-trimming trade in the neighbourhood of Bethnal Green and Spitalfields, added his own "revelations" of the adverse conditions suffered by girls working in the alien sweatshops of Bethnal Green.[59]

In fact the newcomers were already a prime irritant on the ranks of established Jewry. Murmurs of criticism, even open distaste, had reached a crescendo in unison with that of non-Jewish hostility. The previous year this had come to a head in the aftermath of the tragedy at the Yiddish Theatre in Spitalfields. This evoked a strong censure from the *Jewish Chronicle* of "our foreign brethren", warning them of the dangers accruing from their self-imposed alienation from English society.

> We plainly tell... that one of the most direct causes of the recent disaster has been the persistent isolation in which they have kept themselves from their fellow Jewish workmen in all the social amenities of life. When they... want aid in sickness or distress they are willing to claim their privileges as Jews living in England, but in all their social relations they keep aloof from us, and thus forego the advantages of such an institution as the

Jewish Working Men's Club where every practical precaution has been taken to avoid such a calamity as the late panic. The recent event ought to be a lesson to avoid such performances of strolling minstrels acting in the jargon, and helping to keep up the alienation of the foreign contingent. In making these remarks, we are urged by a consideration of the best interests of these brethren of ours... to hasten the process of "anglicising".[61]

The last underlined their fears for their own, recently won, acceptance as British citizens. To protect the whole community's image, the message to the Polish Jew was loud and clear. "Eschew your Yiddish language and culture. Adopt the English language with its civilising customs!" Otherwise attention would be refocussed on the Jews as a whole with English Jews tainted by association with those pariahs, with their repugnant, ie non-British, mores. Throughout 1887 the *Jewish Chronicle* beat the drum incessantly. On 18 March, a correspondent A.L. voiced the response of a die-hard Jewish anti-immigrant: "They are to a certain extend fed and clothed at our expense... We are then brought face to face with the problems, what are we to do with these people for whom we cannot find work, and whom we cannot afford to send back. Would not the wisest plan be to discourage their advent? Let them be shown that in this country there is no room for them!" A letter from "Courtesy", dated 15 March, laments: "Although a Jew, I am likewise an Englishman, and as such, cannot fail to sympathise with the many hardships of our much tried English working classes; and can, therefore, fully understand their just feeling of anger at seeing the work that should be theirs given to foreigners, thereby keeping them half starving."[62]

The Lipski murder case (June-July 1887) in which, after a long and controversial trial, a 22-year-old Polish Jew was found guilty of murdering a fellow immigrant, Miriam Angel, by pouring nitric acid down her throat, was seized upon by anti-alienists to put pressure on the government to halt further immigration.[63] Early in the new year (10 January) at a pre-election meeting in Bethnal Green, the Anglo-Jewish Conservative candidate Arthur Sebag Montefiore voiced the dilemma which had been painfully thrust on him and his caste. "As many of you may be aware, this is an extremely delicate subject for me to discuss. While I cannot bring myself to refuse our free shores to persecuted foreigners, I would do all in my power to dissuade these foreigners from coming to our shores."[64]

It was precisely this attitude which determined establishment policy throughout the year. In his Annual Report of the Jewish Board of Guardians Lionel L. Alexander confirmed that "efforts were made to warn intending emigrants from Russia to England of the congested state of the English labour market and the sufferings experienced by new arrivals here", adding the rider that although "the Board does not favour unwarranted immigration... they seek to check it by warnings rather than advocating prohibition".[65] Nevertheless the difficulties confronting the Jewish hierarchy and their Board of Guardians, that is "to reconcile not only the claims of the poor with its obligation to the Jewish community, but its duty to the needy alien with the part it has to play as a body of patriotic Englishmen", forced them into positions which, at times, proved irreconcilable. Officials' solemn pronouncements responded to the weekly nature of press reports emanating from the Committees of both Houses. While at the AGM of the Board of Guardians on 10 March the President boasted of the Board's policy of discouraging the arrival of their foreign poor, one month later the *Jewish Chronicle* argued that, whereas other aliens came to England to make good and return to their native land, "the Jewish immigrant who comes hither does so with a fixed determination to acquire British nationality for himself and children in as short a time as possible. Such an immigrant as this, bringing with him a certain amount of energy and ability, is far from being a burden on the national resources, but is an appreciable addition to them."[66] This did not detract from the opinion, voiced by the Rev. S. Singer, that "the most profitable occupation for which we could engage during the present crisis (is) to keep them out of the public eye as much as possible."[67] The Board was not slow in publicising its own efforts to "encourage" the aliens either to return to their homeland or to migrate onwards to the USA or Canada.

Powerful figures in Anglo-Jewry vied with each other, in their public utterances, to prove this. In an early interview with the Commons Committee, Mr L.L. Alexander, for the Board, emphasised that his institution had consistently, and successfully, curbed settlement by setting up a transcontinental network of aid centres for those immigrants "influenced" to return ("my Board paying the entire cost of the journeys of the people from London back to their homes, even to Russia, instead of only the fares to Hamburg, as had been the custom up to 1886. The people are now looked after en route by gentlemen acting in Hamburg and Berlin as the agents of the Board"), as well as making special arrangements with the Jewish communities in the frontier towns "for turning back early in their journeys all such cases as should not wander hither".[68] The same Alexander, referring at his Board's committee (18 May) to the honorary service rendered at Hamburg by a Herr Samson in returning Polish and Russian immigrants from London, proposed that a gesture of public recognition should be made to him on the occasion of his forthcoming silver wedding!

On, 15 June the *Jewish Chronicle*, in an article entitled "A Hint to Russia", suggested that, instead of indulging in acts of persecution, the Tsarist authorities should allow their Jews "to be settled in the newly acquired provinces of Central Asia (where) they would bring an element of commercial prosperity... They only need a place where they may earn a livelihood freely, and this they could probably do more easily in Turkestan than in Europe or America" (and thus provide a suitable deterrent to further immigration into the UK.) The following week Samuel Montagu, in a letter refuting charges by the Rev. R.C. Billing that his attempts to repatriate immigrants had been ineffectual, protested: "I have striven for years to keep away from our shores poor Jewish refugees." Since 1881 "I have joined with others in subscribing towards sending poor foreigners back to their country".[69] And so the breast-beating went on. On 26 June, the Board's delegate, F.D. Mocatta, pointed out the desirability of making known to the public that the Guardians had actually come to the end of their resources due to their expending a large proportion of their funds "in sending immigrants away from England". As for efforts to prevent wife-desertion by transmigrant husbands, Montagu went even further by proclaiming that "the Board scarcely granted enough to the deserted family to keep starvation from the door, and did not do anything to prevent them going to the workhouse. The object was not to encourage husbands to leave their families behind in the belief that they would be maintained by the Board. Knowing the strong Jewish dislike of the workhouse, the Board readily allowed any deserted family to drift to the workhouse, so that they would serve as a warning to any husband who thought of going away and leaving his family to burden the Board."[70] By 3 August, the organ of Anglo-Jewry was calling for an International Emigration Commission "which should stop the emigrants before leaving" and "this useless journeying to and fro of persons who should never have left their country". All these pious homilies notwithstanding the terrible acts that continued to be perpetrated against their own co-religionists inside Russia, without any prospects of abatement. Yet three weeks later this same voice, which had so often associated itself with the call for aided repatriation, was shedding crocodile tears over a scene of the "wanderer's return".

> On board the passenger ship Martin of the General Steam Navigation Co., which left London for Hamburg on Thursday 11th, there were a score of poor, woe-begotten Russian Jews, who were being sent back to Russia by the London Jewish Board of Guardians. The appearance of these wanderers excited great commiseration from the other passengers. One aged woman some eighty years of age, particularly created pity, and in the early hours of Saturday morning one of the Christian ladies on board started a collection on behalf of the poor dame, and about 22s were handed to her, much to her surprise and gratification at this last mark of the charity of the English people.[71]

Those who remained were subjected to a barrage of criticism from their anglicised peers. On the one hand the latter put forward arguments to explain, if not to excuse, their foreign brethren's habits of exclusiveness, in congregating together and avoiding close association with the local community. ("In difficulty and danger, it placed him near to friends on whose counsel and help he could confidently rely. It gave him opportunities for indulging in the religious and social intercourse which offered a welcome solace amid the hard trials of mediaeval Jewish life. In proportion, as the world became more harsh and cruel, so the shelter of the ghetto became more grateful, and the tendency to segregation, which it engendered, struck still deeper root."[72]) To end this separatism a concerted drive towards anglicisation was imperative. Since the bulk of East End Jews were synagogue attenders, the *chevras* could prove invaluable in the task of indoctrinating their brethren with the "civilised" mores of the English. "Why should not the lessons of cleanliness, and integrity and thrift, of industry, and truthfulness and 'civicism'... be made the subject of earnest addresses to the congregations that crowd the *chevras*?" demanded the editor of the *Jewish Chronicle*. The Chief Rabbi was not slow in pursuing this line. On 29 September, in a sermon before his elite congregants at the Great Synagogue, he exhorted "those present to become missionaries... to their foreign brethren, to induce them to attend the services organised on their behalf and to give them the example of obedience to the laws of the state, honesty and truthfulness in their dealings, of a right observance of the Sabbath, and abstinence from gambling and quarrelsomeness."[73] Both reveal a presumptiousness in repeating myths conjured up by anti-alienists, as well as a patronising regard for such "inferior" Jews who needed to be redeemed. A letter to the *Jewish Chronicle* (19 October), one of many, echoes a more justified complaint voiced locally:

> Sir,
>
> As one who lives in the district of Whitechapel, I am surprised to find every Saturday hundreds of foreigners (our co-religionists) standing in groups of 5, 10 and as many as 20, in the public footpaths to the annoyance of passers by between Osborne Street and Middlesex Street.
> I do not know for what purpose they loiter in this particular spot, and have often heard very obnoxious remarks made by passers by. I should not at all be surprised that one Saturday they will be stringently interfered with. I must give the police in the neighbourhood great credit for their forebearance. They try all means in their power to remedy the evil, but so soon as the police move them from one spot they collect at another....
> The feeling against this class of people, I am sorry to say, is not of a very friendly nature, and by making themselves conspicuous they may bring trouble to themselves and others.
>
> Yours obediently,
> A resident

Outside the community, the depth and diversity of anti-alien, ie anti-semitic, feeling was evident. Lord Rosebery's public objection to the immigration of pauper aliens (*ELO*, 17 March) was followed by large demonstrations. On 24 March, Spencer Charrington, brewer MP, presided over a mass Conservative meeting at Mile End, in which the usual accusations were made of foreigners undermining employment of British workers by introducing sweating and unfair labour practices. Cases in the courts involving Jews revealed overt prejudices on the part of local magistrates. In June, at Thames Police Court, a Mr Lushington found against the plaintiff, a Polish immigrant, who, having paid £6 to an English solicitor, to take out letters of naturalisation, alleged that nothing had been done to pursue this, and, therefore, charged him with fraud.[74] In September a blatant case of anti-foreign bias by a well-known racist magistrate aroused widespread controversy.

Mr Saunders, magistrate sitting at Worship Street, was strongly criticised for his attitude towards an applicant for summons on behalf of a Polish tailor whose employer, it was asserted, owed him wages which he was unable to get after repeated application.
"Why doesn't the man speak for himself?" asked the magistrate. "He is a native of Poland" was the reply. "Then let him go to Poland," retorted the magistrate, adding however, on the applicant turning to leave the box, that he had better explain the matter. On the case being laid before him, the magistrate observed that the Pole had no business in this country, and that he was taking the bread out of the mouths of Englishmen. You may have your summons," he added, "but I hope you won't succeed."
This is hardly worthy of an intelligent Englishman, much less of a magistrate on the bench.[75]

As the hearings of the two Parliamentary Committees progressed, while the Anglo-Jews were agonising over which stance to take and when, other anti-immigrants were having a field day. On 15 June, the Rev. R.C. Billing, Rector of Spitalfields, in his evidence before the Lords Committee, stated that among the evils accruing from sweating "was a prejudice among Gentiles against working with Jews. He should be sorry to prejudge these people by a sweeping accusation, but they had no knowledge of the decencies of life... Whole streets were now occupied by Jews where there was not a Jew before. If a Jew got into one room he soon got a Jew into another and it became intolerable for the Gentiles to remain... The Jew did not like the Gentile, and the Gentile did not like the Jew." This brought a swift rebuttal from the Chief Rabbi in his speech at the annual prize-giving at the Jews Free School on 17 June, later reinforced in his monthly report at the Board of Guardians meeting of 26 June. In the first he ventured to inform the Rev. R.C. Billing "that there is the greatest anxiety on the part of Christians to obtain apartments in the Charlotte de Rothschild Dwellings, although the greatest number of occupiers are Jews", in the second he firmly rejected Billing's statement. On the contrary, "he found that Jews and Gentiles dwelt peacefully together in the Brunswick Building and in the blocks created by the city corporation... He had seen Christians labouring with perfect contentment in the Jewish workshops, and 90 per cent of the masters, to whom the lads were apprenticed by the Jewish Board of Guardians were Christians!"[76] Rothschild protested at the Chief Rabbi's public criticism of Billing from a school platform "when the proper place to rebut these statements was before a committee (of the legislature)". The Chief Rabbi was probably presenting a picture rather rosier than reality. For the Rev. Samuel Barnett, who had day-to-day experience of local community relationships, noted, according to his wife, that "Gentiles refuse to live in close juxtaposition to Jews, if they can afford to avoid it".[77]

The last observation was repeated by those literati, novelists and journalists, who commented on East End life. Most revealing are the attitudes expressed by characters in Margaret Harkness's contemporary novels. In *In Darkest London*, Miss Hardy, a self-educated radical feminist and reader of Darwin, deplores the current emigration of young English women to Australia. "To send away all these strong, healthy girls, and get in their place the scum of Europe, is a great mistake... I saw a picture the other day of an English port, and over it was written 'Rubbish shot here by order of Prince Bismarck'... The picture showed a lot of those miserable foreigners being shot out of ships to take the bread out of the mouths of us English." The 'progressive' labour mistress is adamant about employing alien Jews. 'No!' she continued, shaking her fist to give her word emphasis, 'I never take on a foreigner. It's bad enough for us English and I won't help to make it worse by giving work to a Jewess.'"[78] Even the unemployed carpenter Jo, hero of *Out of Work* and ostensibly a rational and sympathetic man, fulminates against "them furriners... they'll go to hell". He has succumbed to the myth that they are the main cause of unemployment. "He says hundreds of carpenters are out of work now, men who've been foremen. He thinks Jews and foreigners do jobs so cheap he hasn't a chance."[79]

Such sentiments showed the potency of working-class antisemitism. Even the radical *Commonweal* conceded this in its correspondence early that year in a letter from a Mrs Sairey Brown, who "in search of the truth" was appalled to

> see in the *Telegraph*, which I hear is got up by a Jew that the police is a brave lot... If the Jew, who I hear got the paper up, what says we poor people are failures because we are poor, had his deserts given him he would be more civil. If the working men don't take it out of him and the police he is so fond of, then they deserve to be insulted and knocked about...[80]

In May the same journal described the action of bully boys, hired by the Bethnal Green Tories to break up socialist meetings in Victoria Park, as part of their attempt to silence "blasphemous and seditious speech":

> As the meetings in the park have hitherto been very orderly, the Tories have hired some roughs to try and upset us. Last Sunday (29 April) they appeared on the scene shouting that they were brave and bold Englishmen, and that we were a lot of d**** foreigners. We managed to get one on the platform, when he said that he hated all foreigners, had fought seven years for his Queen and country, that he would sooner starve than work for a foreigner, that he had the chance of seducing the daughter of a German in Green Street, but he hated all Germans so much that he refused it. He was answered by the lecturer, and an English comrade pointed out to him that if the foreigners worked for a living they were quite as good as an Englishman. The Tory reply was a blow on the jaw with the exclamation, "I"m an Englishman, I am!"[81]

Physical attacks on Jews were not uncommon. The immigrant Jewish journalist Winchevsky had warned of the probability of local racial violence four years before. The *East London Observer* reports on a Leah Ginski of 11 Boyd Street who, while sitting outside her door, was approached by 20-year-old John Gerald who, after spitting out 'Jew bastard!", deliberately butted her with his head in her chest causing her to faint, with subsequent rib injuries.[82]

The local press joined in the chorus of denigrating the foreigner, ie the Jewish, immigrant. The *East London Advertiser* was consistently in the forefront throughout and after both Parliamentary Committee hearings. Anti-Jewish quips appeared regularly[83] and on 6 October the paper was lamenting that "notwithstanding all the outcry about the immigration of foreign paupers the cry is 'still they come'". The would-be radical organ of the SDF, *Justice*, under its anti-semitic editor H.M. Hyndman, reached a high point of vilification against Jews generally. In his review of the French racist E. Drumont's "End of the World" (20 November), Hyndman declared that Britons too should "strip off the veneer of hypocrisy with which we cover the misdeeds of our noble and ignoble swindlers and debauchers... (to) reveal the Jew influence in our Cabinets and in our most prosperous journals, and we may well say that here also we are approaching the 'End of the World'", and on 22 December he castigated the Conservative Party for being led by a Hebrew. "How appropriate it is that the sham "patriotic" party shouldn't be able to do without a Jew to lead them. Their last man was Disraeli — a Spanish Jew!" On a more sophisticated level, in a prejudiced article on "East End Labour", Beatrice Potter imposed her own stamp of disapproval on the immigrant Jew. Reflecting on the means of combating sweating, she maintained "that without a constant supply of destitute foreigners, and of women who are forced to supplement their husband's irregular earnings, (sweating) would cease to exist". Her blatant distaste is shown in her stereotyped image of the Whitechapel Jew by reaffirming the so-called characteristics with which history had endowed him:

> It is this passion for the chances of a successful "deal" which tempts the East End Jew into his own vice — gambling. For the machinist may be passing his slack time in a gambling den, whilst the master of the workshop slaves day and night for profit, the presser buys and renovates old clothes for the Petticoat Lane market, and the *greener* hoards his hard-earned pence to buy cheap the coveted watch of the unemployed Gentile. And it is rare for an East End Jewish worker to be content with his nominal profession: hours and days of enforced idleness like the un-spent farthings of the scanty income are turned to profit, unless both alike be dedicated to that vice characteristic of the profit seeker — gambling.

Thus it was that "at the East End this characteristic of the Jewish race has a twofold tendency: to raise the workers as a mass of individuals, and to depress the production industry through which they rise. Hence a Jew may begin at Backchurch Lane and end in Bayswater."[84] All this was in exact accord with her pronouncements in both the Booth commentaries on the

Jews, first in the paper read before the Royal Statistical Society in May 1887 and later in the chapter devoted to the Jewish community in the *Life and Labour of the People of London*.[85]

It would appear that, within a climate of universal hostility, this pariah among pariahs was bereft of any defenders. But this is not so. There was enlightened support from diverse quarters. The local radical *East End News* was cautiously sympathetic. On 6 January, in an article entitled "Sweating 'Whitewashed'", it criticised the "unjust reflections upon Jewish tailors" whose application to the sewing machine ensured that "the extensive clothing industry has been retained on English soil". A week later (13 January) in a report on "Pauper Immigration" it presented the opposite picture to that of the "continental rubbish" portrayed by the anti-alienists: discerning that the recently arrived Jewish families from Kleck near Minsk "belong to the ordinary artisan class, had full employment, and the young male members had all served their military terms of service". It offered as a rational explanation for the Jew's need to quit Russia "the immense attraction of casting himself loose at any sacrifice from the trammels of Russian police laws and a score of petty and exasperating disabilities which clog his natural industry and rob his domestic life of peace and comfort". Though less sympathetic, the *East London Observer* urged restraint on those who prejudged the issue. On 3 March, in a letter from "R.J.W." we read:

> It is quite a relief to find that we are now to have authoritative statistics, and it is no less gratifying to find that wise advice has been given to suspend our judgements and allow things to go as they have done till the Select Committee report is published... it may not happen that the investigations will reveal that the foreign invasion does not cripple us and so... we naturally incite these "aliens" close by us not to work with us for a common good, but to work against us in a ruthless competition. Better far, I say, to make friends with this "mammon of unrighteousness"... The social problem will only be solved when the hearts of all are called into play, and the agent for accomplishing it is... the recognition by the individual conscience that mutual co-operation and not bandying competition is just and right.

By 21 July the *East London Observer* was concerned about attaining accurate and trustworthy evidence for the House of Commons Committee, particularly from those tradesmen directly affected by the foreign influx. The editor conceded that the outstanding stirrer of action against immigrants was the notorious Mr J.V. Jones of the Bethnal Green Vestry, with Bethnal Green living up to its traditional role of providing xenophobic recruits to the racist cause.

Anglo-Jewry, forced perhaps to protect the image of its community as a whole, particularly in the interests of their own recently acquired status of equality in citizenship, adopted defensive tactics on behalf of their foreign brethren. One of their most forceful spokesmen was banker Hermann Landau, himself an ex-Polish immigrant, who exposed to the Commons Committee the falsity of Arnold White's assembly of "witnesses" selected to demonstrate the physical and moral degenerates who, in his view, constituted the majority of aliens. He also pointed out that keener competition in shipping for migrant custom had reduced the rate from London to New York from 6 guineas in 1880 to £3 10s in the current year. The direct run to New York from Hamburg was much more expensive, and it was known that shipping companies "tell them (the Russian emigrants) that they can go via London for much less money". The inference was that less emigrants intended settling in the UK. It was merely a transit point to ensure cheaper travel to the USA. He ended by reiterating that "England as a field of labour, had ceased to be an attraction many, many years ago... My experience is that the bulk of the people coming here are simply passengers going on to America."[86]

The *Jewish Chronicle* (1 June), commenting on the article "The Invasion of the Pauper Foreigner" by Stephen N. Fox in the current *Contemporary Review*, debunked Arnold White's exaggerated estimate of the numbers of incoming immigrants. It repeated the results of the author's investigation, which were basically threefold: "that the clamour raised on the subject of foreign pauper immigration is of the nature of a craze and is unsupported by evidence; that such indigent aliens as do arrive are not found a burden on the ratepayers to any appreciable extent; that the indigent alien has been a source of profit rather than loss to the native worker." Above all Fox had given "emphatic corroboration to the opinions of the Jewish Board of Guardians... that Jewish immigrants do not appear to arrive in any greater proportion than the non-Jewish, and that during, the past year there has been a marked decrease in the immigrant

Jewish poor". On 17 June the Chief Rabbi, speaking at the Jews Free School, claimed that the foreign Jew certainly had a superior morality to "the inhabitants of such localities as St. Giles or the Trongate" (the sort of patronising, insensitive remark he was wont to make), and again denied allegations made by the Rev. R.C. Billing and others "that there existed any feelings of animosity between Jewish and Christian artisans" in the East End.[87] And the *Jewish Chronicle* editorial for the Jewish New Year 5648 (7 September), looking back at the highlights of the year, concluded that the evidence of both Committees proved without doubt that there was little foundation for the alarmist propaganda put out by the anti-alien scaremongers, calling on the "impartial exposition" posited by Mr Lakeman, Factory Inspector, Mr Burnett, Labour Correspondent of the Board of Trade, Beatrice Potter and D.F. Schloss to verify this.

Perhaps the staunchest defenders of the Jewish immigrant could be detected among those diverse groups of radical intellectuals outside the Hyndman circle. Margaret Harkness, as she follows Salvationist "Captain Lobo" through the Jewish quarter, conveys both an impressionistic regard and sympathetic appreciation of the ghetto labourer vis-à-vis his non-Jewish counterpart:

> On the way to Spitalfields... buxom Jewish matrons sat on doorsteps, watching the little dark children who tumbled at their feet. Young Hebrews smoked short pipes and talked their own lingo. Now and then a young girl with jet black hair and flashing eyes ran by, carrying a loaf of German bread under her arm, singing a foreign song or jodelling. There was nothing English about the place, only foreign faces, foreign shops, foreign talk. The Jews looked happy, although they were in a strange land, exiles as their fathers were, crowded into the narrow compass of the East End Ghetto. They had not the down-trodden look of our Gentile population, which seems to enjoy crouching and whining instead of asserting itself with sturdy independence.
>
> The Jews have, it is true, long-suffering faces, but they have hope written in their features, instead of that despair which seems to sodden English East End men and women. Perhaps this habit of looking towards Jerusalem accounts for this, for the synagogues of the East End show men and women full of religious purpose. The down-trodden Gentiles seem to have lost their faith; they speak of death as "the great secret" while the Jew class death "God's kiss", even when it comes to him in the

crowded dens of sweaters or the filthy rooms which he shares with newcomers from the continent. Moreover he knows how to grow rich. He leaves the East End to settle in Bayswater; he does not content himself with husks, like our Gentile swine who fill the public houses. Charity offers him no premium for idleness; so the chosen people hang together, the rich help the poor, and every Jew finds a friend in the Jewish Board of Guardians.[88]

The *Commonweal*, under the auspices of the sympathetic William Morris, a vociferous pro-alien, published three articles in their defence. In "The Blarsted Furriners" (18 April) Frank Kitz purports to analyse the forces behind the current attack:

> They (the Saviours of Society) seek the support of the propertied classes on one hand by asserting that revolutionary socialism is due to foreign immigration, and of the worker on the other that his labour is badly remunerated on the same account. These two antagonistic forces are used as pawns in the reactionary game, which means the total obliteration of the right of asylum, or what is left of it after imprisonment, in 1889!
>
> The "Man in the Street"... lends a ready ear to the wiles of those who wish to distract the attention of the workers from the real causes of their poverty.
>
> The foreign working man landing in a strange land, and speaking a foreign language, finds every man's hand against him on account of this illiberal teaching. Ignorant of the relative monetary values in relation to payment and purchasing power, and in nine cases out of ten desperately poor, he accepts the first offer, and as this is made by some labour-robber or master he comes at once into collision with the English labourer.
>
> Expatriated by persecution he is worse off relatively than he would be at home were he left in peace. Even in the case of voluntary emigration to sell his labour in the best market, he is but carrying out the teachings of those economists whose ardent disciples a number of English workmen are.

In the following edition (5 May) Kitz goes on to deflate the anti-alienists' claim to be as the prime defender of the indigenous working man:

> If by penuriousness or fraud the once pauper immigrant becomes affluent, he would secure the fulsome flattery of those who abuse him now. His foreign blood would not bar him from even the mayoralty of London. If a Rothschild, a Bleichroder, a Goschen, or a Disraeli, he can govern the lives and destinies of myriads of human beings by the power of the purse which knows no country.

> The foreign sweater, oft-times sweated himself, simply takes advantage of commercial conditions as he finds them. With a commercial system which is nothing if not international, and her soldiers forcing her goods at the point of the bayonet into fresh markets, England's outcry against foreign competition is absurd!

The 19 May issue included another contributor, Andrew Scheur, who, commenting on the "New Jingoism", joined Kitz in the attack against the anti-semitic nature of anti-alienism as exemplified in a current article in the *Pall Mall Gazette* (7 May). He argued: "Is there nothing grimly grotesque in this national hypocrisy, in this desperate Jew-baiting as a last attempt to bind the native workers against the real causes of their misery?" He was positive that anti-alienism "is not so to the minds of those workers who look at the social question as one of the power of economic circumstances dividing the population of all the capitalised world into two nationalities and beliefs only — the exploiter and the exploited!" Although his claim that "the number of English working men who take this view is growing fast in spite of the preachers of Social Jingoism, and this is one hopeful sign in the time of shame, hypocrites and petty crusade" could well have been a case of wishful thinking.

The most forceful advocates for the Jewish immigrant were the anarchists. In an editorial in *Freedom* (May 1888) the writer associates himself completely with their interests. Extending the arguments posed by *Commonweal*, he was the only one to define the efforts made by the politicised immigrants themselves in combining with their Gentile co-workers in the national struggles of labour.

> Our socialist comrades amongst the East End Jewish immigrants are doing their level best to bring about this combination. Their weekly paper, *The Worker's Friend*, printed in their own dialect of Hebrew, is obtaining so good a circulation that it has been publicly denounced by the middle-class Jews and determined underhand attempts made to suppress it... Several English groups of socialists gave practical proof how thoroughly they appreciate the total character of the labour struggle by helping *The Worker's Friend* over a financial crisis.
> Our Jewish comrades are not only socialist propagandists, they are energetically occupied in organising trade societies to combat the sweating system, to raise the rate of wages to subsistence level, hold out a hand to a friendless immigrant, who being ignorant of English and English wage rates, are helpless

victims of the sweater and his agents, and to communicate the real state of affairs in the London labour market to their brethren abroad.

Alas support from this quarter, however generous and valid, was more a liability than an asset for its recipient. For the anarchists were a powerless, minuscule group, who, thanks to contemporary myths and newspaper propaganda, were regarded as criminals even by "respectable" working men. Perhaps the most sympathetic regard, and the more influential, came from the less overtly political pen of such enlightened observers of the slum ghetto as architect Robert Williams:

> I do not think there is any part of the world so fascinating in the intensity of its human interest as Wentworth Street, when the market in the street is in full swing... The pen of a Zola is wanted (to describe it)...
>
> A street like this, cut out as it were, from the thick of Jerusalem, is what makes one love old England. The roots of freedom are here, say what we will about the alien. He is welcome, and ever may it be so. He brings his Hebrew Bible with him, and, moreover, he pays for the slum in which he, so often, has to dwell.[89]

In such times of adversity there were institutions already there to aid both newcomer and the settled. Certainly the most welcoming was the Poor Jews Temporary Shelter, founded as an act of pious benevolence by an immigrant baker, Simha Becker, in 1884.[90] It was a centre which, on arrival, offered *ad hoc* hospitality to the poor and weary "greener" and operated as a dispersal agency in which the immigrant was afforded protection from dockside predators as well as assistance in tracing relatives or finding a job in the East End. From its inception it worked in close co-operation with local and government authorities and thus attained official respectability.

But this did not deter Arnold White from adding to his other diatribes an attack on its existence. He contended that "where this helping hand is extended (by the Shelter) so as to put them (the pauper aliens) in a position of successful competition with natives of the country, I cannot help thinking that that institution, and the Board of Guardians, and the great Free School, and the boundless generosity of the community, have between them an immense influence in attracting this class of foreigners to this country".[91] Called to respond to this, Hermann Landau, banker and founding father of the Shelter, offered a convincing defence of its aims and activities.

In his view its purpose was to forward and protect immigrants coming into this country and to pass on non-Jews to other foreign aid societies.[92] The numbers passing through the Shelter in the previous two years (1886-1888) had been 2,192,[93] at a total cost of £814 17s 3d. ("That includes the superintendent's wages, 2 assistants, secretary, gas, rates and taxes, rent, repairs, collectors' commission, postage, printing and stationery, coal and household sundries, and all food for two years since its establishment.")[94] Those admitted were only allowed to stay for 14 days. Most of them were then off-loaded "to their countrymen and they got further sojourn with them for a week of so on the expectation of receiving assistance".[95] Landau had earlier made a side swipe at Arnold White's pertinacious remarks that the Shelter was "one more inducement for immigration" and that objection had been made at the Whitechapel Board of Guardians to the number of Jews who applied for medical relief. His response to the latter was that, considering the large proportion that Jews in Whitechapel contributed towards the rates, he thought the objection particularly ungracious. To the former he countered with the view that "he did not know of any organisation for attracting foreigners unless it was the Bethnal Green establishment for the Society for Promoting Christianity Among the Jews, at which place substantial sums of money were obtained by foreign Jews prior to embracing Christianity." The Shelter recorded specific evidence of the large proportion of inmates who transmigrated to the USA. Landau revealed that between June 1887 and May 1888 "1,364 inmates had passed through the institution, and during the first fourteen days of their arrival and, in the majority of cases, during the first week 270 had proceeded on their way to America and 304 had returned to their own countries".[96]

It was Landau, too, who gave publicity to the hazards confronting the immigrant at the point of arrival at the dockside. The *Jewish Chronicle* summed up his "disquieting statements" which he had previously made to Lord Rothschild before the House of Commons Select Committee.

> It is heartrending to know that poor Jewish immigrants, on landing in London, are made the victims of an organised band of scoundrels, who do not let them out of their clutches until they have fleeced them of the little they possess... in suffering them to be plundered the community is unmindful of its own interests... If proper protection were given to the newcomers on their arrival at the docks, the money which has hitherto been stolen from them would be available for their support until they were able to get employment or until they continued their journey to America.

Landau had estimated that the "proportion of arrivals here of people going to America that are prevented doing so by these robberies is certainly not less than 40%." In detail he gave examples of how the crimps defrauded the *greener* of whatever cash he might have on entry:

> Some of these porters, whom I call loafers, take immigrants who have an address, say to Leman Street, instead of to this address, which is perhaps 1,000 yards from the landing stage, to the home of one of these vagabonds, telling them, "Oh, this place is 260 miles from London and it will cost £2 10s to get there." And they actually have obtained £2 10s and taken them in a roundabout way by the Great Eastern Railway to some out-of-the-way station, and then back again through another route saying, "This is your destination!"... This goes on every day, I assure you.[97]

Such "cruel robberies to which many of the poor ignorant immigrants were subjected" did not diminish as the year progressed. At a meeting in the Shelter on 25 October, Landau spoke of "another of these so-called porters who took 13s from a poor woman for taking her from Fenchurch Street to Brick Lane — a shilling cab fare!" Why had not the victims immediately sought police aid? He went on: "These poor folks feared to call for the assistance of the police because they thought the English police were much the same as the dreaded *Objescik* whom they had just left behind." In any case the local police appeared to have become suspect to the Shelter authorities after a sudden visit from them in June. An official, Mr H.A. Franklin, then reported that the police had seized on a clause of the Shelter constitution "which directed that any applicant who might be deemed able to afford it, should normally pay 3s, and stated that, as money was taken from certain inmates, the institution would have to be registered under the Common Lodging House Act". This forced the Executive Committee to order suspension of payments and "send the class hitherto paying to respectable lodging houses". It also prompted Landau to suspect that the police, in harassing the Shelter, were in cahoots with the riverside crimps, in whose interests it was to prevent immigrants from getting admission to the Shelter.[98]

The role of the Shelter was clearly outlined by its Secretary, Joseph E. Blank, to the House of Commons Select Committee. The immigrants had fled their home country because "matters had been made so uncomfortable for them in Russia through... persecutions". They had come here as a first stop en route for America. The Shelter offered them accommodation and kosher meals for "on an average about 7 days, never exceeding 14. Again the average arrived with about two or three pounds on them, and most were not penniless" (ie paupers). Questioned as to what procedures were adopted to protect their belongings, Blank replied: "Immediately... their clothes have to be disinfected and they have to take a bath; and during that time they leave their money with the superintendent, who gives them a note for the amount; that amount is handed back to them, principally to enable them to get away again; they are always advised to go on", that is, encouraged to move on to America. He contended that most of the newcomers were in transit, but repeated that "a certain amount do remain behind in London because on their journey they have been deprived of the means by which they intended to go forward".[99] Thus the Shelter officials joined in the chorus loudly proclaiming how they, too, had succeeded in the dual exercise of repatriating or transmigrating their foreign co-religionists. At the meeting of 25 October, Ellis Franklin boasted that the Shelter "diverted immigration", thanks to the officers effectively "advising those who were not likely to benefit themselves by remaining in England to return to their native land".[100] The latter was reinforced by a letter to the *Jewish Chronicle* (7 December) from the Anglo-Jewish Conservative candidate Arthur Sebag Montefiore, emphasising his well-known public opposition to the "influx into this country of alien paupers" and his own conviction that "by personal enquiries, the Shelter does not encourage immigration". The last may have been valid. Nevertheless the practical application of its concern for the stranger remains as alive today as it was as its inception. The other centre of aid, though less accommodating, as we have noted, was the Jewish Board of Guardians. Charles Booth, in his contemporaneous study of its function, was quick to point out that it was

> not in any way analogous to the relief administered by a parochial board. Of the £13,000 or £14,000 expended annually by the Board on actual relief, viz. in fixed allowances and in tickets for the necessaries of life; £3,000 a year is lent for trade and business purposes, £1,000 a year is expended in emigration, another £500 in the sanitary inspection of the houses of the poor and in the provision of workrooms for girls. Of the remainder, more than 50% may be considered given in the form of business capital of one kind or another, enabling the recipients to raise themselves permanently from the ranks of those who depend on charity for subsistence.

By inference he exposed the falsity of Arnold White's image of the "alien pauper" as predator on the host community:

> We can hardly, in face of these statistics, describe those relieved by the Jewish Board of Guardians as belonging to the chronically parasitic class of "paupers".[101]

The major force which sustained the immigrant Jew in a hostile *milieu* was religious orthodoxy; and, for the majority, it was from the daily ritual of collective worship within their *stiebl* that they drew strength in adversity. Again, it was Charles Booth who, thanks to a rare sympathetic appreciation by his researcher Beatrice Potter, proffered an objective assessment of the role of the *chevras*, with a moving description of a service to boot:

> The East End Jews of the working class rarely attend the larger synagogues (except on the Day of Atonement) and, most assuredly, they are not seat holders. For the most part the religious minded form themselves into associations (*chevras*), which combine the functions of a benefit club for death, sickness and the solemn rites of mourning with that of public worship and the study of the Talmud. (30-40 of these *chevras* scattered round the Jewish quarter.) Usually each *chevra* is named after the town or district in Russia or Poland from which the majority of its members have emigrated.
>
> Here, early in the morning or late at night, the devout members meet to recite the morning and evening prayers or to

decipher the sacred books of the Talmud. And it is a curious and touching sight to enter one of the poorer and more wretched of these places on a Sabbath morning.

At the conclusion of the service

> the women have left; the men are scattered over the benches (maybe there are several who are still muttering their prayers), or they are gathered together in knots, sharpening their intellects with the ingenious points and subtle logic of the Talmudic argument, refreshing their minds from the rich stores of Talmudic wit, or listening with ready helpfulness to the tale of distress of a newcomer from the foreign home.

Against current attempts by the Anglo-Jewish Establishment to close or absorb the small *stieblech* because of insanitary and overcrowded conditions, Booth defends their retention with the argument that "it is easy to overlook the unseen influence for good of self-creating, self-supporting, and self-governing communities".[102]

With the expansion of East End Jewry resulting from the acceleration of immigration since 1881, *chevras* had mushroomed accordingly. Thus did the refugees from the *shtetlech* remuster their own townsmen in the new ad hoc centres of religious and social intercourse. The newcomers and the established synagogue authorities regarded each other with suspicion. For the foreign worshipper, the nature of the service, the cathedral-like structures of the London synagogues and the almost Gentile stance of the Chief Rabbi were completely alien to his experience of what constituted "true" Judaism. ("East was East and West was West") with a vengeance, the latter more or less regarding the former — outside membership of the United Synagogue — as having "to be provided for" on "eleemosynary lines."[103] There lay the rub, There was a great divide, fully appreciated by the two rival magnates who sought domination over their foreign co-ethnics for their own purposes. Samuel Montagu, the Whitechapel MP, seizing on the alienation of the isolated *stieblech* from the host "United Synagogues", initiated their unity into a separate body, the Federation of Minor Synagogues, on 6 November 1887.[104] Not to be outdone, the grand mogul of Anglo-Jewry, Lord Rothschild, was elected president. Following the climactic proceedings of the

Parliamentary investigations, when the accusations against the Whitechapel Jews were reaching a crescendo, Rothschild requested the Chief Rabbi "to consider well the necessity of building a large Free Synagogue in the East End for the poor",[105] no doubt to ensure the establishment's institutional and spiritual control of the ghetto. Although there was much frenetic discussion and activity, nothing transpired.

That year official attitudes towards the *chevras* and their congregants continued to vacillate between hostility and grudging praise. These views were reflected in the columns of the *Jewish Chronicle*. On 30 March, it noted with satisfaction the Federation's proposal to establish "a system of life assurance" to reduce charity funerals, thereby "promoting the material and moral welfare of the working classes by the promotion of habits of worldly prudence". By 25 May, complaints were reported from the Chief Rabbi, who spoke of "spiritual destitution" among the poor, since he "found that very few belonged to any *chevra* or went to any place of worship", while the Rev. B. Singer fulminated against the "improvident marriages" by those East End Jews "within measurable distance of poverty, that their children had been reared by charity, that their parents lived partly on charity and when they died were buried by charity." On 29 June the Chief Rabbi feared that "if it were spread around that the East End Jews lived immoral lives, it would afford a splendid excuse for Russian persecution". A month later (3 August), in a letter to the editor, the community leader Benjamin L. Cohen was not only condemning the location and condition of certain *stieblech* he had recently visited, but was astounded to find political notices posted on the entrance doors. The following editorial questioned Cohen's exhortation to demolish such dirty, ill-structured minor synagogues. It suggested that one should tread lightly, since "the *chevras*, numerous as they are, do not represent anything like the totality of East End Judaism", and be more practical (here with a bow towards Lord Rothschild) by providing an alternative — "a large free synagogue which might be made a centre of 'mission' work... to which there would be attached an earnest body of men and women anxious to bring to bear the most humanising and ennobling influence upon the Jewish masses of the East End".

Meanwhile, as though the *chevras* were the negation of the civilising process, the Jewish plebs would be uplifted by the privilege of opening the Sabbath service at the Great Synagogue to them, where they could "enjoy" a series of sermons delivered by the leading Rabbis in their own jargon — Yiddish. The first address was scheduled for Saturday, 19 October. A discerning *Jewish Chronicle* reporter noted that, although "the mass who overflowed the synagogue were foreign Jewish Working Men... barely a fifth could be accounted for from those who frequented the poorest class of *chevras*". No doubt the latter preferred that homely intimacy where, unlike the formal anglicised service, the liturgical responses were loud, emotional and traditionally undisciplined. From the pulpit the unfortunate "guests" were subjected to a weekly dose of patronising advice and warnings that aberrant behaviour on their part was affecting the safety of the whole community. Dayan and Chief Rabbi pontificated on what was expected of them. Reporting on the second Sabbath address, the *Chronicle* noted (2 November), with satisfaction, the success of the experiment:

> The congregants last Sabbath were gathered from the lowest part of the East End, and it was not open to much doubt that they were the employed rather than the employers... The half a dozen *Mitzvas* were given to as many of the humble worshippers, and this was the finishing touch necessary to prove that the service was one primarily intended "for the people".

The preacher, the Rev. B. Spiers, took advantage of the occasion to rebuke those who, however needy, worked on the Sabbath. He complained that "it was a source of serious anxiety that so many of their poorer co-religionists would congregate in already overcrowded streets on the Sabbath. Perhaps their homes were not of the most comfortable... But by congregating at street corners they caused the impression amongst the less enlightened that this was the only means of Jewish Sabbath observance, and they were derided." Those who did not care to enjoy the fresh air of the parks were cordially invited to attend his *Beth Hamedresh* (religion classes) on the day of rest "when he expounded the Talmud and other holy writings". He must have been very disappointed that few, if any, took up this "generous" offer!

It was the Chief Rabbi's sermon on 10 November which was the most blatant in its advocacy of social and economic submission on the part of the Jewish labouring poor to the status quo. Even within the contemporary mores it was an audacious plea. He warned his listeners that "they must not set their faces against labour, even though the work be hard and the hours long. The experience of the sweater's hard work is not of the brightest and happiest, but under all conditions of life there would always remain one class harder worked than another. Yet must they be patient and *not rebel*." As for the current Whitechapel murders and Jews "rushing into police courts for trifling disputes", they should assume a low profile and avoid court cases where, by inference, the swindling and lying manifest among them were exposed to the public eye, In short he wanted the focus, and therefore the heat, taken off the East End Jew, to the relief of Jews as a whole.[106]

The heights of insensitivity and patronage marked the sermon delivered on 22 December by the Rev. Hermann Gollancz in an attempted admixture of German and Yiddish for the benefit of his Polish audience. He accused them of operating here as a group of scroungers and importing uncivilised behaviour. "Why in their native lands should they be willing to break stones and carry water rather than beg, and when they come to London try to become a burden to the community?" He would remind them that "what was expected of them was that they should conform to English habits, The text showed that Moses did not wear mean clothes or neglect his person, and he did not wear a distinctive coat or was indifferent to his cleanliness or appearance."[107] It was no wonder that the great divide between East and West remained unbroken by the end of the year; and that some form of conciliation would have to await the passing of more than one generation.

The newcomer was also subjected to a marginally less pleasant onslaught on his religious integrity and un-British mores. He was already the focus of attention by Christian missionaries embarked on an evangelical crusade among the chosen people. What a prize they held out for the true believer! A few had previously succumbed and were employed to carry on the good work among their fellow Yiddish speakers, for they preached in the vernacular. From the moment he or she stepped off the boat the "greener", particularly the young and solitary (and, therefore, the most vulnerable), was the target of the evangelist on the prowl at the dockside. The methods used to entice the unwary were illuminating, as exposed by the volume of criticism that arose from diverse quarters Jew and Gentile.

For the Jew, conversion spelt excommunication from the community. It could even evoke the *kaddish* — the prayer for the dead — from his own kinsfolk, to underline the permanent separation, as of a death, in the family.

Anglo-Jewry was alarmed at the material baits offered by the conversionists. Early in the year Landau was complaining that "a large dispensary had been established in Whitechapel under the auspices of the Mildmay Mission for Conversion, where the attendants were able to converse with the foreign Jews. This was a tempting bait, and it was perhaps not unnatural that recourse should be had by the poor Jew to those by whom he could make himself understood". It was imperative, therefore, to consider "the resuscitation of a *Jewish* dispensary". He had, in the previous year, voiced the anger of his community at the "cunning tactics" employed to entrap the naive foreigner:

> The "enquirers" are fed and lodged. Their religious scruples are as carefully regarded as an angler would study the habits, haunts and natural feeding of the fish he warily seeks to catch. Kosher food is supplied to them, and the Hebrew Grace is muted; they are allowed to say their morning prayers and to lay their *tephillin*. At least one of these missionary traps is styled with shame ful affrontery, a BETH HAMEDRESH (house of learning)![108]

Both he and local-born Jew, Henry de Jonge, complained to the House of Commons Select Committee about such baits set by the missionaries to trap the naive.[109] Even the Passover celebration was used to attract the most needy. The *East London Observer* describes a *Pesach Seder* conducted in a mission hall by a Jewish apostate:

> An interesting representation of the ceremony... was given on Wednesday evening (28th March) at St. Mary's Schools by the Rev. Mr Goldenburg — a very zealous and able missionary attached to the Society for the Promotion of Christianity amongst the Jews. The audience, which was a large one, were each of them supplied with the eggs and Passover cake, while on the platform the Rev. Mr Goldenburg and several friends enacted the scenes we have recounted.[110]

The community fought back. Counter-attacks, led by the *Jewish Chronicle*, were mounted from diverse quarters, both Jew and Gentile. Referring to a current article on "Conversion of the

Jews" in the *Church Quarterly Review*, the *Jewish Chronicle* (25 May) concluded that "in nine cases out of ten the anxious inquirer after Christianity is really an anxious seeker (the bulk of these men are poor men) after his own material welfare... It is strange that they have so strong a hankering after the fleshpots of Christianity." Later (3 August) it reinforced evidence that "conversion traps are baited with gold".

> A circular now lies before us making an appeal for £150 a year on behalf of a convert on the grounds that this would enable him to train for Holy Orders, and this "valuable labourer" would then be secured "for the work of the conversion of God's ancient people". So here is one specimen at least of an indifferent Jew... whose lot has not been of bright promise for some years past, clearly made comfortable for the rest of his days by accepting baptism as the condition.

Charles Booth, in his contemporary survey, joined in the chorus of disapproval in the strongest terms. Christian conversionist societies to the Jews "indirectly have a most pauperising effect and would assuredly achieve the utter demoralisation of the Jewish poor if the work they accomplished equalled to any degree the sum of their expenditure". On the whole the exercise was a waste of money. For though "the process of conversion is very simple: bread and lodging at specially provided houses during the inquiry stage, constant charitable assistance after conversion and the free care and maintenance of Jewish children brought up in the Christian faith... the number of converts is infinitesimal." (And, of these, "anxious to turn to some account that newly acquired 'talent' of Christianity, the youthful proselytes set up business on their own account, collecting and spending the subscriptions of zealous Christians".[111]) Booth's conclusions accorded with those of the Rev. S. Singer who, in a letter to the Bishop of Salisbury referring to the Sion College's subscription to a parochial mission to the Jews fund, suggested that the money could be better spent elsewhere "on the eve of what is likely to prove a trying winter to the poor... on a hundred objects more deserving... than the vain attempt to disturb his Jewish fellow citizen".[112] As for the relative cost of converting a Jew, such an evaluation was recorded, with unconscious humour, by the *East London Observer* on 21 July.

Jewish Jottings

In Smalley's *Cost of the Gospel*, it is said, after an exhaustive comparison of the religious work done throughout the world by the various Christian sects, that the following table illustrates very closely the actual outlay required to bring into any one of the reformed churches each one. of the people named:

An African	14$
An Italian	42$
A Spaniard	55$
An East Indian	60$
A Japanese	80$
A Chinese	100$
A *Jew*	2800$

That is, of course, based on the statistics of American Missionary Societies. In England the cost of converting a Jew is very much higher.

Thus it was that the poorest of the tribe of Israel commanded the highest price for his proselytisation.

To protect the immigrant parent and child from the baneful influence of such non-Jewish "ideologies" as Christianity and socialism, the Anglo-Jewish establishment was well aware of the importance of educational control, if possible through denominational schooling. Throughout the year there was a noticeable flurry of activity in that area. In an editorial plea for aid for the great Jews Free School the *Jewish Chronicle* emphasised this point clearly. It defined the aim and direction of a system imposed from above by an anglicised élite:

> The perplexing problem growing out of the presence in our midst of a large number of foreign poor can only be solved by education. To train the parents in the social and intellectual scale is a task in which, at best, only partial success can be hoped for. The children offer a much more promising field of effort. They, at least, can be rescued from the baneful influence which oppression, and some civilised surroundings, have exerted upon their elders, and which, but for our intervention, might easily leave its traces on their own lives. They, at least, may be taught and helped to practise self-reliance and self-restraint; they may be made into good and industrious citizens and a source of positive strength to the body politic. They may be trained to become elements in the future of the communal well-being, instead of being a draw on the material resources of the community and a danger to its stability. The work is clearly

educational; and the Free School does the bulk of it. Of the 3,000 children within its walls the great majority enter it practically foreigners; they leave it potential Englishmen and women, prepared to take their part in the struggle of life in the spirit of English citizens.[113]

Such views were reinforced by Samuel Montagu MP, who in his contribution to the speeches at the annual prize day (17 June), proclaimed that the school was "a pattern institution... to prove to the public that the Jews had regard for the moral and mental improvement of their poorer brethren", but seem not to have been to the taste of one of its young schoolmasters, Israel Zangwill, who together with a colleague had recently handed in his resignation. Apparently his short-story writing extolling, by inference, the Yiddish-based life style of the immigrants had led to a controversy with the school authority. This was revealed in a joint letter to the *Jewish Chronicle* by the two teachers refuting Lord Rothschild's statement at the same prize day that they "had been forced to resign".[114]

A number of appeals were launched for greater support from the community for other Jewish schools in the area. Considering the needs of the Stepney Jewish School at the AGM of the Jewish Board of Guardians in May, "the committee expressed satisfaction at having succeeded in establishing classes at the People's Palace in metalwork and carpentry for boys, and dressmaking for girls, and hope by these means to cause a number of children to enter mechanical trades and become skilled artisans". On 22 December the *East London Advertiser* reported details of a benefit ball held in the Whitehall Rooms of the Hotel Metropole to attain funds in order "to enlarge the (Stepney) school which since it was built in 1871 for 250 children was wholly inadequate for the 650 children now on the school register". In a speech to the officially non-denominational, but predominantly Jewish, Old Castle Street Board School, the Chief Rabbi, ostensibly lauding the influence of education in combating the sweating system, took the opportunity to attack socialist agitators. Through education, he declared, students "were taught a divine discontent with their lot, not that discontent which sought relief in socialism, but the remedy which taught that every man depended on his lot upon his individual efforts".[115]

Other institutions were currently established to entertain or instruct the immigrant during the few leisure hours open to him. Such was the Jewish Working Men's Club, housed in permanent premises since 1874, whose immediate origins lay in providing free lectures and a reading room for local Jews and their families. By 1888 it had developed into a more sophisticated centre, offering concerts (drama and musical) and lectures or debates, on contemporary issues to which men, prominent in public life, were invited as guest speakers.[116] The *East London Advertiser* reported (3 November) that, on the previous Sunday evenings, the club annual swimming contest prizes were distributed by S. Montagu MP who "spoke of the club which has been in existence for 18 years, and now has a membership of 1,300 both male and female". We learn from a letter to the *Jewish Chronicle* (19 October) by L. Kaliski, Hon. Secretary of the "Kadima Association", of an all-purpose Adult Education and Recreational Institute for "foreign brethren", opened in June by the same MP that "100 members... contribute 2d a week and through the generosity of a few committeemen we are just able to clear expenses of rent and gas. Thus, in pursuing our general principles we keep away poor immigrants from mission halls and other allurements offered in the East End of London by the missionaries." For the less discriminating, a more attractive proposition was the Yiddish play performed at the Hebrew Dramatic Club, 3 Princes Street, Spitalfields, and advertised in the Yiddish press. A weekly drama was forecast in the Yiddish radical newspaper the *Arbeter Fraint* which also ventured critical reviews of the plays in the idiom.[117]

The object of all this national attention and community concern for their cultural "uplift" was further plagued by the diverse "popular" characterisations of their qualities or lack of them. Charles Booth, by way of his "objective" investigations, concluded:

> Social isolation has perfected home life; persecution has intensified religious fervour, an existence of unremitting wile, and a rigid observance of the moral precepts and sanitary requirements of the Jewish religion have favoured the growth of sobriety, personal purity and a consequent power of physical endurance.[118]

John Simon, a Liberal for fifty years, responding to an anti-semitic letter published in 7 May issue of the *Pall Mall Gazette*, declared of the incoming Jews:

> Their emaciated, sickly frames are the stamp of their martyrdom. There is a halo of holiness around them which every true Christian must recognise and respect.[119]

What of the effects of all this on the recipients? It was all, perhaps, old hat. Though subjected to a widespread campaign of vilification and confined involuntarily within the awful parameters of the slum and the sweat-shop, the collective experience and tenacious adherence to their ancient culture endowed the Jews with such qualities as inspired hope, even pleasure albeit ephemeral, within a life of adversity. Their religious ethos, with its accompanying sense of personal fulfilment expressed through traditional communal practice within and without their *stieblech*; the weddings and *simchas*;[120] the emotive *barmitzvahs*[121] and the close-knit family concerns; the picaresque Jewish eccentrics who stalked the main streets of the ghetto to exhort, instruct, but always to entertain; the variety of Yiddish radical clubs providing a latitudinarian fare of political doctrine from the platform, and a social rendezvous for the bright young men and women come to escape from patriarchal restraints; for the secular and observant — all these and past historical imperatives would bind them together with indissoluble ties. It was Zangwill, the great chronicler and intimate of his immigrant folk, with his kaleidoscopic exposure of the picturesque nuances of the ghetto, who conveyed with understanding the dogged will to survive which sustained its inhabitants:

> This London ghetto of ours is a region where, amid uncleanliness and squalor, the rose of romance blows yet a little longer in the raw air of English reality; a world which hides beneath its stony and unlovely surface an inner world of dreams, fantastic and poetic as the mirage of the Orient where they were woven, of superstitions grotesque as the cathedral gargoyles of the Dark Ages in which they had birth. And over all lie tenderly some streaks of celestial light shining from the face of the great Lawgiver.
> The folks who compose our pictures are the children of the ghetto. Their faults are bred of its hovering miasma of persecu-

tion, their virtues straitened and intensified by the narrowness of its horizon. And they who have won their way beyond its boundaries must still play their part in tragedies and comedies — tragedies of spiritual struggle, comedies of material ambition — which are the aftermath of its centuries of dominance, the sequel of that long cruel night in Jewry which coincides with the Christian era.

Footnotes

[1] Booth's estimated total was outlined in May 1887 in "The Inhabitants of Tower Hamlets", p.45. The following year Joseph Blank, Secretary to the Jews Temporary Shelter, reported approximately 33,218 Jews residing in Tower Hamlets in his evidence given to the Select Committee on Emigration and Immigration on Friday 6 July 1888, Minute 2699ff. Both explain the methods by which they derived their estimates.

[2] For both general and detailed studies see Lloyd P. Gartner, *The Jewish Immigrant in England 1870-1914,* pp. 15-56 and William J. Fishman, *East End Jewish Radicals 1875-1914* (London, 1975) pt. 1.

[3] Parliamentary Papers issued Tuesday 6 March 1888. See also report in *East End News* 13 March 1888.

[4] *Life and Labour of the People of London*, vol. 1.

[5] See V.D. Lipman, *A Century of Social Service* (London, 1959) pp. 83-4; *Essays on Jewish Life and Thought* presented in honour of Salo. W. Baron (New York, 1959) pp. 244-5. *The Arbeter Fraint* 24 February 1888, informs its readers that the "shoemaker's pallor and stained hands from blacking shoes were occupational labels, like the tailor's stoop". The Board of Guardians estimates are:

Trade	1882	1892
Tailoring	438	926
Boot and Shoe	187	466
Hawkers	257	316
General Dealers	108	151
Tobacco	146	146
Glaziers	118	75
Woodworking	54	160
Total	1,308	2,240
Total occupied	1,588	2,834

[6] The Inhabitants of Tower Hamlets", pp. 47ff

[7] C. Booth, *Life and Labour of the People of London*, pp. 221-5. See also Myer Wilchinski, "History of a Sweater" in *Commonweal* 26 May and 2 June 1888. A general assessment is presented in W.J. Fishman, *East End Jewish Radicals*, pp. 42-54. Beatrice Webb's article "Pages from A Working Girl's Diary" in *The Nineteenth Century* XXIV, no. 139, pp. 301-14 reveals an impressionistic and somewhat jaundiced description of a Jewish workshop in which she spent two days as a learner.

[8] Report of Select Committee on Emigration and Immigration (Foreigners) House of Commons, 1888 (26th March to 27th July). Minutes 678, 805 and 832.
[9] Ibid., Minutes 2121, 2136.
[10] V.D. Lipman, *A Century of Social Service*, table 1: Main Operations of the Board of Guardians, pp. 278-81.
[11] Minutes 2968, 2969, and 2993.
[12] *ELO* 16 June 1888. The tragedy was also reported with fuller comments in the *Arbeter Fraint* 5 May and the *Commonweal* 12 June 1888.
[13] *JC* 25 February 1887, "The Labour Test".
[14] *ELO* 25 February 1888.
[15] For the refutation of White's figures see *JC* 2 and 16 March. Minutes 450-468 of the House of Commons Select Committee show that, contrary to White, they found that "the foreigner was no additional burden on workhouse or relief except for medical aid", but added "whilst it is possible that local pauperism may be more or less augmented by the crowding out of English labour".
[16] *JC* 7 January 1887, "East London Items".
[17] *JC* 30 November 1888.
[18] *ELO* 7 January 1888.
[19] *JC* 6 January 1888. The previous year the Rev. R. Harris of the Visitation Group reporting to the Chief Rabbi brought up the subject of boys found hawking newspapers and matches in the street and "mentioned that he had recently visited three of these boys in Milbank Prison. They had drifted into crime on account of their being continually about the streets" (*JC* 8 April 1887).
[20] *ELO* 3 March 1888, "The Israelite Marriage Portion Society".
[21] *JC* 6 January 1888.
[22] *JC* 29 June 1888, "The Immigrants Committee" (meeting of 22 June.)
[23] *JC* 20 January 1888.
[24] *JC* 1 June 1888, "Sandys Row AGM Meeting 27.5.1888".
[25] A suggestion for all poor families revived in 1984 by a prominent member of the Thatcher government's "think tank". In a *Guardian* article, Sir Alfred Sherman purported to demonstrate its "viability", within the reborn theology of the free market, in alleviating the costs of poverty!
[26] *JC* 23 November 1888.
[27] See V.D. Lipman, *A Century of Social Service*, Appendix 1, pp. 249-250.
[28] *JC* 21 December 1888.
[29] *Life and Labour of the People of London*, vol. 1, p. 574.
[30] *Poilishe Yidl*, no. 8, 12 September 1884, "The Sad Tale of the *Greener* in London".
[31] Report from Select Committee of Emigration and Immigration (Foreigners) 1888, Minute 2966.
[32] Ibid., Minute 2067.
[33] See above, Chapter 2.
[34] Reported in "The Immigrant Question" (*JC* 3 February 1888) and "Artisans' Dwellings in Spitalfields and Whitechapel" (*JC* 19 October

1888).
[35]See Jerry White, *Rothschild Buildings*, ch. 1, pp. 1-30.
[36]*JC* 2 November 1888.
[37]*ELA* 20 October 1888.
[38]*Spectator* 23 April 1887, quoted above, p. 134.
[39]Lloyd P. Gartner, *The Jewish Immigrant in England*, pp. 158-62.
[40]Report from Select Committee on Emigration and Immigration (Foreigners) 1888, Minute 1392.
[41]*JC* 26 October 1888.
[42]Reported in the *JC* 26 February 1888.
[43]*The Times* 13 July 1887.
[44]*The Times* 30 November 1887.
[45]Letter to Lord Salisbury, 9 November 1887 (Salisbury Papers, Class E).
[46]An excellent account and analysis of the Lipski trial is presented in Martin L. Friedland, *The Trials of Israel Lipski* (London, 1984).
[47]For detailed information on anti-Jewish decrees activated by the Russian government see *JC* 17 February, 20 April, 4 May, 27 July and 10 August 1888.
[48]*East End News* 21 February 1888.
[49]*JC* 3 February 1888.
[50]John A. Garrard, *The English and Immigration, 1880-1910* (Oxford, 1971) p. 27.
[51]*ELO* 18 February 1888, editorial.
[52]*Commonweal* 21 April 1888, "The Sweating System".
[53]*JC* 11 May 1888, "The Stage Effects on the Immigration Committee", and *JC* 8 June 1888, exposing two fake witnesses.
[54]Report of the Select Committee on Emigration and Immigration (Foreigners), 1888, Minutes 1367-1730 dated 8 May.
[55]Ibid., Minutes 1607-1847 dated 5 June, and Minutes 1899, 1909, 1910 dated 15 June.
[56]Ibid., Minutes 2483-2662.
[57]Ibid., Minutes 1101, 1102, 1223, 1228-1239, 1273, 1305-1306.
[58]Ibid., Minutes 2839, 2849, 2852, 2891, 2892, 2945, 2946, 2952, 2956, 2960, 3019.
[59]*ELO* 23 June 1888, "The Sweating System."
[60]On 18 January 1887 a late stage show of the Hurvitz operetta *Gypsy Princess* at the Yiddish theatre in Princes Street attracted a packed audience. There was a cry of "Fire!" from the gallery (later proved to be a false alarm) which led to a mad rush to the exit. During the stampede 17 people were crushed to death, including 12 women and four children.
[61]*JC* 18 February, "Notes of the Week". A postscript to the Spitalfields tragedy.
[62]*JC* 18 March 1887.
[63]See Martin L. Friedland, *The Trials of Israel Lipski*, pp. 195-9.
[64]*ELO* 14 January 1888.
[65]*JC* 17 February 1888.
[66]*JC* 13 April 1888.
[67]*JC* 25 May 1888.

[68] Report of the Select Committee on Emigration and Immigration (Foreigners), Minute 3509.
[69] *JC* 22 June and *ELO* 23 June.
[70] *JC* 27 July 1888.
[71] *JC* 24 August 1888.
[72] *JC* 28 September 1888.
[73] *JC* 5 October 1888.
[74] *ELA* 23 June 1888.
[75] *East End News* 14 September; see also *JC* 14 September editorial.
[76] See *JC* 22 and 29 June for reports on both speeches.
[77] *Canon Barnett*, vol. 2, p. 310.
[78] *In Darkest London*, pp. 109-10 and 275.
[79] *Out of Work*, pp. 63, 64 and 77.
[80] *Commonweal* 24 January 1888.
[81] *Commonweal* 5 May 1888. Such banal rhetoric appears to be in accord with the legacy of racism which has infected parts of Bethnal Green, also reflected in the local support for Mosleyite Fascism in the 1930s and the National Front in the 1970s.
[82] *ELO* 14 July 1888, "Police Intelligence: Butting a Woman".
[83] See *ELA* particularly 16 June (Rambler), 30 June and 8 September (Here and There).
[84] *The Nineteenth Century* XXIV, July-December 1888, "East London Labour" by B. Potter, pp. 161-84 (August 1888). See p. 161 and pp. 176-7 for her definitions of the characteristics of the foreign Jews.
[85] "The Inhabitants of the Tower Hamlets", pp. 47-50 and *Life and Labour*, vol 1, pp. 78-90. In the latter on pp. 589-90, the Whitechapel Jew figures as Ricardo's Economic Man, tainted with "an always enlightened selfishness, seeking employment or profit with an absolute mobility of body and mind, without pride, without preference, without interest outside the struggle for existence and welfare of the individual and the family."
[86] Report of the Select Committee on Emigration and Immigration, Minutes 2193-2204.
[87] *ELO* 23 June 1888, "Foreign Jews in London".
[88] *In Darkest London*, pp. 205-6. Harkness is prone to the usual generalisations about Jews aspiring to riches, etc. Only a few made it to the West End at that time, nor did the Board of Guardians squander its charity indiscriminately!
[89] *London Rookeries and Colliers Slums*, p. 56.
[90] For details of the formation of the Temporary Shelter into a permanent institution see my *East End Jewish Radicals* 1875-1914, p. 40.
[91] Report of the Select Committee on Emigration and Immigration, Minute 1782.
[92] Ibid., Minute 2153.
[93] Ibid., Minutes 2177-2178.
[94] Ibid., Minute 2176.
[95] Ibid., Minutes 2176-2180.
[96] *JC* 20 January and 25 June.

[97] Report of the Select Committee on Emigration and Immigration, Minutes 2186 and 2190.
[98] *JC* 29 June, "Poor Jews Temporary Shelter" Sunday 24 June meeting.
[99] Report of the Select Committee on Emigration and Immigration, Minutes 2713, 2721, 2741, 2742, 2747, 2749, 2780, 2781.
[100] *JC* 30 November.
[101] Charles Booth, *Life and Labour*, vol. 1, pp. 572-3.
[102] Ibid., pp: 567-70.
[103] Joseph E. Blank, *The Minutes of the Federation of Synagogues: a twenty-five years' review* (London 1912), p. 14.
[104] Ibid., see pp. 14-16 for its development and appointment of Minister.
[105] *JC* 29 June.
[106] *JC* 16 November. It was clear that the Chief Rabbi was worried about the possible wider effects of the activities of the East End immigrant radicals. See below, pp. 280-1.
[107] *JC* 28 December.
[108] See Landau's reports to the Jewish Temporary Shelter Committee in *JC* 6 May 1887. It was here that he turned Arnold White's arguments against him. Landau posed the evidence that it was the missions that offered greater centres of attraction to pauper foreigners than the temporary shelter, and suggested that "if means could be adopted whereby the enormous income of the Missionary Societies could be directed into more useful and deserving channels the immigration of foreign Jews would perceptibly diminish... Mr Arnold White might, profitably for Jew and Christian, look up the ways of these missionary tricksters." This was in effect reiterated in his report to the same Committee in January 1888 (*JC* 20 January 1888).
[109] Report of the Select Committee on Emigration and Immigration, Minutes 1160, 2210.
[110] *ELO* 31 March, "A Note on Missionary Tactics".
[111] Charles Booth, *Life and Labour*, vol. 1, pp. 574-5. He refers also to the "magnificent premises" of the mission at Palestine Place, Bethnal Green, which provided a chapel, Hebrew missionary training institute and a Hebrew operative home. But during the year 1887-88 he noted that only "12 Jews were baptised in its Chapel; 40 children (more than 50% of whom were children of Christian mothers) maintained in the school, and 12 converts supported in the operative home". In all a poor return for the mission's spiritual and material outlay.
[112] *JC* 9 November.
[113] *JC* 20 April.
[114] The joint letter with the request for a public apology by Lord Rothschild was published in *JC* 22 June.
[115] *JC* 20 April.
[116] See Harold Pollins, *A History of the Jewish Working Men's Club and Institute* 1874-1912, Ruskin College Library Occasional Publication, no. 2, 1981.
[117] We read in the *Arbeter Fraint*, vol. 111 (1888), lists of forthcoming Yiddish plays at the Hebrew Dramatic Club eg Sunday 8 January "Shulamith", and 14 and 15 January, the popular historical play

"Mechiros Joseph", followed by "Deborah" on 18 January. Weekly notices continue throughout the year.
[118]*Life and Labour*, vol. 1, p. 579.
[119]Letter in *JC* 11 May 1888.
[120]Traditional happy occasions such as family parties to celebrate eg engagements, family successes or honours.
[121]Religious and family celebration which takes place when the boy of the household reaches manhood, ie 13 years of age according to Jewish law.
[122]Israel Zangwill, *Children of the Ghetto* (London, 1892) "Proem" p. l.

Chapter 7
Crime and Punishment

Heredity and the surroundings of the individual are the great cause of social failure; as regards an outburst of criminal display from local causes, some advantage may result from dispersing these centres of population, and building suitable tenement buildings.

Much more may probably be done by altering the surroundings specially in the case of children.

Careless views of the value of human life tend to moral degradation and the prevalence of crime.

Deaths from preventable causes and from infectious diseases similarly tend to lessen the public value of lives. On the other hand improved surroundings, social clubs, recreative evening classes, and the like visible expressions and endeavour to improve humanity, assist in enlarging the subject of thought and cultivating the brains of labouring people, and will produce good effects in the next generation.

"Neglected Population and the Growth of Crime"
British Medical Journal
29 September 1888

We must also remember that this has been a time of sharp distress, and that it is quite evident from the unconsidered trifles that are stolen that the thefts in many cases are not the handiwork of professional thieves but are the deeds of starving men. As long as society can offer no relief to the poor man but the workhouse, who can be surprised if he prefers to relieve himself.

Commonweal
20 October 1888

...for what can be more appalling than the thought that there is a being in human shape stealthily moving about a great city, burning with the thirst for human blood, and endowed with such diabolic astuteness, as to enable him to gratify his fiendish lust with absolute impunity.

East London Advertiser
6 October 1888

Crime and East London have a legendary connection. In an area of continuous deprivation it was evident that such activity provided one means of survival. At climactic periods of economic recession and social discontent the pressure gauge containing suppressed violence was ready to burst. By 1888 it had. In that year the East End was defined as an area plagued with all the sophisticated techniques to deprive illegally the more affluent of their surpluses. This could be expected in a place traditionally peopled by low-income groups, where unemployment and housing shortages were, apparently, insoluble problems. Thus in many families crime was an hereditary way of life. The smug Victorian preachings on the virtues of *laisser-faire* and constant exhortation to self-help were not lost on them. For their grim pursuit of a ruthless appropriation of other people's property is still the credo of a minority of East Enders, nursed in the tradition of crime, who likewise satisfy their own acquisitive urges in a free competitive market!

Yet, that year, the eleventh report of the Commissioners of Prisons records an overall decrease in crime in the metropolis. By November, the ill-fated Commissioner of Police, Sir Charles Warren, was boasting that "London is the safest capital in the world for life and property". Considering his own ineffectual attempts to trap the Whitechapel Ripper, it was a curious statement to make, although he was honest enough to suggest that this was not due "to the superhuman skill of (his) detective department", but rather to the "religious and philanthropic agencies at work" such as "the City Mission, which has been working so hard, and so successfully, especially in the East End of London and against the low-class houses in that district".[1] His pin-pointing of the dangers emanating from the common lodging house was certainly viable. By 6 October the *East London Advertiser* had given a strong endorsement.

> Mr Montagu Williams has done well to call public attention to the infamous conditions under which "common lodging houses" are allowed to exist... the haunts of robber's homes, of pickpockets and hotbeds of prostitution.
> No surveillance is exercised, and a woman is at perfect liberty to bring any companion she likes to share her accommodation... If loose women be prevented from frequenting "common lodging houses", their companions the thieves, burglars and murderers of London would speedily give up resorting to them.[2]

Contemporary advocates of the "flogging" school as crime-preventive were unusually vociferous. In a surprisingly "liberal" article, the *East London Advertiser* scorned such "moral medicine":

Mr Howard Livesay... in a long letter to *The Times*... generously lays his prescription before the world. It consists of the universal application of the birch rod. We are all to be made good by whipping; the nostrum of the nursery is to be applied to adult humanity, and all crime will disappear as if by magic.

It is unfortunate, however, that this specific should be (the) thought of the age. Men have come to feel that corporal punishment, except under exceptional circumstances, degrades and hardens those who are subjected to it.

But perhaps we are all wrong and Mr Livesay will be handed down to posterity as the moral regenerator of his day. There is only one drawback to the system; the habitual criminal will become so accustomed to his punishment that it will cease to have any effect upon him. We allude to what is known in medical parlance as the thickening of the epidermis. Then, indeed, will the expression "hardened sinner" be no longer a mere figure of speech.[3]

However, Mr Livesay's remedy would be to the taste of the local magistrate. A description of the magistrate presiding at the Thames Police Court, who dealt out firm retribution to East End offenders, is given by Margaret Harkness: a portrait of a "beak" in the Dickensian mould. (One suspects that it was the infamous Mr Saunders, the hammer of vagrants and foreigners!) She questions, "Why are London magistrates allowed to sit on the bench until they grow blind, deaf and otherwise incapacitated?" and goes on to set the scene:

> The Magistrate who sat on the bench that morning had snow-white hair, a beaked nose, an irascible voice; his smile might have been described as benevolent, but his lips were firmly set, and he did not relax his features more than once in thirty minutes; a fixed scowl was on his face, and he had an unpleasant way of asking abrupt questions when a witness became at all prolix. This upset the gentler sex, and confused their utterance. The men did not appear to be afraid of him; but the women seemed to feel that tears were useless, and as they had come provided with pocket handkerchiefs, he made them stammer, blush and fidget with their "bits of calico". Possibly these women were the cause of his irascibility; for if there is a sight on earth prone to move a man to wrath, it is an East End woman in the witness box. The female witness has not changed her character since the days of the famous Mrs Cluppins; she still enters into a dissertation on her domestic affairs, and informs the court about the decease of her late beloved, the illness of her last baby, and the wickedness of people in general. It is impossible to make her stick to business...
>
> "Be quiet!" roars the magistrate.

Harkness suggests that the antics of these ancient dispensers of the law are a travesty of justice. "They can merely hear what goes on through clerks and solicitors, and this seems to make them irritable. Occasionally a feeble joke on the part of some limb of the bar puts them in good temper, and then the prisoners get easy sentences; but deaf magistrates are the curse of police-courts."[4]

There were gradations of crime ranging from the petty and non-violent to the extreme of compulsive homicide. One of the most widespread and despised practices among shopkeepers and publicans was the incidence of food adulteration. Milk was commonly prone to this. There were innumerable cases of such offences brought to court. This was endorsed in reports of the Medical Officer of Health of Poplar (annual report ended 1887), the St. George's-in-the-East Vestry (1 April 1888), the Whitechapel Board of Works (16 April 1888) and Mile End Old Town Vestry (26 April 1888). Fines inflicted varied from £8 to 1s. Other items found diluted included bread, flour, sugar, butter, oatmeal, coffee and cocoa, ie those items constituting the necessities of life for the poorest. Even their only "luxury", beer, was widely tampered with.[5] The radical *Labour Tribune*, quoted by *Commonweal*, summed it up in a popular ditty:

> Little drops of water added to the milk
> Make the milkman's daughter clothe herself in silk.
> Little grains of sand in the sugar mixed
> Make the grocery man soon become well fixed.
> Little acts of meanness, little tricks of trade,
> All these pass for keenness, fortunes thus are made.[6]

As a legendary haven for the transient and feckless, vagrancy and begging in the streets were part of the landscape. The preceding lean years had added substantial recruits to the army of homeless who descended on the peripheries of the city. The colder months registered a plethora of arrests and punishments meted out for such offences. A police round-up in early March led to the sentencing of at least one habitual beggar to 14 days' hard labour.[7] Later that month a J. Lucas, aged 33, charged with being drunk (he had been caught singing and dancing to the public's delight along Watney Street!), but, worse still, with habitual begging, was hauled in front of the beak at Thames Police Court. He was promptly sentenced to one month's hard labour.[8] On 26 May the *East London Observer* reported under "An English Crime":

> James Field, 35, John Park, 21, and Frederick Scott, 19, were charged with being found sleeping in the open air. All the men were wretchedly attired and appeared to have been roughing it for a considerable time. About half past three on Tuesday morning (May 22nd) a constable heard a noise of snoring in one of the arches in Frederick Street, St. George's. He then found the prisoners asleep. No money was found on either of the men.

These were fortunate. After being "very properly taken into custody" they were discharged. The police were adept at catching *gregors* (beggars). The latter often employed their own children as decoys to extract alms. (Few among the less impoverished East End folk would resist the piteous sight of a ragged and hungry child pleading for money for food.) It was a profitable ploy until the police moved in. Again, from a clutch of cases the *East London Observer* of 10 March selects one in which a father and child were jointly charged:

> John Bailey, 45, and Alfred Bailey, 5, were charged with begging. Mr Saunders sentenced John Bailey to seven days' imprisonment, and ordered the child to be sent to the workhouse.

The magistrate, the formidable Mr Saunders, showed what was, for him, an uncharacteristic concern for a child. "It is perfectly absurd to charge a child of 5 years of age with begging, because he happened to be in the arms of his father!" For the respectable homeless and unemployed the alternatives for survival were strictly limited. For some the ultimate was "steal or ring the workhouse bell!" — that is, if caught, better the warm cell than the cold Bastille. One such case, brought up in February, exemplified a similar preference.

> After being refused entry into four casual wards — the Borough, Whitechapel, Mile End and South Grove — William Hyde applied to the police sergeant who directed him to the Workhouse, but preferring prison, Hyde threw a stone at a public house window. At Thames Police Court he said he was starving and had to do something.

Hyde was lucky enough to be heard by a more humane magistrate. He was discharged.[9]

The quick hand as the short cut to easy money, such as gambling, was a local vice that cut across class and ethnic bounds. "pitch and toss" in the open brought swift retribution. In April "12 men accused of playing 'public toss' with bronze coins, difficult to catch since outposts were posted to warn the approach of police" were seized by a police posse. Their being caught illegally playing on Sunday enhanced the crime, and magistrate Saunders imposed stiff fines varying from 1s to 5s.[10]

Exploiting the gullibility of a susceptible folk, eager to receive the message of future good tidings that would free them from present misery, was a common predator — the fortune teller. They were dealt with severely. The *East London Advertiser* (3 November) records a typical case:

> Sarah Tanner, a middle-aged woman of Rowsell Street, St. Paul's Road, Mile End Old Town, was charged with obtaining money by pretending to tell persons their fortune. She told the future to a girl for a charge of 6d. The police were notified, and on apprehending her she said she would not do it again. The police found a leaf out of "Napoleon's Book of Fate" and two packs of cards. Mr Lushington sentenced the prisoner to one month's imprisonment with hard labour.

A busy craftsman was the counterfeiter, with his aide the *smasher* (passer of false money), although this turned out to be a precarious occupation. There was always a *nose* (informer) around, and rare is the tale of coiner escaping justice. It was often a family occupation; one husband and wife operating from Limehouse were virtually caught in the act.

A Smasher's Stock in Trade

> Agnes Smith, 33, was charged on remand, with uttering four base coins — three pennies and a halfpenny — with intent to fraud, and with having in her possession two counterfeit pennies; and William Smith, 46, of Dakon Street, Limehouse, her husband, was charged with having in his possession a die punch, a pair of shears, soldering iron, a knife, mug containing spirits of salts, a quantity of silver, sheet of tin, quantity of thin lead, and a quantity of copper, for the purpose of making base coin.
> Committed for trial.[11]

Lowest in the East End criminal's esteem was the practitioner of *kinchin lay* — stealing from children. Young lads, delivering or collecting laundry for their mothers whose only income might be derived from "taking in washing", were waylaid in the street, the linen seized and exchanged at a pawnbroker. In one case the offender was the prosecutor's own grandmother:

> Sarah Bolton, an elderly woman, was charged with stealing a bundle of mangling from Henry Webb of Griggs Court, Stepney. On Friday 9th (March), the prosecutor, who is a cripple, was sent to a Mr Pinkers for some mangling which he received, and while he was walking through Tenter buildings, the prisoner, who is his grandmother, took the bundle from him, and told him to wait until she brought a basket of mangling back. He did so, but she never returned, and he communicated with the police.
>
> Mr Saunders remanded the prisoner for a week to see if the clothes could be traced.[12]

Depriving children of their boots, a highly saleable commodity, could also fetch a pretty penny at the pawnbroker's. This provided a regular source of income for one offender until the police caught up with her. The *East London Advertiser* gave a detailed account of the mode and extent of her operations, a typical example of this crime.

> Ellen Driscoll was charged with stealing boots from different children in the public streets. Rose Burgess said: "I live at 53 Spencer Street, St. George's. On Thursday afternoon about a quarter to two, my little boy, Henry Burgess aged 4 years, left to go to school, and I next saw him at Leman Street Station without his boots. I don't know the prisoner." Anna Norman of 132 Cannon Street Road, said: "On Saturday week I sent my little girl aged 4 years out on an errand and she was brought home at 8 o'clock without any boots. On Thursday last I saw the prisoner in Batty Street with the child Henry Burgess, who had no boots on. I watched her go through a court, and I lost sight of her."
>
> Charles Cooper, manager to a pawnbroker in Cable Street said: "On Thursday last the prisoner brought in a pair of boots, and I asked her who they belonged to, to which she replied, 'A neighbour', who had asked her to pledge the boots. I, however, detained her until a constable arrived, when I gave her into custody."
>
> Morris Cohen, a tailor of 14 Broomhead Street, said: "I lost a pair of boots on Tuesday from the feet of my little boy aged two years. Between 2 and 3 o'clock I saw him wearing the boots, and I next saw him at half past nine o'clock at the station without his

boots. The pair of boots produced by the pawnbroker were his property."

Inspector Brady of the CID said that was as far as they proposed to go today...

Further evidence had already revealed that the prisoner had previously served 6 months' hard labour for stealing 14 pairs of boots from children in the street. She was therefore committed for trial in the high court.[13]

The age-old practice of purse-snatching was being challenged by "shootflying", ie watch-chain snatching. This was generally carried out on the run or by depriving the victim of his watch and chain under threats of violence. It could prove lucrative. A gold Albert chain seized from a surgeon in his Whitechapel pharmacy was valued at £5. Another with a 20$ piece attached, an attempted snatch from a Whitechapel tailor, was worth £7 16s. Even a silver watch and chain could fetch £2. A successful operation could therefore provide good pickings for thief and fence alike; it was a popular pursuit among local *gonophs* (minor thieves). Such cases were brought before the Thames Police Court with tedious regularity; with the inevitable sentence of three months' hard labour being inflicted on the offender.[14]

The narrow, dim-lit courts and alleyways leading from the Thames to the main thoroughfares were the natural haunts of such predators as the waterside *crimps* and *sharks* on the prowl. Woe to the unwary stranger venturing alone south of the Commercial Road towards the docks. Seamen were a natural target for the local whores. The game was to lure them into a brothel. (Devonshire Street, St. George's seems to have been a major haunt of these women, for many of those who were arrested gave an address there.) The evidence of the hilarious capers that the women and their unwitting dupes got up to was lost on the solemnity of the court. Two examples among many illustrate the perverse humour conveyed by recounting such escapades. This may have unconsciously affected the lugubrious Saunders, for it led to some glaring inconsistencies in his sentencing.

Robbing a Sailor in a Brothel

Mary Ann Regan, 39, Alice Crawley, 28, and Mary Ann Shea, 38, were charged with being concerned in stealing a jacket, scarf and knife, value 35s belonging to Henry Bloom, seaman, staying at the Sailors Home, Well Street, Whitechapel. The prosecutor said that on Saturday night at 11.30 he met the prisoner Shea, and accompanied her to a house at No. 3 Angel Court, Shadwell. Regan appeared and said she was the "missis" and he would have to pay 2s for the room. He did so and went into the room with Shea. Witness paid the latter 2s 6d and took off his coat. About 10 minutes later Shea left the room, and as he heard a man's voice he was scared and stayed upstairs. Crawley then came up and wanted him to go to bed with her, but he refused, and she went away. Witness was in bed alone and when he awoke the next morning he missed his coat and its contents. He went downstairs and saw an old woman whom he asked for his coat, but she denied having it. He then gave information to the constable — Constable 346H said that on Sunday morning the prosecutor told him something, and while they were talking Crawley came along. Prosecutor gave her into custody, when she said she knew nothing of the coat. The other prisoners came to the station and were charged. Regan had the coat under her shawl.

Mr Saunders said there was no case against the prisoners and discharged them!

That same day he tried a Julia M'Cartin of no fixed abode for stealing 11s from the vest pocket of a Mr Louis Barrett, a boot and shoe maker of Wolsey Street, Stepney. It was almost an identical case to the sailor's, "and the constable who apprehended her said she frequented the company of women infesting the neighbourhood who were known as trippers up and waylaid drunken men and robbed them". M'Cartin got short shrift. Saunders sentenced her to 6 weeks' imprisonment with hard labour. One month later a similar prosecution evokes a scene from a comic farce:

> Kate Turner, 28, and Kate Anderson, 28, charged on remand with stealing a watch and chain and cardigan jacket value £2 8s, a £5 bank note, and 6 sovereigns from William Lander, a seaman. About midday Sunday (April 22nd) accosted by the two women in Ratcliff Highway, he accompanied them to a hat shop, and, sent into an upstairs room, took off his coat, cardigan jacket, in which were his watch and chain, and went to bed with Turner. He was very tired and went to sleep (?) When he woke, two hours later, he found Anderson in bed with him and the other prisoner gone.
>
> Lander got up and then missed his cardigan jacket, watch and chain, and the bank note and sovereigns from his trousers pockets... Turner was eventually committed for trial.[16]

Women were not the only villains in on the act. Male *mutchers* were naturally more adept in avoiding arrest. But in April, one John Wheeler, aged 39, was actually caught by a policeman while in the process of relieving a drunken sailor of his money in a dark recess of a hoarding in Nightingale Lane, Wapping. (This narrow lane leading to the Thames, was, until the 1930s, reputed to be a major crime alleyway. Normally no one, policeman or otherwise, dared venture there alone!) He was summarily committed for trial in a higher court.

Minor nuisances, short of criminal intent, were widely manifest. The devil found work for idle hands along the Bow Road on Sundays. This was the infamous "Monkey Parade", when gangs of young lads, aged between 15 and 20, marched up and down the main highway between Grove Road and Bow Church molesting passers-by, especially young women on their way to Sunday Service. Early spring brought the louts out in force, and their pranks were enumerated in court; such as "pushing respectable people off the pavement". "Some of them had lamp black on their hands which they placed on young girls' faces, whilst others whitened their hands and clapped girls on their backs." Magistrate Saunders was not amused. He dealt out retribution accordingly, with fines ranging from 2s to 10s per offender according to age, and threatened prison without the option of a fine if the nuisance persisted. But, in spite of his declaration of intent, the Monkey Parade went on unabated throughout the year. One perceptive correspondent put the blame squarely on the style and content of church services that repelled modern youth (his recipe for keeping the young off the streets strikes a perennial note):

> Moroseness and seriousness may do very well for older folks, but until the church is able to introduce something gay, sprightly and laughter-making, it is foolish to expect any radical improvement in Bow Road... The only hope, seems to me, to be in the opening up of our schools, halls and churches, and providing in them, free of cost, things pleasant, instructive and amusing. Anything like laboured attempts at lecturing and sermonising ought to be discarded, and, as music is always appreciated, it ought to be judiciously seasoned, secular and sacred... I am not going to believe that the young men are worse than at any other time, and I see in the rowdyism on the "Parade" the pent-up reaction that comes because no other place can be had, and no inducement for anything else to do.[17]

Considering the over-concentration of music halls in the area, one non-violent form of protection racket was alive and doing well that year chirruping. A rare and amusing description of how the villains operated is given in the *East London Advertiser* (10 March):

> To extract money from music hall artistes beforehand under the threat that unless a bribe be paid the *chirruper* will interrupt the performance. A case in front of the Lambeth Police Court in which the *chirruper*, the head of a large gang which makes a habit of hanging around music halls "when a well-known artiste was about to enter by the stage door he was accosted by one of the band, and told that unless he paid 'blackmail' his performance would be interrupted; but that if, on the other hand, he consented to part with a portion of his fee beforehand roars of applause would reward his efforts to amuse." The merry game had gone on for some time with great benefit to the *chirrupers*, but at last the police got wind of it, and took prompt measures to suppress the practice, which the police magistrates rightly designated as a very shameful one.
>
> We hardly think that *chirruping* is of native growth; it has been practised in Paris from time immemorial by bands of youths known as *siffleurs* and *claquers* and has probably been imported with many other Parisian fashions in England. It is very hard on music hall singers who, except the stars, are not a well-paid class; and it must make Mozart and Handel, not to mention Bach, turn in their graves at the thought that some exquisite combination of musical genius and lyric beauty — like "Two Lovely Black Eyes" for instance — might have been lost to posterity by the sacrilegious disapproval of an unpaid body of *chirrupers*.

The romantic illusions of East End "low-class" life attracted the permanent involvement of a number of off-beat upper-class eccentrics, who essayed to go "native". Such adventures invariably ended in disaster; and Tower Hamlets was often the terminal point in the careers of those déclassés come down in the world through drink and crime. One widely publicised case was that of a Thomas Demalynes, aged 62, a miserably clad man, occupation given as ex-surgeon, of no fixed abode, charged with obtaining under false pretences charitable contributions to the amount of 2s 6d from the Rev. Edward Matthews, Secretary of the British and Foreign Sailors Society, Mercer Street, St. George's. It transpired that he was a "fallen" surgeon who had embarked on a career of fraudulent deception in India. There he had been in turn artilleryman (court-martialled and imprisoned for theft); fakir or religious mendicant; policeman (dismissed for drunkenness); apothecary and assistant in several druggist shops; arrested for forgery and acquitted. In 1882 he returned to England and ended up as a wandering *dosser* in the East End. The magistrate sentenced him to two months' hard labour.[18]

An unusual assault by a crazed suitor brought an unexpected touch of humour to the pen of the editor of the *East London Advertiser*:

Love's Artillery
Mr Frederick Tott has been hauled before the Police Court for persecuting a lady. To demonstrate his love, his plan consisted of throwing weights through the dining-room window of the lady. He has, however, grasped one of the fundamental principles of amorous or warlike attack, which is that the last assault should be always more vigorous than the preceding one. He commenced with a 4lb weight and on the next occasion sent a 14lb weight crashing into the room where the family were sitting at luncheon. This is indeed a novel form of "love's artillery" and calculated to bring a mantling blush to the brow of the most brazened fair, especially if one of these modern specimens of cupid's darts speeds true to its mark and comes in contact with the face of the lady... In the present instance, however, there is some reason for supposing that hate and not love was the motive force which nerved Mr Tott's arm. He gave, as an excuse, that he suffered from "electricity to the head!"... A solution, however, is to hand. When Mr Tott was asked what he had to say, he replied that he didn't think that other people were right in their minds. It is obvious, therefore, that according to popular theory he must himself be mad. Like government of the people, madness is only a question of the majority. If mad people preponderated, the sane portion of the world would be all committed to lunatic asylums. In the meantime the game is with us, and we imagine it is about time that Mr Tott should be shut up literally as well as metaphorically![19]

The workhouses contributed their own quota of law breakers. Recalcitrant paupers were dealt with severely by magistrates. In February seven able-bodied young men aged between 18 and 20, inmates of the casual ward of St. George's Workhouse, were charged with disorderly conduct, namely shouting and using filthy language. As they refused to stop, the labour master gave them into custody. Saunders sentenced them each to 14 days' hard labour.[20] An inmate of the same workhouse, William Sterling, aged 32, was charged with neglecting to perform his allotted work task. On 10 March after a spell of illness in the infirmary, he was discharged as fit to return to the backbreaking labour of picking oakum. The charge reads: "On Monday he was given 3lbs of oakum to pick, but he only picked 1¾lbs. On Tuesday he only picked ¾lbs of oakum and was then given into custody." It could well have been that he had erroneously been diagnosed as fit for work, but this cut no ice in court. The penalty — seven days' hard labour![21] Given the conditions within for the able-bodied, it was no wonder that absconding from the Bastille was a daily exercise. "Dropping over the workhouse wall" in front of sympathetic outsiders, escapers were often helped by locals to evade their pursuers. If caught, they could expect no mercy. A minimum of 7 days' hard labour and a forced return to the House was the norm for the first offence. A pauper, accused of being consistently idle, could anticipate the same treatment. In one case, William Johns, a 60-year-old, was charged with refractory conduct in that he refused to perform work allotted to him in the bakery of the South Grove Workhouse. This prematurely worn-out inmate was sentenced to one month's hard labour.[22] From the casual wards there were cases of overnight or short-term entrants destroying their own clothing and thereby compelling the Guardians to replace them from workhouse stocks. In two instances involving the St. George's-in-the-East Ward, two men explained that the place they slept in was filthy and that there was no means available for them to disinfect their clothes. Both were sentenced to 7 days' hard labour. An even less fortunate pauper, tried for a similar performance at the Mile End Workhouse, offered the same plea before the unbending Saunders, who promptly sentenced him to 21 days' hard labour![23]

As though frozen in time, Harkness presents a scene in the Lower Thames Police Court of a woman and her baby just released from the Union to find her old bedstead distrained by her landlady in lieu of arrears of rent.

> "I've just come out of the Union", the complainant said, taking the pauper's cap off the baby in her arms, "and I thought I'd pawn the bedstead to get along. I'll pay her the rent, and the bed's mine, and you can't take away my bedstead; it's all I've got in the world, your worship. My husband left me after this blessed infant was born, and we've both been in the Union. I must have my bedstead."

You can't have it," the magistrate said. "It's distrained for rent."

She was hauled down by two policemen, who hustled her out of court. A minutes later screams were heard in the adjoining passage, and she was led back again, followed by the landlady whose face was bleeding. "She fell on her like a tiger, your worship," said one of the policemen. "She wasn't outside before she flew at the other woman, and if I hadn't been close she'd have dropped the infant."

"I shall send you to prison for two days for contempt of court," growled the magistrate. "You're an incorrigible woman..."

"That's just what I wanted," said the prisoner, wiping away her tears. "I'm much obliged your worship, now I'll get something to eat."

The author, obviously well-cognisant of the ways of such women, presages a gloomy future for both:

> She followed the policemen to the cells, carrying the baby in its pauper dress. It slept soundly, for its mother had pawned an old shawl to buy drink, and she had drugged it. Its white, sickly face contrasted strangely with the red cheeks of its angry parent. She wore a short, ragged dress, and a hat adorned with a gaudy feather. The expression on her face was both angry and defiant, for much of her life had been spent in fierce feuds with landladies, and she did not like to be "worsted". In the cell she would go to sleep, and when released she would travel on from casual ward to casual ward, dragging her infant with her until death — whose merciful sickle cuts down so many slum babies — came to release the child from earth.[24]

The toughest survived; and the more aggressive (the East End was not short of women of this calibre) sometimes provided a sort of comic relief in court. Such was the case of Ann Golding, aged 44, a South Grove pauper, who, when body-searched on admission, was found to harbour "two packages containing indecent manuscripts" which were confiscated. The next morning Ann demanded their return, and, on refusal, hurled foul abuse at the labour master and threw a pannikin through the window "breaking a pane of glass value 3s, the property of the Guardians". Giving evidence, the Master added that she was the most violent and turbulent woman that ever came into the workhouse, threatening both female and male officers with physical assault that she had previously inflicted on the last Master and for which she had been sentenced to two years' imprisonment. Magistrate Saunders responded accordingly. Declaring that she was more fitted for a lunatic asylum than a poor house, he nevertheless sent her off to serve two months' hard labour. "The prisoner, upon leaving the dock, ejaculated, 'Good luck to you, old cock!'"[25]

The old demon drink, with its traditional hold on the labouring poor, certainly exacerbated local crime. Charles Booth was, perhaps, the first to assess the realities of the "evils" resulting from its consumption. His conclusions reversed the accepted view that drink was the cause of the downfall of men and their families. Men drank because they were poor; they were not necessarily poor because they were drunkards. (In 1888, he wrote: "To those who look on drink as the source of all evil, the position it here holds as accounting for only 14% of the poverty in the East End may seem altogether insufficient.") His evidence on the importance of "questions of employment" as a determinant of poverty was his most significant discovery.[26] He also depicted a curiously attractive scene of benign respectability when he proffered a general description of pub life.

> Anyone who frequents public houses knows that actual drunkenness is very much the exception... Go into any of these houses. Behind the bar will be a decent middle-aged woman, something above her customers in class, very neatly dressed, respecting herself and respected by them. The whole scene is comfortable, quiet and orderly.[27]

A dubious interpretation, certainly not applicable to those bawdy drinking dens that infested the side streets and alleyways off the Whitechapel and Commercial Roads and those by the dock-side! For the records show that drink and mayhem were regular associates throughout that year. This was manifest in a variety of incidents centred around pubs and illicit drinking dens. Of the latter, which would appear superfluous considering the numerous "legal" houses around, we read of a bogus club at 23a Princess Square, whose proprietor was summoned for using his premises without a licence for selling port, beer, whisky and tobacco — caught by an official *nark*, ie a supervisor of the Inland Revenue posing as a customer.[28] Drunken drivers, of horse or donkey carts, were regularly hauled into court. A comic episode was recalled in early February, when a Joseph Jacques, aged 30, was accused of being inebriate when in charge of a donkey and barrow. On Monday, 29 January, his cart was seen careering aimlessly around the streets, with Jacques hanging on to the saddle of the donkey, helplessly drunk. Saunders was not amused. The prisoner was fined 5s or 5 days' hard labour.[29]

A serious public scandal, which broke in June, concerned the case of the drunken Public Vaccinator. With vaccination unpopular enough at that time because of the harsh way it was carried out locally, the case made national headlines. It first came to light in a report issued by the *East London Observer* on 16 June:

> It was alleged that Dr Thomas Loane (who resigned his position as Public Vaccinator to the West Ward of Mile End) on the previous Wednesday was in such an intoxicated condition that parents were caused "to fly from the room"; while, judging from the arms of four children whom the doctor had attempted to vaccinate, and the blood spilt upon the register, there was no doubt whatever as to his condition at the time.

A more detailed account was outlined in the *East London Advertiser* (18 August). One parent, a Mrs Elizabeth Koll of 7 Cope Street, was horrified to perceive at once that "when Dr Loane vaccinated the child he was very intoxicated... She was not satisfied with the way he vaccinated her child; she thought he did it in too many places!" We can only surmise what must have been the terrible consequences of such overdoses of vaccine. They were certainly not recorded. As for Loane, his plea was that he had had a glass of wine and was quite sober before entering the centre; "but not being very well, it took effect on him when he got into the heated room of the vaccination station".

Drunk and disorderly behaviour was the most common offence attributed to the "lower-class" inhabitants of Tower Hamlets. All evidence suggests that it was more widespread. While the respectable, that is the more secure, working men and women filled some of the churches on Sundays, the labouring poor found solace in their one place of freedom — the pub — offering nightly the vulgar camaraderie of the bar. But comradeship, often short-lived, soon turned to drunken violence. It was within the precincts of the pub that vicious assaults on men and women became part of a continuing street show. It resulted in a daily parade of offenders and victims before the

Thames Police Court. They provided permanent copy for the local press. We read early in the year of "an assault by a man killer in Chrisp St., Poplar, on another man outside a pub. The prisoner had served eighteen months for killing a man, and was just out of jail after a 6 months' sentence for cracking a man's rib." The attacker, a William Whitwell, aged 26, got two months' hard labour. In March, there was reported another case, among many, of a particularly vicious assault on the proprietor of a pub on the Isle of Dogs, which warranted the same sentence.[30] Minor assaults by violent customers often took the form of smashing the costly decorative plate-glass windows which adorned the front of the pubs. The punishment for this offence was normally up to one month's hard labour. Sometimes less violent, but more disorderly behaviour resulted from a drunken mob indulging in high jinks. On 21 July the *East London Advertiser* described the antics of some hooligans enacted outside the Bow cemetery:

> After the ceremony of interment a disgraceful scene occurred outside the gates. Some twenty roughs of the lowest order, who were under the influence of liquor, indulged in rough horseplay to the danger of the public. The language used was shocking. They had to be quieted by the police.

An everyday sight in the streets was a shabby form, sprawled across the pavement, "drunk and incapable", to be scooped up by a patrolling handwagon, and carted off to the local police station. Thomas Jackson, local Methodist preacher and philanthropist, watched the removal of a drunken woman, who had lain herself down on the ground, by "that horrible vehicle, a police hand ambulance... the woman was strapped into it and carried away shrieking and cursing; a dehumanised thing, as morally insensate as the beasts that perish, and far less clean."[32]

The dread of every young and well-informed constable was to be posted to East London's "H" Division, with its legendary no-go areas where the men on the beat were continually exposed to the dangers of physical attack. This can be seen in the reports of the *East London Observer*, which ran a weekly watching brief on police activity. These reveal a multiplicity of incidents involving drunken assaults on police, and are exemplified by the following charges brought before the Thames Court magistrate:

Threatening to Settle a Police Constable

William Bennett, ship steward, drew an unloaded revolver after a Police Constable tried to stop him entering the Queen's Palace of Varieties in a drunken state. The PC "requested" him to go away; he drew the revolver and said, "I'll settle you at once." The gun was wrested from him by the aid of another and the prisoner taken into custody. The prisoner claimed that he was drunk and did not remember what had happened.

Mr Saunders fined him 40s.

Bennett: "I have no money."

Mr Saunders: "Then you must go to prison for one month with hard labour."[33]

Actual violence was perpetrated in most cases; two of the worst were reported in June.

A Malicious Man

Daniel Hickey, 40, was charged with being drunk, disorderly and with assaulting Constable 37H while in the execution of his duty. On Saturday night the officer saw the prisoner behaving in a very disorderly manner in Great Alie Street, Whitechapel. He was drunk and used filthy language, and as he would not go away he was taken into custody. Hickey then became very violent — kicked the officer several times in a dangerous part, hurting him at the time, but the pain has now gone.

Prisoner, who said he recollected nothing of the occurrence, was sentenced to 10 days' hard labour.[34]

Stoning a Constable

John Canavan, 20, charged with being drunk, disorderly and assaulting a policeman. On Sunday night the prisoner, who was drunk, and others were singing an indecent song in Burn Street, Limehouse. ("The neighbourhood was a most dangerous one, and it was not safe for a constable to go there alone".) On attempting to arrest Canavan, the latter struck the PC, wrenched himself free, and he and seventeen others proceeded to stone the constable, who was alone. Another PC arrived on the spot, when all the men ran away but the prisoner was caught.

The accused was fined 40s or one month's hard labour.[35]

In Tower Hamlets, therefore, the policeman's lot was not a happy one. It was certainly hazardous enough when pounding the beat through the foul alleyways and dimly-lit cul-de-sacs that bordered the river. There were moments of light relief, however. "Treading on a constable's corn" described what happened when one Saturday, outside the Old Commodore pub in Poplar High Street, one George Brown, aged 23, fell on Constable 218K and trod on his toe. The painful outcome must have roused Old Bill to a state of frenzied belligerency; for, in terms of the evidence he presented, it "led to a violent exchange of blows". Accident or no accident, Brown paid for the mishap. He got 7 days' hard labour.[36] Later that year the whole of the same police precinct seems to have been infected by summer madness and the example of their local "clients". In the *East London Observer*'s "Run and Read Notes" of 21 July we read of an orgy of drunken revelry at a police party which upset some law abiding church goers:

> It seems that the Poplar Police would do well to remember the reputation they once had. Such scenes as those which occurred after the garden party in the recreation ground on Thursday week (July 12th) when intoxicated guardians of the peace lent themselves to assault and uproar are begetting feelings in the neighbourhood so different from the esteem in which the local police were at one time held, that it is perhaps fortunate for the police themselves, as well as the public, that the Chief Commissioner has interposed, and that the whole matter is to be gone into at the Thames Police Court.

It was not surprising that, in another column, a correspondent also complained of the absence of police along the Bow Road at night and was perturbed that the East End was "not getting fair value for its contribution to the police rate". And their subsequent antics during the Ripper murders would justify his concern.

With violence the norm, so was the incidence of unaggravated assault. In April the press recorded the case of a gang attack on the proprietor of a common lodging house. He was beaten up by five or six thugs "led by Messrs Odell and Robinson because he refused to employ one of Odell's friends as a watchman". Saunders rewarded Odell for his "ruffianly conduct" with a sentence of two months' hard labour. Later that month (21 April) along the Canal Road, Mile End, four men set upon a fifth without cause as he was returning from the theatre, and broke his leg. Violence often erupted in tramcars mainly over the collection of fares. One fracas was caused by a passenger attempting to avoid payment. It was a typical ploy by a fare-dodging thug and ended in a dangerous assault.

A Violent Passenger

Thos. Lillywhite, 27, was charged with refusing to pay his tram fare, and with wilfully breaking a window, value 3s, belonging to the North Metropolitan Tramway Company. On Saturday afternoon the prisoner got on a car, which was journeying from Aldgate to Stratford, at Whitechapel Church. When asked for his fare, he said his friend would pay. The man, whom the accused said was his friend, refused to pay the fare, saying he was a stranger. Lillywhite then struck the man and knocked his head through one of the car windows. He was given into custody.

Saunders ordered the prisoner to pay 3s 8d, or in default, three days' imprisonment with hard labour.

A week later another brutal attack arose out of a docker's attempt to smuggle a stolen shirt through the dock gates.

Assaulting a Gatekeeper

Thos. Green was charged with unlawful possession and violently assaulting Mr Chambers, a gatekeeper at the London Docks.

When stopped by a policeman "noticing his bulky appearance" he struck the gatekeeper a severe blow on the left eye, nearly stunning him and kicked him... He was held by two Custom House Officers who gave him into custody. A shirt was found to have been stolen from the ship lying in the dock.

Previous convictions having been proved against the prisoner, Mr Saunders sentenced him to two months' hard labour.[38]

Walking the streets at night, even through the main roads, could be dangerous. Nocturnal predators were on the prowl, ready to pounce on some naive victim who ventured out alone. A German innocent, John Kolisky, was strolling along the Commercial Road at 4.30am, the morning of 12 February. He was followed silently by a William Ryan, who suddenly seized him by the throat, struck him a violent blow in the eye, and with the aid of an accomplice, cut his pockets and extracted all his money (£4 14s) Fortunately a PC Arthur Petts saw the action and gave chase after Ryan, caught him and delivered him into custody, At his trial the villain was found to be an old offender with convictions for felony going back at least two years. He got 6 months' imprisonment with hard labour. Again it was the dockside quarters that offered greater scope for such activity. At least two cases were recorded round there, but fortunately the thieves were caught. One was of a man attacked in Wellclose Square, his watch stolen and later retrieved; the other was an account of a past midnight assault in Turner Street, where a Nathan Henry

was jumped upon by two men and relieved of all his money (4s). However, smart police action in both incidents ensured the prompt return of their property to the victims. Again seamen constituted a prime target for wharfside "sharks", In May, under the title "East End Ruffians", our local correspondent describes one of many such attacks that took place
during that year.

> Thos. Sullivan, 30, was charged with assaulting George Jacobs, ship's fireman of steamship "Aurora" lying off Wapping, with intent to rob him. He and three others waited for him at the corner of Old Gravel Lane as he came along "a little under the influence of drink". They surrounded him, struck him on the mouth and rifled his pockets, watched by Constable 383H. The time was 11 o'clock Monday night. He got two months' hard labour.[40]

Threats of highway robbery at night persisted. An early warning letter in the *East London Observer* (7 January) quoted an increase of such incidents in Stepney Green and St. Peter's Road, demanding, as a remedy, the installation of "more lights" there. Not that it would have helped, since day-light attacks were equally sustained throughout the year. For example, in *The Times* of 14 September a letter entitled "The State of Whitechapel" appeared to confirm the every-day dangers confronting those who ventured to pass through the side streets of Brick Lane.

> Sir,
> May I add to what has already been said on this subject? Yesterday at 11am a gentleman was seized and robbed of everything in Hanbury Street. At 5pm an old man of 70 years was attacked and served in the same manner in Chicksand Street. At 10am to-day a man ran into a baker's shop at the corner of Hanbury Street and King Edward Street and ran off with the till and its contents. All these occurred within a hundred yards of each other, and midway between the scenes of the last two horrible murders.
> Yours obediently,
> J.F.S.
> September 13th.

On 21 January, the *East London Advertiser* proclaimed that "the burglary season" was at its height. The East End was a "natural" training ground for "professionals" and "non-professionals", and, until the recent demolitions, in certain homes, in certain streets, burglary was a family occupation, the techniques and tools handed down from father to son. Here the knights of the "jemmy" and the crowbar were astir; noticeably during the late winter and early spring nights. According to the *East London Observer* court reports many a felon was caught in the act.

On 7 January, two customers who hid in the cellar, after closure of the Anchor beerhouse in Grove Street, Commercial Road, were foolish enough to leave the exit flap open, which attracted the attention of the policeman on his rounds. They were each sentenced to 7 days' hard labour. On the same day three Jewish burglars (not the type of activity normally attributed to Jews), Abraham Levy (33), Adolph Golding (34) and Simon Cohen (29) were charged with "breaking and entering the premises of Jacob Spiegel, trader of Plummers Row, Whitechapel, and stealing therefrom 39 overcoats, value £20, the property of the prosecutor. They were inveigled into distributing their booty by an informer." A spate of burglaries were recorded in March, the unsuccessful ending up in court. Such was the case of two young thieves, Alfred Nash (14) and Henry Gower (15), who were charged with loitering with intent outside a house in New Martin Street, St. George's. "When taken into custody Nash was found to be in possession of a bunch of false keys, and each had a box of silent matches." Saunders sentenced them to one month's hard labour.[41] A week later one Benjamin Barrett (45) was charged with breaking into the Primitive Methodist Chapel in Chrisp Street, Poplar, and stealing a table cover. On his arrest at the Salvation Army refuge in the West India Dock Road, he exclaimed, "Ah, thank God, I am innocent." But when the police witness informed him that a man answering to his description was seen climbing over the chapel wall, he broke down. Begging pitifully, "Are they going to charge me? It is only away for a shilling", he produced a pawnbroker's ticket relating to the table cloth. The unbending Saunders placed him on remand for committal.[42] One attempted burglary ended up as a comedy act. This is described in a letter to the editor of the *East London Observer* dated 20 January, entitled "Caught by the Leg".

Sir,
This morning an attempt was made by a burglar to enter our premises, situate as below. About half past two this morning we were awakened by our dog barking furiously, and upon looking out of the window we perceived a man mounted upon the railings, (which we use instead of shutters), trying to get upon the ledge above the facia, but we suppose, hearing us open the window, he intended making off, and, in doing so, his foot slipped and he crashed through the plate glass front, and got one of his feet entangled in the railings; and, in spite of all his endeavours to get loose, he had to remain in this extraordinary position until he was kindly released by a constable and two of our assistants. He was taken and charged at the Thames Police Court and committed for trial by Mr Saunders, the sitting magistrate.
Arter Brothers
484 to 486 Cable Street,
Shadwell.
March 20th, 1888.

Another audacious attempt, albeit abortive, was made by John Leary, a dock labourer, who had the courage to break into two houses very near the Thames Police Court, and was, accordingly, caught in the act. On the same day three youthful burglars were tried for breaking into and stealing from the match warehouse of the Millwall Dock Company. The punishment imposed was harsh. They were each sentenced to a birching to be followed by a stretch of five years in the reformatory.[43] There was a singular case of suspected burglary involving the future international star of the Yiddish theatre, Jacob Adler, who had returned for a short trip from the USA. Adler, on going to bed in a friend's lodgings, had dropped his purse in one of the boots, which, at his own request, were placed outside to be removed for cleaning. On their return he found the purse missing. The shoeblack concerned was charged with its theft, but the case was dismissed on the plea that "the boots were passed through hands before reaching the bootblack who was an army pensioner".[44]

Pockets of the respectable, that is the more affluent parts, such as Stepney Green, Beaumont Square, and the more salubrious thoroughfares off the north side of Bow Road, provided a profitable range of targets for local cracksmen. The anger and frustration of the victims was summed up in a letter to the *East London Advertiser* (8 December) by a Mr James Bartlett, of Antill Road off Grove Road. It was appropriately headed "Burglars' Paradise".

> The neighbourhood in which I have the honour to reside appears by some means to have become a perfect hunting ground for the vile wretches, who, stealthily sneaking about, and by the exercise of that cunning (probably begot of strictly secular education, and the lack of any moral training in their younger and possibly school board days)... suggests that a stranger knocking at the door should be treated with suspicion, that a policeman's whistle should be kept at the ready etc. There is also another point for the consideration of our ruling powers, and one upon which there is a very strong opinion among those who are not therein included, and that is this: if the same means were adopted in regard to burglaries as were applied for the correction of those whose profession was known as "garrotting" it would have a more salutary effect than simply a short or even long term imprisonment, perchance with hard labour in addition thereto. It is monstrous that in these times with our advanced civilisation and boasted freedom, it should be necessary for some vigilant sentinel to be on guard during the hours of night, in order that a household may enjoy well-earned repose, after the labours of the day, without being plundered and molested by these midnight marauders and disturbers of the peace.

Supreme among Victorian values was the concept that private property was sacrosanct. Woe betide those who trespassed. Petty larcenists were dealt with severely. In March, George Burton, aged 40, charged with stealing a blanket worth 6s from a common lodging house in Pennyfields, Poplar, got six weeks' hard labour. Dockers' "winnings", that is stealing on the job, was widespread. In June, a Sergeant Flynn of the dock police, while patrolling the wharves on a Saturday night came across several men "with a cask of wine ripped up, while the prisoner William Mew, 40, was drinking out of the bung hole. Witness then arrested him. The other men were waiting their turn to have a drink from the cask, but witness prevented them from doing so." Mew, the sacrificial lamb, was sentenced to 7 days' hard labour. Previously, in March, two men, John Murphy and Ralph Waites, were caught in the docks attempting to make off with two large boxes containing cheeses worth 30s, the property of the London and Liverpool Steam Company. They were promptly committed for trial at the High Court.[45]

The busy, overcrowded pub could also provide ample opportunities for the enterprising thief. But in January one inside job came to a sorry end. It was the case of a potman charged with stealing 6d marked money belonging to his employer, a Mr Hugh Douglas, proprietor of the Crown, Rhodeswell Road, Limehouse. The accused had been employed for nine months, receiving 12s per week. Takings had declined dramatically, so Douglas marked a coin, a sixpence, and when the accused was leaving the pub he was asked to turn out his pockets when the marked coin was found. His reward was one month's hard labour. In March one of two men who attempted to lift a gold watch, valued at £16, from Englebert Schlingemann, owner of the Castle pub on the main Commercial Road, received 8 months' hard labour.[46] From the punishments meted out it would appear that crimes against property were deemed more serious than those against the person!

Food stealing, as already noted, was a popular crime. For the hungry and penniless, it was necessary for survival. Bread stealing from baker's shops, street vendors or shoppers, was commonplace. Two cases of the many brought to court illustrate this. In January we note:

> James Cadderley, a promising youth... crawled on his hands and knees into a baker's shop in Bromley Street, and was returning in the same way with a loaf in his hand when a PC relieved James of the loaf and his liberty. There was a sound of weeping and wailing in the vicinity of the police court shortly afterwards, as 12 strokes with a birch rod were administered to James.

With such civilised grace was a hungry lad dealt with. In March two young girls, Catherine McCarthy (17) and Elizabeth Welch (16), were charged with committing an unprovoked assault on a respectable young woman, a Miss Beatrice Empleton, along the Shadwell High Street, and snatching two loaves from her basket. The magistrate ordered each to pay 40s or do 21 days' hard labour. This was no choice for the likes of them. Like many other East End youngsters they would make their criminal debut in a state prison.[47] For stealing 5lb of beef from a butcher's shop in Cannon Street Road, St. George's, on 10 March, William Ford (25) was fined 10s or 14 days' hard labour. Illustrative of another thieves' exercise, that of purloining food from a delivery van, was an account given by the arresting officer:

> James Woodhouse, 20, was charged with stealing 15lbs of margarine and a basket value 15s, the property of some person unknown.

> PC Harvey, 52H, said that on Tuesday evening he was in Cornwall Street, when he saw prisoner and two other men run behind a covered van and take the basket of margarine off it. Witness followed and caught Woodhouse with the basket under his arm. On the way to the station he was very violent, and threw witness twice to the ground.
> He was remanded for the owner to be found.
> Prisoner: "Good luck to you. I hope I shall get five years!"

Perhaps the *cri de coeur* of a poor man, beyond despair, who could plead for such harsh retribution. Of course there are extensive records on the compulsive thief. One, Jane Emmsworth, aged 73, was locked up overnight in the Shadwell Police Station for being drunk and incapable. On being baled out next morning a large bundle was detected under her shawl. She had tried to make off with a pillow, that is police property valued at 2s 6d; a piece of audacity which cost the old woman 7 days' hard labour.[49]

Child criminality and corruption was another potent factor that forced national attention on to this locality. A nineteenth century commentary articulated public concern. "Children, who under circumstances probably never before paralleled in this country, are now completing their education for future practice as 'dangerous classes' by sitting up half the night with persons of every vice, half naked, drunken, obscene, and quarrelsome."[50] Five years earlier William C. Preston in his *Bitter Cry of Outcast London* had confirmed the widespread prevalence of "child misery" which accorded with the dramatic exposés of Dickens and Mayhew. William Booth warned of the "gangs of lad thieves in the low Whitechapel lodging houses, varying in age from thirteen to fifteen, who live by thieving eatables and other easily obtained goods from shop fronts (and whose) al fresco lodgings are found in the seats outside Spitalfields Church".[51] Although the young Constable Leeson's career in "H" Division commenced a little later, his description of child criminals on charge, and the consequences thereof, is relevant.

> There were not even juvenile courts in those days and I have seen small girls and boys herded together in the same cell with old convicts whilst waiting their turn to go before the magistrate. Here they listened and learned the significance of such terms as *snowballing* (stealing wet clothes from lines in backyards), *dipping the lob* (stealing from tills), *parlour jumping* (entering

through the window of the front room from the footway), *busting* (burglary) and *screwing* (house-breaking).

When convicted the punishment was either birching or a spell in the industrial school or reformatory... I have seen the inside of these places... I could never see there any hope for the reform of the child criminal.[52]

Public records on the activities of child burglars and petty thieves abound. Two youngsters brought to court on the same day in May illustrate this. The offenders had the misfortune to be tried by magistrate Saunders. The first, "Frederick Horn, aged 9, was charged with breaking and entering the premises of William Lindon, manager at Fergusson's Wharf, Millwall and stealing therefrom three books, a purse containing 7d, a pair of earrings and brooch valued at 5s. The boy was caught by the manager at 3-3.30pm on Monday previously and, on being challenged, replied, 'Mother sent me to see if you had a room to let!' Some keys were also found on him." The second, Joseph Duxberry, aged 11, was charged with "stealing 1s belonging to Elizabeth James of 74 Tarling Street, St. George's. The prisoner lived in the same house as the prosecutrix. On Saturday morning (28 April) she missed 1s from the table (out of 3s left there) and the prisoner had gone. On return the boy admitted the theft of money 'with which he had bought some sweets'. He was given into custody." Both boys were ordered to be flogged.[53]

Local crimes against children were widely in evidence. Dr Barnardo was currently engaged in a national campaign to end child abuse. His biographer noted that, from the victims' complaints, "a factor which rises again and again in these early admission reports is that one or other parent was a drunkard". Mothers could be the worst offenders since "gin was the reported remedy for unwanted pregnancies... when knowledge of contraception among the poor was practically nil... This seldom worked so the woman was left with the worst of both worlds, a child she didn't want and couldn't support, and a craving for the spirits."[52] One of Harkness's impressionistic descriptions illustrates this:

> Nelly knew how it was on the staircases; babies lay there in one another's arms fast asleep, with their heads on the stone steps, waiting for their parents to return and unlock their "place". It was terrible to hear them crying at midnight, when their fathers and mothers came home drunk, and gave them cuffs and kicks...

> Men who at other times were civil and pleasant enough, became like wild beasts the night after they received their wages, and women who worked hard to make husbands comfortable and keep children tidy during the week, grew rough and reckless on Saturday night.[55]

A more extreme case of "a diabolical treatment of a child" as described in the *East London Observer* (17 and 24 March), was that of Teresa Smith, aged 24, charged with "shockingly ill-treating" her five-year-old illegitimate son, Henry. According to a neighbour, who stood as witness, six months before the mother "smashed the child's head open with a quarter pot". The previous Wednesday the same neighbour observed another horrific assault on the child.

> The prisoner forced him to the ground and then jammed filth into his mouth. She then put the poker in the fire until it was red hot. In the meantime, she put soil in a cloth and tied it round the child's mouth so that it went down its throat. She then took the poker from the fire and, having stripped the child, applied the weapon to the bottom of his back, burning him severely. She kept the poker in one spot for about three minutes. Prisoner then knocked the poor child down, and kicked him about the ribs, and afterwards jumped on him with all her force. She also knocked the child's head across the door so severely that a Mrs Sullivan, who lived in the next room came out. The same day witness saw the prisoner bite a lump out of the child's arm while he stood by the fireplace. Witness had seen the prisoner assault the child every day since.

A doctor, called by a police constable, confirmed the terrible nature of the injuries inflicted on the victim. The magistrate ordered the mother to be remanded for two consecutive weeks. There is no record of the child being removed from her care!

Instances of straightforward child neglect or ill-treatment frequently recur towards the end of the year. On 30 September Elizabeth and John Tobin were charged with neglecting their two-year-old son Dan, who was found starving and had to be removed to the workhouse. The father was a confirmed drunkard.[56] In November, Margaret Anson, aged 34, was charged with being drunk and disorderly and with cruelly ill-treating her male child (14 months old). A witness was shocked to see the child half-clad and wet throughout in the cold. On her arrest Anson declared that she was "Jack the Ripper's wife"![57]

Given the over-congested conditions exacerbated by scarcity in domestic housing and the need to accommodate lodgers who brought in extra cash, children in poor families were exposed to the dangers of incestuous or other sexual assaults by adults. In January, one Philip Jacobs, aged 25, committed an indecent assault on baby Leah Gowshawski, aged 2½, at the house of her parents. That same evening the child complained of Jacobs' behaviour. Medical witnesses were called, who soon found that child had contracted a venereal disease consequent of the outrage perpetrated on her. In March, a denizen of the infamous Canal Road at Mile End, clerk Charles Clarence aged 28, was placed on remand for attempting to "carnally know" his daughter, Ethel, aged 4, and "thereby communicating a frightful disease to her". He was bound over for prosecution at the next session of the Central Criminal Court. In May two cases of indecent assault were brought to the Thames Court. One involved a lodger, John Oakley, a labourer aged 48, who committed a sexual offence against a 7-year-old, Rose Johnson, living at 4 Boarded Entry, St. George's. The little girl, who was very bright, described how the accused had lured her into his bedroom and offered her two spoonfuls of sugar. "He then placed her on his bed and committed the deed with which he was charged, afterwards rewarding her with a half-penny." The other was that of a tailor, Richard Tabb, aged 20, of 165 Turners Road, Mile End, who was simultaneously committed for trial for similarly assaulting a 15-year-old, Susan Boswell.[58]

Locally, the crime of infanticide was legendary; not only as a result of an attempt to escape from the social stigma attached to a "fallen woman" and an illegitimate child, but also out of sheer economic necessity. The pressures on a young, single girl, deserted by her lover and rejected by her own folk, were overwhelming. Relief could be attained by disposing of the child, permanently. An alleged shocking child murder that briefly dominated the headlines before the advent of the Ripper, was described in detail. It concerned one Florence Lovett, aged 25, of 175 Skidmore Street, Mile End, who murdered her newborn child.

> The baby, recently delivered, was found in a box by a Dr Barton. The child was pinned in a bundle. There was a piece of tape round the child's neck, and it was tied in a knot, which the

doctor cut... Witness tried artificial respiration, but failed and rigor mortis had well set in. Witness arrived at the conclusion that the child had lived for an hour or two, separate from the mother and that death was due to strangulation... She must have had a painful delivery and she still required the assistance of a medical man. It was possible for a woman to be in such pain through a delivery as to lose her reason for the time being. It was possible to use a tape for the purpose of self-delivery.

The magistrate would brook no plea for diminished responsibility, although her father's evidence disclosed that there was insanity on both sides of the family and that she had recently been subject to hallucinations and fits of depression. She was committed for trial at the next session of the Central Criminal Court and ordered to be taken directly to prison.[59]

In the final count, self-destruction offered the hard way out for many an East Ender — man and woman. Throughout 1888, attempted and successful suicides abounded. The proximity of the Thames or an adjacent canal provided the place and the opportunity as a point of exit for the desperate. In January, Henry Englefields, a would-be suicide in the Old Ford Canal, was forcibly saved by two bargemen. In the same month, the more "popular" Old Gravel Lane Bridge, Wapping witnessed two attempts by young women. Here, in February, another two women were prevented from taking the same action. The second incident, reported in full by a police constable who saved the woman, confirmed the major cause which drove women to kill themselves. At 2.00am on Sunday 5 February, a Mrs Katherine Connell, aged 25, was poised on the bridge rails, ready to throw herself in, when the PC seized her and pulled her back; at which point she cried,

> "Let me do it. I've had a row with my husband." It was with great difficulty she was got to the station, where she wanted a knife to cut her throat. Prisoner now said her husband was continually ill-using her and she was sick of it. On Saturday he was locked up in the city for loitering and, when he got discharged he abused her for not bringing him some food, and when he got home he beat her in a brutal manner. Her mother interfered, and he struck her about the face, bruising it frightfully. She (the prisoner) then went and attempted to drown herself.
>
> Mr. Saunders, having given the prisoner some good advice (?) allowed her to be discharged.[60]

Discharged, without any legal restraints being imposed on the vicious husband? The insensitive Saunders would thus guarantee that she would try again, and succeed, the next time.

So, too, with others. According to her niece, a husband's ill-treatment of his wife was behind the attempt by Eliza Pritchard, aged 40, to drown herself off Midland Street, Ratcliff in May. At court on the same day, Julie Donovan, aged 22, was charged with the same crime. According to a police constable he intercepted her by the riverside. She pleaded, "Let me go. I want to die. My mother is starving and my father has got two months." Both had certainly been drinking and both were discharged with a caution — to return to the very misery, from which, in an act of final despair, they had tried to escape.[61] Other attempts were more successful. In May, Mary Woolger, aged 20, of 27 St. Thomas's Road, Mile End, disappeared "on the evening of that day she left home, having previously bidden goodbye to her little brother, saying she was going to drown herself". Her body was never recovered. Later that month "Robert Barber of 153 St. Leonards Road in Bromley, a fishmonger, locally known as Bob, committed suicide by jumping into Bow Creek near the Bromley Hall Board Schools, in the presence of his brother whose efforts to rescue him were unsuccessful". The report made evident what drove him to suicide. "He was a hard-working man, who had endured much to support a widowed mother, and a widowed sister and her family, as well as to his own wife and child."[62]

Violence between women was a daily phenomenon played out in the streets, and it often ended in bloodshed. One "rare virago", Catherine Dooley, aged 40, commenced her onslaught on a Catherine Sullivan who had tried to protect her own daughter from assault. Dooley then simultaneously attacked mother and daughter with an iron poker, as well as belabouring Mary Carey who had intervened, her victims all receiving severe injuries. In court "Stubbings, the assistant gaoler, said he had known Dooley for twenty years. She was a pest in the neighbourhood and had been convicted many times at that court." Saunders sentenced her to four months' hard labour, at which "prisoner fell down in a faint and had to be carried from court... For some time the prisoner was heard screaming in the cells."[63] Fighting harridans there were galore: many of them robust daughters of Erin, who, once on the rampage, could only be stopped by calling in the unsung peacemaker of the Irish ghetto — the parish priest. A repeat performance on record that day in court was that of Mary Kennedy — aged 32, who violently assaulted Mary Ann Scully of Star Street, Commercial Road. It was a case of a fall-out between "sharks" over the spoils.

> Prosecutrix, whose head was enveloped in surgical bandages, said that on Tuesday evening (31st Jan.) she went to the Victory public house at the corner of Watney Street with some friends. The prisoner came in and had half a pint of ale. When she drank that, Kennedy deliberately struck witness with the pot across the head, cutting it severely. She then left, and witness followed, when the prisoner again struck her across the head with the pot, saying "I will do for you and Martha Lappidge." Witness then gave her into custody. Her head was severely cut and was dressed at the police station.

What motivated the attack eventually came out.

> The accused said that the grievance was that a fortnight since she and the prosecutrix robbed a sailor in Devonshire Street, and Scully was guilty of what they called in their slang "whipping", which meant that she did not properly share the proceeds.
> Mr Saunders sentenced Kennedy to one month's hard labour. Kennedy: "Thank you, sir, I"ll see you later, Mary Ann!"

Similar incidents of drunken and violent attacks by women on other women went on unabated throughout the year. As already noted, men were also on the receiving end. Given the natural toughness of such women (they had to be to survive) their men often found themselves in the reversed role as battered spouse. One of many examples was a case brought before the Thames Police Court when a husband pleaded for release from a violent wife who was brazenly consorting with another man.

> Margaret Murphy, 27, was charged with assaulting husband, James Murphy, of Backchurch Lane, Whitechapel, and Patrick Cottrell was charged with rescuing her from custody. The wife struck him at 12 o'clock at night in a public house with a pewter pot and cut open his head. His wife had previously cut him with a pewter pot and stolen money from his pockets. All he wanted was a separation.

PC 148H arrested the prisoner and on the way to the station Cottrell tried to rescue her and caused her to become violent. He had also to be arrested. The female accused was a very violent woman.[64]

The following month another vicious attack by a wife might well have been a case of tit for tat. Bridget Gamble, aged 36, was charged with assaulting her husband William. The couple lived at 26 Star Street, St. George's, a notorious slum inhabited by the "criminal class". It appeared that at 9.30pm on the previous Monday, the prosecutor was working at home when the accused came in and struck him on the head with a soldering iron. He struck her back, when she pulled out a pair of scissors and stabbed him in two places. In consequence he lost a quantity of blood. The wife, when asked for her version of the affair, said that her husband had been ill-treating her for about seventeen years, and she was covered with scars where he had stabbed her. She had black eyes from him every week! The magistrate, Mr Lushington, ordered the accused to find one surety in £10 to keep the peace for six months, or on default, to be imprisoned for two months. (The prisoner replied, "Good luck to him!")[65]

Earlier an unusual case from the Jewish quarter was reported: that of Leah Gealish, aged 30, Polish immigrant Jewess, charged with "unlawfully cutting Aaron Rason, a tailor at 5 Duncan Street, Whitechapel". From the evidence of a third party, a quarrel broke out in the kitchen, when the woman picked up a knife and deliberately stabbed Rason in the calf of the leg. According to M.H. Ghys, house surgeon at the London Hospital, the wound was of considerable depth and it narrowly escaped the main artery in the limb. The case aroused concern among the Jewish community, since it was only six months since the Lipski affair had drawn hostile attention towards the immigrant Jew, as well as invoking adverse publicity for their womenfolk. According to legend they were notoriously religious and law abiding,[66] but the truth of this was further called into question by press exposure of the recruitment of immigrant girls from Whitechapel to the white slave traffic, especially along "the road to Buenos Ayres"!

Certainly Tower Hamlets offered a ready market for the procurement of human flesh, and Jews were by no means absent from the trade.[67] The *Jewish Chronicle* "Notes of the Week" (20

July), in commenting on the work of the Jewish Association for Preventive and Rescue Work among Women, lamented "a dark side of Jewish life (when) only mischief can result from covering up a wound in the body politic... Most of these unfortunates are foreigners, and immediately on setting foot in England have been entrapped and ruined by the miscreants who are ever on the watch for such easy prey. Coming here with no vile intent, they have ignorantly been betrayed by wretches who — we blush to write it — are members of their own race. Even married women, coming here alone and unprotected, are not safe from such fiends." What was intolerable to the respectable Anglo-Jew was the sight of Jewish prostitutes openly soliciting on home ground. A Michael Zeffertt, in a letter to the *Jewish Chronicle* (12 October) from fashionable 12 Clifton Gardens, Maida Vale, complained that many city men, as anxious as he was, were unable to "pass through Liverpool Street and other parts of London, without witnessing the degradation of our sisters", and warned that "the amount of immorality daily growing among the women is a blot upon our community at large". This warranted a sharp reply in the *Chronicle* (19 October) from S. Singer of 12 Petersburgh Place, W. who chided men *qua* men for daring to put the onus for both their downfall and reclamation solely on women. "Shall I be pardoned for suggesting that in this matter the "blot" rests not upon our sisters alone? The work of purification in Israel, if it is to be effective, must not be entirely one-sided. How many of our brothers, even when indignation is hottest against their degraded sisters, would not, if they spoke the truth in their heart, be compelled to confess, 'She is more righteous than I'!"

Gentile pimps were more numerous and ranged country-wide to inveigle village girls into the East End brothels. In March, Eliza Smith, aged 26, giving a Worcester address, and Eliza Mullings of Ernest Street, Mile End were charged with "attempting to procure" for prostitution a Worcester girl, Kate Spencer, who was under 21 years of age. Smith set the bait to bring the girl by train to East London, but Kate soon realised that she had landed in a brothel. That night Mullings ordered her "to get men, and get money". She accompanied Smith to the Paragon music hall, notorious as a pick-up rendezvous for "clients", and then quickly broke away to find a policeman, ostensibly to help her contact a relieving officer. After questioning at the local police station, itinerant Inspector Towley went off to arrest the would-be abductors. They were duly sentenced at Tower Hamlets Police Court: Mullings to 2 years and Smith to 1½ years' hard labour.[68]

It was the local quixotic crusader against vice, F.N. Charrington, who brought to book another "shocking case" of procuring, this time of a minor. It involved a Minnie and James Luxon of 24 St. John's Place off the notorious brothel-ridden Nelson Street. However, it was revealed in court that the 16-year-old Emma Fursey's own mother was a prostitute and, before the girl's association with the Luxons, she had already experienced six weeks as a working prostitute in a low brothel at dockside Albert Street, Shadwell. Charrington had "rescued" the girl and taken her to his refuge in Stepney Green. At the same hearing, publicity was given to another indictment being prepared against a pimp who had forced a young girl of 15 on to the streets, where she too was found and "saved" by Charrington.[69]

Fifteen years later, young Jack London diagnosed the continuing degradation suffered by many East End women (especially those categorised by Charles Booth as under "on or below the poverty line") as resulting from the brutal treatment inflicted on them by their menfolk.[70] That year the list of known assaults, ie those reported in court, was limitless. Rape may have been common enough, almost accepted as the norm among the other aberrant practices in the slums. There were exceptions, and at least two cases achieved wide publicity, appearing simultaneously that April. One was that of Arthur Haslem, aged 45, a general dealer of 35 Ocean Street, a man of some affluence who was charged with raping his 17-year-old servant Jane Ryan. The other, a medical student of the London Hospital (whose name, significantly, was not disclosed), was summoned for attempted rape of a religious girl, Emily Bevan, occupied as a servant and resident in the same premises at 63 Philpot Street.

Statements by both parties exposed the assumptions of the "superior" class offender vis-à-vis his "inferior" victim. It transpired that on that evening the student ordered her to fetch his tumbler in a rude manner, whereupon she refused and turned to leave. She was pounced upon, dragged back into the room and forced into a sitting position on the sofa. The girl struggled and was then pulled to the floor by her assailant who tried, against strong resistance, to seduce her. Forcing him to free her, she ran to her chapel at St. George's and brought back the lady officiant there, Mrs Aireson, to confront the student. In response to the girl's face-to-face accusation he replied, flippantly, "You know what these girls are. It's for them to say 'No'." But, on examination by hospital doctor Morrison, Emily was found to have been severely bruised, and the student was charged accordingly. The case closed with him being remanded for one week with bail accepted on one surety of £25.[71]

Daily assaults by men on women were so numerous that, in many charges, only a legal quibble separated them from attempted murder.[72] Wife bashing was such that those brutes who indulged in the practice gave as their excuse that the recipients expected it (on the maxim, "If he don't beat me he don't love me" — an obnoxious myth perpetuated until recent times!) Harkness dispels the myth in her description of a court case.

> A young woman stepped forward, dragging her two miserable children after her, and kissed the dirty Bible. She planted herself, with her back to the individual she had taken "for better, for worse", and produced some torn papers.
> "There is my lines, your worship. I"m properly married to him, and he goes at me something shameful. He's hit and kicked my children — just look at this girl's mouth, your worship — and I can't stay with him any more, the policeman's my witness."
> "You want a separation, I suppose," said the magistrate. "I shall order him to pay you 10s a week."[73]

The wife would be lucky if she ever received her allowance. The husband might disappear or, if unemployed, truthfully plead inability to pay. Thus for the majority of battered wives whose husbands were in employment, it was better to endure a personal hell by staying put in return for her man's income, which would enable her, at least, to feed and clothe their children. Of course there was always the danger of homicide. Strangely enough, in the two murders of women before the Ripper's onslaught began, both victims were immigrant Jewesses. The first was perpetrated by a jealous husband; in the second, the body was found with "shocking injuries" in the tunnel between Aldgate East and St. Mary's, Whitechapel. It was in this setting of everyday violence against women that the

Whitechapel murderer found his natural habitat and struck accordingly.

The Whitechapel (Ripper) murders

By 1888 East London was an overpressurised ghetto of immigrants and internal and external displaced labour, where the perimeters of poverty and hunger were expanding. In the East End outbursts would manifest themselves in two distinctive patterns: by a peak crime wave and by radical demonstrations, mainly separate responses to the same stimuli but, in one major incident, a fusion of the two. This was the Sidney Street siege of 1911, the second great East End legend which achieved international fame.

The first was that of the infamous Whitechapel murders of 1888, performed, according to most researchers, solo by that ubiquitous surgeon of the night, Jack the Ripper. For East Enders he still remains one of the great anti-heroes of their locale. Had his identity been discovered and had he been brought to trial, his exploits would merely have registered another sordid tale of a murderer brought to justice, such as that of wife-dismemberer Dr Crippen or the Boston Strangler. But he was never caught, and his identity still remains the greatest enigma in the annals of unsolved crime.

Exactly how many victims fell to his knife is still a matter for conjecture. So far most "Ripperologists" estimate that there were six, spread over the three-month period between 6 August and 9 November. The dark, cobbled alleyways, habitat of patrolling ladies of the night, provided an ideal setting for murder by an insane (?) killer. (The Whitechapel Board of Works were debating the extension of gas lamps into the dimly-lit alleys and culs-de-sac of Spitalfields on the eve of the Ripper's first attack!) It was in the early hours of a hot summer morning on 7 August that a policeman was passing an unlit archway along the Whitechapel Road (now Gunthorpe Street, still untouched by time) when he was confronted by an agitated waterside labourer who had stumbled over the bloody corpse of a woman on the landing outside his lodgings in George Yard Buildings. (Adjacent to George Street, according to a police spokesman "one of the most dangerous streets in the locality... has for years been a regular rendezvous and hiding place for deserters... Old bayonets can, at any time, be bought in Petticoat Lane, and at the old iron stalls there, for about a penny each, and they have frequently been seen as playthings in the hands of children!")[74] The constable, no stranger to extremes of local violence, was, nevertheless, shocked at the sight. The body resembled a human pepper-pot, the torso oozing blood from the cuts of innumerable knife wounds. The victim was soon identified as Martha Turner, aged 40, a street walker of the "cheapest type".[75] Such was the manner and ferocity of the attack, that only four days later on 11 August the *East London Advertiser* was anticipating the probability of more to come, thus presaging the reign of terror which would spread beyond the community:

> The circumstances of this awful tragedy are not only surrounded with the deepest mystery, but there is also a feeling of insecurity to think that in a great city like London, the streets of which are continually patrolled by police, a woman can be foully and horribly killed almost next to the citizens peacefully sleeping in their beds, without a trace or clue being left of the villain who did the deed.

These fears were justified. Three weeks later, in the early hours of Saturday, 31 August, only half a mile away at Bucks Row (now the same desolate Durward Street), the second body, that of worn-out prostitute Polly Nichols, was found. The corpse appeared to have been deliberately placed across the regular route taken by the night policeiaan on that beat. Her wounds were equally frightful:

> Her throat was cut from ear to ear. The wound was about two inches wide and the blood was flowing profusely.
> She was immediately conveyed to the Whitechapel mortuary where it was found that beside the wound in the throat the lower part of the abdomen was completely ripped open and the bowels protruding. The wound extends nearly to her breast and must have been effected by a large knife... Some of the front teeth have also been knocked out, and the face is bruised on both cheeks and very much discoloured. Her clothes are torn and cut up in several places bearing evidence of the ferocity with which the murder was committed.[76]

And it was evident that the killer had a substantial knowledge of the human anatomy, particularly that of the female. On 8

September the *Advertiser* again warned that "the murderous lunatic, who issues forth at night like another Hyde to prey upon the defenceless unfortunate class" would attack again, and that "three successful murders will have the effect of whetting his appetite further". Again, it anticipated correctly. On 8 September, the mutilated body of "Dark" Annie Chapman was found at the rear of 29 Hanbury Street in Spitalfields. It was revealed soon after that the police were receiving letters, purporting to have come from the killer, under the signature of "Jack the Ripper", in which he brazenly outlined his intent. By this time a great fear, bordering on panic, had spread throughout the streets of East London and beyond. "Respectable" women dared not walk alone at night, and thoroughfares were eerily deserted except for a sudden sortie of police patrols, often in plain clothes. When they failed to catch the Ripper a body of local vigilantes was formed, their venue significantly a Whitechapel pub: an urgent exercise in self-help to catch the maniac, whose activities were forcing customers to stay indoors at night, thereby reducing the income of publicans.[77]

While Samuel Montagu MP offered a £100 reward for the detection of the Ripper, smart entrepreneurs, other than burglars, seized the opportunity to extract profit from the murders. After the third incident our local correspondent lamented that "with all our boasted civilisation and increase in education facilities the morbid tastes of the poor still come to the front, or we should not hear of hundreds of persons paying a penny each to view the back yard of the house in Hanbury Street where the poor unfortunate woman, Annie Chapman, was hacked to pieces".[78] A more respectable attempt to profit from the event was revealed by the curator of London Hospital's Pathological Museum at the coroner's inquest "against police advice". Apparently an American had called upon the museum requesting information about the exact portions of Chapman's body which were found missing, in order to illustrate some medical publication, and "he was willing to pay £20 for each specimen". The coroner was furious. "Is it not possible that the knowledge of this demand may have incited some abandoned wretch to possess himself of a specimen?" "Rambler" in the *Advertiser* (29 September), musing in the same vein, opined further: "The police have thus got a clue of the greatest value... It is a grisly thought that the whole of this awful series has arisen out of the American craze for sensational advertisement." But this theory was soon to be discounted, when, in October, vigilante George Lusk received by post a cardboard box containing a portion of a human kidney analysed as "belonging to a person who had drunk heavily", which tallied with the organ missing from the fourth victim, Catherine Eddowes, a known alcoholic.

Apart from the usual spate of false confessions and arrests, one interesting piece of evidence that emerged was a description of the last man seen accosting Chapman at 5.30am outside the house where she was murdered. He was closely described as "a foreigner of dark complexion, over 40 years of age, a little taller than the woman, of shabby genteel appearance, with a brown deer-stalking hat on his head, and a dark coat on his back" — the latter garb, as we shall see, would be appropriated as part of a contemporary literary creation. Further horrific and baffling features of the atrocities were compounded, in the early hours of 30 September, by the discovery of a double murder of prostitutes known to be acquainted, their places of execution within a few hundred yards of each other. It appeared that the frenzied assassin was speeding up operations. For the first victim, "Long Liz", Elizabeth Stride, was found only just dispatched (the Ripper was actually interrupted) at the rear of the International Working Men's Club, 40 Berner Street, off the Commercial Road; the second, only 35 minutes later (1.35am) in the south-west corner of Mitre Square, Aldgate, underneath a hoarding attached to a picture-frame workshop. The next day, the Rev. Dan Greatorex, in his address to the Whitechapel Board of Works, was voicing the anxiety of a whole nation:

> Whitechapel has become notorious all over the world as a place to be shunned and feared, and if the supposition once gains a hold that it is unsafe for a woman to be in Whitechapel Streets after nightfall, the result must be utter ruin to all trade.[79]

Adding to the complexities faced both by the police and by the public in their attempts to identify the killer, was a publication venturing a supernatural dimension to explain the affair in Mitre Square. "Rambler" in the *Advertiser* (24 November) reported on the author of *Curse of Mitre Square*, who declared that he had discovered the following by accident while consulting an old historical manuscript:

> It seems that there was an old monastery in the sixteenth century on the spot where Mitre Square is now situated. As was not uncommon in those days, the morality of the monks was not of the highest order and in addition to many other crimes one of the fraternity put the finishing touches to his wickedness by murdering a woman whom he had smuggled into the monastery at the foot of the altar. A curse was pronounced on the spot, and it was on the same place where the altar used to stand that the unfortunate woman, Eddowes, was murdered. The writer of the story asserted in his letter that there is a plan of the old monastery in the British Museum, which enables the spot to be accurately identified.

Hardly had the hue and cry subsided after the double killings when the Ripper struck again, albeit for the last time. (It was as though it were a final and most horrific act of defiance by the Grand Guignol as he quit the stage.) On 9 November, the corpse of Mary Jane Kelly, the youngest of all the sacrificial victims, was found in a filthy one-roomed dwelling at No. 9 of the enclosed Millers Court off Dorset Street. The body had been subjected to the most extreme mutilation, and while it had been thoroughly dissected, there was, as usual, no trace of the instrument employed. The poignancy of the crime against a young woman with no known home or relations provoked a mass demonstration of sympathy among the local poor, particularly the womenfolk, who could identify with a kindred spirit whose short life had been so brutally terminated. Her funeral provided the occasion, and her exit signalled the end of the Ripper saga.[80]

Who was the Ripper? Views on his identity were, and still continue to be, speculative.[81] Given the contemporary scene, these terrible tragedies engendered some real-life comedies. The East End was never short of criminal homicides. After the third murder, any passer-by who aroused the suspicion of a street crowd was forcibly seized and hauled into the local police station. On 22 September the *Advertiser* noted two "further arrests of suspicious characters". One was Charles Ludwig, a respectably-dressed German, who was charged on 18 September at Thames Police Court with being drunk and threatening to stab an Alexander Finlay at an Aldgate night coffee stall. "Another constable stated that, earlier than this, he heard loud screams of Murder! proceeding from a dark court in the Minories. The court led to some railway arches, and was a well-known dangerous locality." Here he found the same man with a prostitute, who claimed that he had pulled a knife on her. That he had one was confirmed when he was arrested after his second attack. However, in tracing his movements during the previous three weeks, it proved impossible for him to be identified as the Ripper. The report on the second arrest conjures up the scenario of a minor black comedy.

> The Holloway lunatic, who is detained on suspicion in connection with the Whitechapel murders, is a Swiss, named Isenschmid. Some time ago he kept a pork-butcher shop in Elthorne Road, Holloway, and he is known in the trade as a "cutter-up". Some years ago it seems, he had a sunstroke, and since then he has been subject to yearly fits of madness. These fits have usually come on in the latter part of the summer and on several occasions his conduct has been so alarming that he has been carried off to Colney Hatch... One of his delusions is that everything belongs to him — he has called himself the King of Elthorne Road. On several occasions he had threatened to put certain people's lights out, as he expressed it, and more than once the landlord of the shop had been warned not to approach his lunatic tenant. One of the alarming practices of Isenschmid when he is mad is his continual sharpening of a long knife, and his disappearance from home for a few days has not been unusual. He went mad some weeks ago, and his frightened wife got an order for his detention in a lunatic asylum, but Isenschmid could not be caught... It may be only a curious coincidence.

but the mad pork butcher closely answers the description of the man who was seen on the morning of the (third) murder near the scene of the crime with bloodstains on his hands.[82]

With homicidal mania dominating the news a spate of the most bizarre diagnoses of its causation, medical and otherwise, followed. *The Fortnightly Review* of October published a curious article by a Dr Savage, proffering a new view on the origins and features of the illness. He warned that children pulling off the wings of flies should be carefully watched, and went on to suggest:

> As might be expected we find that natural heredity has much to do with these bloodthirsty propensities. Professor Benedikt of Vienna has been making an exhaustive comparison of the brains of criminals, and has devoted special attention to the cerebral development of murderers. He has weighed, measured and done everything but taste the brains of scores of malefactors. The result is that he has demonstrated satisfactorily that the brain of

a murderer frequently resembles that of a lower animal "in certain definite ways"... it is fair to suppose that thieving and a monkey-like condition of the brain go together... According to Professor Benedikt, murderers' brains have a special likeness to those of bears!

This brought a witty response from the *Advertiser* (6 October). "A man with a bear-shaped brain should therefore be avoided — unfortunately there is considerable difficulty in telling the shape of your friend's brain while he is still alive. The number of interesting, though blood-curdling, themes brought forward by Dr Savage are enough to form the material for a score of 'shilling dreadfuls'."

Such unique horrors were bound to evoke theories based on folk superstition or the supernatural. In October at least four national journals were seriously discussing the latest theories from Vienna explaining why the Ripper persisted in removing parts of his victims' anatomies, which provoked a more sceptical response from the *Advertiser*:

> It seems that internal organs, such as were abstracted from the unfortunate women, have been used for many centuries for the manufacture of what are known in Germany as *Diebslichter* or thieves' candles. There is a superstition that the light from these candles throws anyone into a deep sleep on whom it falls. Therefore, as might be imagined, they are in great request among the burgling fraternity. In the 17th and 18th centuries it appears that several statutes were passed inflicting severe penalties — and no wonder — for the making of these candles, and that the superstition is not dead is shown by the fact that in 1875 a trial took place in Galicia in which the prisoners were accused of using the prohibited candles. We shall, I suppose, hear soon of a series of mysterious burglaries. I commend the idea to Sir Charles Warren. He refuses to adopt any reasonable suggestions; there is, therefore, hope that this one may be to his taste.

A supernatural element was again evoked in the evidence given by Elizabeth Stride's sister at the inquest. She told the coroner that she received "an occult warning of her sister's death. 'About twenty minutes past one on Sunday morning I felt a pressure on my breast and heard three distinct kisses.' Now this was just about the time at which her sister was giving up her life under the hands of the awful being in Berner Street." Here, the same reporter took a more serious view and suggested the need for investigation by the Psychical Research Council on the premise that "the late Mr Edward Gurney, in his *Phantasms of the Living* gives several instances of telepathy, or thought transference, occurring at the moment of a person's death".[84]

It is not surprising that suspicion fell on local doctors, and rumour had it that such notable practitioners as Dr Barnardo and Frederick Treves were both under surveillance. P.E. Halstead, a doctor at the London Hospital, also claimed in his reminiscences: "I became aware that I was being shadowed by the plain clothes men... a whole year after the search was tenaciously kept up. I must be the only man living to have been suspected of being Jack the Ripper." He went on to recollect a series of murders in Central America which might have been perpetrated by the same killer. ("In 1889 a series of atrocious murders were reported from Managua — the capital of Nicaragua — and, as far as we could judge, the method and execution was identical to that of Jack the Ripper.")[85] On 9 November, a medical man, who was foolish enough to pose as a detective in mufti on the prowl, was surrounded by a mob and "conveyed to the Leman Street Police Station amid a scene of wild excitement".[86]

A further American connection arose out of the conviction that he could be a slaughter-house worker, and police enquiries revealed that several of these had quit their jobs during the murders. Two suspects were found to have gone to the USA, one to Chicago, the other to Kansas City. Pinkerton agents commissioned by Scotland Yard actually caught up with them, questioned them thoroughly and judged them innocent. In December, a letter was sent from Colorado by an ex-employee to a Mr Thomas Porter of Hucknall Torkand, who immediately handed it over to the county police. The writer claimed: "You will be surprised to hear it is me and a pal of mine doing this work in Whitechapel... since leaving Colorado have been carrying on a deadly line here in East London. I feel at this moment as if I could burn or blow all those dens down, and all those filthy low women in them... Oh, how I wish I could do without any more of this sort of life I have been leading of late, but I must go on, or my pal would do for me..."[87] It was signed "Jack the Ripper's Pal".

The weirdos, the eccentrics, the perverts and the inadequates had a field day. "Rambler" recalled "the strange encounters which one hears from one's friends concerning people suspected of being the Whitechapel murderer".

> There is an extraordinary person, who appears to haunt the Croydon district, and to terrify people with wild glaring eyes, and ensanguined discourses about the murders. His practice seems to be to elaborate his own theory with a ferocity which reduces his hearers to complete acquiescence in his views, whatever they may have previously thought. If any question is raised, he cuts it short by saying, "Sir, I have been studying the science of murder for twenty years, and I repeat to you that the employment of bloodhounds is **** nonsense." And this eccentric individual, casting a stony glare around on the shivering company, disappears like a nightmare. It is quite possible, of course, that he is a practical joker of a particularly ferocious kind, but his appearances are by no means regarded in a mirthful spirit.[88]

There were many more of the same kind. During the week following the last murder the number of suspects detained rose dramatically. One tramp in the Holborn Casual Ward, "a rough-looking fellow named Thomas Murphy", was arrested for behaving suspiciously. At King's Cross Police Station he was searched and found to have in his possession "a formidable-looking knife with a blade ten inches long". A loner of no fixed abode, it was his type that prompted "further inquiries at lunatic asylums and workhouse infirmaries, to attain lists of those recently discharged as cured within the last few months who had previously been afflicted with dangerous mania". Police records that same week also show that "several men who, while drunk, had charged themselves with being the murderer, were brought before the magistrate... and sent to gaol for 14 days with the option of paying the fine". To plague them further, "on Friday night (9 November) there was found in the pillar box at the corner of Northumberland Street and Marylebone Road a letter addressed to the police. 'Dear Boss — I shall be busy tomorrow night in Marylebone. I have two booked for blood — Yours, Jack the Ripper. Look out about 10pm, Marylebone Road.'"[89] "Normal" or sober prowlers accosted by women of the streets accepted at their peril. There were plenty of false scares "resulting either from approaches to "respectable" women, or where a prostitute, for her own reasons, cried "Murder!" against an innocent client.

Of course, it was in accord with current belief in British pride and moral superiority, that no Christian Englishman could have perpetrated such abominations; therefore it must have been a foreigner. Easiest to pinpoint were the Russians, settled locally, and one commentator referred to an article in a Russian paper naming a Russian anarchist, Nicolai Vassilyev, who emigrated to Paris in the 1870s where he shortly went insane and, after murdering several prostitutes, was incarcerated in a lunatic asylum. His mania was driven by the conviction that fallen women could only atone for their sins and obtain redemption by being killed. Shortly before the first Whitechapel outrage he was discharged as cured and crossed over to East London. After the Turner murder he went underground.[90]

It was inevitable that suspicion would fall on the old scapegoat, the foreign Jew. After the Hanbury Street crime, a poor Polish boot-finisher, Jacob Pizer, nicknamed "Leather Apron", and associated with "a man of sinister appearance, wearing a leather apron, who terrorised women of the streets", was arrested. A collection of long-bladed knives found in his house were ostensibly tools of his trade, but a series of impeccable alibis proved his innocence. This did not prevent a minor outbreak of Judeophobia which a local editor observed under the heading "A Riot against the Jews":

> On Saturday in several quarters of East London the crowds who assembled in the streets began to assume a very threatening attitude towards the Hebrew population of the District. It was repeatedly asserted that no Englishman could have perpetrated such a horrible crime as that of Hanbury Street, and that it must have been done by a Jew — and forthwith the crowds began to threaten and abuse such of the unfortunate Hebrews as they found in the streets. Happily the presence of a large number of police... prevented a riot actually taking place.[91]

Anti-semitism was prevalent in the hierarchy of the Metropolitan Police. Sir Robert Anderson, appointed Assistant Commissioner and head of the CID in September, was convinced that the Ripper was a Jew. (His chief, Sir Charles Warren, who disliked him, took the opposite view and was determined to refute anti-Jewish accusations.) After the Hanbury Street affair, the ill-timed publication of an article in *The Times* by its Vienna correspondent heightened such suspicions. It referred to a Galician cause celebre concerning one Moses Ritter, who had only just been acquitted of raping a Christian girl "and in order to destroy all evidence of the fact had caused his victim to be murdered". The real criminal was proved to have been a Christian peasant, only after Ritter, his wife and a Polish Christian stockbroker had been in prison for more than two years pending trial. Nevertheless the correspondent added that "there was no doubt that Ritter was innocent, but that the evidence to this superstition was never wholly disproved", implying the possibility of the age-old anti-Jewish libel of ritual murder. The Chief Rabbi promptly protested:

> The impropriety and injustice of the libel is only equalled by the danger involved in telegraphing it... no one knows what an excited mob is capable of believing against any class which differs from the mob majority by well-marked characteristics. Many English and Irish workpeople in the East End are inflamed against the immigrant Jews by the competition for work and houses, by the stories of the sweaters and the sweated. If these illogical and ignorant minds should come to believe in the report heedlessly spread by a writer who is not quite just nor well informed himself, the results might be terrible.

Letters to *The Times* from both the Chief Rabbi and the equally respected Rev. M. Gaster rejected, with the full force of Talmudic erudition, the myth that a Jew could attain spiritual absolution by murdering the Christian woman with whom he had fornicated. Rabbinical fears were subsequently borne out by events. On 6 October *Commonweal* reported that "the excitement caused by the murder outside the Berners Street club prevented the usual meeting here on Sunday (30 September)". Whoever the Ripper was, it certainly suited him to cast suspicion on the Jews. For the fourth murder was committed within the precincts of a predominantly Jewish club; and, after the fifth, it was he who wrote on the walls of the model dwellings in Goulston Street inhabited mainly by Jews, a message in large chalk letters: "The Jews are the men who will not be blamed for nothing." Thanks to the initiative of the metropolitan policeman who first discovered it, another violent outbreak against Jews was scotched. He consulted his superiors, who agreed to order its immediate removal.

There was no shred of evidence that the killer was a Jew. On the contrary, Margaret Harkness, declaring her own views in the contemporary novel *In Darkest London*, completely exonerates the Jews. A dying slaughterer confesses to the Salvation Army officer that he is the Ripper, and explains the evil dynamic that drove him to commit murder:

> people must eat and someone must kill beasts; but to kill makes a man like a cannibal, it gives him a thirst for blood, and I got to feel at last that nothing would quench my thirst but human blood, human flesh.

His blood lust reached saturation point when he "could not go on butchering" and sought some kind of sanctuary in the ghetto:

> I hid myself here among the Jews who hate blood and never spill it. I'm not a Jew. I'm a Gentile.[94]

This accords with the peculiar horror entertained by Jews of any mutilation of the human body before or after death, an act strictly forbidden by Talmudic Law.

Speculation on identity persisted and rumour was rife. Some even deduced that it could be a woman, perhaps a midwife who had knowledge of anatomy and could have explained away her presence in the streets at night in bloodstained clothing. Suspicion of evil in high places was currently fed by the nocturnal activities of the young Duke of Clarence; and later, in retrospect, a theory was put forward which detected the masonic hand behind the murders, perpetrated according to ritual to protect the Duke, and through him the integrity of the monarchy. Whoever the Ripper was, his deeds had ramifications both locally and beyond their time or place.

One casualty along the way was public respect for the police, which deteriorated as the killings went on. Well before the first outrage the *East London Observer* was questioning the efficiency of Old Bill on the beat. Such doubts were strongly voiced after the third murder. A powerful attack on the Police Commissioner, Sir Charles Warren, was mounted by the *East London Advertiser* on 15 September. It described him as "a martinet of apparently a somewhat inefficient type" who was guilty of

> the double folly of weakening his detective force and strengthening his ordinary police force from the ranks of reservemen and others of a military or semi-military type that

> destroys two safeguards of a community... It deprives it of a specially trained force, consisting of men of superior intellect and specially adapted powers for detective purposes... It substitutes for the old parish constable the man with the few years military service but with no other qualification for serving the public... Nothing, indeed has been more characteristic of the hunt after the Whitechapel murderer than the want of local knowledge displayed by the police. They seem to know little of the bad haunts of the neighbourhood, and still less of the bad characters who infest them.

By the third murder there was, according to the *Advertiser*, already "no confidence in the police". On 17 September a Mile End Vigilantes Committee was formed at the Crown, 74 Mile End Road, under the auspices of a Mr Baron. A letter to the Home Secretary was drafted demanding the offer of a reward, which was rejected on the basis that "the practice was discontinued... because experience showed that such offers tended to produce more harm than good". This prompted the *Advertiser* (*Economist*, 29 September) to follow up its attack with the accusation that "the police force of 13,000 men in the metropolis was inadequate and disproportionally distributed — the most patrolling the richer districts, a consequence of which was that the low, crowded and vicious districts within it are insufficiently guarded". The age-old complaint was repeated that "when a crime has been committed the police come so late that criminals have had every advantage in their efforts to get away". After the fifth murder the *East End News* (5 October) added insult to injury:

> The marvellous inefficiency of the police in the detection was forcibly shown in the fact that in the very same block as that containing Mitre Square, in the great leading thoroughfare, and at a moment when the whole area was full of police just after the murder, the Aldgate Post Office was entered and ransacked, and property to the value of hundreds of pounds taken clean away under the very noses of the "guardians of peace and order"!

Such was considered to be the state of lawlessness and terror that on 2 October the Whitechapel Board of Works was bemoaning the injurious effects on trade. One coffee-house keeper informed a member that "emigrants were refusing to be located in Whitechapel en route for the West", while the Rev.

Dan Greatorex went further, declaring that "Whitechapel was becoming notorious all over the world as a place to be shunned and feared". The *Advertiser* added the suggestion that, given police attitudes towards prostitutes, their very presence inadvertently helped the killer. "Constables are carefully watched off their beats by these poor wretches, and so the victim and the murderer are in a kind of conspiracy to accomplish a murder."[97] At the meeting of the Whitechapel Vestry on 3 October such criticisms of police ineptitude reached a crescendo. Attacks centred on the person of Sir Charles Warren, who was censored for not agreeing to offer a reward, with the Rector of Whitechapel demanding that "bloodhounds should be employed with the object of tracking the murderer". (Warren subsequently carried out an exercise on Tooting Common involving two bloodhounds, which proved a fiasco and rendered him the laughing stock of London.) The radical press joined the fray. For the "real" causes of the Ripper phenomenon their diatribes centred on the evils of society and the antics of its current "protector", the Police Commissioner. *Justice* (6 October), was quick off the mark. In a humorous article, meant for serious application, H.M. Hyndman, leader of the Social Democratic Federation, slated the "cant" exhuded by "bourgeois" attitudes towards the murders, followed by a scathing denunciation of poor Warren:

> The very people who are now the most vehement in their denunciation of this almost certainly demented murderer don't turn a hair when hundreds or even thousands of women of the same class as his victims rot to death with syphilis in a Lock Hospital... Who cares, too, how many young girls have their jaws eaten out of their heads by phosphorous in order that matches should be sold cheaper and shareholders should get a higher percentage for their investment? Not even a fraction of those of the non-producing classes who are harrowing up their feelings so pleasantly with the details of the unlicensed dissections in the East End of London.
>
> All this hysterical cant will die down, as it has died down time after time before, and men, women and children will be left in precisely the same conditions of life as those which render these murders possible.
>
> None the less, however, these murders and the impunity of the murderer teach a plain lesson to the police. They are paid to protect the public... instead of this they batter in the heads of their real paymasters, the working people, with truncheons, let

> murder after murder pass undetected in our midst... If the assassin of Whitechapel is cranky on the uterus or has gone daft on the purity question, the South African filibuster is certainly clean "off his head" at the prospect of the anniversary of the French Revolution.

In the next issue (13 October) he contemptuously dismissed Warren's letter urging the Whitechapel Board of Works to "dissuade the unfortunate women about Whitechapel from going into lonely places in the dark with any persons, whether acquaintances or strangers".

> A more lamentable ignorance of the true position of these women could scarcely have been made public. Everyone, we should think, save Sir Charles Warren, must know perfectly well that the vast majority of East End prostitutes are compelled to earn the 3d or 4d for their bed before they can obtain a night's lodging. There are no comfortable brothels for them like those at the West End. Thus, if these poor unfortunate creatures are not to run the risk of murder and mutilation by "going into lonely places in the dark" they must walk the streets all night, and it is questionable whether, even then, the danger will be in any way avoided... And, be it remembered, one at least, of the women who had fallen a victim to the maniac's knife went on the streets only when driven to do so by sheer dread of starvation.

William Morris's *Commonweal* was also in bantering mood before putting in the knife. Its "Notes and News" referred to the latest theory accusing Warren of arranging the murders to back up his demands for more police. Conceding that this was not credible, the writer went on, "but if he is not a scoundrel he is at least a fool", whose folly was now revealed to all. Thus

> the gentleman who occupies his spare time in mutilating and murdering in the neighbourhood of Whitechapel, has quite intentionally done society a service. By his latest masterpiece he has made Sir Charles Warren's position almost untenable, and it will probably not be long before the London Socialists will bid adieu to their best friend.

For, on the other hand, his departure could be to the detriment of the coming revolution that all "true" radicals were striving for. Therefore, it bemoans, albeit sarcastically (and prophetically), his imminent dismissal:

> His loss will leave us inconsolable.. Oh, if he could stay another year and give us another Trafalgar Square performance! The small radical remnant who have not yet accepted the gospel of revolution at his hands might then be driven, by dint of hard knocks and furious charges of mounted men into our ranks... to the only religion which any sane person professes.[98]

There was also severe criticism from the highest in the land. Queen Victoria personally intervened to offer royal advice. On 10 November, she wired the Marquis of Salisbury from Balmoral. "All these courts must be lit, and our detectives improved. They are not what they should be." In the follow-up correspondence she repeated that "the detective department is not so efficient as it might be" and outlined practical suggestions on how to improve methods of investigation.[99] Her last words on the matter spelt finis to Warren's career. On 17 November the editor of *Justice* joyfully announced that on Tuesday 13th the police commissioner had "been ignominiously kicked out of office by the same Tory Home Secretary amid the jeers and execrations of the whole community". The nature of his dismissal brought the internal wranglings and rivalries within the hierarchy into the public eye: that is, the antagonisms between Warren and Home Secretary Matthews and between the metropolitan and city forces. It meant a loss of confidence in the police which precipitated an overall scrutiny of their operations culminating in the major reforms of 1894.

The social implications of the murders endured well after the hue and cry had died down. Discussions on the Ripper phenomenon persisted as a national disease. Locally there were immediate repercussions. Hooliganism increased as youths, pretending they were the killer, went on the rampage frightening old women and girls. Drunken attacks on women were stepped up, notably violence against prostitutes. While police efforts were concentrated on catching their prime target, the burglars successfully increased their operations on the periphery of the Ripper's killing ground. This was all good copy for the press and high drama for the popular theatre. *Punch* pointed an accusing finger at the latter for helping to exacerbate the incidents of crime:

> It is not within the bounds of probability that to the highly coloured pictorial advertisements to be seen on almost all the

hoardings in London, vividly representing sensational scenes of murder, exhibited as the great attraction of certain dramas, the public may be to a certain extent indebted for the horrible crime in Whitechapel? We say it most seriously; imagine the effect of these gigantic pictures of violence and assassination by knife and pistol on the morbid imagination of unbalanced minds. These hideous picture-posters are a blot on our civilisation and a disgrace to the drama.

> **"On Horror's Head Horrors Accumulate!"**
> Here are a few clippings from one day's papers:
>
> "Shocking murder of a servant"
> "The Italian stabbing case"
> "Cruelty to a child"
> "Knocking a man's eye out"
> "Revolutionary murder in Whitechapel"

On the positive side, the Whitechapel incidents certainly led to greater emphasis on socio-economic and environmental causes rather than character defects in considering the poverty of human and moral propensities supposedly inherent in East End life. They helped register a more favourable climate for the reception of Charles Booth's findings and provided a catalyst to unify all reform interests with others hitherto unconcerned with the problems of deprived areas. *The Daily Telegraph* (6 October), commenting on the murder of Annie Chapman, focused the issue:

> She has forced innumerable people who never gave a serious thought before to the subject to realise how it is and where it is that our vast floating population, the waifs and strays of our thoroughfares, live and sleep at night and what sort of accommodation our rich and enlightened capital provides for them...

It was indeed the Ripper terror which persuaded authorities to embark on improvements in both health and housing for the "lower classes". The *Lancet* (6 October) conceded that "modern society is more promptly awakened to a sense of duty by the knife of a murderer than by the pens of many earnest writers". It was the Rev. Samuel Barnett's letter to *The Times* on 19 September that forcefully projected the desperate social problems of East London on to the national stage. He posited four practical suggestions: efficient police supervision; adequate lighting and cleaning, and the control of tenement houses by responsible landlords ("At present there is lease under lease, and the acting landlord is probably one who encourages vice to pay his rent" for "vice can afford to pay more than honesty!")[101] Henrietta Barnett's petition to the Queen, signed by over 4,000 "women for the labouring classes of East London", pleading that she call on her "servants in authority to close bad houses", brought a favourable response and, no doubt, reinforced Barnett's urgent demands for local improvements.[102]

The first priority was to light up the dark alleyways and courtyards. As early as February the Commercial Gas Company was informing both the Whitechapel and St, George's Board of Works that the price of gas for public lamps was being reduced to £3 9s per annum.[103] The offer had little effect until the killer struck. On 18 August the *East London Advertiser* noted that the Whitechapel Board voted "that lamps with double the illuminating power be fixed at the corner of the following streets, viz. Wentworth Street West Corner, Thrawl Street, Flower and Dean Street, Vine Court, Quaker Street, Worship Square, White Lion Street and Spital Square". By November the same Board had appointed a standing Lighting Committee with powers of spending up to £2,200 (until March 1889), the third largest expenditure allowance for the district. But the prospect of electric lighting for Whitechapel was already in the offing. On 10 December, the Works Committee "reported that they had under consideration the bill introduced into Parliament by the London Electrical Supply Corporation for the supply and sale of electric light in various parishes of the metropolis under the Electric Lighting Acts of 1882 and 1888, the area of Whitechapel being included". By the last month of the year street lighting had been extended in both the Mile End and Limehouse districts.[104]

The murders led to the escalation of new housing policies. *The Lancet* (6 October) was in the forefront urging for new public health legislation relevant to improved housing. In a milder reiteration of Shaw's terse polemic it conceded that "modern society is more promptly awakened to a sense of duty by the knife of a murderer than by the pens of many earnest writers". Gauldie confirms that the crimes engendered two important Acts.

i. The Housing of the Working Classes Act 1890 was a comprehensive Act consolidating all previous Housing Acts. It opened the way for progressive local authorities to begin the development schemes... Its most useful provision was to allow authorities in the Metropolitan Area to purchase as much land as might prove necessary for the long-term planning of an effective improvement scheme.

ii. The Public Health Amendment Act 1890 extended the provisions of the 1875 Act to empower every urban authority to make by-laws about the keeping of WCs supplied with flushing water, the structure of flows, hearths and staircases and the height of rooms, the paving of yards, the provision of means of access for refuse removal and to forbid the use as human habitations of rooms over privies, middens, cesspools and ash pits.[105]

Their implementation was made possible by the terms of the Local Government Act of 1888, which created both the structure and the permanent officials to design and construct mass low-cost housing within the auspices of the new-born London County Council.

At the local level there was an immediate response, especially by the increased activity of the Warden of Toynbee Hall. Practically all the remainder of the foulest enclaves within the Flower and Dean Street complex were demolished. The 4 per cent Dwelling Company purchased the north-east side and erected Nathaniel Dwellings, completed by 1892, with 170 apartments accommodating 800 people. From the rubble of the rookeries rose Stafford House on the north side of Wentworth Street, thanks to the land-owning Henderson family eager to dispose of their property in the locale, tainted by association with the recent horrors. In the 1890s demolitions continued between Flower and Dean and Thrawl Streets where Abraham Davis, a speculative builder, added a further six tenements, each four storeys high, with ground-floor shop fronts. Thus within the parameters of Flower and Dean, Lolesworth and Thrawl Streets a further 168 flats were constructed. The historian Jerry White concurs that "within six years Jack the Ripper had done more to destroy the Flower and Dean Street rookery than fifty years of road building, slum clearance and unabated pressure from the police, Poor Law Guardians, Vestries and sanitary officers... by 1897 the area was entirely dominated by the tenement blocks".[106]

Another positive outcome was the re-focusing of national attention on the plight of children in the common lodging houses. The social backcloth revealed by the murders stimulated renewed concentration of effort to alleviate the terrible incidence of homeless and abandoned children — a running sore of the metropolis. Their role as perpetual recruits to criminal gangs had been underlined by Dickens, and Barnardo had helped pioneer the movement to rescue them from the streets. He was quick to seize this opportunity. In a letter to *The Times* (6 October) he emphasised the dangers threatening young children forced to live in lodging houses, He demanded government intervention to rescue "boys and girls from the foul contamination of these human sewers" and to "make it illegal for the keepers of licensed lodging houses to which adults resort to admit young children upon any pretext whatever". He stressed that "provision is urgently required for the shelter of young children of the casual or tramp class, something between the casual wards of the workhouse and the lodging house itself, places where only young people under 16 would be admitted", and ended with the forceful plea that "surely the awful revelations consequent upon the recent tragedies should stir the whole community up to action and to resolve to deliver the children of today, who will be the men and women of tomorrow, from so evil an environment". In fact Barnardo had caught the current mood. His exhortations certainly provided ammunition for those involved with him in child aid, and had both the immediate and long-term effect of mobilising public concern for the welfare of deprived children.

"A great empire could not develop its potential strength while its own heart was weakened by disease. This disease was the poverty to which the crude existing social system condemned so many." This was brought home vividly to the young Lloyd George, who had caught a glimpse of it when, with a fellow Welshman, Sir Alfred Danes, the Caernarvon-born Superintendent of the Metropolitan Police, he made an expedition to the scenes of "Jack's" recent operations. He was apparently fascinated by "this Hogarthian Picture... and appalled by its degradation". There is no doubt that this experience helped to foster a passionate concern for the poor which he later transformed into practical welfare legislation.[107]

As for the fundamental causes to which such horrific crimes

could be attributed, that depended on the religion, class or politics of the would-be analyst. Radical opinion played on the socio-economic implications behind the murders. Hyndman's *Justice* had a field day. "Whoever may be the wretch who committed these sanguinary outrages, the real criminal is the vicious bourgeois system which, based on class injustice, condemns thousands to poverty, vice and crime, manufactures criminals, and then punishes them!" After the Hanbury Street affair, it poured scorn on the fears of local middle-class sermonisers, as reflected in the warning expressed by the Rev. S. Barnett that "if they don't look out — that's the moral of it — the rich will get their throats cut and their carcasses mangled like the poor wretched women of the slums", rejecting such "mawkish twaddle" with the argument that nothing will be done by "individual effort" save by an "organised and vigorous social democracy". In the SDF's reckoning the current "unemployment meetings in Hyde Park, which have received so much of police attention, and the Whitechapel murders which have received so little, are both effects of the same cause". William Morris, in his *Commonweal*, was even more explicit, in his condemnation of the bourgeois mores that perpetuated such infamies: that is "the exclusive culture of those whose sensibilities are so shocked by the brutality, the responsibility for which their greed and cowardice evades... and when the dark side of this inglorious inequality is thrust on their notice, they are shocked and read moving articles in the newspapers — and go on eating, drinking and making merry, and hoping it will last for ever — Whitechapel murders and all". Yet a month later a contributor, H. Davis, concedes that "at length our masters are aroused, and behold! a Royal Commission is enquiring into the particulars of the housing of the poor... and that in our age of contradictions and absurdities, a fiend murderer may become a more effective reformer than all the honest propagandists in the world".[109] Certainly one outcome of the murders was the focussing of national attention on East London which, together with other current political "happenings" there, would give rise to a wider sympathetic appreciation of the dockers' case in their strike the following year, another important factor in the making of the New Unionism.

Diagnosticians from the respectable middle classes reckoned the Ripper phenomenon as a symptom of other social diseases.

Theologians posed such simple arguments as the reading of sensational French novels and detective thrillers, habits that activated hitherto suppressed murderous instincts in a criminal. Would-be social psychologists, quoting the current popularity of "Dr Jekyll and Mr Hyde" at the Lyceum Theatre, were wont to concur with the clerics, yet were curiously suspicious of the Salvation Army "blood and thunder" dramatics as a possible stimulant for bloody deeds by a religious maniac. Social workers in the field put forward a confused mixture of causes: the lack of good housing; educational facilities which excluded any appreciation of aesthetics as well as the need for improvement of normal schooling; and, of course, drink and the lack of thrift which must ultimately result in a state of dehumanisation that could produce such a monster.

In a letter to *The Times* the aristocratic polemicist Lord Sydney Godolphin Osborne blamed the Society for the Propagation of the Christian Gospel for dereliction of duty among those on its own doorstep:

> I believe nearly half a million of pounds is yearly raised in this country by societies having their headquarters in London to propagate the gospel in foreign parts, to support the established church system, to send missions to convert the heathen in other lands... all this within cheap cab hire of that portion of eastern London, which for many years has been known to have been in a social condition utterly devoid of the commonest attributes of civilisation, so saturated with all that can contribute to heathenise as to be a standing shame to the nation.

After the third murder he warned: "Wealth and station in its embodiment may at one moment be inclined to cry, 'Ah, ha, I am warm'... In my poor opinion these are just the days when apathy to the condition of the lowest classes is most fraught with danger to all other classes." Such sentiments expressed by outsiders on the East End did not go unopposed by local worthies. The *East London Advertiser* had quickly responded to the hiatus following the first murder. The editor referred to the Mrs Grundy ("who has every sympathy for those 'rich in the world's goods'") attitude towards "the poor savages in the howling wild corners of the East End" where "the inhabitants of particular parts are all ruffians and viragos who acquired a taste for thieving and violence in their mothers' arms". He counter-claimed that statistics of criminal offences were no greater or less than any other part of the metropolis or Great Britain. On the contrary, East London was "not in a moral and social downgrade... but surely being reached by the influence of a better age and truer charity".[110]

Such definitive postures proved inconsequential as the Ripper got into his stride. Other acts of extreme violence and homicide continued unabated, reinforcing the insalubrious image of the East End. A case of fratricide in Watney Street in July, an attempted murder of a chemist in Berners Street in early September, made the national headlines. On 12 August a brutal murder took place on the Isle of Dogs, where an old eccentric, "Mad Dick" Bartlett, battered his wife to death with a hammer. There was no let-up in criminal high jinks during the Christmas festivities. The *Advertiser* summed up the score:

> **Holiday Charges**
> Of course there is always the swing of the pendulum, and at the Thames Police Court on Wednesday there were 38 charges arising out of Christmas Day, and four remands down for hearing, which is about the average number on Monday mornings. The former consisted of 14 on account of drunkenness etc, 8 for wilful damage, 6 on account of assault, 1 for being drunk in charge of a pony and barrow and furious driving, 1 for drunkenness and violent assault, 1 for drunkenness and arson, 1 for unlawful possession, and the remainder were felonies.

Two days later the body of a strangled woman, a known prostitute, was found in the early hours of the morning by a patrolling Police Sergeant in Charles Yard, a grim rookery off the Poplar High Street. Such news aroused fear and trembling locally. It wouls appear that Old Jack was back in business and boded ill for the coming New Year.[112]

Footnotes

[1]See *ELA* 10 November, "The Decrease of Crime", and *East End News* 20 December, "Crime in London" for overall statistics.
[2]*ELA* 6 October.
[3]*ELA* 20 October, "The New Birch Rod Remedy".
[4]*In Darkest London*, pp. 180-2.
[5]For adulteration of foodstuffs see Local Government reports in *ELO* February, 3 March, 7, 21 and 28 April, 30 June. Also *ELA* 21 February.

For beer adulteration see *ELO* 18 February and 7 April.
[6]*Commonweal* 23 June.
[7]*ELO* 10 March.
[8]*ELO* 31 March.
[9]*ELO* 18 February.
[10]*ELO* 28 April and 5 May.
[11]*ELO* 3 and 10 March.
[12]See *ELO* and *ELA* 24 March. Another case is reported in *ELO* 26 May.
[13]See *ELA* 3 March and *ELO* 10 March. Also see *ELO* 14 April when a similar charge of robbing boots off children was brought against Mary Ann Griffith. Magistrate Saunders sentenced her to two months' hard labour.
[14]For examples see Thames Police Court reports in *ELO* 21 January, 17 March, 19 May, 2 and 9 June.
[15]*ELA* 24 March.
[16]*ELO* 28 April. For other similar cases see *ELO* 10 March, 7 April, 5 May, 26 May, 30 June.
[17]Letter by R.J.W. to Editor, *ELO* 17 March. For details of the weekly "nuisance" see *ELA* 3 March, *ELO* 24 March, 7 April, 28 April, 19 May.
[18]See *ELO* 24 March. The case is fully reported in the *ELA* 31 march under the "Strange Career of a Surgeon".
[19]*ELA* 4 August.
[20]*ELO* 4 February.
[21]*ELO* 17 March.
[22]See, for example, *ELO* 12 May re absconding charge brought by St. George's-in-the-East, and *ELO* 16 June for two cases by Mile End Old Town Workhouse. For the case of William Johns see *ELO* 9 June.
[23]For charges brought by St. George's-in-the-East see *ELO* 17 March. For Mile End Old Town see *ELO* 4 February.
[24]*In Darkest London*, pp. 184-5.
[25]*ELO* 21 April.
[26]According to T.S. & M.B. Simey, *Charles Booth, Social Scientist*, pp. 180-2. See also Brian Harrison, "Pubs" in *The Victorian City, Images and Realities* (London, 1973) ed. H.J. Dyos and Michael Wolff, vol. 1, pp. 164-5. Booth found that "in the one mile of Whitechapel Rd. from Commercial St. to Stepney Green there were in 1899, no less than 48 drinking places"; a map on p. 164 of Harrison's article shows their exact location.
[27]*Life and Labour* (1st ed.) pp. 113-14.
[28]*ELO* 14 April.
[29]*ELO* 3 February.
[30]See reports in *ELO*, "Police Intelligence", 28 January and 3 March.
[31]For examples see *ELO* 31 March, 7 April and 30 June.
[32]William Potter (C. Tirling), *Thomas Jackson of Whitechapel* (Liverpool 1929) p. 77.
[33]*ELO* 4 February.
[34]*ELO* 9 June.
[35]*ELO* 30 June. Other violent attacks on police reported up to July are recorded in *ELO* 7 January, 17, 24 and 31 March, 7, 21 and 28 April, 5

and 12 May.
[36]*ELO* 21 April.
[37]*ELO* 14 and 21 April respectively.
[38]*ELO* 3 and 10 March respectively.
[39]See reports in both *ELA* and *ELO* dated 10 March.
[40]*ELO* 4 February and 19 May.
[41]*ELO* 3 and 10 March respectively.
[42]See both *ELO* and *ELA* 24 March.
[43]*ELO* 18 February.
[44]The full process of this case is reported in *ELO* 31 March and 7 April.
[45]*ELO* 10 March and 2 June.
[46]*ELO* 21 January and 31 March.
[47]*ELO* 21 January, and *ELA* and *ELO* both dated 17 March.
[48]*ELO* 25 February.
[49]*ELO* 28 April.
[50]*The Nineteenth Century* XIV, p. 252.
[51]*In Darkest England*, p. 26.
[52]Sergeant (ex-Detective) B. Leeson, *Lost London* (London, 1934) p. 119.
[53]*ELO* 5 May.
[54]Janet Hitchman, *They Carried the Sword* (London, 1966) p. 38.
[55]John Law, *A City Girl*, pp. 54-5.
[56]*ELA* 6 October.
[57]*East End News* 16 November.
[58]See *ELO* 14 January, 10 March and 19 May respectively. For further cases of child molesting see *ELO* 9 and SO June. For indecent exposure Saunders sentenced a Joseph Ebinay, aged 40, to two months' hard labour — report *ELO* 7 April.
[59]Recorded fully in *ELO* 11 February.
[60]*ELO* 7 January and 11 February.
[61]*ELO* 17 March.
[62]*ELO* 5 and 26 May.
[63]*ELO* 4 February.
[64]*ELO* 5 May.
[65]*ELO* 16 June.
[66]*ELO* 25 February. Other assaults by women on men are reported continually throughout the year. See, for example, violent attacks on policemen: *ELO* 7 and 21 January.
[67]For an insight into the problems of Jewish prostitution in London, see Edward J. Bristow, *Prostitution and Prejudice* (Oxford, 1982) pp. 236ff.
[68]*ELO* 3 and 25 March.
[69]*ELO* 17 March, and see below, pp. 249-55 for Charrington's "war against vice".
[70]See above, pp. 120-1.
[71]Both cases are described in *ELO* 21 April.
[72]The numerical preponderance of such cases is evidenced in the Police Intelligence Reports in the *ELO* and the Thames Police Court News in the *ELA* throughout the year.
[73]*In Darkest London*, p. 182.

[74] *ELA* 18 August.
[75] For a full contemporary report on the murder and subsequent inquest see *ELA* 11, 18 and 25 August. In the same week and following other recent murders, only a brief mention is made of five other violent attacks on women and children which were contemporaneous with the Turner murder. It was the nature and ferocity of the latter that afforded it the top headlines and reportage in the national press.
[76] *ELA* 1 September, "Another Whitechapel Mystery. Horrible Murder in Bucks Row".
[77] In one case a publican claimed that he had become bankrupt. See D. McCormick, *The Identity of Jack the Ripper* (London, 1959) p. 74.
[78] *ELA* 15 September, "Rambler — Here and There".
[79] See *ELA* 6 October for details of murders and *East End News* 5 October for Rev. Greatorex's speech.
[80] For descriptions of the murder and the emotional scene at the funeral of Kelly see *ELA* 17 and 24 November
[81] Although the late Stephen Knight's *Jack the Ripper: the final solution* (London, 1976) offers the most plausible evidence in identifying the killings as a series of ritual executions carried out under the direction of freemasons in high places to protect the Prince of Wales' son, Albert Edward, and thereby the monarchy (which at this time was at its lowest ebb in popularity), from exposure to a public scandal.
[82] *ELA* 22 September.
[83] *ELA* 13 October. The other journals were the *Pall Mall Gazette, Spectator, Saturday Review* and *Punch*.
[84] *ELA* 6 October.
[85] P.E. Halstead, *Doctor in the Nineties* (London, 1959). "Rambler" in the *ELA* of 6 October refers to a report telegraphed in by a Mr Bishop, *Daily News'* correspondent in New York, of series of murders, accompanied by similar atrocities, recently perpetrated in Texas. "The criminal was never caught, and the suggestion is that he has come over to England, and is at his old work in Whitechapel."
[86] *ELA* 17 November.
[87] *ELA* 1 December. One of the many theories was that the Ripper was a butcher employed on a cattle boat transporting live freight to and from the continent, thus periodically appearing and disappearing. According to one coroner the knowledge of physiology possessed by a butcher would be sufficient to enable him to locate and cut out the parts of the body which were abstracted (*ELA* 17 November.)
[88] *ELA* 20 October.
[89] Ibid. 17 November.
[90] *ELA* 1 December, "'Jack the Ripper' — in Russia".
[91] *ELO* 15 September.
[92] See *JC* 5 October for comments of Chief Rabbi on the Ritter case, and notes on the two Rabbinical letters to *The Times*.
[93] For details of the murders see accounts given in L.W. Mathews, *The Mystery of Jack the Ripper* (London, 1948). On the Jewish association see pp. 48, 82 and 93. For contemporary information on the Jewish factor see also *JC* 12 October, *ELA* 13 October and *Commonweal* 20

October.

[94] *In Darkest London*, p. 208.

[95] See above, n. 81.

[96] "One of the East End representatives might do service by looking into the police arrangements in the East End of London, for there is room for grave doubt whether our end of town has its fair return for money in the matter of police protection." It went on to evidence assaults by night where "the guardian of the night" was notably absent. "Where was the police?" it demanded.

[97] See *ELA*, 6 October, "The Mysterious Atrocities", and "Here and There — Rambler" in the same issue.

[98] *Commonweal* 13 October.

[99] See *The Letters of Queen Victoria*, third series, vol. 1. 1886-1890 (London, 1930).

[100] *East End News*, 14 September. Reporting on the *Punch* article of 11 September.

[101] The full text of his letter to *The Times* on September 13th is well worth scrutiny. His major object was to press for an immediate rehousing programme. Barnett was resolved to rebuild the "whole bad quarter" (letter to FGB 20 October 1888).

[102] *ELA* 27 October reproduced a copy of the letter.

[103] See *ELO* 11 February.

[104] Note Local Government Reports in *ELA* 8, 15 and 22 December.

[105] Enid Gauldie, *Cruel Habitations*, p. 293. In effect the murders helped to create a climate ready to reassess means of ending overcrowding in the slums and thereby re-directed a thrust towards the greater need for municipal housing rather than philanthropic projects as proposed by Octavia Hill, etc.

[106] Jerry White, *Rothschild Buildings*, pp. 29-30.

[107] Frank Owen, *Tempestuous Journey: Lloyd George and His Times* (London 1954) pp. 63-4.

[108] See *Justice* 15 and 22 September, pp. 63-4. 13 October for its observations on the Ripper murders.

[109] *Commonweal* 6 October and 3 November. In the 29th issue, anarchist David Nicoll rejects the charge by "renegade" radical paper the *Echo*, that the murders "have their origin in the incendiary speeches of Trafalgar Square agitators".

[110] *ELA* 25 August, "Crime in East London".

[111] For the case of fratricide see *ELA* 21 July, the attempted murder *ELA* 6 October. Bartlett's crime is reported in full in the *ELA* 25 August, and his subsequent trial and sentencing to death on the 27 October.

[112] See *ELA* 29 December for the reports on Christmas charges and the murder in Charles Yard.

Chapter 8
The Saints

> It is very difficult to give any adequate idea of the extent of the religious and philanthropic effort that has been made in the Whitechapel District. No statistical device would be of much avail to measure the work done, and description fails to realise it. Great as the effort is in many other parts of London, it is greatest here.
>
> Charles Booth, *Life and Labour of the People of London*, vol. II, pp. 50-1.

The one growth industry in East London, at this time of social distress, was charity. Armed with the Bible and the bread basket, an army of individual and institution-based philanthropists marched across the city borders to aid (and, as some suggested, abet) the growing armies of the poor. As we have seen, middle-class field workers were recruited from a variety of the more affluent groups.

Attitudes towards such seemingly overt acts of mercy were not uncritical. One of the earliest pioneers, Samuel Barnett, regarded "indiscriminate charity among the curses of London... I would say that the poor starve because of the alms they receive." The effect of charity was that "the people never learn to work or save; out relief from the House, or the dole of the charitable, has stood in the way of providence, which God their father would have taught them." These were his observations as a recent arrival in 1874. That year a committee consisting of the Rev. and Mrs S. Barnett and three others, sat in judgment on an applicant for relief every Friday. Their policy was to offer the supplicant "efficient assistance in the shape of a substantial gift or a loan, or perhaps the most hopeful way of helping him will be by a stern refusal". The latter sentence often led to a crowd attack on the vicarage, such that the Barnetts were forced to have "a door cut from our house into the Church through which the Vicar could slip out to fetch the police". By 1877 the Barnetts were still maintaining in their Parish Report that "the principle of our work is that we aim at decreasing not suffering but SIN".[1] However, continual exposure to the horrors of poverty, and the growing recognition of the innocence of most its victims, led them to modify such notions of an "undeserving" poor.

Radical opinion, expressed by Harry Quelch in *Justice* (7 January) was more forthright. Commenting on the Jubilee Year, just ended, with its promise of a revival in trade, he dismissed it "as fresh evidence of the utter uselessness of jubilee junketings, of charity doles, of soup kitchens and Mansion House funds to effect any change for the better". Following another tack, the *East London Observer* turned its attention to that current prime dispenser of aid, the Charity Organisation Society. With a magnificent piece of irony, its observer castigated the delegates at the annual gathering in the fashionable Willis's Rooms.

> Mr Lock opened the ball by reading a bilious effusion from Lord Derby abusing those who could not swallow the gospel of Buckingham Street, describing them as "dishonest or ignorant" and concluding with the more important and practical remark that the Society might rely on his continued fiver — "support" was the word used by his lordship — but in referring to the accounts for 1887, I find that it is typified by a donation of exactly five pounds... "One of the accusations against us," he (the chairman) said, "is that out of a pound we only spend a very few shillings in charity. Well, a great many of the principal supporters of the Society urge — rightly — that, as it is, <u>we almost spend too many shillings in actual relief</u>. That is not the object of the Society." Then his lordship (Stalbridge) continued: "Another charge brought against us is that we are too inquisitorial, and that, after having asked questions, and searched for information, we do nothing. That, I admit, is perfectly true, and is in accordance with the constitution of the Society." Oh, ye gods, what a Society!...

In like vein he went on to debunk this "sapient council of respectable mediocrities" for their confusion of aims and methods. "There is no general rule of the Society that able-bodied persons temporarily out of work shall not be assisted", and their instructions then went on to emphasise that "the temporary relief that is usually given to the unemployed, whether by work tickets or doles, is a mere delusion and only increases every year the burden of pauperism". The reporter confirmed that the finer feelings of human nature among these charity organisers were subordinated to the dictates of "red-tapeism and a costly system of centralisation", and contemptuously dismissed their conclusion that "the want of thrift and careful living is probably the chief cause of distress!"

> It will be seen at once... in the study of economics and sociology what a deal the charity organisers understand of social questions. They coolly assume that it is possible for the thousands of men out of work, and unable to procure it through no fault of their own — even dock labourers and numerous other unskilled men, with wives and families dependent upon them to be or to become thrifty, though when they are in work they never earn enough to live on decently, are compelled to overcrowd their dwellings and live under the most demoralising conditions![2]

In an evocative article, one week later, a correspondent, "J.H.J.", went beyond denigration of such dispensers of charity to condemn outright the social and economic conditions which debased giver and supplicant alike. The latter faced the more painful hazards:

> If the impecunious "stranger" is not careful as to the manner in which he makes his necessities known, he may speedily find himself in the arms of a Christian policeman, zealous for the inviolability and sanctity of the law in this year of our Lord, one thousand eight hundred and eighty eight. If the indigent one, who has fallen from healthy estate, seeks relief in accordance with the magnificent provisions of the laws of a "civilised" country he can get relief inkind, of a kind, on surrendering his liberty to a great extent, or until he shall have performed certain laborious and worthless tasks which our parochial wiseacres have imposed for the supposed protection of those who do not require relief. If the "stranger" applies to a Christian professor, or leader of a Christian church, he will probably be told that, not being one of the "faithful" or "elect" nothing can be done for him, but if he goes to some fashionable charity (but not charitable) society they will, probably, "enquire" into his early life — as to what age he was weaned, when he ran alone, and so on — and see if his "sin spots" are ineradicable; if his hunger ought to be appeased; if his future is worth considering, and if his soul is worth saving. And by the time the "enquiries" are completed and the charitable committees have solemnly decided to refer the applicant to the hospitality of the Poor Law, the unfortunate and impatient stranger may have flitted or passed away.

The correspondent, having "determined to spend one or two hours with homeless, destitute outcasts and see for myself what sort of a day Good Friday was to them", entered Reuben May's Mission Hall in Great Arthur treet. There "700 or 800 men and lads with perhaps a score of women", hungry and homeless, were packed into a small area with "scarce an inch of standing room. And all for what? Simply a mess of pottage — a tin of lentil and oatmeal porridge some 3lbs in weight!" With emotional fervour he embellished a portrait of misery on the bread line:

> Mr Reuben May was speaking a few words of cheer from a platform under the pulpit and as the assistants were bringing up the porridge from the basement, he unfurled a sort of bannerette on which was printed an appropriate thank-offering, and which, to the incongruous tune of "Home Sweet Home" the men sang off as grace in capital style, proceeding without more ado to do justice to what was set before them. Verily it was a SORROWFUL SIGHT that large, hideous mass of suffering humanity. Here were a few young lads but 14, 16 and 18 years of age, who only required to be taken kindly in hand at that moment, perhaps to lead honest, industrious, respectable lives; perhaps to be made brilliant men of service to others as well as to themselves. Yet no one seems to care a fig about them in this competitive strife, where it is "each for himself, and the weakest to the wall". By far the large majority of those present were young and middle-aged men — many "horny-handed sons of toil" who had been maimed and worsted in their encounter with the world... There can be no doubt that those who are blessed with an abundance of this world's goods have some duty to perform to the oppressed and to the unsuccessful in life's stormy battle. Even Lord Derby has said that he does not believe in the gospel of success, as it is a gospel that can be preached only to the few![3]

Later (9 June), a pertinent touch was added by an editorial musing on "poverty's perpetual presence". This was regarded as a "disease", in the treatment of which "both skill and attention should operate through legislation". Not through institutions of elaborate architectural beauty, chiefly concerned in maintaining a highly-salaried staff could this be effected, but those resting on the principles of "equity and economy", justifying their existence on their ability to "lessen the horrors of poverty". As for the proper mission of a charitable society, it was primarily to assist

> the industrious poor of either sex, to find employment for them and to see that they are kept employed under no stigma whatever arising from the fact that they have been recipients of relief and under conditions favourable to their moral and physical development. Such conditions, of course, imply that the workers are neither overworked nor underpaid, and that their interests as employees are strictly safeguarded by a system of state supervision.

It was a far-sighted proposition, well in tune with those ideas currently gathering strength in the movement against the hitherto sacrosanct Social Darwinism.

Considering state intervention as the best means of remedying the defects of private charity, Charles Booth predicted that the substitution of governmental direction would not negate the demand for the latter. In doing so he dismissed the sentimental bleats of those romantics who clung to the bankrupt illusion of the colourful vagabond of song and legend.

> What could we lose by such a change? We are always losing something of the poetry and picturesqueness of the past. The rags of the beggar, his rare orgies, his snatches of song and merriment, his moments of despair, his devil-may-care indifference to the decencies of civilised life — all these touch the imagination and lend themselves to art; they are excellent theatrical properties, less imposing but not less attractive than the personal state and impulsive changes of feeling of the absolute monarch, or the loyal devotion of the feudal dependent, and a hundred characteristics of a fallen society gone, never to return. Yet audacity, daring, generosity, devotion, impulsive affection still exist and flourish among us; the setting alone is changed. In the same way, there would be no less room than now or than always for charity, whether the stately generosity of endowment or self-sacrificing service of man or pity which seeks its exercise in the relief of suffering; all these would find their way in softening the inevitably hard action of the state, but would be required to fall in line with it.[4]

Whatever the academic arguments on method, that year there was a plethora of "stately generosity" and "self-sacrificing service" on the part of practical-minded individuals dedicated to alleviating suffering in Tower Hamlets. It was during the cold months that relief was the most pressing. Again it is in the local press that we learn of the extent of the nature and incidence of charity. Thus from January to March much space is devoted to such concerns.

We are struck by the diversity of the sources of benevolence. From all quarters of the East End the feeding of the hungry went on continuously. The type of operation is exemplified by two reports in the New Year issue of the *East London Observer* (7 January).

Friday 30 December
The annual tea for the lodging house poor took place at the Schoolroom, St. Mary's Street, Whitechapel, when about 400 men of the Chicksand Street lodging houses partook of a substantial tea provided by the Whitechapel Lodging House Mission. After tea the number increased to about 600, when an entertainment was given, which was much appreciated by those present.

Saturday 31 December
Dinner to "deserving poor" at the Town Hall, Poplar, was given by Mrs A.B. Marshall of the School of Cookery, Mortimer Street, Cavendish Square, consisting of soup, roast beef, potatoes and Xmas pudding — to between 250 and 300 of the deserving poor of Poplar and Limehouse... The Bishop of Bedford, after grace had been said, "thought... he might ask them to show by their applause how grateful they were to Mrs Marshall;.. These were hard times for many of them. His heart was often sad on this account and he could assure them that never a day passed over his head without his thinking very sympathetically of their case." Afterwards a conjuring performance was given, varied by the vocalism of some friends of the hostess.

And much more in the same vein during the succeeding months from locations, including church halls and public houses, sited all over the area[5]. Other varieties of charity were on offer. *The Illustrated London News* (11 February), under the heading "The Playhouses" informed its readers that "Mr Alec Yorke, one of the Queen's household, and Mr Charles Bethune have started a charitable institution "down East" called "The Shelter", where they hide the poor from the inclement weather and feed them with bread and water. Mr Beerbohm Tree has determined to do something for this excellent institution and proposes a benefit at the Haymarket Theatre early in March... A capital programme like this might draw all London and give 'The Shelter' a little capital of £400."

The advocates of self-help had an eloquent spokesman in A.H.D. Acland MP who, at a meeting at the Bow Coffee Palace on 16 March, called for wider support for the newly opened Tower Hamlets Co-operative Society at 227-229 Bow Road. He emphasised that "if London is to improve, especially among the working classes, it will be by genuine efforts, and I know no better work than co-operation".[6] But what of those living and working on the margin of existence? For them, such prospects of mutual aid could only exist as a fanciful misconception! It was towards relieving this mass residuum of the poor, "deserving" and "undeserving", that a quartet of great philanthropists directed their life-long efforts and, in the process, projected the East End of London on the international scene.

Dr Thomas J. Barnardo

The first, whom we have already noted, was Thomas J. Barnardo, the greatest benefactor of destitute children, who began his operations in Stepney.[7] That year gave him his hour of opportunity to focus attention on his enterprise, and thereby attract more resources for expansion. For by 1888 he had "achieved universal recognition that (he) dealt with children whom the nation had left derelict, yet his homes had so moulded their lives as to make them an asset to society". The same recorder also observed that the "Barnardo family in the homes in 1888 was six times greater than in 1877", and that by 1888 "he had migrated 3,773 children to the outposts of empire where, in his terms, 98% had settled successfully".[8] In that year, too, we detect the finalisation of his creed and the aim and direction of his labour. For, whatever his real motivation, he pronounced his *raison d'etre* in his *Three Tracts*, 1888.

Barnardo asserted, against current middle-class belief, that the "seeds of the righteous were among the children of the poorest". The dangers confronting them at birth were "due to their environment rather than any individual tendency to evil". To succour the homeless was, for him, a sacred duty, hence the notice "NO DESTITUTE CHILD IS REFUSED ADMISSION" inscribed in bold letters over his door in Stepney Causeway. Thus, too, the joyful relief on the face of the dying pauper Mrs Clarke when, on learning that Barnardo had accepted her two children, exclaimed, "I have no workhouse fears for them now!" His daily task was to snatch "waifs and strays" off the streets, already proficient in crime themselves and probably the future progenitors of criminals ("a process of degeneration taking place around us every day in squalid London") and to rescue "such poor bairns from impending ruin before it is too late". He outlined a record of child reclamation that spoke for itself. He had received four new children every day throughout 1886 and had emigrated to Canada 622 of those trained in his English homes during the same year. By January 1887 he had a total complement of "1,700 boys and girls under my care requiring daily food, education and clothing", while the last figure (Christmas 1887) stood at 2,149! "Yet all this is but a drop in the ocean to the great needs of so vast a city as in our modern Babylon," lamented Barnardo.

It also provided publicity to back his plea for greater contributions. He wrote that he "required £83 a day to feed 1,800. £16 will support one healthy child for a whole year in any of our London homes. £1.10s will provide the means by which 100 homeless children can be gathered from the lodging houses and the streets to a SUPPER, at which the most needy may be selected for the permanent benefits of the institutions." As a ploy to add effect to his personal testament in succouring the army of innocents, he concluded in verse

> In cellar, in garret, in alley and court,
> They weep and they suffer and pine,
> And the wolves of the city are prowling near,
> Back wolves! For the children are mine.[10]

The verse might be pithy, but the versifier knew his audience. It was the religious, the sentimental, the compassionate who responded accordingly, with profitable results for Barnardo's.

On 10 January the *East End News* reported that the annual supper for destitute children was held on 5 January at Barnardo's Edinburgh Castle Mission Hall, Rhodeswell Road, Limehouse. "About 2,000 waifs and strays, collected by night searchers in the streets, in the market places, by the riverside, in the common lodging houses, casual wards and sleeping places of the destitute poor, sat down to a good substantial supper. A glance at the boys and girls showed what was represented of them, for many were without headwear or boots, and had evidently not seen soap and water for a considerable period." In fact, as Barnardo confirmed, "the numbers (2,213) and appearance of the children present a poverty deeper and more widespread than marked the previous annual musters of the children of the streets... never since 1872, when the Educational Act was vigorously enforced, have I had so many young children at one of my annual suppers." And to enhance his message to would-be sympathisers he added that, on this occasion, there were "400 girls among the waifs and strays... as a rule at our street children supper, we seldom have more than 100... the great majority of the female children present had that undescribably draggled-tailed appearance which told plainly of lodging house and beggar life."[11]

Children were not the only recipients of the doctor's beneficence. On Friday 27 January a hot dinner for 1,200 adults was arranged by Barnardo at the Edinburgh Castle. These were "poor and aged folk, men and women collected from various lodging houses, casual wards of the Union workhouses, and night refuges in different parts of London. They were regaled with roast beef, potatoes, pudding and a cup of tea, at the cost of the committee and benevolent subscribers. The hospitable repast was followed by the singing of hymns and by short addresses of an encouraging nature."[12] The last no doubt to add spiritual uplift to the feast! At the end of January the annual factory girls' tea was held with Barnardo contemplating offering "further meals to the blind, to tramps and vagabonds and to East End omnibus and cabmen respectively".[13]

The urgency of his work among the homeless children was brought home dramatically, when 362 fresh cases of destitute boys and girls were admitted in the first two months of 1888. ("February showing the highest record of work ever accomplished in any one month in the history of the Institution", with 202 being brought in during the first 25 days of the month.) We read: "Some of these were little cripples; some deaf mutes; some quite blind; some had other grievous maladies; some were so far advanced in disease that they were admitted only to die...". He had, in effect, set up one of the first hospices dedicated to ease the last days of those most vulnerable to rejection by other welfare bodies. It also registered his change of policy towards blind children, hitherto refused admission and sent on to other societies who offered specialist aid. Thenceforth he declared himself "fully committed to the resolve not to use any really destitute blind children who apply... and am now making steps to arrange for the formation of two small families of blind children, who shall be taught carefully, and receive that technical training which goes so far to relieve the helplessness, sadness, and incapacity of a life so sadly deprived".[14]

His practical concern for crippled children was, in the context of his time and place, marked by genuine compassion and effective application. While a new Cripples Home was being built locally, "feeble cripples", that is those not requiring surgical aid, were temporarily boarded out in rural districts pending transfer to his Felixstowe Home where they would remain during the winter months. A second class of cripples "who although deformed are not in pain or in feeble health, are unquestionably best circumstanced when allowed to mingle freely with their healthy brothers and sisters". Here Barnardo, drawing on his own experience, showed remarkable prescience in implementing ideas only recently claimed as "newly discovered". A third group, the "feeblest", defined as "those who suffer from abscesses, sinuses and open wounds, and were thus unfit either to be boarded out or placed amongst healthy children", would, of necessity, be placed in his infirmary under constant medical care.[15]

An itinerary of aid rendered was listed in his Winter Report of 1887-1888. From his Deaconess House, lady helpers went forth to seek and relieve countless cases of privation, while at the Edinburgh Castle food tickets and money payments provided instant relief to supplicants in dire distress. Healing and help went hand in hand at his Medical Mission, whose applicants were the miserable inhabitants of "empty garrets and cheerless attics". At his Copperfield Road Free Schools "the daily ministration of warm meals has put new heart into legions of pallid-faced little scholars". Yet Barnardo was quick to qualify his activities in accordance with the current mores. "Our resources have not been frittered away over undeserving loafers, nor have I in any way permitted a breach of the scriptural law, 'If any would not work, neither should he eat'"[16]

Barnardo was puzzled by the fact that many of the street urchins were reluctant to succumb to the attraction of the permanent warmth and security of his homes. In May he recalled:

> At our supper to Street Arabs (ie 5 January) this year my attention was drawn to two boys, evidently brothers... who, clad only in the most wretched rags, and having a genuine lodging house and doss out upon the street look from top to toe, were nevertheless the life and soul of all the circle of boys who sat near them, whom they kept in convulsions of laughter with their witticisms and street fun...

> The eldest of the pair was but 13, and the youngest only 10. They were half starved, their cheeks were hollow and sunken, their faces pale and thin. Their dress was torn here, there and everywhere, while for shoes the covering on their feet was indeed but a poor apology. Nevertheless the boys were merry, so merry that a good friend of mine could scarcely keep the tears back as she watched them, and observed the infinitely pathetic contrast between their outer and their inner circumstances... they, alas! had neither father nor mother, nor friend in the world apart from each other.[17]

It was this perverse independence and comradeship of the streets that eluded Barnardo. Yet to those in dire need who were under legal parental control and outside his jurisdiction, he still offered clothing, especially to the bootless nippers. But a pair of boots was a status symbol and, thus, a saleable commodity. He soon caught on that some of these ended up in the pawn shop with the proceeds spent on drink. He therefore issued them as "hired" to the parents, with an indelible stamp on each boot. Should anyone attempt to dispense of them, the Barnardo mark would thereby open them to the charge of theft. The threat alone was in most cases adequate. With winter approaching he was appealing for "night dresses, knitted stockings, warm jackets and ulsters, either new or left over by the ladies, which are often stronger than new articles of the same class in cheaper makes".[18]

Barnardo was also preoccupied with the problem of juvenile crime, traditionally prevalent in the East End. He concluded that prevention was better than cure, citing his own methods of attaining "rescued cases" and evidencing "how much less it costs to make honest citizens out of wastrel youths than to keep them, when once, through our neglect, they have joined the criminal classes". He outlined his balance sheet:

1. Bread, water, shame, flogging; cost per young criminal in prison, <u>£80 per annum for all the term of a lost life</u>.

2. Meat, bread, honour, the Bible, Christian teaching; cost in a Christian workshop and training home, and then emigration, <u>£19 once and for all</u>.[19]

He agreed with current opinion that children inhabiting cheap lodging houses were those most exposed to criminal influence.

Others of the same kind, with no fixed abode and found wandering in the streets, were liable to be charged and sent to prison, where they would receive further education in crime. Barnardo quotes the case of an 18-year-old admitted that year to his Labour House.

> George was an orphan, and literally friendless and alone in the world. The first fact I learned about him that he had been to prison... Well, what was it for? And the answer was, "For being homeless!"... So our wise world shut him up, and thereby set a life-long mark upon him, whereby his only society would be gaol-birds and criminals! He had spent his life in the workhouse, and in the sick ward, and on the streets; and now, with the broad arrow stamp upon him, his peril of bad companions bade fair to ruin his future.

The Doctor claimed that he had stepped in in the nick of time and the lad now had "the probability of Canada before him, and of eating there the bread of self-respect and honest labour".[20]

The Ripper murders gave him the opportunity to highlight the moral dangers threatening those children frequenting lodging houses. Commenting on the "horrors of great darkness" that had befallen East London, he pointed out that of the victims "three... were regular habitués of the common lodging houses" where children of the streets are "condemned to the vilest associations... degraded by constant contact with fallen women, with thieves, with criminals of every type, and with persons who are veritably the pariahs of society". He had, in fact, inspected 32 Flower and Dean Street, a known rendezvous for prostitutes, shortly after the first murder. One of the women he had spoken to there he later identified on the slab of a Whitechapel mortuary. It was the fourth victim, Elizabeth Stride. In November he acquired two houses — one in Flower and Dean Street, the other in Dock Street, Stepney — and had them duly licensed as Common Lodging Houses for Children.

He intended these as exploratory innovations which had to work. (He had recently been pestering the local authority to establish such places, advocating the provision of special shelters for young children of the tramp or casual class — something between the common lodging house and the casual wards of the workhouse.) Only children under 16 would be admitted, and they should be free to enter and depart... If successful he hoped it would result in legislative enactments on a national scale. It was the Ripper who enabled him to put his ideas into action. That they provided a sanctuary for those who feared the oncoming of night is recalled by Barnardo's chronicler:

> A nominal admission charge of a penny per night was made and a hot meal was provided at the cost of a halfpenny. No needy child was sent away, even if the penny for admission was not forthcoming; but it was necessary, the doctor explained, to keep up the form, and even to appear inflexible in carrying out the demand for the night's fee. Women with children were admitted, as well as children who were alone. The doors were open in the evening about 7 o'clock. A few particulars, name, age, address of previous lodging etc., were obtained from each applicant and duly recorded. A simple nourishing meal was provided, evening prayers followed, and then all retired to bed. At 10.30 the doors were closed and locked for the night, and the lights lowered.
>   Perhaps a dozen times in the night some poor girl would come to the door and call aloud for admission. "Of course it was against the rules," said Dr Barnardo, "but we dare not keep them out." Sometimes a policeman would come and beg that a young girl, or perhaps a mere child whom he had discovered on his beat, sitting homeless in a market place, or walking wearily through the streets, might find admission.[21]

By 1888 in accord with one aspect of Board of Guardians policy,[22] Barnardo was "deeply convinced that of all methods of training children none are so advantageous, none so economical, and none so successful in every way as boarding out". By the end of the year he boasted that "500 of our bairns are so placed". He decreed that the best foster parents were found among the respectable labouring classes in country villages, given that certain safeguards were met: first, that the local clergyman be willing to assume the position of chief superintendent of those children placed in his parish; secondly, that a small committee of at least six women would undertake the whole burden of visitation of the children at the home of their foster parents; thirdly, that foster parents of the "humbler labouring class" must be Christians, should be fond of children and should have an assured income from other sources. There were other criteria that necessitated the existence of a good parish or national school in the village and that foster parents should have no children of their own or any others boarded out to them. Children selected, aged between 5 and 7 years, had to be free of any serious illness, "of good character and conduct, having, as a rule, received some little training first in a (Barnardo) institution". Thus the interests of both parties were protected. A fully qualified woman doctor, a Miss Walker, had been appointed as overall inspectress "to pronounce upon questions affecting the children's health". She always made surprise visits, and after an inspection that was "full and searching in character", would submit a "minute and exhaustive" report on each boarder. Barnardo boasted that "no better scheme exists for bringing up little children of the destitute class in a homely, common-sense and economical way."[23]

There were other ways of emptying the East London streets of their human "dross". Barnardo's intimate knowledge of London's underworld early acquainted him with the diverse means by which children were exploited. Expansion of British settlement in Canada and Australia needed colonists — raw materials to help fructify the vast open plains of both continents. Emigration, voluntary or otherwise, was the order of the day. The push and pull of social and economic conditions within and without Britain demanded it. By discriminate selection the most "suitable" of the slum dwellers of Whitechapel could be exported to make their labour available for the vast new farmlands of empire. Barnardo had already foreseen the possibilities of emigration policy. He noted that "it was in the year 1882 that we organised our first party of emigrants for the Dominions". Previously occasional groups had been sent out under the charge of employers and emigration agencies. On adopting his own scheme he selected "the flower of our flock", defending his support of emigration on the grounds that "by training the boys in the mechanical arts I could only place those... in situations in Great Britain by turning out of employment many now hard at work for their living". So off to Canada with the children "we have drilled and tested; they have no family responsibilities to handicap them. They are decent, honest and industrious."[24] For Barnardo was convinced "that nothing so permanently lightens the burdens of the old country, nothing so surely attacks, at the very roots, the Upas Tree of social distress and discontent... as this... scheme of juvenile emigration".

His binding excuse for speeding up emigrant numbers that year was to make room for the overwhelming demands of fresh destitute youngsters seeking admission to his Stepney Homes.

Thus on 29 March, 200 trainee boys sailed in the steamship Polynesian to Canada, with an additional 400 boys and girls set to follow between May and June. According to Barnardo the demand for farm labour there was "practically unlimited". "Farmers flock almost on to the trains and shipboard in their eagerness to secure a lad." A system of distribution was centred in a large house in Toronto, which also served as a temporary residence for boys who had lost one job and were seeking another. The empty plains of Manitoba were chosen for settling older boys, specially trained in the Youth Labour House at Stepney. One such Barnardo farm comprising 8,960 acres was located at Russell in the Shell River district and served as a main agricultural training school. It extended for 14 square miles, and a large house, resembling an army barracks, was built to accommodate up to 200 boys. The immediate aim was to create a creamery and cheese factory, but the overall objective was to discipline the ex-slum lads to undertake "continuous hard work" under "pure and healthy conditions", that would ensure them "an abundant livelihood with future prospects of independence".[26]

Whether Barnardo succeeded in thus transforming the lives of all his overseas charges to better purposes is questionable. There were difficulties on the way. His enthusiasm, and that of the British press, in advocating emigration as a means of relieving the poor rates was already counter-productive as far as Canada was concerned. For years earlier the *Toronto Globe* had voiced fears which would exercise the public mind for the following two decades: "Street waifs and inmates of reformatories, refuges and lodging houses... are not the classes with which to build up a strong nationality."[27] Barnardo, by 1888, could justifiably reply that "the injudicious emigration from this country, of which they (the Canadians) very properly complain, does not include the... children I send out, but that these complaints refer solely to the indiscriminate dumping upon their shores of adults of the poorest class, mostly from city slums, many of whom are without character, and few of whom have any means of earning a livelihood anywhere, except by begging". He pointed out that boys and girls placed in employment overseas were levied one dollar a year out of their wages as a repayment to Barnardo's Homes for aid rendered. In 1887 he received a total of 300 dollars from a majority obviously in stable employment.[28]

But, as Lady Wagner reveals, there were other problems affecting the well-being of the young emigrant: in Britain the question of tearing a child away from its roots, that is from bonds of family — inadequate or otherwise — and the permanent psychological damage resulting therefrom; and on arrival the animosity of the Canadian labour unions who resented the incursion of cheap juvenile labour that could depress the wages of the average adult farm worker. There is evidence of the ruthless exploitation of children by farmers which eluded the notice of inspection, given the shortage of inspectors whom Barnardo constantly needed to fulfil his obligation to monitor the condition of all his charges. Hence the number of absconders, who, in desperation, took to the wilderness to escape from a cruel master. The advantages, therefore, of this compulsory emigration of the young (since under Barnardo's authority they had little command over their own fate) are still open to debate. Only assiduous scholarly research will put into perspective Barnardo and his acolytes' enthusiasm for transplanting "a young and struggling life from the overcrowded wilderness of London to the fresh soil and gracious surroundings of a Canadian farm".

Barnardo's firm belief in personal charitable action through the Christian Witness led him to reject the growing view put to him that "the state ought to take the work up" and assume total responsiblity for the welfare of its citizens in need. He replied, "Well, one often longs for the adoption of some form of that suggestion, especially when one reads that the money invested by the state in a single man of war represents a larger sum than has reached my hands during the whole twenty-two and a half years of my work in East London." Yet "it would be a sad business if the Church of God allowed its work to be done by the nation. The relief of the poor and the rescue of the children is as much a necessity for the healthy life of the Church of God as the realisation of experiences of sorrow, suffering and chastisement are to the development of the brightest graces in the individual Christian life".[29] In like terms, and with one eye on his affluent religious benefactors, he also publicly rejected the socialist panacea of a reconstructed society based on a forced redistribution of wealth. On 17 January, addressing an audience of 1,300 unemployed dockers at the dinner given to them at the Edinburgh Castle, he argued by giving his assurance of the deep sympathy of Christian people generally with their unemployed brethren, if it meant anything, meant that there is a narrower gap between "classes" and "masses" than some persons imagine. Proceeding amidst the closest attention to a little talk about remedies, he decried some of the theories of socialism, notably on the subjects of community of property and the nationalisation of the land, and showed how property, like snow, if it lay level today would be blown into drifts tomorrow! Socialists ascribe most of the evils from which the community suffer to purely legislative causes. But alas! many of the wrongs that call for redress are solely due to moral causes; they demand reform in the individual heart, and conduct rather than in the civil constitution.

Nevertheless he concluded that no one had the right to live on the misery and degradation of others. For the younger men, the one great hope for the future lay in emigration.[30] Thus Barnardo allied himself with those who espoused philanthropic acts as a religious imperative. As such, like the others who ministered to the East End, he could neither comprehend nor concern himself with the underlying socio-economic aberrations that perpetuated an uncaring and brutalised society.

However, that year his operations diversified into fresh areas. He sniffed out and brought to safety young females, bought and sold in the lodging houses as candidates for child prostitution. Often cruelly beaten by their keepers, they were also hired or sold to tramps, their natural parents being the lenders or vendors. Wee mites were easily made to appear pitiful and hopeless by sheer neglect, and so the greater was their appeal and their ability to evoke sympathy as aids to begging. Pick-pocketing was frequently taught by parents "and many a tiny child looking the picture of innocence was thrust out upon the streets with the stern injunction not to return empty-handed!" Even more evil was the inhuman trade practised by some entrepreneurs, who "bought" the custody of unwanted babes, took out insurance policies on their lives, and then proceeded to terminate their existence quickly by physical abuse and starvation.[31] Against all these, especially the baby "farmers", Barnardo fought a ceaseless campaign, even employing illegal tactics to rescue the innocents.

His normal activities were substantially rewarding. In his annual report ending 31 March 1888, Barnardo boasted that it was his most successful year to date with 6,402 receiving benefits and the rest of the year already presaging an even higher intake. The New Children Fold at 82 Grove Road was ready to receive "100 lame, crippled and deformed children, who are destitute and who need special surgical and medical care", while at the Free Ragged Day and Sunday Schools, Copperfield Road, "1,900 of the poorest children receive education and free meals". His first munificent gesture of the year was the annual offering at Christmas. 1,300 Barnardo "clients" ranging from mere children to young men and women sat down in the great hall at the Stepney Causeway homes to a dinner of "Brobdingnagian scale". For the founder it provided a good opportunity to publicise another year of success. Benefactors were invited and other interested parties who came as onlookers "were provided with seats in the gallery and a platform underneath, (and) evinced much interest in the proceedings".[32]

But this was no mere exercise in salesmanship. One biographer, Janet Hitchman, noted that many of the ease-loving affluent Victorians came to loathe him. His policy of direct personal approach in their own homes brought "the smell of the slums into the drawing-rooms". He touched their consciences and their pockets, and they resented it. Fortunately many more were fired by his compassion and gave willingly to the cause. For the wealthy donor who offered good riddance payment, "the man had no taste, no feeling for the fitness of the occasion, and he was Irish to boot!" — the very characteristics that endeared him to his outcasts of the East End.[33]

The Rev. Samuel Barnett

The second great benefactor, the Rev. Samuel Barnett, as becomes a Church of England clergyman, was more amenable to the establishment and, therefore, less successful in establishing a close rapport with the itinerant poor. At first he had supported the policy of the Charity Organisation Society in opposing indiscriminate relief. The Society's narrow and continuously hardening dogma ultimately repelled him, and his breakaway in 1886 "sent a thrill through the philanthropic world of London".[34] As outlined above, 1888 was also his year of opportunity for furthering his ambitions both in slum clearance and, as a member of the Whitechapel Guardians, for projecting his scheme of Agricultural Training Homes for the Unemployed which was widely disseminated and aroused national debate.[35] He had finally discovered that some of those old Whitechapel folk, impoverished though they might be, "were verily the moral aristocracy of the poor". To uplift them, and their less fortunate fellows, spiritually and culturally, was a further aim to be pursued. Such views were constantly evoked during the year and backed up by practical demonstration.

On Saturday 14 January, the Clothiers Company invited the East London Branch of the University Entertainment Society, plus 300 Toynbee Hall residents and local members, to a night's festivity and musical recital. Between 7pm and 8pm the company élite and their East End guests indulged in refreshments and social chit chat. This was followed by the rendering of madrigals, the inevitable Lost Chord, and finally a speech by Warden Barnett. He viewed such social meetings as "good in bringing people together; employer and employed meet face to face. They help to remove the artificial barriers that divide class from class!"[36] The last was more a wish than a reality. Henrietta Barnett recalled how he organised musical concerts at Toynbee Hall, bringing in West End voluntary choirs including future greats such as Lady Colin Campbell and Madam Clara Butt; as well as lectures on Milton, Carlyle and Wesley attended by at most 100, or at the least, 20 people.[37]

Barnett claimed that it was all an exercise in mutual aid — profiting student residents and local labourers alike. In February, those housed in the Wadham House in Wentworth Street celebrated its first birthday with a dinner. Barnett, proposing the toast "the health of the House", dwelt on the promise accruing to all engaged in this experiment of a University transplant in the East End. He pointed out that "the residents' lives were fuller for the sense of comradeship and the keen intellectual air of college life. They were not only gaining an education of the best kind, but taking part in the social movements around them." He revealed that, currently, the student intake consisted of those "who are engaged in business during the day as schoolmasters, clerks and artisans, have each a separate room, with a common room for meals. The cost of a furnished room with attendance and use of a common room is 7s a week."[38] What was on offer for the likes of the aristocracy of labour rather than for the most gifted but needy of the working men!

It was in an important speech at the fashionable St. Philip's Church in Regent Street that Barnett outlined the purpose of his creation. He reported that the Hall now had 20 inhabitants operating as a centre of education to which some 1,000 learners were drawn every week. It was very revealing, in so far as his own attitude towards class was defined and his optimistic reference to bridging class differences and, thereby, lessening mutual suspicion and hostility.

> Toynbee Hall was simply a club house, of which the condition of membership was interest in the poor, and goodwill towards their needs. The house and its green quadrangle formed an oasis of quiet in the midst of noisy, crowded and grimy streets.
>
> The Toynbee Hall men connected themselves with that large class just above the degraded poor, by joining boards and relief committees to whose action they had given warmth through their sympathy. By their conduct they had induced officials to treat the pauper with the respect due to a man. Others had worked at education. Some had taken classes or reading parties, some had become managers of Board Schools... Some had joined men's and boys' clubs, had tried to teach them the art of self-government, had given lectures or taken them out of narrow rut. Having made friends... entertainment was a large feature of their life. The best rooms were daintily furnished and set apart for their purpose... These rooms were well used week after week by friends who came to share what was best in pictures, music or the privilege of meeting the well-born, the well-clad and the well-learned.

Barnett regarded his University Settlement as a link between the centres of industry and learning, each of which suffered from want of the other:

> As Ruskin said, "Life without industry is guilt, life without art is brutality"... The life of the East Londoner needed to be painted in sober tints and those had done him wrong who painted it in the strong colours of vice and starvation. He had, however, no conception of the past, no imagination of the future, no language in which to express emotion or hopes.

At that point he broke off to make, by inference, an unexpected attack on the well-breeched audience who had invited him:

> ...the West End amply showed that life without industry was guilt. Here there were thousands who had no work to do and who

killed time by purposeless calls and weary pleasures. They had a sort of culture selfishness; they wore out emotion in talk, and they got a new sensation today from the revelations of the Committee on Sweaters, tomorrow from the rebukes of a popular preacher. They spent lightly what had been made at the price of blood, they made conversations of that which should make their hearts bleed. They were deaf to the most piercing call, or the still small voice of suffering humanity. They were hard and cruel, and all this because they had no work to do.

He ended his forceful condemnation with a plea for a link "between the East and West... The growing enmity of classes, the unwisdom of the well-meaning was their trouble. Enmity would not be softened by missionaries and gifts. It could be done away with by the sharing, the breaking of bread in common." His University Settlement had pointed the way and "shown that rich and poor could live together. A few had done what many might do".[39] Although his sense of paternalism still showed through (the poor's privilege of meeting the well-born), Barnett had come a long way from the stern advocate of charitable aid only to the deserving poor. By that year he was already warning the Anglican establishment that "when the poor be goaded to make a reconstruction of values, so please God they will some day, then the church may find out it has overslept itself."

Meanwhile his plan for the cultural uplift of his Whitechapel flock, under the aegis of an intellectual and artistic elite, proceeded accordingly. On 20 March the eighth annual art exhibition was opened at the St. Jude school rooms, Commercial Street, to remain on show daily, Sundays included, until 8 April. It was noted by the press, that of the large company attending on the first day "the bulk... had come from the West to East to show their approval of the effort to bring some of the finest works of art under the notice of the people of East London". It was a superb show. The 250 exhibits included works by leading contemporary artists such as Watts, Rivière, Millais, Leighton, Holman Hunt and the Israels. Barnett, in his opening address, declared that the aim of the promoters was to "make common the best" and to feel "that rich and poor meet here in good will". Holman Hunt was then introduced, and proceeded to offer some interesting points on the contribution that ordinary working men could make to the creative arts.

> Mr Holman Hunt... after more indignant criticism (of the present state of art)... said that the best hope of curing what was wrong was in the co-operation of the working classes; and he looked forward to the teaching of design, so that inventive art should take the place of current imitation. The art world had been kept to a little section of society, but the sons of labour had a healthy instinct for art, and, therefore, he was glad to learn of the practical work that had been commenced by Mr Ashbee in the Technical and Art School at Toynbee Hall, especially, as he thought, that in the line of decoration, we might look for improvement in art.

The company then adjourned, some to view the pictures, others to inspect the dining-room, which was currently being decorated by Ashbee's students. This comprised the painting of a design in freehand on the wall, *repoussé* work in metal, modelling in *carton-pierre* and gilding, and the making of a frieze of shields — bearing the arms of all the colleges of Oxford and Cambridge — that had been modelled in clay, cast in plaster and then painted and gilded. This remarkable décor is still intact, illuminating the dining-room as it did nearly a century ago.[40] With his penchant for mustering a number of such art exhibitions and public lectures for the locals, and the opportunity provided by the Ripper murders seized upon to accelerate the drive for slum clearance, it was, on the whole, a good year for the Vicar of St. Jude's.

Frederick Charrington

It was also a reasonably successful year for the East End's home-born crusader against sin Frederick Charrington. Heir to the local brewer, he had voluntarily rejected his filial role as inheritor (but not its income!) to espouse the cause of Christ, teetotalism and, above all, the extirpation of vice. In the winter of 1887 our "Valiant for Good" began "a furious, God-inspired onslaught upon the dens of East London".[41]

At the time a 37-year-old bachelor, he appeared obsessed with the evil of sexual immorality, perpetuated, in his reckoning, by the existence of so many brothels in the area. Under the Criminal Law Amendment Act of 1885 a citizen could report to the police any house illegally operating as a brothel, in return for which a money reward was offered for this gesture of "public duty". The record does not show many takers. No doubt the fear of being discovered and marked by the brothel interests as an informer overrode the attraction of a "squealer's" fee! For Charrington, however, the act could be used as a weapon to destroy them. Armed with a large black book and a respectable witness, he crept through the streets to seek out "the foulest sinks of iniquity". The nocturnal prowling of this "purity crusader" had a salutary effect on his enemies. According to his chronicler "the bullies, the keepers of evil houses, the horrible folk who battened on shame, and enriched themselves with the wages of sin, feared Frederick Charrington as they feared no policeman, no inspector, no other living thing...". Certainly 1888 was a busy year for this local Quixote's onslaught on the bordellos. On 2 February he applied for a warrant for the arrest of two persons for running a brothel at a house in Nelson Street, Mile End. A summons was issued and, as a result, a Mrs Gibson was sentenced to one month's hard labour which, the *East London Observer* confirmed, "struck terror in the hearts of those keepers" who "did not dream that those (Charrington's) threats would be carried out". In a series of articles entitled "The Raid on East End Brothels", an *Observer* reporter outlined the extraordinary revelations and hilarious escapades that the *procureurs* got up to in order to elude their tormentor.

Charrington's antics had a disastrous effect on the local flesh trade. On 11 February came a report of his attack on Devonshire Street, "The Bullies Starving", with a preamble recounting his successes to date throughout the borough.

> It may be recollected that Lady Lake's Grove — one of the most notorious nests of immorality — was first cleared; Cottage Grove followed soon after, and the individual who owned a large number of houses of a similar character in Oxford Street took fright and decamped with all her tenants. Thomas Street, in Whitechapel, was looked after next and the result was ... that the then occupier of the houses there also beat a retreat in the dead of night. Then came the grand *coup* on Nelson Street and "Jack's Hole" — two notorious localities near Commercial Road; and after considerable difficulty and continual visits extending over several weeks, during which time Mr Charrington was so frequently and seriously attacked that police protection had to be given him, most of the houses there were cleared.

Constant beatings up by the ponces had, temporarily, put him out of action. But he was soon back, determined to pursue his moral crusade, come what may. His next target was the infamous Devonshire Street off the Commercial Road.

> This is, notoriously, one of the blackest holes of immorality and villainy in existence. The girls and women living in this street are nothing more or less than a gang of thieves, whose business it is to decoy sailors into their houses, there to stupefy them with drink and drugs, rob them of all they possess, and bundle them into the street. Should resistance be offered — as it sometimes is — there are in every house a number of *bullies*, who quickly settle the business by knocking the poor *tar* on the head. The street is in a condition of the greatest disorder both night and day; if it is not a sailor who is loudly protesting against his pockets being rifled, then it is a free fight between some of the women who had been detected in what is technically known as *whipping*, or cheating the other members of the gang out of their share of the proceeds of some robbery. The majority of these houses are owned by a wealthy brewer and, taking advantage of the clause in the Criminal Law Amendment Act, which makes it incumbent on the landlord of premises that are made known to him to be disorderly, to abate the nuisance complained of, Mr Charrington served the necessary notices on him...
>
> The houses are tenanted also by a number of *bullies* whose profession is that of thieving... The other night, at the suggestion of Mr Charrington, a raid was made by the police on some of the houses, with the result that no less than seven well-known characters who have been wanted by the police... were captured and conveyed to the police station there to be identified and charged.

The recorder goes on to specify how, like an avenging angel, this eccentric son of a brewer smote the brothel-keepers hip and thigh without respite. Many were so demoralised

> that in sheer desperation, they have returned to their old quarters, caring little whether they have to appear in a police court or not — such is the state of destitution at which they have arrived. The *bullies* who formerly led an idle life on the proceeds of prostitution are in a similar plight, and it was only the other day, in Clark Street, Stepney that one of the fraternity was captured for stealing nuts, with which — so he said — to satisfy his hunger!

Landlords often professed to be totally unaware of the way in which their property was being misused. (Most were in cahoots with their shady tenants, deriving greater rents from the trade.)

One tenant, a madam, popularly known as Becky, when given notice to quit by an irate landlord, protested her innocence, assuring him that of the three girls living with her, two were her daughters, the third "a young lady who went to business during the day"![42]

The raids revealed some public scandals which were promptly exploited by the press. Following the cleansing of the Commercial Road redoubts, Charrington turned his attention to Railway Place in Shadwell, "a lane scarcely six feet in width and, in some places, not more than three, running parallel with the Great Eastern Railway from Shadwell Station". This rookery was again infested with thieves and prostitutes. Charrington, to his horror, discovered that the property belonged to a prominent member of an East End chapel and was managed by an agent:

> Within a very short time the whole of the occupants were cleared out. In pursuing this inquiry the curious facts were elicited that another agent having the management of a large number of disorderly houses in the district was a well-known member of a church in Stratford, and also that actually adjoining a chapel in the Commercial Road — next door to it in fact — was a disorderly house of the worst description. Some of these facts may, perhaps, account for the spirit of deprecation on the part of certain "pious and religious folk" respecting the raid on these places!

The ubiquitous Becky was pursued mercilessly. Anticipating discovery in one place, she had a carefully devised system of opening business in another. A person was employed to "keep it warm" for her, and a large house off New Road was opened under the auspices of an agent. But Charrington was on to this; and Becky was quickly forced to make a moonlight flit to escape the inevitable police raid.[43]

By late February Charrington's fame had spread well beyond the borough. His post at the Assembly Hall was flooded with letters of support. The local press noted that "some were piteous in the extreme; others plead for the closure of houses which have ruined their sons; and wives appeal for the closing of others which have ruined and broken up their homes". All information received was meticulously recorded in his black book and passed on to the magistrates. By springtime the Charrington crusade was projected on the national scene, with dire consequences for the local prostitutes, who were forced to take to the streets or move elsewhere.

It was the latter effect that aroused strong criticism, reflected in the many letters of protest in the local press. On 13 February "Misericordia" from Mile End voiced his indignation at "the merciless employment by Mr F.N. Charrington of the modern "whip with six strings" and at "religion armed with penal knuckledusters which drives the 'moral malady' from hitherto isolated spheres to be more disseminated and circulated..." True religion consists, indeed of "keeping oneself unspotted from the world", but not in adding to the misery of unhappy women, already grievously injured and wronged by men.[44] In like vein "Explicit" complained of Charrington's religion "of which persecution appears a part" and which, as a result, drives the evicted unfortunates out into the severe weather or, as they are forced to move to other localities, "serves but to spread the moral contagion".[45] The message was also received by correspondents to the *East London Advertiser*. While the editor himself condemned Charrington for his "libelling of East London" by unsavoury missions that made stock headlines (and thus inferring that the area teems with vice),[46] a local observer confirmed the charge that even greater evil resulted from Charrington's exploits:

> A friend in "The West" thus writes to me: "The result of your neighbour Charrington turning the women adrift is, that the East End workhouses are too full; and a great number came up to St. James's, and we had quite enough here before."
> There seems to be in his use of a black book, a grim tinge of burlesque of "The Recording Angel" (mentioned in *Tristram Shandy*), and the result of his campaign reminds me of a domestic sweeping carpets and omitting wet tea-leaves spreading.

He concluded: "But Mr Charrington deserves praise for establishing a refuge and perhaps some of the deserted houses could be used with a view to finding finding honourable occupation for former inhabitants."[47] This was fair comment, since for many of the East End girls it was either prostitution or starvation for themselves and their families.

Charrington's nightly sorties often led to some real-life tragicomedies. One of his victims was Mrs Rose, "a procuress and brothel-keeper of the worst description". She was told that

Charrington had her name in his black book and was approaching. She turned to run indoors, collapsed on the floor and died instantly. This summary punishment, according to his narrator, was "surely the power of God, approaching in the person of His servant, who pressed God's lamp to his breast that struck down this woman as a terrible example". (Or was it the <u>certainty</u> of the application of the Criminal Law Amendment Act, via its most forceful advocate, that felled her?) Another escapade of his ended in a startling exposure. Accompanied by two detectives disguised as water inspectors, he set out to rescue a young girl, forcibly detained in a brothel. The invaders burst in, quickly rescued the girl and, while searching the rest of the house, the evangelist came across a large portrait of himself hanging on the wall of the main reception room. The detectives explained quickly that his picture could be seen displayed in <u>every</u> brothel in the East End since "the keepers of these places wished to have a ready means of identifying the man who was breaking up their dreadful trade"![48] Yet, in the end, Charrington's raids (according to his biographer) accounted for the closure of 200 brothels in Tower Hamlets. If true, it was no mean feat for this arduous campaigner against vice!

For the ex-brewer, the second deadly sin was drink; hence his parallel activity in the movement to achieve universal temperance. By February 1888, he apparently boasted that he had "ruined 13 public houses", while pleading for funds to further this cause, It brought an irate response from a local resident who, under the signatory "Fair Play" rejected his plea with the argument that "many would prefer to assist edifices which do not seek to ruin, such as the People's Palace, the Working Lad's Institute, or Free Library in Bethnal Green, to which might be added the Saturday night entertainment movement at the Assembly Hall, Mile End".[49] This would not deter Charrington. In the same Assembly Hall on 13 March he was sharing a platform with Dr Barnardo, who was presiding over the annual meeting of the Tower Hamlets Band of Hope Union, dedicated to extirpate drink. In June he was busy organising a teetotal demonstration to take place in Hyde Park on the 2nd, against the compensation clauses of the Local Government Bill. An unsympathetic reporter "Rambler", in the *Advertiser* (2 June), informs us that

> We are promised an imposing array of cold-water drinkers from all parts of London, and the publicans near the Park and on the line of route are especially requested not to supply the thirsty demonstrators with anything
> stronger than ginger pop.
>   Of course there must be the sensational element introduced into the procession in order to make it draw. They will consist of a van filled with ragged woe-begone children from St. George's-in-the-East, the division represented by Mr Ritchie upon which will be printed in large type "WHO IS TO COMPENSATE ALL THESE".[50]

In fact the demonstration proved effective. The sight of those poor mites exposed in this real-life exercise in dramatic protest deeply moved the vast audience assembled there. For the rest of the year his involvement in the anti-drink campaign matched his activities against vice. Yet in advocating the former he appeared to be more circumspect. While strongly deprecating the annual drink allocated to workhouse paupers at Christmas, he deliberately absented himself on the day so that the beer could be served without fuss. "Rambler" remarked sceptically, "His (Charrington's) soul soars above pewter pots and their foaming contents; not so, however, the inmates of the Union, who seemed to consume their beer with even greater gusto, knowing that the fiat at one time was to stop the allowance."[51]

It is for the diversity of his more positive and creative labours on behalf of the local working class that Charrington deserves recognition. On Thursday 19 April, a public meeting was held at the Great Assembly Hall to inaugurate the Rock Co-operative Society under Charrington's presidency. From the rostrum he set forth its aims:

> The Society has been formed by working men for the purpose of social, moral and intellectual improvement in the conditions of the masses generally by mutually combining in the wholesale purchase and distribution of commodities amongst the members, and by social intercourse in which they would consider social problems in relation to capital and labour.

A registered office was set up within the hall; enrolment and meetings were held every Tuesday evening, and within three weeks the Society had mustered nearly 100 members with over £80 capital subscribed.[52] His philanthropic deeds were interspersed with serious social commitments. On 12 July he opened his hall to 1,300 striking match girls "assembled there for the purpose of having their names placed on a register", the latter used to lay the foundation of the Matchmakers Union, the largest in England, composed entirely of women. Only two days before he had organised and led the monster annual day's outing for the local poor to Clacton, when two special trains were chartered to transport 1,700 men and women for a day's junket by the sea. A colourful description of the event was given by the *Observer* reporter.

> On arriving at Clacton, a procession was formed, headed by the Crusaders Brass Band belonging to the hall, and the whole marched to the pier where the company dispersed to engage in the various amusements usually afforded at sea-sides — some driving around the country, others taking short sailing excursions, while others went down to the edge of the sea to play with the sand, or dip the tips of their toes in the salt water.
>
> A cricket match was played in the afternoon between teams chosen by Mr Kerwin and Mr Richardson. The band at intervals played selections and at 6 o'clock took up their positions in front of the flag staff. A conveyance was hired and this made the platform. Mr Charrington then gave out one of Sankey's well-known hymns, which the band played and the company as well as visitors sang heartily. After prayer, short addresses were given by Messrs. Harrison, T. Richardson and Charrington, after which the band took the lead and played as they marched to the railway station for the return journey, the train arriving home about 10 o'clock, the whole party having thoroughly enjoyed their day at the seaside.

Charrington had tremendous amount of compassion for the needy and, although ostensibly apolitical, when the time came he was active on the side of the dispossessed. In December he supported 82 parents who defaulted in having their children vaccinated, declaring it an abomination that ordinary citizens should be prosecuted because they conscientiously objected to it. One year later (28 December 1889) he was to open his great hall for a mass meeting held to inaugurate the first all-Federation of

East London Labour Unions. In an era of harsh utilitarianism he proffered charity with a human face.

General William Booth

For the fourth member of the quartet of publicised "saints", General William Booth, 1888 also proved a year of opportunity. On 18 February he opened the first Salvation Army Hostel in the building of a former warehouse at 21 West India Dock Road, "for the purpose of lodging and feeding the extreme poor of the East End".[54] The local press provided him with wide coverage:

> The design is to afford decent and comfortable sleeping accommodation and wholesome food at a price which, it is thought, even the needy and miserable men who have now reluctant recourse to the casual ward can pay: and although the Salvationists themselves will give away no free tickets for admission to this shelter, others may do so. Sleeping accommodation is provided for 150 males at the outset, and besides this, two wholesome meals — one at night and one in the morning — can be had for three pence. The warehouse has been adapted for its present use at a cost of £700, of which about £90 remains unpaid. The rental of the premises is £180 per annum. Upon the ground floor, there is a restaurant where a basin of soup or a cup of tea or coffee may be got for a halfpenny and, in the case of juveniles, for a farthing. Despite these small charges, it is confidently believed that the experiment will answer, and the institution prove self-supporting. In that event, kindred institutions will be established in other poor localities of the metropolis, provision being made for women as well as men.[55]

A prophetic judgment. The ad hoc building would be the archetype — the model for future Salvation Army Hostels round the world.

Criticism was levelled against Booth's project from many sides. Of course his low-priced tariff would rouse the antagonism of local café owners and lodging-house keepers, who accused the General of unfair competition in the market for cheap food and accommodation. The Stepney Board of Guardians led the rest in censoring the new Shelter. They argued that it acted as a magnet, attracting outside paupers to the area who, when penniless, added to the army of applicants for admission to East London workhouses and infirmaries, an increase that was "calculated to prove most injurious to the ratepayers of Stepney". Evidence was afforded by relieving officers in the form of certificates stamped "Salvation Army Quarters" produced by new applicants to the workhouse, who had spent the night before at the Army's hostel.[56]

The Stepney Guardians' indignation reached a peak when, on 10 May, a strong resolution listing complaints was moved to be sent to General Booth. These included concern that the Shelter's objects were not carried out "considering that carmen, stevedores, organ men, and others, well able to pay a fair price for their food, were supplied by the Shelter to the injury of the rate-paying eating houses in the neighbourhood. Also that paupers from all parts were attracted to the place, afterwards coming on the local rates; also that a large number of boys intercept foot passengers, begging for money to enable them to get food tickets thus causing annoyance and obstruction..."[57] They were not concerned with the humane services rendered to the needy poor that was the Shelter's *raison d'être*. The local Bumbles were more obsessed with the cost effectiveness of the house bill than with Christian responsibility for "transient paupers".

Booth's "feeding place" expanded so rapidly that by March the reporter for *Justice* calculated that to-date "4,000 men and women had been fed in the place and 500 farthings had been taken from children for basins of soup". The homeless continued to flow in throughout the year so that, by late December, Booth was exploring the possibility of "state aid for an extension of his scheme for food and shelter depots."[58] It is Margaret Harkness, the correspondent for *Justice* and also personally involved with the Salvation Army, who presents us with a sympathetic description of the new venture, explaining why it was a more attractive alternative to the common dosshouse or local spike.

> The sleeping accommodation is very cheap; by paying one penny a man can get a clean bed, for the sheepskin he has round his neck and his mattress are constantly baked, the only way in

which they can be kept from vermin. Many a respectable man "out of work" prefers to sleep on a doorstep, if the weather is at all fine, rather than lie between the filthy sheets in a dosshouse. A dosshouse bed costs 3d or 4d; Salvation beds cost only one penny. The room is heated by water pipes. The officer in charge (an ex-business man who gave it up to devote his life to the Salvation Army) has exactly the same mattress and sheepskin as the lodgers. Only men can, as yet, be accommodated; but later on they hope to have accommodation for women.

Perhaps readers may think that a man who sleeps in a Salvation bed is pestered about his soul, is kept awake by prayers and thanskgivings. This is a mistake. He may be asked if he is saved... but the officers are busy men, and have not time to spend in pestering sleepy people about salvation.

On the possibilities of extending new hostels she continues:

It will be interesting to see if this Salvation feeding place really becomes self-supporting. The soup is good, and has meat in it. Coffee and tea are of the same strength as Lockhart's: and other provisions resemble the fare that Lockhart's put before the public.[59] A man can live there for threepence a day, and get a bed for another penny. Men are free to come and go; no restraint is put on anybody.

She makes a side swipe at a well-known academic critic, obviously a nineteenth-century replica of one of our modern counterparts on the New Right!

Of course people like Professor Leone Levi will say that such a place does mischief, by keeping alive the scum of London. But the scum does not come there in any appreciable quantity... the scum consists of parasites not hungry men and women.

And parasites were, by definition, not only found among the East End loafers. They were equally recognisable amongst the idle rich:

After a fortnight I learnt to know the East End loafer's face as well as I can recognise a West End masher by his dress and movements. Both are parasites, both have an inane expression on their countenance that seems to say, "I ought to be swept clean off the face of society."

Harkness concluded that the new hostel was the "most communistic place in London!", and added pertinently:

I am not aware what socialists think of Salvationists, but I know the latter are very favourably disposed towards "the servants of men". General Booth has lately expressed his respect for socialists in public. The two organisations ought to work together more than they do at present, for they have many points of common interest. From our respect the Army teaches us a great lesson. It has never split up. It is one large labour union.[60]

But Hyndman, editor of *Justice*, was not impressed by this. A letter from Harkness in answer to his criticism underlined a fundamental difference in approach to socialism that has always plagued its ideologues. Harkness considered the moral basis as sacrosanct:

> Sir,
> I am sorry my article on Salvationists and socialists led you to think that the "feeding place" in the West India Dock Road is "*à la* Lockhart". It neither overworks its hands, nor does it attempt to make a profit. I called it communistic because it is carried on in the socialist spirit.
>
> "We are all socialists now," a young stockbroker said to me last week at the headquarters of the Army in Queen Victoria Street. Socialism must be looked at from its moral, as well as its economic aspect. Men and women cannot be left to starve whilst socialists are waiting for a social revolution, or laying siege to a ballot box. Nothing saps a man's energy like being hungry.
>
> The theory that the worse things get the more people will become socialists is not true with regard to hungry men and women. They grow hopeless. A man cannot be fed or housed at present by economics. But let a man of normal strength see that socialism must come, because it is the next step in the evolution of society, and he will work for it, he will influence other men to become socialists.
>
> The real enemies of capitalists and landlords are men above the line of starvation. Much energy is wasted among such men at present. They know what they want; but they do not <u>know</u> how to get it.
>
> Yours fraternally,
> Margaret E. Harkness

Hyndman's response was significant. He posed the argument that first priority must be the introduction of <u>state</u> social welfare schemes to aid the poor, which would be delayed precisely because these were currently met by such philanthropic bodies as the Salvation Army.

> We quite agree with our correspondent in what she says about starving men and women, but we believe that the provision of food — and work — for these should be made a public function, and the fact that such organisations as the Salvation Army provide cheap or free meals in the worst district is likely to militate against the, provision of free meals all round. As to the place being "*à la* Lockhart" our correspondent told us that the meals were of the same quality as those provided by the well known caterer of cheap — if not nice — food and drink. We understand, too, from our correspondent that the man in charge works 16 hours a day! — Ed.[61]

It was a typically ungracious commentary by Hyndman. Earlier that year *Justice*'s roving reporter noted William Booth's personal sympathy for socialists who were practically concerned with alleviating poverty.

> The socialists were said to have a plan for the raising of the race apart from religion. He (Booth) took the opportunity of saying that he respected all socialists who were in earnest according to their light. He would not utter a word against them; his sorrow and anger were, on the contrary, reserved for those who did not care and did not feel for the appalling amount of vice and misery by which their daily life was surrounded.[62]

It could be argued that, unlike Hyndman and co., who theorised on a future millennium for the poor, Booth was practically involved in saving as many as possible from hunger and degradation, there and then!

Opposition to Booth came from other quarters. Local established and even reform clergy were antagonistic. On 22 April, the Rev. J. Atkinson, while sermonising on "The Fast Young Man" at Sion Chapel, Whitechapel, was interrupted by the clashing of cymbals and blaring trumpets of a passing Salvation Army band. He paused angrily: "I hear music (within); better music than that which went past... We should stop that if it is repeated often; we have had to do so several times in different parts of the country!" The Rev. W. Adamson of Old Ford, giving evidence on 12 May before the House of Lords Committee on Sweating, accused the Salvationists of competing with the poor by setting up their own match factory and thereby reducing labour cost of production from 2¾d to 2¼d a gross. This was refuted in the Army's journal, *The War Cry*, which concluded with the prayer "from envy, hatred, malice and uncharitableness (ie of the official clerics) — Good Lord deliver us!" Support for Booth came from an unlikely quarter. Bryant and May, the largest match manufacturers, dismissed the accusation in a letter to *The Times*.[63]

Within the peripheral East End borough of Shoreditch, and voluntarily ensconced in the infamous Old Nichol rookeries (which marked him as the heroic padre in Arthur Morrison's *Child of the Jago*), The Rev. A. Osborne Jay fulminated against "the blasphemous ravings" of the Army preachers. Harkness deduced that he was after the funds of those outside benefactors who might otherwise contribute to Booth's mission.[64] Against the trio of the East End's contemporary "saints" Booth appeared as the odd man out. There was enough fierce competition for the bodies and souls of the *lazzaroni* of the streets. It could be that Booth's message was the more potent. For the proletarian army that he had been called to muster would march with him to Eternal Glory on full stomachs and well-shod feet. Not for the Salvationist the fashionable distinction between the deserving and undeserving poor. For them, to be poor was to be deserving!

It was Margaret Harkness, working so closely with them, who presents us with an all-embracing tableau of Salvation Army life. In her *In Darkest London* (sub-titled *Captain Lobo, Salvation Army*), written that year, she conveys real characters against the day-to-day situations which confront them. The description of the hero (based on an actual East End officer) is that of a young man, self-sacrificial in his devotion to the poor, living in a sparse barrack room in Army accommodation, and subsisting on one pound a week:

> But to give half away and live on ten shillings is a problem that would have baffled Euclid... He was no milk-and-water religionist... He did not preach about hell and then go home to enjoy a good meal of roast beef and plum pudding. If he consigned a sinner to the burning pit, he gave the sinner half of his own dinner to eat on the journey, and recognised the fact that a man's soul has an intimate relationship with a man's stomach. He hated sin in the abstract; but he loved sinners, and most of all he loved his Whitechapel people. Even the loafers were dear to him. And the roughs were good lads, he said, lacking opportunities.[65]

She explains why the appeal of the Army was more acceptable to the labouring poor than to their betters:

> Salvationists do not attempt to reason, they appeal to a man's heart, and think the intellect a little thing that requires wheedling. Consequently, few educated men and women join their ranks, and they cannot point to one scholar in their camp of any importance. But in slums and alleys their work is a real force, for the inhabitants of these places recognise their sincerity of purpose, and do not approach them in a critical spirit. Such people feel sin, and fear to sink into the burning pit by reason of it; such people are not educated enough to find hell in an uneasy conscience.[66]

A moving description is given of the slum saviours, young women Salvationists who sacrifice their lives for the cause. Harkness perceives that no labour commands so much devotion as slum work. The girls choose to live among the filth and vermin, in imminent danger of contracting a fatal disease; while their acts of compassion are ignored by respectable folk who regard them as fanatics or lunatics.

> They go to the slummers with a Bible in one hand, with the other free to nurse the sick and help the helpless. No room is too filthy for them to work or pray in: no man or woman is too vile for them to call brother and sister. They penetrate into cellars where no clergyman or priest has ever ventured and spend hours among people who frighten policemen. Directly they see any danger ahead, instead of running away they fall down on their knees and begin to pray. So it comes to pass that not a single Salvation lassie has been hurt anywhere, for the slummers say, "They are so plucky!"[67]

One pair moved into two vacant rooms in the infamous Angel Alley, which they fitted up as a sanctuary for battered women found on their patch. It was expected of a saviour to go about "from morning to night, nursing the sick, and feeding the hungry with her own scanty rations, until early death crowned her efforts".

Of course such saintliness was too often infected with prudery. On Sunday evenings, at the back of Angel Alley, could be heard the cacophony of a mixed drum and fife band from the church playground, a recreational facility provided by the Rev. Samuel Barnett. The neighbouring slum lassie was indignant at such high jinks perpetrated on the Sabbath. "I think it's a sin to spend money on music and lamps while people are starving, and that a clergyman should try to save souls instead of letting sinners dance straight from Whitechapel into hell." Responding to a politically-conscious labour mistress, who defended Barnett for attempting to uplift the poor culturally by bringing flowers and colour into their lives, she declared: "There's a dear woman lying dead not far from this house. She talked just as you do about flowers and pictures when she was well; but she sent for us on her death bed, not for Mr Barnett or his curates. That sort of religion may be right enough for those who understand it, but I say that for an East End clergyman to countenance it is to place a stumbling block in the way of ignorant men and women. I daresay that Mr Barnett is a good man, but he should go to the West End, where people can understand him." It was the more sophisticated artisan who was repelled by an approaching crone "bent almost double by age and wrapped in rags from head to foot" while the Salvationist greeted her warmly with a blessing. Yet the labour mistress had a point. "They (the Barnetts) thought it best to give them (the poor) a little happiness here, instead of bothering them about the hereafter."[68]

Almost certainly it was during that year that William Booth, with his intense East End activities, finalised his social creed. This was laid down in his book *In Darkest England* (published in 1890) and confirmed him in the role of dedicated advocate for the poor. He denounced the annual vulgar display of pomp and wealth instituted by city financiers:

> But as we have Lord Mayor's Day, when all the well-fed fur-clad city fathers go into state coaches through the town, why should we not have a Lazarus Day, in which the starving, out of work, and the sweated half-starved *in-work* of London should crawl in their tattered raggedness, with their gaunt, hungry faces — emaciated wives and children, a procession of despair, through the main thoroughfares, past the massive houses and princely palaces of luxurious London?
> They stretch out their grimy hands to us in vain appeal, <u>not</u> for charity but for <u>work</u>.

Work was the first priority, and he made a passionate appeal with a message that transcends time and place:

> A man's labour is not only his capital, but his life. When it passes it returns never more. To utilise it, to prevent its wasteful

squandering, to enable the poor man to bank it up for use hereafter, this surely is one of the most urgent tasks before civilisation.[69]

He angrily rejected the stern, unbending free-market ideologues at a point where they were already facing other political and social challenges:

"Let things alone", the laws of supply and demand, and all the rest of the excuses by those who stand on firm ground salve their consciences when they leave their brother to sink.
We want a Social Lifeboat Institution, a Social Lifeboat Brigade, to snatch from the abyss those, who left to themselves, will perish...[70]

Yet, in contradiction, he could not distance himself from the Social Darwinism of his time:

I am labouring under no delusions as to the possibility of inaugurating the millennium by any social specific. In the struggle of life the weakest will go to the wall... All that we can do is to soften the lot of the unfit.

He also stressed the obvious, that he was not offering a means of transforming society, leaving to "others the formulation of ambitious programmes for the reconstruction of our social system". In his own case he had found no use in merely "preaching the gospel to men whose whole attention is concentrated upon a mad, desperate struggle to keep themselves alive". In the final count, therefore, he was less concerned with theorising than with the immediate practical demands of succouring the poor.[71]

In this he was incomparable. By 1888 he headed the list of contemporary "saints" operating in East London, who gave unstintingly of their labour and devotion to those whom society preferred to ignore. He also fortified the area's reputation as a haven of caring where the socially maimed would always receive help with compassion.

***

Within the pantheon of local philanthropists there were many more unsung heroes and heroines of the same kind. One was Miss Mary Steer, who founded the Ratcliff "Bridge of Hope"

Mission in Betts Street, St. George's. She had arrived with two companions nine years before "to devote her life to the rescue of the social outcasts and pariahs of the district". Starting from a small slum cottage in the foulest of streets, she raised enough money to extend this to "a large palatial building (containing) a laundry and night shelter for fallen women". The foundation stone was laid by Lady Ashburton, a friend of Frederick Charrington, on 8 February and the completed building ceremonially opened on 1 November. An indefatigable worker, Steer had, by 1888, already rescued hundreds of young girls and children from the streets, and directed them into a new life, either to be trained as servants or as emigrants to the colonies.[72]

A letter, a *cri de coeur* from Mr J. Rolfe Asher, Minister of the Burdett Road Congregational Church, joined the chorus of other worthies of East London making a public plea for the urgent needs of their poor. "Day by day I meet with the wailing cry of hundreds of starving little children, half clad and utterly miserable, and the quiet, heartbreaking appeal of the pale, wan faces of heart crushed men and women." He was anxious to provide a soup kitchen offering ½d dinners to famished children and unemployed men and women. Only "£1 is sufficient to provide an ample and nourishing meal for 250 persons". The mission and relief work was unpaid and every case was investigated so that "sheer want is the only qualification for aid". Such funds would only be used to supply soup, bread, coals and clothing to the really deserving poor.[73]

Demands for public soup kitchens and charity dinners increased as Christmas and the cold weather approached. From the Vicarage, Old Ford, Mrs Adamson wrote: "I hope once more to relieve the semi-starvation of thousands of children. Last winter the cost of the dinner (including plant and pannikins, coals and coppers) which we gave to the poor children connected with three Board Schools in the neighbourhood was £79; the number of dinners were 10,225... My husband's parish alone numbers over 11,000 persons, most of whom crowd together in small tenements." Mr Edwin H. Kerwin, Chairman of Charrington's Assembly Hall Christmas Fund, was again preparing "to brighten Christmas Day by sending into our back streets and alleys a Christmas dinner, so that hundreds will be fed in their own home who would otherwise go without". From the Lady Superintendent of the Mother's Lying-in Hospital,

Shadwell, came a request for contributions to provide inmates of the home, known to be destitute and deserving, a dinner on Christmas Day; to be joined by the Secretary of the East London Hospital for Children, also in Shadwell, who publicly appealed for funds to hold a Christmas Party for the inmates on Wednesday 2 January. ("100 children who have been in-patients at the Hospital will be invited and provided with tea, cake, fruit and a comic entertainment. Gifts of clothing of all kinds... will be gratefully received.")[74]

So with Christmas came the opportunity for the great public shows of beneficence fully reported in the local press. On Monday evening, Christmas Eve, the Lord Mayor and Mayoress attended the annual distribution of Christmas dinners to 12,000 of the very poor in the Harley Street Independent Chapel, Bow Road. (The Mayor was pleased to note that last year's recipients had been 10,000 "but this year's funds have permitted an extension of invitations and the members of 2,345 families were enabled to participate.") To add to the evening's entertainment he was glad to deliver this after-dinner homily to his impecunious audience:

> Emigration (is) good if properly organised, but the government (has) cut the ground from under (your) feet by not retaining more of the Crown Colonies than they (have) done... The unemployed and surplus population (may) be sent away, but it would be a fatal error to take out only the best-skilled artisans and the strongest and healthiest portion of the community — in fact the prime members of this country.

Having enlightened his audience on how their future might be better secured — by transplanting them elsewhere — the Mayor went on to the Charrington party at the Assembly Hall, where we learn that the distribution consisted of 2,000lbs beef, 1,475 loaves, etc — in all 6,665lbs of foodstuffs to be consumed. Charrington was quick to point out to his guest the necessity for all this. Of the applicants present, the largest number of unemployed "belonging to the shoe trade, next came dock and casual labourers and amongst the women assisted were those who went out 'charing'". Contrary to the optimistic musings of the editor of the *East London Advertiser* (who declared that there was "less pinching poverty among the masses than so sadly prevailed... December last") he reckoned that the present distress was the worst since the winter of 1879-1880. Overcrowding was rife. Families that had once occupied two or three rooms were now obliged to "come down, with 5 or 6 in a family to live in one room each".[65]

Finally, charity at its best, administered by the most compassionate of donors, was that rendered by the Sisters of Mercy at the Providence Row Night Refuge in Crispin Street, Spitalfields. It still stands, a dark and gloomy citadel without, but within a sisterhood committed to serve indiscriminately the lonely and the desperate. On Boxing Day, 700 men and women of the most destitute class sat down to a dinner of soup, beef and plum pudding. The institution was unique in that it was conducted under the auspices of a Catholic community whose unsectarian stance attracted Protestant financial support. Genuine unemployed were allowed to remain for one month while enquiries were made both to check their *bona fides* and to procure work for them. Throughout 1888, in this refuge, 2,100 night lodgings with supper and breakfast had been supplied weekly "to the destitute from all parts, without distinction of creed, colour and country".[76]

But with all this uncoordinated enterprise, such creditable activity by individuals was merely scratching the surface. Both William Booth and Samuel Barnett partly got the message that state concern and intervention were vital for alleviating the terrifying incidence of poverty. Even they were only tilting at society's manifestations not its substance. It needed more than these fragmented, albeit noble, efforts to tackle the problem of 85% of East Londoners (ie of the total population of 456,877) who, by 1887, were categorised by Charles Booth as living on or below the poverty line; and of whom 13% were deemed so chronically distressed that "decent life is not imaginable".

For a group of radical élites supported by a minority of local working-class autodidacts, it would appear that such philanthropy and social tinkering was a mere diversion. They preached the inevitability of the socialist millennium; and, together with their trade union affiliates, took to the streets in direct action to play out their role as political harbingers of the New Society.

Footnotes

[1] See H.O. Barnett, *Canon Barnett*, vol. 1, p. 75. Barnett declared in his report of 1877, "In my eyes the pain which belongs to the winter cold is not so terrible as the drunkenness with which the summer heat seems to fill our streets, and the want of clothes does not so loudly call for remedy as the want of interest and culture. It is sin, therefore, in its widest sense against which we are here to fight. Sin in the sense of missing the best."

[2] *ELO* 31 March 1888, "The Charity Organisation Society — Its Philosophy and Pretension" by "Diogenes".

[3] *ELO* 7 April, "Good Friday with Fallen Humanity" by "J.H.J." It could be argued that such criticism of the political establishment's mores is as applicable today as it was then; although there is a much more compassionate service rendered to the needy on the modern bread lines.

[4] *Life and Labour*, vol. 1, pp. 170-1.

[5] The *ELO* and *ELA* give extensive coverage to these in the early months. For further reports see *ELO* 14, 21, 28 January and 4, 25 February; and *ELA* 3 March.

[6] *ELO* 24 March.

[7] See above, Chapter 5. For Dr. Barnardo's formative years and subsequent career see A.E. Williams, *Barnardo of Stepney* (London, 1943); Jessie Powell, *The Man who Didn't Go to China* (London, 1947); Janet Hitchinan, *They Carried the Sword* (London, 1966); G. Wagner, *Barnardo* (London, 1979) and *Children of the Empire* (London 1982).

[8] J. Wesley Bready, *Dr. Barnardo, Physician, Pioneer, Prophet* (London, 1935) pp. 156 and 162.

[9] *Three Tracts* (1888), pp. 2, 4 and 18.

[10] Ibid., see further pp. 20-38.

[11] *Night and Day*, vol. XII, pp. 5, 6.

[12] *Illustrated London News* 4 February 1888, p. 109.

[13] *Night and Day*, p. 23.

[14] Ibid., pp. 24 and 27.

[15] Ibid., p. 109.

[16] Ibid., p. 48.

[17] Ibid., pp. 45-6.

[18] See Janet Hitchman, *They Carried the Sword*, p. 18; *Night and Day*, pp. 136 and 137.

[19] *Night and Day*, p. 153.

[20] Ibid., p. 63.

[21] Ibid., pp. 101-2. Also see *East End News* 16 November. For details of description of the new houses founded by Barnardo see A.E. Williams, *Barnardo of Stepney*, pp. 138-9. It was imperative that such houses be introduced on a large scale as Barnardo estimated that no fewer than 50,000 found shelter in lodging houses each night, of whom 25% were children!

[22] See above, Chapter 4.

[23] *Night and Day*, pp. 140-1; and, on the role of Inspectress, p. 110.

[24] Ibid., pp. 147, 152 and 153, for statistics of Barnardo's emigrants to-

date. Before 1882, 856 boys and girls were emigrated. Between 1882 and spring 1888, a total of 2,937. Between spring and December 1888, a total of 2,773. In Barnardo's own reckoning only 1½% were failures of the 3,773 sent to Canada.

[25]Ibid., p. 27. He confirmed that "all the emigrants were over 12 years of age, (and) have received practical industrial training before being sent out".

[26]Ibid., pp. 147-53.

[27]*Toronto Globe* 9 October 1884. For an informed criticism of Barnardo's emigration schemes in Canada see Gillian Wagner's *Children of the Empire* ch. 8, "Only the Flower of the Flock".

[28]Ibid., pp. 69, 84 and 85.

[29]Ibid., p. 105.

[30]Ibid., p. 28. Extracted from *The Christian March* 1888.

[31]A.E. Williams, *Barnardo of Stepney*, pp. 84-5.

[32]For a detailed description of the festivity see *ELA* 29 December 1888.

[33]Janet Hitchman, *They Carried the Sword*, pp. 14 and 19. She records, "Forty years after the foundation of the homes, when Dr Barnardo died 59,384 children had passed through their doors. At his death (1905) 8,000 children were being maintained of which 93 of that year's admission were crippled, blind or deaf mutes."

[34]Beatrice Webb, *My Apprenticeship*, pp. 178-9; C.L. Mowat, *The Charity Organisation Society* (London, 1961), p. 127. The latter confirms that Barnett's views had changed by the early 1880s when he declared that state intervention was vital.

[35]See above, pp. 223-4 and his practical suggestions during the Ripper murders, of which some were quickly implemented.

[36]*ELO* 21 January.

[37]*Canon Barnett*, vol. 1, pp. 93 and 97.

[38]*ELO* 3 March.

[39]This was fully reported in both the *ELA* and *ELO* dated 23 June. The lecture was delivered on 17 June.

[40]See *ELO* 24 March.

[41]For a background account of his life and work see Guy Thorne, *The Great Acceptance: the life story of F.N. Charrington* (London, 1912) and pamphlet *An Oasis in the Desert — Frederick N. Charrington*, L.C.C. published by the Great Assembly Hall, Mile End Rd. (1889). Also W.J. Fishman, *The Streets of East London* (London 1979) pp. 63-7.

[42]Reported fully in the *ELO* 11 February. Lady Lake's Grove, running parallel to the Mile End Road, is described by Guy Thorne as "notoriously the most disorderly and the most irreclaimable of any of the streets of East London". It contained about eight houses, and near the middle of the Grove running off at right angles was "an infinitely smaller lane only some four feet in width known as Cottage Row, nearly the whole of the houses in which were devoted to the trade of whores and their ponces" (*The Great Acceptance*, p. 160).

[43]*ELO* 3 and 31 March, and 14 April give further extensive coverage to Charrington's raids on the brothels. In one case he discovered that not only clerics but also policemen were involved as clients in the nefarious

trade!

[44] *ELO* 18 February.
[45] *ELO* 3 March.
[46] *ELA* 14 April.
[47] *ELA* 28 April.
[48] *The Great Acceptance*, pp. 165-7.
[49] *ELA* 25 February.
[50] *ELA* 2 June, "Rambler".
[51] *ELA* 29 December.
[52] See *ELO* 21 April and 5 May respectively.
[53] *ELO* 14 July.
[54] Perhaps the other "first" was the Rescue Home for Women, opened in 1884 in Hanbury Street, and totally destroyed in the Blitz during World War II.
[55] *ELO* 25 February.
[56] *ELA* 3 March, "General Booth does the ratepayer an ill-turn".
[57] *ELA* 12 May.
[58] *Justice* 24 March and 22 December.
[59] "Lockhart's were public restaurants — a sort of forerunner of Lyons tea houses.
[60] *Justice* 24 March, "Salvationists and Socialists".
[61] *Justice* 14 April.
[62] *Justice* 21 January, "Tell-tale Straws".
[63] See *ELO* 28 April and 12 May.
[64] Rev. A. Osborne Jay, *Life in Darkest London — A Hint to General Booth*.
[65] *In Darkest London*, pp. 10-11,
[66] Ibid., p. 33.
[67] Ibid., pp. 29-30 and 93.
[68] Ibid., pp. 140-3.
[69] William Booth, *In Darkest England*, pp. 31-2.
[70] Ibid., p. 43.
[71] Ibid., pp. 44-5. Although here agreeing with the Social Darwinists that "no amount of assistance will give a jellyfish a backbone" nevertheless he added, "How can we marvel if, after leaving generation after generation to grow up uneducated and underfed, there should be developed a heredity of incapacity, and that thousands of dull-witted people should be born into the world."
[72] See *ELA* 3 November, and *Night and Day*, November 1888, p. 111. The whole cost £4,000 with accommodation for 140 women nightly.
[73] *ELA* 17 November.
[74] *ELA* 15 December.
[75] For the editor's assessment see *ELA* 22 December. "The Visit of the Lord Mayor to East London" is reported in full in the 29 December issue.
[76] *ELA* 29 December.

Chapter 9
Politics

Socialism is in the air. It is the talk of the workshop and club, alehouse and street corner, throughout the civilised world. It is whispered in drawing rooms and seriously discussed in professional lectures and scientific assemblies.

Freedom
January 1888

Socialism is in the air, it is touching everyone and tingeing everything. Many who abhor the name are greater socialists than those who hold socialistic tenets. Some professing socialists seem to think that a man is orthodox if he wears a red tie and blacks his own boots; that a woman is a sincere believer if she cleans her grate, and wears a gown tied with a string round her waist. Such people are a poor sort of advertisement. With their help — or in spite of it — socialism is growing every day both the sentiment and the economic theory...

John Law,
In Darkest London,
p. 158

The New Gospel
Get all you can, and keep what you can,
Is the Gospel of Squeez'em and Tease'em;
And most people think it an excellent plan
The clever idea seems to please them.

The Old Gospel
Lay not up for yourselves of silver and gold,
But wherever you suffring may see,
Give lovingly, freely, and promptly. "Behold",
I will say, "thou hast done it to Me".

East End News
10 February 1888

Just as the philanthropists seized on the many opportunities for doing their good deeds in this running sore of the metropolis, so did the radicals discover there fertile soil for agitation and propaganda. The events of Bloody Sunday (13 November 1887) had destroyed "the illusion that revolution was just round the corner, and the futility of playing at revolution (was) accepted". Demarcation between sects had begun with the crucial two-day socialist debates held in Fleet Street in September 1886, when the Fabian Society, in its earlier stage of being free from constitutionalism, broke with the anarchists. They concluded, prophetically, that British socialists would develop into two movements — anarchist and collectivist. The latter mobilised under the leadership of H.M. Hyndman, who initiated the Social Democratic Federation in 1884. His authoritarian manner alienated many of his fellow ideologues, the outcome being the splintering of the movement and the foundation of a separatist, more libertarian association, the Socialist League, under the aegis of William Morris. By 1888, diverse esoteric groups, anarchist, Socialist Leaguers and SDF, had set up branches in the side streets of Tower Hamlets. They all operated under a common delusion that by bringing political and social consciousness to the local masses, they could thereby direct them onwards to the promised land.[1]

There were a number of Speakers' Corners where the crowds would gather. Victoria Park was a popular rendezvous and offered a variety of secular and religious orators on Sunday afternoon. J.H. Rooney, correspondent for *Harpers Magazine*, presents us in the February 1888 issue with a lively description of scenes enacted there.

> On the big central lawn are scattered numerous groups, some of them very closely packed. Almost all the religious sects of England and all the political and social parties are preaching their ideas and disputing...
>
> On this lawn the listener, as his fancy prompts him, may assist on Malthusianism, atheism, agnosticism, secularism, Calvinism, socialism, anarchism, Salvationism, Darwinism, and even, in exceptional cases, Swedenborgianism and Mormonism. I once heard there a prophet, a man who professed to be inspired by the Holy Ghost; but this prophet ended by being locked up in an asylum, where he will have to convert the doctor before he can recover his liberty.
>
> The anarchists, who are rare, declare the uselessness of all government, demand the absolute liberty of all citizens, will not admit any intellectual differences between man and man, but affirm, on the contrary, that we were all born with equal facilities, only different in form.
>
> At last here we are in the midst of a strong group in socialistic discussion. One notices a number of foreigners, especially Germans. One red-haired orator, with a vigorous, square-chinned face, and an expression of tranquil obstinacy is contravening the doctrines of the collectivists. He is perched on a stool and sprinkled over with specks of sunshine filtered

through the foliage overheard; he gesticulates slowly and regularly with both hands. "You want to reduce man to a state of slavery worse than that of those nations who live under the yoke of a tyrant. You want to destroy the finest privileges of truly civilised men, namely liberty and individuality."

His socialist adversary soon cuts in to claim his right to reply; and mounting the stool "he shows his nervous face and sharp eyes, and begins to talk rapidly".

> "Our friend here accuses us of wishing to convert men into slaves and machines; our friend accuses us of wanting to stop the development of brains. Our friend is mistaken... We ask our friend where he sees the liberty of a workman who works ten hours a day for a morsel of bread. We ask him what sort of liberty is that if the man out of work has to go and knock at the door of the workhouse. We are curious to know what he thinks of the poor girls who are reduced to sell themselves in our streets. Does not our friend know that labour is the source of all riches? Doesn't he know that a big capital cannot be created without one man oppressing another?"

A frenzied argument proceeds between the two primary antagonists, both drawing on analogies to prove or refute each other's precepts while "from all sides newcomers crowd up to bring their intellectual obiter to the fight, until at last calm is restored, and a new point of discussion springs up and enables the orators to resume the monotonous seesaw of their speeches".

The narrator ends with a splendid evocation of the dying fall of speech day in the great park, as the audiences gradually disperse:

> But slowly here is twilight creeping over the edge of the park; the light glides away harmoniously, rose, orange, and coppery clouds rest on the western horizon and the sparrows chirp vigorously, and fly in wild flocks above the trees and garden plots. The fading light seems to glide over the grass as it quits the leafy summits of the trees. The roof of the rose granite monument seems to be covered with pale ashes, and in the water of the little pond, where a weeping ash bathes its drooping branches, the swans stop and seem wrapt in sweet reverie...
> Silence invades the vast lawn of the park; the summer constellations appear among the clouds; a thicker mist clings around the streets and trees, and outside in the adjacent streets the lamp lights begin to flicker; a luminous rosy red of dust obscures the sky, and forms that strange glowing canopy which

will hang over the monstrous town until daydawn, marking its site afar to the country people. Now the disputers issue out through the four great gates; the more thirsty go and refresh themselves in the neighbouring beer saloons; others in desperate earnest continue to crush each other with argument as they walk along the street. And soon they are all once more in their homes in those peace-making English homes whose soothing influence makes the anarchist patient and the sectarian tolerant.[2]

Indeed! These were peaceful antagonists since, as Beatrice Potter, another onlooker, quickly pointed out "for the most part they were men in full employment, and their speculative interest in social reform was not whetted by positive hunger".[3]

Nevertheless the authorities, no doubt fearful of radical agitation, and with the Trafalgar Square riots in mind, tried to curb the activities of these open-air orators. By June, the Metropolitan Board of Works who controlled the park had secured the consent of the Home Secretary to a bye-law forbidding collections to be made in the park. Since this was common practice among all socialist groups as a source of income it was obviously aimed at them, as well as at the Salvationists! It would appear that a citizen's petition had been got up to go still further and demand a ban on these Sunday meetings "because of the bad, seditious, blasphemous and disgusting language used". The canvassers approached passers-by and informed them that anyone could sign, irrespective of age. The result was a collection of singatures belonging largely to churchgoing women and their children. The Socialist League took the initiative and responded accordingly.

On 10 June a protest meeting was called for 3.30pm that Sunday afternoon. (The previous two Sundays' collections were deliberately taken by League speakers S. Mainwaring, F. Charles and W.B. Parker, and consequently their names were taken by the park keepers.) The main speaker, Mrs Annie Besant, was greeted, with prolonged applause by a crowd estimated at 2,000. She was followed by other socialist leaders such as Mainwaring, Mrs Schack and J. Carr of the National League, and the meeting lasted for three hours supported by the large, enthusiastic audience. Mrs Besant, after her address, made a collection, to ensure that her own name was added to those facing prosecution. Over the following weeks money continued to be collected in defiance of the bye-law which apparently died an ignoble death, since no one was charged.[4]

The two major socialist groups vied with each other in propaganda campaigns to gain recruits. The SDF, whose club rooms were located in 339 Burdett Road, publicised meetings at Dod Street, Poplar (evenings at 7.30pm); the Mile End Waste (11.30am); outside the Salmon and Ball (7.30pm Sundays after 24 November) and opposite the Great Eastern Railway Station, Bethnal Green (Sundays 11.30am). Open-air meetings in the East End assumed the role of free public theatres in which the audience could participate. Able and controversial speakers were stars who could always attract a large crowd. *Justice* reports a succession of these addressing mass audiences throughout the year. In March a great meeting was held at the Great Eastern Railway Arch where the chief orator was one Power, his objective being to attract recruits for a new local branch of the SDF. Hyndman was in great demand. Although he was an impressive tub-thumper, often seen performing on the Mile End Waste, it is doubtful whether many of his listeners could keep up with his verbose ramblings. The watchword was agitation. Herbert Burrows put it succinctly in *Justice* (9 June). "Our great work after all is by agitation to assist the people to educate themselves and to combine for a distinct and definite purpose, and that purpose is a revolutionary one."

The Match Girls Strike and the proceedings of the House of Lords Sweating Committee prompted a joint radical anti-sweating demon- stration at Hyde Park in the late afternoon of Sunday 22 July. Details of the march were outlined in *Justice* (21 July), in which participating contingents were defined including both SDF and Socialist League groups from East London. The line of march began at Beckton Road, Canning Town, at 1.00pm to arrive at the East India Dock Gates at 1.15pm; thence via Burdett Road to stop at the Mile End Waste at 2.15pm to meet the Limehouse Branch of the SDF, the Bethnal Green Socialist League, the East London Tailors and Machinists Society and the Berner Street International Working Men's Club. The next point of arrival was at Gardiners Corner to join up with groups emanating from the Triangle, Hackney at 2.45pm. The joint procession then proceeded by way of Leadenhall Street and Cornhill, Mansion House, Cheapside, Newgate Street, Holborn Viaduct and Circus, New Oxford Street and Oxford Street, thence direct to Hyde Park. The SDF organ gave a colourful description of the processionists on the great march and its aftermath at the Park.

For variety of colour, the number of banners, flags, bannerets, mottoes and designs, this procession could hardly have found its equal. One curiosity which caused much attraction, was a match box carried by the girls, with a list of prices paid for the work inscribed on each side.

The crowd behaved admirably, consequently there was no disorder. Several branches of the SDF carried large and imposing banners; also a huge match box, out of the top of which the effigy of a clergyman protruded, with hands raised in the attitude of prayer, his supplication printed on the end of the box being "O Lord, increase the dividends" it was obvious that he was also a shareholder...

At No. 3 platform the proceedings were opened by John Burns who acted as chairman. Just as he commenced his speech a part of the East End contingent with the match girls passed and received an ovation from the crowd which they readily answered... George Bernard Shaw moved the resolution in a speech full of force and eloquence... Mr. Newman (President of the International Society of Journeyman Bootfinishers) then spoke warmly and passionately on the foreign labour question, saying that this tale of the "foreigner" was got up simply to set race against race to make them better tools for the capitalist classes (cheers!).

At No. 5 — Herbert Burrows presided. The largest assemblies of the day attended probably owing to the presence of the match girls. "Hobart moved the resolution... called upon the men to emulate their (the match girls') example, saying that if his fellow trade unionists had only been united as the girls, the 8-hour day would now be an accomplished fact... Mrs Besant followed and in her usual impressive and eloquent manner dealt with limitation of child labour, her remarks being received with great applause.

No. 6 platform was given to the Socialist League, who had their own resolution. They were also reinforced by the foreign section, who, with their two bands, one from St. George's-in-the-East and the other from Fitzroy Square, together with the various branches, made a very large meeting... The proceedings commenced by singing "The Starving Poor of Old England" the chorus being backed up well by the enormous audience. The resolution was moved by William Morris which runs thus:

> That this meeting, while protesting against the extortion practised under what is known as the sweating system, points out that this is a necessary result of production for profit, and must continue until that is put an end to, and it therefore calls upon all workers to combine in order to

bring about the social revolution, which will place the means of production and exchange in the hands of the producers.[6]

One of the highlights of SDF activities that year was the Hyde Park demonstration mustered in aid of the match girls. Yet the party's official attitude, voiced by SDF correspondent H.W. Hobart, was not supportive of strike action *per se*. "Strikes, generally, we do not believe in — they invariably mean very hard times for the strikers and no particular hardship for the employers. But one great strike, one final blow — the SOCIAL REVOLUTION — has yet to be undertaken, and before this can be entered on with any degree of success the workers must follow the example of the match girls and unite."[7] The SDF's most popular speaker, Annie Besant, was out and about spreading the socialist gospel to whoever would listen. In late February, at the Tower Hamlets Liberal Club in the Mile End Road, she held forth to a full audience on "What Socialism Is" as promulgated by her party. All should labour; there should not exist a rich and idle person. No man should work more than eight hours per day; railways, banks, canals and docks should be the absolute property of the people. Every child should receive a thorough education provided by the state, free, as a matter of right. The lecturer would give the franchise to all adults of 21 years of age, both men and women. The affairs of the nation should be governed by the people, for the people, and each representative should be paid for his services. International affairs should be dealt with by a council, and all matters of disagreement referred to arbitration.[8]

Party policy, issued as a parliamentary manifesto of the SDF on 28 August (and published in full in *Justice* on 1 September) confirmed Besant's ideological precepts. It stated that, during the elections, "with respect to supporting candidates, no candidate should be supported by the SDF or any of its branches who does not definitely admit:

1. The existence of a class war between the wage earners and the classes which own the the means and instruments of creating wealth.
2. That the only way in which this antagonism can be removed is by the complete socialisation of all the means and instruments of production, including the land, under the

control of the entire adult community, all being called upon to do their share of work."

It was an old party stalwart who stressed the moral basis of a humane socialist creed, a proposition that has caused dissension amongst self-styled socialists ever since. J.C. Kenworthy wrote in the last issue of *Justice* that year:

> If every socialist, becoming convinced of the truth and being desirous of propagating it, would first set his own house in order — become honest, just, kind, helpful — we should find our case progress as by magic... When once we, as a body, feel the necessity that is laid upon us, of being, now, as individuals, such men and women as the New Society must be composed of, then our progress will be measured not by inches but by leagues.

It would appear that the rival Socialist League was the more actively engaged in agit-prop exercises in the East End. Its organ *Commonweal* records the many venues of meetings called during the year. A major branch was located at the spacious Mile End Radical Club at 108 Bridge Street, and weekly open-air meetings were held outside the Salmon and Ball in Bethnal Green on Sunday mornings and in Victoria Park the same afternoon. The predominantly Jewish International Working Men's Club in Berner Street was open to Socialist League branches, and William Morris could be heard lecturing there to mixed ethnic groups.[9] On Tuesday 27 March, his play, *The Tables Turned or Nupkins Awakened*, was performed here as part of a benefit concert in aid of the Yiddish radical newspaper *Arbeter Fraint*. Concentration of propaganda amongst the East End workers was initiated by a letter to *Commonweal* (12 May) by F. Charles of 38 Ainsley Street, Bethnal Green, who notified comrades that "the members of the East End branch of the Socialist League... have decided to throw themselves more energetically than ever into the spread of our ideas amongst the huge mass of workers living in all degrees of misery in the East End of London". Why here? Because "the system had crushed them into such a deadly state of apathy and indifference that we feel it is necessary to go to and amongst the people instead of expecting them to come to us...", that is to bring social consciousness from without to what would otherwise remain a torpid mass. With the assistance of "our foreign comrades" the local Leaguers had already mustered first a bill-posting parade to deliver posters and leaflets into every local court and alleyway, secondly other voluntary bands to distribute house by house the four-page leaflet *What Socialists Want* by William Morris together with a list of 25 or more indoor and outdoor places where future regular meetings of the Socialist League could take place. The letter ended by stressing (much more strongly than the SDF!) their solidarity with the immigrant worker "and especially in view of an anti-foreigner agitation (we) urge all our comrades to come and throw themselves heartily into the English propaganda and show that the international solidarity of labour is something more than a fine theory". In practice the Socialist Leaguers were much more sympathetic to their "alien" comrades than the SDF.

East London activities continued to top their list throughout the year. For example on week days in May Socialist League speakers could be heard addressing large crowds on the Mile End Waste (Tuesdays 8.30pm) at Philpot Street (Thursdays 8.30pm), Union Street, Commercial Road (Fridays 8.30pm) and Saturdays again at the Mile End Waste at 8.00pm. On 3 June the main speaker at Mile End was a Mr Parker and, at Leman Street, the Jewish trade union leader Lewis Lyons. That same month the star orator at Victoria Park was William Morris, who also continued to hold forth to predominantly Jewish immigrant audiences at Berner Street. On 17 June his *Tables Turned* was repeated at the Princes Square Club to a crowded house, after which "recitations and songs both in English and German, with dancing which was continued to a late hour, concluded a very successful entertainment on behalf of the East End Fund".[10] The Leaguers did not live for politics alone. They were ardent socialisers. The traditional radicals' excursions to Epping Forest, to which all manner of socialists were invited, were organised by them. Their correspondent recorded the lively jollifications in the bush as well as the peculiar antics indulged in by a police snooper in plain clothes:

> Last Sunday an enjoyable outing was spent in Epping Forest by members of the various socialist bodies in London. Besides singing, revelry, songs in different languages, dancing and other games, a meeting was addressed by Mainwaring, Rochman, Blundell and others. A lot of "Weals" and other literature was sold. During the day we had a good illustration of the work our "admirable police" are paid to do. There was a large number of

police, both mounted and on foot, at different points en route, besides several detectives in plain clothes. One of them wore a red tie, and represented himself as a member of some German drinking club, watched for about two hours by some comrades he tried by all means in his power to get a ticket for some member for drink, displaying to the full the well-known abilities of "moral miracles" in lie telling. He at last persuaded a woman comrade to sell him a ticket, obtained her name, and promised to summon them for contravening the Licensing Acts, and so departed, no doubt well pleased with the idea that the police would be able to lighten the profits of the day and so shorten the share of them which is to be devoted to the East End propaganda.[11]

For them the outdoor demonstration was the order of the day. On 1 July a Trafalgar Square mass rally with main speakers Messrs Coneybeare MP and Sanders demanding free speech was attacked by "Warren's Wolves" (the police). Two boys and one man were arrested and "while being conveyed to King Street Police Station the crowd followed, hooting and jeering. Near the Horse Guards an attempt was made to rescue the prisoners, but after a severe struggle they were got to the station".[12] As we have seen, the anti-sweating demonstration at Hyde Park on 22 July brought out the Socialist League as a major participant; more noticeable was their supportive coverage for foreign comrades (currently accused of being voluntary perpetuators of the sweating system — even by fellow socialists in the SDF!), by publicising in full the anti-sweating resolution passed by the immigrant workers' contingent that day.[13] The East End meetings — purporting to spread the message — continued unceasingly throughout the summer and autumn, the élite speakers appearing on the same weekly platforms. In Victoria Park on 18 November a vast demonstration was organised by the League to commemorate the first anniversary of the execution of the Chicago Martyrs. *The East London Observer*, through a prejudiced recorder, described the proceedings:

> Two extemporised platforms in the shape of excursion vans were placed in position round which immense crowds soon congregated. The chief attraction at the one was Mrs Lucy Parsons, the wife of one of the Chicago anarchists who met his death at the hands of the law. She was a dark — almost mulatto — looking woman, attired in black, and her utterances, displaying a limited knowledge of grammar, were listened to with

the deepest attention. At the other platform the cynosures of all eyes were Mr William Morris and Mr Cunninghame Graham. From both these platforms such arrant nonsense was cast forth about the "down-trodden working men" and "tools of the wealthy" which, of course, was cheered to the echo.[14]

Disdain for such nonsense accorded with Gladstone's speech in late December claiming that the efforts of the Liberal Party during the last 50 years in setting free "both capital and handicrafts... have resulted not in a uniform but in a very general and large improvement of the conditions of the working community". This brought an indignant response from *Commonweal*'s David Nicoll:

> What! Are there no sweater's dens? No women compelled to sell themselves for a night's lodging? No East End filled with swarming misery? How is it then that with all these beneficent labours of the Liberal Party that in this great city alone there are 179,000 starving men crying for "work or bread"?[15]

As for the élite purporting to give aim and direction to the local rank and file, they are revealed by Harkness (whose everyday involvement with them entitled her to speak with authority) to be riddled with factionalism. Through the medium of her hero Captain Lobo, the Salvationist, she castigated both the characters and relationships between the self-styled leaders. Their influence is negated "because they are so jealous. They cannot work together. They split up into small parties and spend their time quarrelling." The same rhetoric is expounded to the same people on the same street corners "unless the lecturer happens to be an anarchist". Of the latter he quoted, as an example, "a charming little lady" speaking to 80 practical working men about anarchism. "When she was pressed to say how the change would come about she told them that she had not come to the lecture hall with any solution of that question, but that she supposed some day everyone would rush out into the streets, a revolution would take place, and we should all become anarchists." Harkness gauges the reaction of a typical audience. At the woman "the men laughed, of course, for Englishmen like to see the next step, and even then hesitate to take it". To the socialists "they listen rather scornfully... because they do not think that the socialist programme comes within the sphere of practical politics. Anarchism is to them a farce, unless it has dynamite behind it. They look upon English anarchists as amiable lunatics."[16]

Harkness's estimate of the strength of the SDF accords with the statistical record of members and affiliated branches to date.[17] Noting that the SDF "has branches all over the country, and talks very big; but its numbers are few, and its funds are next to nothing", she concluded whereas a few years ago the federation used to frighten respectable folk, it was now

> a mere bogy. Its clubs... like butterflies
>
> Born in a bower,
> Christened in a tea cup,
> Dead in half an hour.

She further derided the intellectual ideologues as well-meaning but constantly at war with each other over the question of doctrinal purity. Only William Morris the "grand old poet" comes in for favourable comment; while the Fabians met to listen to an erudite lecture every fortnight, so that at the end they could "tear the lecturer to bits and flap their little wings over his carcass".[18] Finally, with rare insight, Harkness sharply disposes of what she considers to be those earnest and humourless Robespierrists of either sex who espouse <u>causes</u> through vague, unbending principles.

> You may see the same expression of the faces of men and women who live not for themselves or for their families, but for causes: who are animated by the wish to serve humanity rather than self, or a limited circle of friends or relations. Many of these people never find an outlet for their sympathies and aspirations. Not a few dash themselves upon the rocks because they seek their ideals in individuals. Some discover a way to serve humanity, and after long years of self sacrifice are obliged to confess that they have crucified themselves to no purpose.[16]

In response to the problem of sweating, at this time associated with the alien Jews and achieving national prominence, the East End Jewish radicals fought back. On 4 February a packed meeting of "sweaters' victims" was held in a Brick Lane school (probably Christ Church, Church of England Junior) "to protest against the cruel and inhuman sweating practised in England".

After a moving speech evidencing the terrible conditions in the sweatshops, Lewis Lyons, the Jewish trade union leader, urged that the following reforms be implemented by government decree:

> that no factory should be established or worked without previous notice given to the Home Office, and that particulars both of the industry to be pursued and the number of employees should be notified. Sanitary arrangements for the benefit of the workers should be provided by the manufacturers who should be punished by a continuous fine so long as this was neglected. Eight hours a day should be the limit of the work. Employers supplying articles to the employees should do so at cost price. The factories should be registered and the register open to the public. If new machinery were used, the labour should be reduced in proportion to the work done by the machine. Any employer breaking the rules laid down for his guidance should forfeit his licence. Fines inflicted in the factories should be divisible twice a year among the workers. A voluntary commission elected by ballot for a year should superintend the work of the factory inspectors.

A resolution was proposed endorsing the report of J. Burnett, labour correspondent to the Board of Trade, on whose evidence on sweating Lyons had based his plea. A commotion broke out ending in a fist fight as A. Cohen, a Master Tailors' representative, tried to move a counter-resolution that the meeting reject the report of Burnett as "a flagrant untruth, being one-sided and... only suggested by a prejudiced person", seconded by M. Marks, the largest and most unpopular tailoring employer in the area. On order being restored, Lyons' resolution, when put to the meeting, was carried with loud cheers.[20]

The supposition that Jews *qua* Jews were a unified body was also dispelled by an article in the *Jewish Chronicle* of 2 March, based on a government paper on the "Sweating System" by a Mr Lakeman. Commenting in this report on the Social Conditions of Factory and Workshop Female Operatives in the Central Metropolitan District (a Blue Book issued on 1 March), he concluded that there was a sharp division of interests between sweater, sweated and wholesale merchant. He drew the obvious conclusions that:

> the Jewish merchants are not in complete sympathy with the Jewish sweaters. The capital in money seems to war with the

capital in labour: the maxim that "All Israel are brothers" is not adhered to in the sweating trade, but rather the Ishmael life is exemplified and intensified by immigration whence fresh sources of discontent are sprung, prices kept down, the middleman as potent as ever, the sweater as powerless and the merchant smiling through all, gazes upon his enormous stock ready for shipment and home distribution.

In the final analysis the cause of sweating was attributed to the shrewdness of large manufacturers who took advantage of the stress of competition among the workers to beat down prices in every way by playing off the middleman against one another.

But, as we have seen, the victims in this predatory scenario were already astir. Spurred on by the false image projected through the deliberations of both Parliamentary Committees, immigrant radical leaders took the offensive. With Leeds' tailors out on strike in May, the Jewish East End tailors responded accordingly. On Saturday 26 May, an anti-sweaters parade took place to collect funds for their northern comrades. At 1.30pm the procession, numbering about 200, took off, headed by a band behind which a black banner was unfurled displaying in gilt letters the slogan "Down with sweating. Help the Jewish tailors on strike at Leeds". They marched through Aldgate, the City, High Holborn, Chancery Lane, Fleet Street, Queen Victoria Street, London Wall, homeward bound via Bishopsgate Street, returning to the Mile End Waste where a public meeting was held. The *East London Observer's* account exposed its own ambivalent attitude to such "alien" politickings: no sympathy from the locals who betrayed "the most venomous hostility to the intruders into the London labour market. One little woman in particular gave expression to her feelings in language which seemed in the main to express pretty accurately the estimation in which the foreign Jews were held by those around her. "There was no getting rooms for them", she said, "for they were always ready to underbid you; while they were always eager to snap up any thing in the way of charity." These denunciations were heartily endorsed by a surrounding mob at the start line, with insults flung at the assembled Jews "who neither resented nor answered in any way. Many of the Jews could not understand them properly; there were many who could, however, but they simply let their assailants rail and held their peace." Yet the recorder felt bound to add that it was a demonstration well calculated to arouse sympathy. "The black flag, the small forlorn looking party, the puny, seedy, unwholesome look of the majority of the men, could not fail to recall vividly to mind much that has been made public of late as to their sufferings and wrongs, and the fact of most of them being refugees from tyranny and persecution"; and the rousing speeches by Lewis Lyons and Annie Besant at the end were reported without any adverse commentary.[21]

Not only immigrant tailors were prompted to take industrial action. On 14 May, 300 East End journeymen bakers struck against excessive hours of labour. It started off when a select few quit their bakeries and marched through the streets stopping at every baker's shop in the area and appealing to the men inside to join them. The strategy was repeated throughout the week, the procession increasing each day accompanied by a brass band playing stirring music. It was noted that the strike was "confined almost entirely to Jewish and German journeymen whose average wages are about 13s per week and who demand an increase of another 5s per week". There appeared to be some success in the drive towards unionisation. On 10 August the *Jewish Chronicle* observed that Jewish journeymen bakers held a public meeting "last week and it was decided to agitate for sanitary places to work in, for a reduction in the hours of labour, for an increase of wages, and for the non-employment by master bakers of non-union men". The tailors never let up on their own anti-sweating campaign. On 28 June at the Goulston Street Hall a packed meeting was addressed by Mr Coneybeare MP and Mrs Annie Besant. A motion seconded by dockers' leader Ben Tillett was passed calling upon the introduction of a "new Factory Bill to contain clauses which shall provide for the registration of workshops, and that no workshops be open for more than 8 hours during every 24", to which Jewis Lyons added a second resolution condemning the Merchant Taylors' Company "for its wilful and persistent neglect of the interests of the working tailors for the promotion of which the trust funds administered by the City Company were bequested", which was also carried unanimously. The mounting wave of protest found even the despised Jewish sweaters in the boot trade calling a meeting in late August, to commence united operations against the manufacturers for an advance of wages. Throughout the rest of the year, immigrant tailors, boot, stick and cabinet makers were preparing for united action. In 1889 these activities climaxed in a series of strikes that shook the complacency of the Anglo-Jewish establishment.

It was the International Workers Educational Club in Berner Street, a narrow slum thoroughfare off the Commercial Road, that provided both a power-house for ideas and a mobilising centre for workers' demonstrations. It was predominantly Jewish but opened its doors to all ethnic groups. The founders had become patrons of the weekly radical Yiddish newspaper, the *Arbeter Fraint*, which offered a sounding-board and news-sheet for diverse immigrant radicals and trade unionists settled in Britain.[22] A unique description of a night's activity in the club is captured by libertarian novelist J.H. Mackay, who was currently exploring the area with a companion, a necessary safeguard, especially at night. The narrator Auban recalls the scene as his German comrade Tropp is invited to address the meeting.

> They ascended the narrow stairs to the hall, which was completely packed with people. It was of medium size and held hardly more than a hundred and fifty persons. Plain benches without backs stretched through it crosswise and along the walls. Everywhere extreme poverty but everywhere also the endeavour to overcome poverty. On the walls hung a number of portraits: Marx, Proudhon, Lassalle overthrowing the golden calf of capitalism; a cartoon in a black frame: "Mrs Grundy" the stingy, greedy, envious *bourgeoisie*, which, laden with treasure of all sorts, refuses the starving the pittance of a penny...
> At the front, the room was enclosed by a small stage. There Tropp was standing beside the table of the chairman. He spoke in German... Auban felt the tremendous passion flooding the meeting in hot waves from that point. Breathless, anxious not to lose a single word, they hung on the lips of the speaker. An electric thrill passed through these young people, hardly out of their teens; those women tired and crushed by the burden of their ceaseless toil; those men who, torn away from their native soil, had found each other here doubly and trebly disappointed. Rarely had Auban seen such devotion, such burning interest, such glowing enthusiasm as shone from those faces... Questions that among the children of the west would have at most formed matter for calm interchange of opinion, were discussed here as if life and death depended on them; in contrast with their own sorrowful, depressed, narrow life only the ideal of paradise! Nothing else! Highest perfection in communism: above all peace, fraternity, equality! Christians, idealists, dreamers, fools — such were these Jewish revolutionists of the East End — stepchildren of reason, banner-bearers of enthusiasm.

The evening ended with a stern rendering of the "workingmen's Marseillaise", in Yiddish-Deutsch:

Tod jeder Tyrannei!
Die Arbeit werde frei!
Marsch, marsch,
Marsch, marsch!
Und wärs zum Tod!
Denn unserer Fahn' ist roth![23]

This absolute dedication by a small band of political enthusiasts was reflected in the columns of the *Arbeter Fraint*. It publicised lectures at the club, union meetings, sales of current socialist literature in Yiddish and English, monitored world news of Jewish concern, especially in Russia and the USA, while printing leading articles by the prominent Yiddish radicals Philip Kranz and Benjamin Feigenbaum. On Tuesday 5 June, when giving evidence to the House of Commons Immigration Committee, Arnold White quoted it as having a widespread malevolent influence — through a weekly sale of 1,700 copies! (This was immediately refuted by Samuel Montagu who estimated sales at a mere 200, informing the same committee that a week before the paper itself had declared "through want of funds we were unable to issue the paper last week".)

While attracting the support of the anarchist's *Freedom* and William Morris's *Commonweal*, the Jewish radicals antagonised established Anglo-Jewry whose rabbinate thundered against them from the pulpit, and whose organ, the *Jewish Chronicle*, took a jaundiced view of the image that they were projecting in a hostile milieu. Perturbed by the national publicity focused on Jews in the sweated industries, the Chief Rabbi called a meeting of the Committee for the Visitation of the Poor in April to discuss means of suppressing the system. He made special reference to the so-called *Arbeiters Freund*, "a revolutionary paper said to be largely read by these poor folk but whose circulation was very limited". He concluded that "as soon as some means of bettering the condition of the sweated were devised, doctrines propagated by such sheets... would not to any extent be held".[24] The Berner Streeters had crossed swords with the Chief Rabbi before and continued to provoke the orthodox with their anti-religious antics. The worst was an advertisement in the *Arbeter Fraint* publicising a secular ball to be held on the same day as *Yom*

Kippur, the most solemn of Jewish high holy days. Officials of the *stieblech*-based Federation of Minor Synagogues were incensed. Their secretary, Mr J.E. Blank, drew attention to a Yiddish pamphlet inviting Jews to a dinner on *Yom Kippur*. He declared that "such people... who issued the invitation, were not recognised as Jews but were merely outcasts of our creed".[25] A United Synagogues' senior cleric, the Rev. E. Schewzok, followed suit in his Sabbath address to a largely immigrant audience at the Great Synagogue on 8 December: "how deep was the degradation of the Jews he did not know until a few days ago, when a printed paper was put into his hands calling the Jews to a dinner on the Day of Atonement. Was the race to be cursed for a handful of outcasts?"[26] As for the reaction of established Jewry to socialism in any form, this was appropriately summed up in an article entitled "Practicable Socialism" in the *Jewish Chronicle* on 2 November. Responding to an essay by the Warden of Toynbee Hall, who by now was expressing sympathy as well as posing arguments for that cause, the editor called for

> charitable enterprises based on compassion by the haves rather than the impractibility of what is understood by socialism... This professional follower of the communist who said it was easier for a camel to pass through the needle's eye than for a rich man to enter the Kingdom of Heaven, admits that it is useless to discuss state workshops, nationalisation of the land, division of income... He might have also pointed out that they would destroy all our existing order, won by centuries of painful progress, with the certainty of failing to provide anything of value in its place.

Anglo-Jewry's Rabbinate and its mouthpiece were firmly on the side of the status quo!

After all the marches, rallies and demonstrations led by the immigrant radicals that year, the outpouring of the *Arbeter Fraint* at the end of the year fuelled the anxieties of Anglo-Jewry. Feigenbaum, in an article "Frank and Free", accused the religious of living on murderers and exploiters, and of perpetuating ignorance and, therefore, subservience among the masses. He poured scorn on the clerics:

> Where can you find a godservant who has put the wind up the ruling class of all times against the shedding of blood, which permeates all episodes of the Good Book. Why didn't religion prevent its servant, the Inquisition, from performing such

atrocities? Its whole story is warped with such horrific deeds that it makes our limbs tremble to read them.

The editorial of 28 December ended on an ominous note. "The workers must once and for all realise that they alone can free themselves from all burdens, that is through the social revolution that will eliminate all parasites who sucked their blood for centuries and saddled their yoke". The next day the Berner Street Club featured a lecture by Mr Gould of Limehouse Branch SDF on "Will parliamentarianism help to bring about the social revolution?" For the Jewish establishment the gloomy foreboding of that year might well be fulfilled in the next — the centenary of 1789!

By 1888 it would appear that many who benefited from the capitalist system were, nevertheless, perceptive enough to foresee the dangers inherent in dogmatic belief in the infallibility of *laisser-faire*. According to *Commonweal* on 26 May, the possibility of "legislative social reform" was mooted by "a large number of MPs on both sides of the House (who) have long been dissatisfied with the apathy of Parliament on social questions". The practical application of such ideas was given a dramatic thrust by the coming of Jack the Ripper. Charles Booth had already reached the decision that somehow socialism and social welfare were synonymous and believed that combined systems of public and private enterprise could ultimately effect a more equitable society. Dismissing fanciful solutions to the problem of unemployment, he ventured his own:

> For the state to nurse the helpless and incompetent as we in our families nurse the old, the young and the sick, and provide for those who are not competent to provide for themselves — may seem an impossible undertaking. BUT NOTHING LESS THAN THIS WILL ENABLE SELF-RESPECTING LABOUR TO OBTAIN ITS FULL REMUNERATION AND THE NATION ITS RAISED STANDARD OF LIFE...

He concluded that "if this class were under state tutelage... the balance would be more favourable to the community". With this as a basis of policy he proposed an extension of the Poor Law (which he regarded as a limited form of socialism!) by way of labour camps for the unemployed, the scheme currently proposed by the Rev. Samuel Barnett. These, in his view, would constitute

> A socialistic community (with aid from outside) living in the midst of an individualist nation (where) life offered would not be attractive. Some might be glad to exchange their half-fed and half-idle and wholly unregulated life for a disciplined existence, with regular meals and fixed hours of work (which would not be short).

He outlined the preliminary objective as making "the dual system <u>socialism</u> in the arms of <u>individualism</u>... more efficient by extending somewhat the sphere of the former and making the division of function more distinct". Within his definition the introduction of Board Schools, hospitals and charitable bodies were all socialistic innovations. But the real clue to his partial embracing of so-called socialistic measures is revealed in his concluding argument that the introduction of limited socialist projects would, paradoxically, strengthen, not weaken, capitalist society. His argument ran thus:

> Individualist system breaks down as things are, and is invaded on every side by socialistic innovations, but its hardy doctrines would have a far better chance in a society purged of those who cannot stand alone... interference on the part of the state with the lives of a small fraction of the population would tend to make it possible ultimately to dispense with any socialistic interference in the lives of all the rest!

From this "small fraction" would be conscripted the unemployed for labour in the new industrial settlements. Here, "there need be no competition with the outside world. It would be merely that the state, having these people on its hands, obtained whatever value it could out of their work. They would become servants of the state." This rationale was received as a result of Booth's investigations in East London.[28]

Other demonstrations of social protest were continuously manifest. On 8 February a full meeting at the Stepney Meeting House, presided over by the Liberal candidate for Stepney, B.T.L. Thomson, learned of the evictions of poor crofters in the Highlands by corrupt landlords. A crofter's spokesman, Donald Macrae, addressing a sympathetic audience in "a homely and vigorous Scotch" outlined the terrible injustices inflicted on the victims:

> How their women had been dragged from their Highland homes and thrown into Edinburgh prison; how animals now occupied the land which God had intended for the people... He exposed the fraud perpetrated upon the Highlanders by the Crofters' Act by which, although it proposed to carry out the recommendation of Lord Napier's Ccommission that more land should be given to the people, not a single inch had been added to any croft in the Highlands. He spoke of terrorism exercised by the landlords where interviewees feared to tell the truth, whilst the Lord's agent was present, lest he be punished later... Mr Macrae declared that the people in the Highlands were now literally starving. The women and children... are almost naked and their only food is potatoes and salt.

The East Enders responded with "groaning and hooting" as the names of the despotic clan lords were announced, and registered their solidarity with the other poor by unanimously passing a resolution "That the East End people desire the Government to do its duty to the poor wherever they may be found in the three kingdoms".[29]

The same year another incident projected East London onto the international stage: the historic Match Girls' strike at Bow. On 15 June at a meeting of the Fabian Society, Mrs Clementina Black, after lecturing on her researches into female labour, urged the formation of a Consumers League. Members would be pledged to deal only with shops certified clean from those known to pay unfair wages. In the discussion that followed H.H. Champion revealed that Bryant and May Match Company was a prime offender while paying out enormous dividends to its shareholders. (The value of the original £5 share was currently quoted at £18 6s 6d.) Annie Besant was moved to intervene. She and her companion Herbert Burrows went down to Bow to interview some of the girls to obtain a list of piece rates and charges. They were horrified at their findings; and Besant records

> A typical case is that of a girl of 16, a piece worker; she earns 4s a week, and lives with a sister, employed by the same firm, who "earns good money — as much as 8s or 9s a week". Out of the earnings 2s a week is paid for the rent of one room. The child lives only on bread and butter and tea, alike for breakfast and dinner, but related with dancing eyes that once a month she went to a meal where "you get coffee and bread and butter, and jam and marmalade, and lots of it". [130]

She immediately published an article "White Slavery in London" in the *Link* on 23 June, attacking Bryant and May and appealing for a boycott of their product. On 26 June she and Burrows stood at the factory gates distributing the article to the girls as they came out.

The company's response was a threat of libel action against Besant coupled with an order by management that the workers refute her charges individually by signing a statement certifying that the accusations were untrue. They refused and three girls, suspected of having provided information to Besant, were promptly sacked. On 5 July the whole factory downed tools in sympathy, and 1,200 girls from the wood match-making department and 300 from the box-making adjunct marched out. In traditional style, East Enders, from all classes, rallied to their support. The next day Lewis Lyons was arrested for obstruction while addressing the strikers outside the factory. (On 13 July he was duly fined 14s or 14 days imprisonment.)

The causes of the strike went far deeper than the immediate provocation. The girls had struck before in 1886, ostensibly over a wage cut, but as much over unhealthy working conditions. The company had gained a dominating position in the industry by cutting its labour costs during the recession of the 1880s. Any opposition to this or the breaking of strict work rules laid down by the management was punished by fines which reduced the take-home pay of many to a minimum. Above all the nature of the work itself was a health hazard. "Phossy jaw" (phosphorus necrosis) was a common disease causing intense pain from inflamed teeth and jaws, and ultimately terrible disfigurement. In effect it reduced the rate of production through illness, and sick girls on the bench who were unable to fill their quota would be sacked. There were many dayworkers forced to moonlight as cheaper outworkers when, with husbands unemployed, they were the only breadwinners. For those employed during the day, the prospect of being discharged and forced to rely only on the miserable pittance of an outworker was a fearful one.

Annie Besant took charge. On Sunday 8 July a group of speakers mobilised on the Mile End Waste. They included Herbert Burrows, the radical priest Stewart Headlam and Women's Protective League representative Clementina Black, all under the chairmanship of Besant. On 14 July the scarcely sympathetic *East London Advertiser* attacked the intervention of the socialists and cast suspicion on their use of money collected on behalf of the strikers. ("Disputes seem generally to have arisen with regard to the distribution of the money collected... the girls say they have received very little of it.") It noted a threat by the firm to import labour from Scotland. The SDF's immediate response was to telegraph all branches in Glasgow appealing for joint demonstrations against the export of blackleg labour. A complete day-to-day coverage of the first week of the strike was outlined in the 14 July issue of *Justice*. Certain incidents would prove of long-term importance to both the women's and the general trade union movement. It was at the mass meeting on the 8th that a resolution was passed calling on the matchmakers to form a union. On the following Tuesday, after a march along the embankment, a deputation of 56 girls was invited into Besant's house at 84 Bouverie Street to be provided with tea, bread and butter. Twelve of them were selected by the girls themselves to proceed to the House of Commons in order to present their grievances via two sympathetic MPs, Cunninghame Graham and Coneybeare, to Parliament.

Meanwhile Annie Besant continued to press their cause as a national issue in letters to the newspapers and public rallies, while organising the collection of funds to sustain the girls during their struggle. On the Wednesday morning, 11 July, the *East London Advertiser* noted that Frederick Charrington had "granted the use of his halls at Mile End, and 1,800 girls of the wood and safety matches departments were assembled there for the purpose of having their names placed on a register"; and that during the course of the day various collections amounted to about £80. Help was also forthcoming from local Jewish tradesmen who "subscribed several pounds among themselves, and at a public house thereby, distributed large quantities of bread, cheese and beer to the girls".[31] Of course some of the girls succumbed to the usual pressures to return to work: no money for rent and food meant the threat of homelessness and hunger. On 14 July the *East London Observer* publicised Frederick Bryant's intention "not to take back strikers especially those of the Victoria factory which contained the ringleaders", and on the same day the *East London Advertiser* announced, with obvious satisfaction, that on the morning of Monday 9 July, 160 girls had returned to work.

"Poor as we are," they informed our reporter, "we ain't come to cadging yet." On Tuesday 50 more resumed — it is anticipated on good grounds that the movement must collapse in a few days. The £120, which it is announced has been received for the strike fund, will not go far among such a large number of girls.

It was a piece of wishful thinking on the paper's part. The strike went on as 600 of the girls took off to the fruit fields and the rest were promised strike pay on the following Saturday. Thanks to Besant and her aides, public opinion was mobilised in their favour. This was best illustrated by the fact that in such a traditionally affluent and conservative haven as Tunbridge Wells, a few workmen succeeded in collecting in one week between two and three pounds, in sums ranging from a penny to a half a crown.[32] The boycotting of Bryant and May matches with leaflets exhorting people to buy the rival Wilson and Palmer product, since "the firm treats its girls decently", the intervention of widely respected public figures such as the Rev. Barnett, who led a delegation from Toynbee Hall to meet the directors of Bryant and May in an effort to influence them in the strikers' cause; Bradlaugh's questions in Parliament, which aroused the sympathy of the House and "stirred up the constituencies in which shareholders were revealed as members", Sidney Webb moving the National Liberal Club to action while the Fabians offered such heavyweight orators as Bernard Shaw and Stewart Headlam, who stomped the streets of the capital and its environs enlisting support in clubs and pubs — all this was too much for the beleaguered Bryant and May. Within a fortnight the London Trades Council was called in as arbitrator, and the firm virtually capitulated.

The details of the settlement were spelt out in *Commonweal* on 21 July:

> On Tuesday 17 a deputation from the London Trades Council, accompanied by the girls' strike committee, had an interview with the directors of Bryant and May's. After a long discussion the following terms were agreed upon for submission to a meeting of the strikers who were awaiting the result in Charrington's Hall:
>
> 1) Abolition of all fines;
>
> 2) abolition of all reductions for paint, brushes, stamps etc;

3) restitution of "pennies" if the girls do their own racking or payment by piecework of boys employed to do it (the result of this latter will be more than equal to the penny);

4) the packers to have their threepence;

5) all grievances to be taken straight to the managing directors without the intervention of the foremen. The firm further said that they would as soon as possible provide a breakfast room so that the girls will not be obliged to eat in the room where they work, and also expressed a strong wish that the girls would organise themselves into a union, so that further disputes may be officially laid before the firm. These conditions were submitted to the meeting at Charrington's Hall by the Strike Committee, and the girls unanimously decided to agree to them, the payment of boy helpers by piece work being accepted as a full equivalent for their pennies. The waxworkers returned to their work on Wednesday and the wooden match workers on Thursday. All the girls and boys to be taken back, no distinction being made to ringleaders.

While William Morris regarded the victory of the girls as small change,[33] the historic consequences of their strike tactics were soon apparent. It was an act of mass solidarity by unskilled workers, which set off a new pattern of unionisation, its effects extending well beyond the boundaries of East London. A week after the strike ended the committee met to draft the rules of a Matchmakers Union. It was attended by Messrs Cooper and Steadman of the London Trades Council, Miss Clementina Black of the Women's Provident and Protective League, under the leadership of Besant and Burrows. A code of rules was drawn up and submitted to the representatives of the women on the following Friday evening, 27 July, at the Stepney Meeting House in Garden Street off Stepney Green. The girls were "full of enthusiasm and earnestness" in their readiness to create a union — from one of the most difficult sections of workers to organise —the largest of its kind in England composed entirely of women.[34] With characteristic vigour, Besant directed her energies towards strengthening the Union by the acquisition of money from diverse sources. One was the organisation of a ticket benefit show at the Royal Princess's Theatre, Oxford Street, for the last five days of August, the proceeds to go to the Union Building Fund. At the first quarterly meeting of the Union at the same Stepney Meeting Hall on 15 November, the secretary reported that the total membership had reached 678 while subscriptions had amounted to over £60. It was then that it was decided to alter the first rule so as to admit male workers.

An immediate offshoot of the strike itself was a dispute at the Paces Factory in Bromley-by-Bow, a branch of Bryant and May. On 24 July 100 women, most of whom were box makers and outworkers, refused to continue working. Apparently a half-a-dozen girls had been brought in from Glasgow, and it was alleged that they were being paid 1¼d gross of boxes instead of 2¼d, paste and hemp however being provided in addition to the wage. The local women struck against the importation of outside labour and appealed to Besant for help. The rumour of cheap labour proved unfounded. The "Scotchies" had merely come short term to teach them a new way of working and were then to return, so the local girls were easily persuaded to treat them as friends. More important was a meeting called for 31 July, that is only two weeks after the successful ending of the strike, to form a new General Labourers Union. The letter sent by the founder to *Justice* (11 August) is self-explanatory, while the effect of the match strike is evident.

> Comrade,
> I, with others, called a meeting of navvies and unskilled labourers of London at Sydney Hall, Battersea, on July 31st, for the purpose of forming a General Labourers Organisation, which could include all grades of unskilled labour... A Committee was elected to draw up rules for presentation to the members at a meeting to be held at Sydney Hall on Thursday, August 9th. From that time the society will be in actual existence. Now is the time for unskilled labour to prove it is not the useless aggregation of incapacity that some of the "aristocrats" of labour would have us believe. All communications should be addressed to the secretary at the address below. Having been boycotted by *Reynolds*, we now fall back on "Labour's Tribune", the organ of social democracy to give notice of this very important step on the part of unskilled labour in England.
>
> Yours fraternally,
> John Ward, Sec. Pro Tem.
>
> 16 Bramford Road,
> York Rd., Wandsworth.
>
> PS The name of the society is the "Amalgamated Society of General Labourers".

The momentum for union building gathered pace and entered the political arena with Annie Besant at the forefront. She recalled the aftermath of the Bow strike:

> Then came a cry for help from South London, from tin-box makers, illegally fined, and in many cases grievously mutilated by the non-fencing of machinery; then aid to shop assistants also illegally fined... a vigorous agitation for a free meal for children, and for fair wages to be paid by all public bodies; work for the dockers and exposure for their wrongs, a visit to the Cradley Heath chain makers, speeches to them, writing for them; a contest for the School Board for the Tower Hamlets division and triumphant return at the head of the poll. Such were the ways in which the autumn days were spent... lectures... meetings... and scores of articles written for the winning of daily bread.[36]

All these gave an additional fillip to Ben Tillett's efforts to unionise the dockers. His recently formed Tea Operatives and General Labourers Association (July 1887) experienced its first opportunity for action in late October, when the dockers struck at Tilbury for an increase of 1d an hour. The lessons of solidarity were not lost on East Enders. On 24 October a meeting of local dockers under the auspices of their Union at the St. Mary's schoolroom in Whitechapel passed a resolution supporting their brethren at Tilbury. Two days later, at Charrington's Assembly Hall, a huge audience was informed by Tillett that the most satisfactory feature of the strike was the response of the West India dockers, who refused to go to Tilbury and perform blackleg labour. The strikers were out for a month, but in the end, as the *Justice* reporter perceived, "the pallid faces of the wives and children, and the craving of their own stomachs were too much for them. It is satisfactory to know, however, that the men, although temporarily defeated, are determined to strengthen their organisation in preparation for a more extensive fight." For lessons had been learned. The key issues were wider public, and thereby greater financial, support and absolute solidarity between all co-workers. Tilbury provided the dress rehearsal for the great dock strike that broke out the following year.[37]

Momentous happenings that year, particularly for women. Following Besant's initiative their incursion into the East End was dramatic. As already noted, such middle-class foragers included Eleanor Marx-Aveling and Margaret Harkness. The latter submits a unique sketch of a new breed of recruits — self-educated working-class radical feminists locally involved in either the SDF of Socialist League. There is a patronising, almost contemptuous description of her subject — a labour mistress — that reveals her own class prejudices and the superficiality of her overt egalitarian stance!

> The labour mistress is living in this year of grace 1888, and is a fair specimen of a strong-minded proletarian spinster. She would attend women's rights meetings if she knew where they take place, and agitate for the enfranchisement of her sex if she knew how to agitate. Her ideas about socialism are vague, for she has no time to study and little time to think, but she believes in justice and hates the capitalist. A string of words and phrases, such as exploitation, bloated aristocrat, white slavery and the emancipation of labour, dangle like charms before her eyes. She sees the words but they elude her grasp, for they were not written in her School Board lesson book, and she has no money to buy a new-fashioned dictionary. On Sundays she tries to "improve her mind" with the help of a circulatory library which contains many three-volumed novels and a few standard works. The latter she has long since finished. Such libraries are not meant for strong-minded proletarian spinsters, but for clerks and young ladies in business. She lives far away from the British Museum reading-room, where she might graze among a herd of like-minded ladies.

An attempted dispassionate presentation of current feminist argument is flawed by ending on a note of cheap sarcasm that is usually attributed to men.

> The reign of muscular force is said to be well nigh finished, and men having prepared the rough ground for women, are now, we are told, making way for the gentler sex in all places, even in politics. Untamed instincts are being trampled underfoot, and we are about to see "a glorified humanity". This being so, women must begin to emulate the few virtues which men have left: they must no longer indulge in eavesdropping and gossip![38]

If the East End women, led by Annie Besant, had made history with their July victory in the match strike, they were soon to do so again with Besant's successful election as Tower Hamlets member to the London School Board on 26 November. Like her comrade, the Hackney candidate Rev. Steward Headlam, she was adopted by such diverse groups as the Liberals and Radicals as well as the Socialist Central Democratic Committee. Frustrated by her inability, as a woman, to stand for the newly created London County Council, she was resolved to play a leading role in any public institution that had power to legislate for change. Her election address was a blueprint for educational reform. Revolutionary in its time, her aims would, henceforth, be fought for item by item until implemented throughout every local authority in Great Britain.

> Free, secular, compulsory, technical education for all. Education should be for all classes alike, so that it may break down class divisions and lay a basis for real equality. The common school system is the foundation of true democracy.
> Extension of education and school management in favour of Evening Continuation Schools and the opening of higher education to the poor. I shall never consent to starve either the schools or the teachers; teaching is arduous and exhausting work, and those engaged in it should always be treated with consideration and sympathy. I am in favour of putting the Board School at the service of the public... and the throwing open of the playgrounds to all children during the hours of daylight after school time and throughout the holidays. No more <u>hungry children</u>. Children sent to school without breakfast and given but little dinner, cannot profit from the education you pay for. They are blamed for stupidity and inattention when they are only hungry, and they break down under what is called "over pressure", but what is really underfeeding. If we force them to learn, we must make them <u>able</u> to learn. Until Parliament gives us power to provide a free meal we must be content to organise voluntary effort... Not a penny will be added to the rates, but to the misapplied city charities and, taking these, we will use them for filling the stomachs of thin children instead of gorging the paunches of fat aldermen. "Over pressure" both on teachers and children, also arises from our present system of payment by results, and I am in favour of its abolition.

She reinforced her plea to the electorate with a personal statement of intent.

> I shall, if elected, steadily oppose any work of the Board being given to firms who treat their workpeople unfairly, or who pay less than trade unions rates of pay.
> I am strongly in favour of the appointment of working men and women as managers of our Board Schools.
> Lastly, I ask the electors to vote for me, and the non-electors to work for me, because women are wanted on the board, and there are too few women candidates. Women have proved themselves useful, especially in connection with administrative

details, whenever they have been elected to offices of public trust, and, as a woman, I ask you to elect me.[40]

The last was a bold demand, considering the person, the time and the place. A woman, a socialist and atheist to boot, who had walked out on her parson husband and advocated birth control, was enough to send the local clergy into paroxysms of rage and miles of print against the scarlet woman. Not only had she ranged against her three sitting members who were clerics of the Anglican, Primitive Methodist and Catholic persuasion and an ex-army colonel, but also the scion of the old Jewish aristocracy and Conservative candidate Claude Montefiore, who purported to represent the Jewish vote. The latter could have constituted a formidable threat by alienating the support of local Jewry, had it not been for the intervention on her behalf of the irrepressible Lewis Lyons, a much more popular figure among the immigrant poor. His action must have more than marginally swung their votes in her favour.

For the conservative (and rabidly anti-Besant) *East London Advertiser*,[41] while lamenting the "apathy of the people" ("The work at one station in Wapping was phenomenal. At 12 o'clock just 12 persons had voted, 8 an hour"), was quick to note that at "St. Jude's School, Commercial Street, the officers... were the busiest of any station... a fact which was doubtless owing to the proximity of so many Jewish people". There were additional bonuses, such as the novelty of a woman candidate standing in a rough, male-dominated constituency, and her own charismatic personality. During the campaign she drove a dog-cart throughout the length and breadth of the East End, immediately recognisable, a glamorous figure with a bright red ribbon in her hair. The less conservative *East London Observer*, after commenting that her dress was indistinguishable from that of other women, was ready to concede that "there was that in her browned and tanned face and in the firm, thin lips and knitted brows, which unmistakably told of a woman of courage and determination". In spite of the Church Party's attempt at defamation of character (one Rev. E. Hoskyns of the Rectory, Stepney, refused to apologise under the threat of a libel suit, but acceded to her demand that he otherwise contribute £50 to the London Hospital!), supported by some spurious letters to the press from local mothers, the outcome was dramatic. Annie

Besant topped the poll with 15,926 votes, while the second place went to the erstwhile favourite, the popular Liberal Sir Edmund Hay Currie, who gained 13,150.[42]

One immediate result of her victory was to encourage a Miss Jane Cobden to extend the struggle and attempt to challenge the man-made rule of male candidates only for the forthcoming elections to the newly created London County Council. On 29 December the *East London Advertiser* informed its readers that Miss Cobden, a Women's Equality Candidate "comes forward (for Bow and Bromley) at the invitation of the Liberal and Radical Association and, if returned, the question will be raised as to the legality of her claim. In her address, she, in the first place, believes that women ought to have not only a vote, but a voice, on all questions affecting the housing of the poor." The fight for women's suffrage was on, to be given an important impetus by the incursion of these doughty activists into the East End.

Equally important were the number of educational reforms pressed for by Besant and executed by the new School Board. On 15 December *Justice* noted jubilantly that Besant, aided by Stewart Headlam, had succeeded in introducing one of her election aims, that is to defer tenders for Board work until it was ascertained that the firms selected were paying a fair wage. Early next year the Board went further to pioneer the order demanding that trade union rates be paid by firms seeking Board contracts. On 30 January 1890 it passed the historic act, introdueed as a resolution by Besant, declaring that schools receiving state grants should be free. This example by the London School Board prompted an Act of Parliament the following year implementing free elementary education for all. *Punch's* cartoon of 1 December 1888 backed up Besant's contention that hungry children made poor learners. The following month a motion was passed by the Board to inquire into the number of undernourished children in the metropolis. The survey found that one in eight school attenders suffered from malnutrition, and as a result a London Schools Dinner Association was founded to provide meals for the needy and funded by charitable aid.[43] In the nation's record 1888 registered a watershed of change. Where East London led, others followed, particularly in the unionisation of the unskilled and the education of the poor.

There were other less salubrious but more hilarious aspects of politicking in the East End that year. One was the scandals that broke involving members of the Mile End Vestry. Accusations against them varied from drunken behaviour to corrupt practices concerning the disposal of property left by deceased inmates of the infirmary. At the centre of the furore was the grand Inquisitor Frederick Charrington, and his aide-de-camp the formidable M.T. Richardson, known locally as the scourge of the Vestrymen. The campaign was opened by the "reforming group" at a rally in the Assembly Hall on 31 January as a protest against the Vestry's attempt to bar ratepayer observers from their meetings. Richardson recalled election night, when he and his colleague Kerwin entered the Vestry. They were confronted by

> gentlemen seated around a table and imbibing something which was not bitter beer. One of the said gentlemen was evidently very far gone, for he got up, and staggering towards them said "Mister-hic-Kerwin — I'm very glassh to shee you" (laughter). Mr. Kerwin made a remark to the effect that he would have been much more pleased to have seen that gentleman had he been a little more steady!

Richardson went on to deplore the terrible reputation that these people had brought on their parish:

> A great cry had gone throughout London at the idea of Mile End Vestrymen indulging in whisky and brandy, but Mile End Vestrymen had better tastes than that. They could get twopennyworth's of brandy or whisky at any time, but the world ought to know that they indulged in their Hockheimer, their Verstiza, their Most and their Perrier Jouet. It was really unfair to say that the Mile End Vestrymen did not know their choicest brand, because they did, and they drank of them much and frequently at the ratepayers' expense.

He then exposed further corrupt practices which involved a public servant, the surveyor, who was receiving, in excess of his salary, commissions for public works that were contrary to his contractual obligations. The latter was also involved in the acquisition of an iron weighbridge from Messrs Schwarz, sugar refiners, that had been condemned as unfit for use but bought by the Guardians for £130 and still lying around unused. The speaker proceeded to enlighten his audience on the scene he witnessed during the audit of the Overseer's Account. It would appear that fiddling the books was normal practice:

> In the centre of the room sat the auditor, and then sitting all in a row, were the three overseers — the three superior Bumbles. While he was standing there — for they had not the good manners to offer him a chair — he heard the auditor say, "I can't pass this; I must have more particulars." Hallo, thought the speaker, what's that? He eyed those superior Bumbles, and they looked at him in a very savage manner — the auditor also added, "With regard to these brothel cases, I have not anything like the evidence I want. I cannot take them... I cannot pass them now." And, as to those brothel cases, they all knew how Mr Charrington had cleared the whole of Lady Lake's Grove at an expenditure of something like a guinea, but here were some of the amounts spent by the overseers: George Raynor, reward for information of a disorderly house £10; Slones, Morris and Stone, reward £10; Mr McHaffey £15; Mr Chidgey £15; Mr Jutson, for brothel cases, judgement, debt and costs £426 19s 4d. That was astounding and scandalous... and it was a wonder that the ratepayers did not rise as one man for some kind of attention in their local laws by which men should not, as now, dive here and dive there, for money — grab, grab, grab all round — taking the bread out of the ratepayers' mouths simply to feed positions which were good without it.[44]

It was the beginning of a battle against the "corrupt Guardians" which paralleled that against vice, led by the same protagonists. The following evening, the *East London Advertiser* noted a vast attendance of the public at the Vestry Hall in Bancroft Road. Richardson confronted the members and, repeating his charges against them, demanded a detailed explanation of their expenditure in public. The *Advertiser*, no friend of the reformers, ruefully commented on "the great high jinks" instigated by them in the solemn halls of a local authority, but ended with satisfaction that "the clerk and officers effectively defended themselves against the onslaughts of Messrs Richardson and F.N. Charrington. The meeting eventually adjourned amid lively scenes. From the railing outside... Mr Richardson continued to harangue an audience of about 200 on the events of the evening."

Under the patronage of a reforming duo — the Mile End Ratepayers Protection Association and the Municipal Reform

League — Richardson proceeded to harass the old guard, whom he characterised as "gluttons and drunkards". He fulminated against the pickings accruing to the clerk, surveyor and rate collectors: the present incumbents defined as predators feeding on the body politic. Having secured the Vestry Hall for one night on 7 March, his accusations in front of a packed audience culminated in a famous "Sticks of the Dead" speech in which he disclosed a particularly odious practice only recently brought to his notice:

> Mr Richardson said it was well known that it was customary with some persons when they were ill to go into the infirmary, and not wishing to break up their homes, the furniture was stored with the Guardians. Some few years ago, a large quantity of furniture had accumulated, owing to the death of the owners in the infirmary, and the Guardians determined to sell it. Now he wished to know if one gentleman went to another gentleman, and said, "I want you to do a little business for me", and if, before going, gent No. 1 said "Remember this is my business, and you're not to go above £5." He wanted to know if these two gentlemen went and viewed the furniture at the back of the workhouse and whether gent No. 2 said, "I'll give you £5 for the lot" and whether the original gent said, "I'll give you six guineas" and whether they were knocked down for six guineas — (a voice: "yes") — and he wanted to know if, when coming out of the yard, gent No 2 said to No. 1 "I'll give you £40 for the lot!" (sensation, and cries of "shame"). Yet it was said the Guardians were all right. Notice the hard-heartedness of the circumstances. Not content with doing injury to the ratepayers, they were down upon the "sticks of the dead" squandering them away in that ruthless fashion.[45]

This led to two resolutions, passed unanimously. The second, moved by the agent for the local Radical parliamentary candidate, was to prove the more pertinent. ("That this meeting pledges itself to use its utmost endeavours to return men to the Board of Guardians at the next election who will study the interests of the ratepayers in avoiding all extravagances, at the same time having due regard to the welfare of the poor.") In spite of convincing evidence produced in their defence, the old guard were doomed. On Monday 9 April the Ratepayers Protection League tried its "prentice hand" at the elections for the Guardians of the Poor. The Friday before saw trouble at the hustings, when pandemonium broke out as rival parties from adjoining meetings clashed in the open Stepney Green. To the surprise of all, not least of the reformers themselves, 14 of their 18 candidates were elected, with F.N. Charrington topping the poll with 3,227 votes.

Certainly, for Mile End, there were changes in the air. The fight against old corruption was pursued relentlessly. Open-air meetings were now the vogue, Richardson exploiting the success of his reform caucus with public declamations on street corners. On 14 May, at the end of a monster torchlight demonstration held at Stepney Green, he accused the old Vestry clique of allowing over 1,000 houses in the parish to remain without water. The feeble excuse offered was "that the sanitary inspector was agent for these houses". When the official was called before the new Vestry, his answer was that a water supply was pending and that he had been agent for these houses long before he came to the Vestry considerably over 20 years before. Two days later, at a meeting outside the Edinburgh Castle in Rhodeswell Road, Poplar, Richardson continued his invectives against the remaining "guzzlers" and "greedy gormandizers", attacking also the local East Ward rate collector for receiving, due to illicit payments, over £500 a year. It was Charrington who set the pace. When the new Board met on 19 April, he quickly manoeuvred his group into control with his own men being elected Chairman and Vice Chairman accordingly.

The ex-brewer was soon riding his other hobby horse — drink! At that first meeting he initiated a resolution that was passed condemning those clauses in the Local Government Bill advocating compensation for publicans. A ding-dong battle between the old and new Vestry men persisted throughout the year, with accusations and insults bandied about and recorded in public. One positive outcome that would influence other parishes was the demand for a strict control on jobs put out to tender; though the two major newspapers in the area, whose political leanings were both Conservative, were noticeably sceptical of the "rancorous rantings" that they attributed to the reforming group.[47]

In the mainstream of party politics during 1888 both liberals and conservatives were consolidatirig their bases in the East End against the onslaught of socialists and radicals. Two party controversies centred round the Irish Question and Jewish immigrants, notably on the latter's potential effect on the vote, and thereby how to attract their support. Qiven the mass of Irish and Anglo-Irish constituents within the borough, liberal speakers could command a captive audience. On 5 February a large demonstration gathered at Tower Hill to protest against the imprisonment of Wilfred Blunt, W. O'Brien MP and T.D. Sullivan, the Lord Mayor of Dublin. The meeting had been convened to attract the majority of liberal, radical and Irish clubs and leagues in the East End. It was an impressive gathering, and from the account of an on-the-spot reporter, would be long remembered by police and demonstrators alike:

> From 3 to 4 o'clock there was to be witnessed from the meeting place procession after procession marching from every street and road emerging on to the Hill, their banners gaily flying, and their bands playing, the rear being invariably brought up by a waggon or brake containing the speakers... the great black and green (sashed) mass representing some 15,000 people... At the extreme edge of the crowd were gathered posses of police comprised of the City and H Divisions but at no time from the gathering of the processions to the termination of the meeting were their services required... At the principal platform was Mr J. Hall (of the Whitechapel Liberal and Radical Association, who acted as Chairman). At the next platform, presided over by Mr Lewis Lyons, faced by the artisans and some Bethnal Green clubs were Mrs Shark, Messrs Ellis (the Peckham and Dulwich delegate to Ireland), A. Flint (the Stepney delegate), Dalziel and Ambrose. The Socialists were addressed from their platform by Messrs Parker, Lane and others. The dimensions of the crowd were so large, however, as to prevent many present from coming within hearing range.

After a common resolution (condemning the cruel treatment inflicted on the political prisoners as "un-English and unworthy of a civilised country" and calling on the House of Commons "to intervene on behalf of justice and humanity") was put, the processions re-formed and marched away headed by their bands to the tunes of *God Save Ireland* and *The Wearing of the Green*.[48]

The Irish Question was a good vote catcher for East End Liberals. On 7 March they called a meeting at the St. Paul's Hall, Goulston Street, to hear a recital of experiences by local delegates who had recently visited Ireland. George Lansbury, representing the Bow and Poplar Branch, was a member of the deputation which travelled north to visit the Nazarene, Shirley and Andrews Estates. His report was a terrible indictment of landlordism with its ruthless policy of evictions. On the Nazarene properties the majority of peasants had been cast out. He witnessed one case on the Shirley Estate:

> Peter Ward, with his wife and children was evicted from his house while the snow lay thick on the ground. He went to Mr Shirley and asked if he and his family could have shelter in an old barn on his farm, and the answer was "You had better go and ask your English friends to keep you." In desperation, Ward and his family went to Garrick-on-Cross, and took shelter in a wretched little hovel there, where, a day or two afterwards, the man died of a raging fever as the result of the privation through which he had gone...[49]

Fenianism and Home Rule could always find dedicated recruits in the "Irish" docklands. On 15 December Gladstone's progress in his carriage to speak at Limehouse Town Hall developed into a triumphal procession through dense crowds from Aldgate eastwards. A packed audience — 1,800 within, 5,000 outside — greeted the champion of Home Rule. An onlooker described the scene as Gladstone left the hall:

> There was a block of movement at the exit... no passage for traffic, the carriages of the distinguished visitors were immovable, the police were powerless, while above all the struggling and confusion, rose the strains of the Irish band, *God Save Ireland*. In the midst of this, way was made for Mr and Mrs Gladstone, several of the stewards charging down the steps of the hall with violent force into the crowd. Another ovation was made as the parties took their seats in the carriage, the crowds melted as if by magic, the gleams from red and blue fires gave a weirdness to the scene, and followed by a yelling and cheering crowd, the carriage drove off towards Aldgate. So ended the only visit Mr Gladstone has thought fit to pay East London.[50]

Given the current hysteria provoked by the so-called alien invasion, it was not surprising that the East End immigrant was used by either party as a stick to beat the other. While the *East London Observer* (14 January), quoting the *Echo*, agreed that the S.W. Bethnal Green Conservatives had acted judiciously in selecting Mr Arthur Sebag Montefiore as their candidate, since Bethnal Green contained a Jewish vote that was well worth conciliating, the *East London Advertiser* (28 April) poured scorn on Liberal MP Samuel Montagu for exhibiting "so much affection for the foreign immigrant" as a ploy to secure their vote.[51] Yet in May, in a report in the same paper, Colonel Trench, Chairman of the Conservative and Constitutional Association, was defending himself against a similar charge by Montagu ("that he had spent a large amount of money to publish a circular... in the Hebrew-German dialect, praying and entreating those foreigners who could not understand a word of English to vote for him") with the plea "I do not see anything grave in this charge. When I came here I found that a great number of voters who were ignorant of the English language were on the register, and therefore entitled to vote, (they) should understand what they were asked to vote about!"[52] The same Colonel Trench had only just realised that the aliens were major supporters of the Radical factor in East London. He asserted that, in an unguarded moment, John Hall, the Radical agent, had boasted to him that "they would have 2,000 more of them on next time" — that is that he would swamp the register with alien voters, presumably in his interest.[53]

Curiously, the question of Irish Nationalism emerged as a factor on both sides in their attempt to win over the Jewish vote. On 6 June, at a crowded meeting in the Jewish Working Men's Club in Alie Street, held to elect 46 Liberal delegates to represent the South Ward of St. Mary's, Whitechapel, Montagu emphasised his party's opposition to coercion in Ireland. He advised his audience that, as Jews, who formed a large proportion of the population of Whitechapel and who themselves "had suffered in recent times by repeated attempts... to crush out their national spirit, (they) ought not to forget their own history, nor desert those who were suffering the same oppression".

The Conservatives responded accordingly. At a Primrose League meeting at St. Paul's Hall, Goulston Street, on 4 July, Trench attacked Montagu for endeavouring to "raise prejudice on the part of the Hebrew community against their Anglo-Saxon brethren". He, however, "would open the eyes of the Jewish community as to the real feeling of the National Party in Ireland towards them and their brethren out there". He held in his hand two or three reports listing the persecution of the Jews in Limerick in 1884 and again at the end of 1887; and clinched his evidence by quoting a report from the Cork correspondent for the Dublin *Daily Express* as recent as 9 March, in which the

Cork Trades Council unanimously demanded that the Jews should be hunted out of the city, on the ground that they were ruining honest trade. One delegate characterised the Jewish community as "crucifying gypsies" and said that they should be exterminated! While the *East London Advertiser*'s editorial on 14 July backed the truth of Trench's disclosures with a warning to the Jews that, after such loathsome insults cast at them and their religion, they should not soil their hands by any such alliance, Montagu refuted allegations of mass anti-semitism in Cork. Trench's reports, he explained, were observations obtained solely from two artisans. This was verified by a personal letter he received from the Mayor of Cork who "actively repudiated sympathy in connection with attacks on the Jews".[54]

While the Jews continued to be wooed, albeit reluctantly, by opposing groups, rivalry between the Liberal and Conservative parties, along with the mainstream of national politics, continued to dominate the local scene. The Conservatives' mouthpiece, the *East London Advertiser*, seized every opportunity to promote its party's cause and to denigrate its opponents.[55] Its rival, the *East London Observer*, although tending towards the Conservatives, was much more circumspect, adopting a balanced approach to political issues, particularly those concerning the welfare of all citizens within the borough.

1888 was a year of political stirrings. New ideas and challenges, emanating from the East End, were to have both short-term and long-term consequences nationally. Apart from her leadership of the successful match girls' strike, which would lead the way to the unionisation of the unskilled, Annie Besant brought to wider public notice the need for educational reforms as mooted by the social democrats. This stimulated debate among all sorts of radicals, liberals and socialists alike, the terms of which are still valid a hundred years later! On 13 October *Justice* published a socialist programme that was adopted, and fought for with limited success, by Annie Besant during her term of office at the School Board. Social democracy's demands for education were spelt out by Herbert Burrows:

> For compulsory free education — free of fees — one free meal a day for the needy — abolition of payment by results ("the blighting influence which the routine and cramming have on the

minds of the children"). In all, training cannot be attained by anything short of compulsory, free, secular, physical and industrial education for all classes of the community.[56]

There were strong doubts, even among sympathisers. In the same issue, one self-styled "aristocrat of labour" instanced the curse of apathy amongst workmen: "They seem to be dead to everything but a sordid kind of self-seeking: but that is in accordance with their education, which teaches them, above all things, to get on in life, that is 'to look after number one'." Harkness, with patronising contempt, pours scorn on the would-be self-educated working men and women drawn to progressive causes:

> The East End is full of people who seek to educate themselves with the help of secularist and socialist lectures, Sunday discussions in the park and circulating libraries. They pore over the stalls of second-hand book shops in the lane, and finger old volumes outside the shops of literary merchants... The pain these men and women suffer from mental indigestion can be witnessed in lecture halls on Sunday evenings while they listen to things that are beyond their understanding. They carry away words and phrases to puzzle over during the week, and sometimes they give the things they have heard quite a wrong interpretation or use them in an exaggerated sense that takes away their meaning.[57]

Justice, with Toynbee Hall as its target, proclaimed its own response to meddling upper-class do-gooders, who came in from outside to educate the barbarian:

> It seems to us that if the East End of London could and would return the compliment and send a colony of the workers to the universities to teach the gilded youths on the Isis and the Cam how to do a little useful work and how to live on something less than £300 a year, that would be a much better arrangement... How the aesthetic young dons would descant, in mincing epigrammatic phrase, on the necessity for having creatures like these as hewers of wood and drawers of water for the superfine of the earth![58]

Nor would *Justice* have subscribed to the sentiments expressed above by one of its contributors — Margaret Harkness. Had the editor known (the novel in which they appear was published the following year) she would have received short shrift.

Despite the factionalism within the ranks of the secular radicals and religious reformers, 1888 registered successes in many of their endeavours. The rigid doctrine of Social Darwinism with its concomitant "blessings" of *laisser-faire* had been effectively challenged. There was no going back. Reliance on enlightened self-interest, that is on private initiative alone to effect public progress, was found wanting. Signs of the changing climate were reflected in the "respectable" press. At the formation of the new London County Council, the *East End News* welcomed the innovatory public service open to men "of leisure, industry and integrity with a practical knowledge of the real needs of London", that is "sanitation, street improvements, artisans dwellings, gas and water supply, protection from fire, open spaces and the purification of the Thames".[59] In December the *East London Advertiser*'s editorial urged the introduction of a National Insurance Act, which, although state imposed, would be beneficial to all classes of society.[60]

As the year closed, and in anticipation of the next, the centennial of the great French Revolution, SDF leader Hyndman warned "that our own governing classes may read some lessons to themselves as they enter the year 1889. As the aristocrats of France were "played out"; so are the plutocrats and capitalists of England and of Europe effete and useless today". Quite wrong about this, he was far-sighted about one area of their activity: "They are gathering in their 'Trusts' and 'Syndicates' to create monopoly in place of competition and to prepare the international organisation of the industry of the world."[61] 1888, with events in East London acting as prime movers, proved a landmark of change in the nation's social and political thinking. But the lessons were not lost on the established classes. They were well entrenched and resilient enough to meet and contain any changes that might threaten their hegemony.

Footnotes

[1]Dona Torr, *Tom Mann and his Times* (London, 1956), vol. 1, pp. 263-9.
[2]The article "Among the Socialists — a Scene in Victoria Park" is reproduced in the *ELO* 4 February. As a boy I went to such meetings there, albeit over forty years later, and the scenes so marvellously

evoked by this narrator remained very much the same.
[3] *My Apprenticeship.*
[4] See reports in *ELO* 16 and 23 June.
[5] See, for example, *Justice* 24 March. A series of local meetings was advertised throughout the year. A meeting was notified for Tuesday 8 November to be held at the Crown Office Tavern at Bethnal Green "to consider the best means of forming an East End Socialist Club for socialists of all shades of opinion" (*Justice* 3 November).
[6] A full report of the combined meetings was published in *Justice* 28 July.
[7] Ibid., 21 July.
[8] *ELO* 3 March, "Mrs Annie Besant at Mile End".
[9] For examples of speakers, dates and places of public meetings see *Commonweal* 24 March, 14 and 28 April, 19 May, 26 May, 2 June.
[10] Ibid., 23 June.
[11] Ibid., 30 June, "Socialists in Epping Forest".
[12] Ibid., 7 July.
[13] Ibid., 28 July."
[14] *ELA* 24 November.
[15] *Commonweal* 29 December.
[16] *In Darkest London*, pp. 153-4.
[17] According to *Notes on Labour Statistics* by P.A. Watmough total members and branches in London were

	Members	Branches
1887	568	22
1888	333	16

[18] *In Darkest London*, pp. 154-6.
[19] Ibid., p. 237.
[20] A full report is given in the *Pall Mall Gazette* 6 February, and in both the *ELO* and *ELA* dated 11 February. Lewis Lyons (1864-1918) was born in London and educated at the Jews Free School, Bell Lane. He contributed to many radical journals including the *Anti-Sweater* and, later, the *Daily Herald*. A Jewish tailors' trade union leader in the 1880s and 1890s, he was befriended by, among others, George Lansbury, Bradlaugh, Annie Besant, Eleanor Marx, and Kropotkin. He met his wife Fanny at a Trafalgar Square protest meeting in 1887 when they held hands to meet the onslaught of the police. According to his daughter he "refused to pay rates and often had his house effects distrained and he was imprisoned for seven days while neighbours looked after the family" (Interview with sole remaining daughter Lily Singer, 20 February 1984 — W.J.F.).
[21] *ELO* 2 June.
[22] See W.J. Fishman, *East End Jewish Radicals*, pp. 153-62.
[23] J.H. Mackay, *The Anarchists*. See pp. 183-7 for a full description of the Berner Street Club.
[24] *JC* 20 April.
[25] *JC* 23 November.
[26] *JC* 14 December.

[27]*Arbeter Fraint*, 21 December, which also issued notice of a "church parade" in Whitechapel, "to which our club had been invited and will take part", for Sunday 23 December, organised by the Bethnal Green Branch of the SDF. Its object was "propaganda for socialism".
[28]Charles Booth, *Life and Labour*, vol. 1, pp. 165-7.
[29]*ELO* 11 February, "Crofters' Meeting in Stepney".
[30]Annie Besant, *An Autobiography* (London, 1893) pp. 334-5.
[31]*ELA* 14 July.
[32]*Justice* 28 July.
[33]*Commonweal* 28 July. In "Notes on News" Morris wrote "When one sees how small the gains to the girls are, how small their demands were, one is struck aghast at the miserable cheeseparings by which great fortunes are made."
[34]Detailed reports of the meeting are given in *Justice* 28 July and *ELA* 4 August. According to the latter "800 girls had assembled... Mrs. Besant submitted the rules to the girls who called out "Yes" and waved their hands in approval as each rule was read. The elder girls agreed to pay twopence per week and the younger ones one penny. A weekly allowance of 5s is to be made in case of sickness, or want of employment, and it is stated that a recreation room for these girls will shortly be opened. The society is to be called The Union of Women Match Makers" and its object is to protect the rights and privileges of the trade. All girls over 14 years are eligible for membership. The executive business is to be conducted by a committee of 12 women in the trade. Mrs Besant was elected the first secretary and Mr Burrows treasurer..."
[35]For information on the Benefit Shows see the 25 August issues of *Commonweal* and *Justice*.
[36]Annie Besant, *An Autobiography*, p. 338.
[37]For details of the strike see *ELA* 27 October, 3 November, 15 December and *Justice* 27 October, 24 November and 1 December.
[38]*In Darkest London* pp. 117-18. For a further description and doctrines of the labour mistress, see pp. 103-9. For a critical study of Margaret Harkness's novels putting forward an explanation for her ambivalent attitude towards certain socialist and feminist activists, see Eileen Sypher, "The Novels of Margaret Harkness" in *Turn of the Century Women*, vol. 1, no. 2, pp. 12-26 (Winter 1984, published by the University of Virginia Press).
[39]The London County Council was created as a result of a Bill introduced by local MP D.C. Ritchie for the Tories in March 1888.
[40]The address was printed in full in *Justice* 17 November.
[41]For the *ELA*'s consistently anti-Besant propaganda see issues dated 20 October (The Coming School Board Contest"), 10, 17 and 24 November, 1 December.
[42]For an excellent account of the election see D. Rubenstein, "Annie Besant and Stewart Headlam: The London School Board Election of 1888", *East London Papers*, vol. 13, no. 1, summer 1970, pp. 3-24.
[43]As Dr. Rubenstein points out, "Early in 1889 an angry ratepayer wrote to the board to protest that the children of well-to-do tradesmen attended Board Schools, excluding the children of the poor. Annie

Besant supported the Board's reply declaring that all parents had an equal right to send their children to Board Schools and that there was "considerable advantage in having children of all classes attending the same schools". Dr. Rubenstein rightly concludes "Support for the concept of the common school was an unusually radical stand at the time and was prophetic of an era which was to unfold after both Mrs Besant and Headlam were dead" (ibid., p. 24).

[44] A full report of the Assembly Hall meeting is given by the *ELA* 4 February "The Mile End Vestry".

[45] *ELO* 10 March.

[46] Fully described in *ELO* 14 April.

[47] See *ELO* 26 May, 16 June ("Reformers' at Work"); and *ELA* 10 and 17 March, and particularly 28 April ("Politics in Local Affairs").

[48] *ELO* 11 February, "Irish Demonstration on Tower Hill".

[49] *ELO* 10 March.

[50] *ELA* 22 December, "Mr Gladstone's Visit to Limehouse". In the same issue note the caustic anti-Gladstone poem, "The Gladstone Fog", exemplifying its own anti-liberal stance; while *Justice* (22 December) decried his coming to the East End and making a speech "without a word in it on the social question".

[51] The *ELA*'s blatantly Tory reporter "Rambler" wrote, "I now see through it all. They form the bulk of his constituents, and go to make up the "free and independent electors" who give so much trouble as "aliens" in the *Revising Barrister* every year."

[52] *ELA* 12 May.

[53] *ELA* 21 April, "Rambler".

[54] For opposing appeals to local Jews over Irish Nationalism see *ELA* 9 June and 7, 14, 16 July.

[55] It publicly advertised the aims of the Conservative's Primrose League and offered information on how to apply for membership (28 April); openly attacked Gladstonian Liberalism in the same issue ("Politics in Local Affairs") and on 17 November, in "For Whom to Vote", supported the "old" Conservative members for re-election, calling for voters to reject the "forces of radicalism, extravagance, unbelief and socialism". It was particularly scathing about Gladstone's visit to Limehouse.

[56] This was a follow-up to the Editorial Education Programme outlined in *Justice* 8 September.

[57] These views were expressed in *In Darkest London*, pp. 170-1. As for the working-clase voter, he is exemplified in George, a character in *A City Girl*. He visits the Radical Club "because his friends belonged to it" but votes Conservative "because they had the most money, so it was best not to offend them!"

[58] *Justice* 27 October.

[59] *East End News* 18 September.

[60] A long rational argument for such a scheme is outlined in *ELA* 29 December.

[61] *Justice* 29 December.

Chapter 10
Leisure

They should be told that here in East London... there will be found numerous centres of social and educational importance which will stand comparison with those of other metropolitan districts and provincial towns.

East London Observer
14 January 1888, editorial in response to adverse criticism of East London in an article in the *Manchester Guardian*

Let us never forget that the temptation to drink is strongest when want is sharpest and misery the most acute. A well-fed man is not driven to drink by the craving that torments the hungry and the comfortable do not crave for the boon of forgetfulness. Gin is the only Lethe of the miserable.

William Booth,
In Darkest England, p. 48

To portray the East End as one sombre mass of unmitigated woe would be a travesty. Given the gradations of poverty there, the pursuit of leisure, where this was possible, varied considerably. Among the casuals and the unemployed, the culture of poverty, gloomy and precarious as it might seem, was not devoid of relief, expressed in rituals of uninhibited joy and the devil with the consequences. What many earnest social investigators failed to perceive was the resilience, the sort of esoteric humour that sustained the East End cockney in adversity. While both Charles and William Booth identified much of their vulgarity and irresponsible fun-making with fecklessness, littérateurs, with a more catholic perception, caught glimpses of the reality.

For the majority of the labouring poor, freedom — the pub — lay at the corner of the street, offering its nightly sessions of joy amid the brash glitter and warm camaraderie of the bar. A cluster of drinking dens could be found bordering the main thoroughfare, such that along the one mile of Whitechapel Road from Commercial Street to Stepney Green, there were, in 1899, no less than 48 drinking places, and these so strategically placed as to provide "the working man with breakfast on his journey to work and with refreshments on his journey home".[1] As a "leisure" centre they attracted the widest class of clientèle.

Among the poorest the most popular drink was three ha'pence

of gin, known as *blue ruin* or *jacky*. Harkness describes some beggars outside a pub near the docks, patiently waiting until they had cadged sufficient coins to buy their "threepenny worth of gin (which) would cost less than supper":

> At the door... crouched two old women, like sphinxes. Wrinkles were cut deep in their tough yellow skin, thin locks of grey hair fell over their red inflamed eyelids. Their bony hands clasped their tattered petticoats. They looked on the ground heedless of passers-by, except when a man or woman dropped them a halfpenny. There they sat day and night, these sphinxes.[2]

The novelist was well aware that outside these dock pubs also "congregated the lowest dregs of the East End" who preyed on seamen, and she describes a typical operation carried out by *sharks* in cahoots with the publican.

> Directly a jolly Jack-Tar came swinging past (the worse for drink) a vampire dressed in a gaudy skirt, with a string of blue beads about her neck and a fringe of greasy hair on her forehead, had him by the elbow. Then a siren in a velvet jacket put her arm round his neck, and led him into the gin pit, out of which he did not return, depend upon it, until he had been robbed of his last sixpence.[3]

As Dr Harrison points out, it was these shenanigans and the wide incidence of drunk and disorderly behaviour that led to the respectable middle classes associating heavy drinking with the slum dwellers of Tower Hamlets; "when the slums had been cleared from St Giles, the East End became identified with everything feared by the well-to-do, and the drinking habits of the poor were regarded with a mixture of fear and fascination".[4] By 1888, Charles Booth had arrived at the unfashionable view that men drank because they were poor, and were not necessarily poor because they were drunkards, stressing that adverse socio-economic conditions were more likely to be a strong causative factor leading to drink. "Who can wonder", stormed William C. Preston, "that the public house is the Elysian Field of the poor toiler!"[5]

There was a healthier, more positive side to the pubs. They sold wholesome food, and, according to the degree of respectability of the house, hired out backrooms for musical concerts and dances, where pianos plus a tuner and even an orchestra could be supplied. One aspect of working men's culture was exemplified by the weekly Friday night meeting of the St. George's Musical Union held at The Refiners' Arms in Buross Street off the Commercial Road. An onlooker noted

> fair attendance, members being ably assisted by a contingent from the East London Workmen's Club, Jamaica Street. Amongst the gentlemen who contributed to the programme of the evening: Mr Gus Mercer, who played a cornet solo, "Queen of my Heart" in capital style, also solos, songsters of folk ballads, plus a really splendid reading by Mr Chas. Cox entitled "The Captain's Colt" which completely enthralled its hearers.[6]

Harkness observed that people did not "frequent public houses solely for the sake of drink; they go there to enjoy each other's company, to hear some new thing, to joke and to gossip." In effect they appeared to take the place of clubs for poor men and drawing rooms for their women. In most East End pubs "the only well-dressed people... were the publicans and barmaids. Warmth and light attracted customers inside the doors, and the sight of women in satin and velvet, of men with diamonds on their fingers enlivened the scene after people had said what they wanted. Coloured glasses stood on the shelves: red, blue and yellow bottles were reflected in the looking glasses. Sleek men in broad cloth took pence at the bar, well-fed women handed gin and beer across the counter."[7] Inside a more ornate and spacious gin palace past the bar and up the stairs was located the dance hall where "two or three musicians sat at one end of the room, playing the latest East End gallop on brass instruments, and on the sanded floor whirled girls and men round and round, in and out, backwards and forwards, keeping time with the music".[8]

Pubs also acted as rendezvous for Friendly Societies, as centres for mutual aid. Charles Booth noted that five well supported Friendly Societies met in Whitechapel pubs, as well as "loan and investment societies" who, operating on pub premises, were referred to as "publican's thrift". It was customary for local branches of political parties to hire a room for social or propaganda events. One active Conservative Association was that of Limehouse, Shadwell and Ratcliff, which gathered at the Silver Tavern, Burdett Road, on Thursdays to hold a smoking concert offering such popular entertainment as a piano solo, songs and recitations. Likewise the Stepney West Ward

Conservative Association, whose supporters were mainly non-immigrant Jews (names like van Gelder, Seigenberg, Levy etc. dominated the membership) held similar functions. On Monday 3 January, for example, the usual imbibing was accompanied by songs and recitations including "Christmas Day in the Workhouse" rendered by J.L. Van Gelder, and a negro dialogue by Messrs Myers and Steinhadt (which) afforded much amusement".[10]

Clubs were an integral part of East End life. By 1888 Charles Booth could cite 23 extant in the Whitechapel precincts alone — classified generally into four groups. The first, titled proprietory, were mainly illicit, catering for gambling and betting, limited, of course, to members only. The second group was political, meeting mainly in party premises but also using selected pubs. They offered drink, nightly entertainment, concerts, indoor games, lectures and debates. The third was philanthropic, usually held under the auspices of a local church or mission hall. (There were six in Whitechapel alone!)

A detailed description of one popular club, located in the most insalubrious rookery bordering Tower Hamlets, Jays Club for Jago Men in Shoreditch, was given by its founder who was present from its inception until the last day of its existence. Considering that its supporters were drawn from the Old Nichol patch, ie mainly street villains and burglars, its rules were few and unwritten, yet all the more rigidly enforced by the vicar, the Rev. A. Osborne Jay. He explained these and outlined the extraordinary variety of activities on offer.

> No one can join under 18, the subscription is a penny a week, and as far as possible, all members must be parishioners. The number on the roll is a little under 500 and... at least 100 members use the club every night. It is an absolute rule to shake hands with me both on entering and going away. I never myself take part in any game, but spend all the time walking about and talking to the members... games of all kinds are provided on small tables — cards, draughts, dominoes and even chess. A large table is set apart for books, illuminated papers and other literature.
> Below the club is a gymnasium much used, and in the club room itself we have a flying trapeze, rings, parallel bars... but besides gymnasts and acrobats of whom we have many, all more or less "artists", at least on the boards of small places, and rejoicing in such professional names as "Levano, Artelle, Nero

and Neroni", "The Unrivalled Tricolini", we have naturally a large number of members who box.

He went on to criticise the cant and hypocrisy of some churchmen and establishment figures who dismissed boxing as a gross habit that is against the need to refine and elevate the masses, yet secretly lent their support to prize-fights; and countered their censure by informing the affluent West Enders that

> Shoreditch is called "the cradle of pugilism" and its men and boys will box whether you like it or not; if not in the club, in some low *booza*, and as far as most are concerned, the knowledge of the art of self-defence never harms but raises and improves...

He used the club as a vehicle for his own socio-religious aims and applications. A Sunday club and Bible class thrived on the dual premises that no hymn book was issued and men were even allowed to smoke. Jay claimed to attract 300 men weekly when applicants "not only compete to get a place in church but enter most heartily into the service when there". The way in which some hundreds of voices thunder out 'The Church's One Foundation' or 'Onward Christian Soldiers' should convince any hearer that church hymns, with definite teaching, are as much liked as undenominational ones." Male solos were encouraged and the sight of a brutal looking ex-con belting out a Sankey's hymn with obvious gusto had to be seen to be believed. The Bishop of London, on one occasion only, was graciously disposed to come down and address the club for "fifty minutes on the duties of renunciation to a congregation who have but little to give up!"[11]

Muscular Christians emanating from the Church and Oxbridge elites were astir, eager to engage their energies in inducing physical and spiritual uplift among the youth of the slums. P.E. Halstead, who spent many years as a doctor in Whitechapel and Bethnal Green, was one of the many self-appointed club leaders who found that the East End offered unlimited opportunities for them to test their convictions. This is evident in his reminiscences:

> We turned the ground floor and garden of our house in Palestine Place into a boy's club and recreation centre. There was already

> a boy's club of sorts in Whitechapel, which was run by a well-meaning clergyman, but he had no control over them, and they had no respect for him, so he agreed to hand the boys over to us... We were both firm believers in the good effects of the physical discipline provided by athletics and so we set out really to put these boys through it, and I don't think any of them ever regretted the treatment we gave them.
>
> Every Saturday night, the dining-room became a gymnasium, with a boxing ring established in the middle... we were able to profit from the enormous reverence such boys had for athletes like ourselves... so that there was never any danger of the place becoming a rough house. They were mostly aged between eight and fourteen, and most of them had left school early, and were going out to work.

Money was urgently needed. At first generous contributions were received from local firms and eminent philanthropists, but Halstead intended to make the club self-supporting:

> We made the boys themselves put by a penny a week... The point of levying this token sum from the boys was to teach them not to expect something for nothing; it helped to make them self-reliant, and taught them the principles of paying their way in later life.

An attractive feature on offer was the annual camp by the seaside. There Halstead and his co-leader Wilfred Grenfell would put to sea in the latter's fishing smack *Oyster* with a crew carefully selected from the ranks of the young campers.[12]

Of course the model recreation centre for young adults was the Working Lads Institute in the Whitechapel Road. Built by charitable trusts and opened in 1885, it was considered the loftiest building in the East End. "From its roof may be seen the ancient buildings of the city — and to the north the Alexandra Palace marks the limits of vision. Looking eastwards... in the remote distance are traces of Epping Forest's greenery."[13] According to the January report by founder and hon. secretary Mr Hill, lectures, recitals, entertainments, Friendly Societies, even an employment register were on offer there, with additional facilities including an indoor swimming bath and a gymnasium. Membership was limited to working lads only, not to destitute boys; and qualifications for entry were strictly defined by the secretary on the occasion of the opening of a new lecture hall by Princess Christian on 21 April:

> The institute... was for the benefit of the great army of working boys between 13 and 18 years of age, who were employed as errand boys, apprentices and factory hands or engaged in shops and warehouses and whose wages varied from 6s to 10s a week. Such boys were usually released from work at 7 o'clock in the evening, and as they were not wanted at their homes or lodgings till 10 o'clock, it was sought by this institution to utilise spare time that otherwise might be less profitably spent.

For a small subscription a member could be entitled to attend evening classes, lectures and concerts. One memorable example of the latter was a performance given on the evening of 30 January by boy prodigy, Victor Aaronson, aged 10, of 77a Whitechapel Road, who played two classical violin solos to a packed audience. Orphans, or those living at a distance from home or friends, could stay at the Institute which offered 25 beds for overnight accommodation. Chess was a popular activity. On the first Saturday night in May the chess club held their annual supper after the termination of a very successful season, having won 10 out of a possible 13 games in an inter-club tournament. As was the custom "the evening was agreeably enlivened by vocal and instrumental music as about 25 sat down to supper". But it was local MP Samuel Montagu, speaking at a *conversazione* held there on 31 January, who emphasised the possibility of social mobility open to working-class youngsters who used the club facilities wisely.

> He considered it to be especially valuable from the fact that it dealt with lads at an age when they were particularly liable to be led into bad ways and associations. It took such lads in hand, gave them wholesome recreation and enjoyment and the advantage of a great many evening classes, and with the aid of classes such as those, and in a country like England, there was no position in life to which the lads at that Institute might not attain. All they needed besides was hard work hard work and perseverance which turned copper into silver, silver into gold, corduroy into broadcloth and the tradesman's cart into a carriage.[14]

Such opportunities were, of course, denied to those destitute lads who wandered the streets. This would be remedied by the Rev. Thomas Jackson who converted the Institute into a haven for homeless boys when the Methodist Mission took possession only a few years later.

Together with those instituted by Barnardo, F.N. Charrington and the Salvation Army within their own establishments, and others sponsored by local churches and mission halls, there was a variety of clubs scattered around the East End catering for young factory girls of every grade. A rare report on some of their activities was offered by a journalist in *The Echo* (3 January) who summed up his findings after a series of nocturnal excursions into the area. Although tainted with the usual patronising attitude, his descriptions are valid. He found a "decidedly rougher set of girls" in one Evening Home in Alie Street, Aldgate. There "young women wear no hats, have an all-pervading fringe and are untidy and ragged", and pay 1½d a week for the privilege of membership. The reporter was duly "encouraged" by the sight of twenty or so girls sitting round a table, busily engaged in making straw frames and coloured paper chains. In an adjoining room there was a swing, while in a third religious instruction was, to his amazement, actually in progress. These girls were mainly employed as feather workers, rag sorters and cinnamon washers; they were perpetually in and out of work. When unemployed, which occurred more frequently than the reverse, they appeared to exist by pawning their possessions and "doing little jobs for the Jews on Friday nights", such as lighting their fires or cleaning their homes in time for the Sabbath. He was moved to learn of the close comradeship and mutual aid existing among them. "Mrs Antrobus (club leader) told us that not very long ago a former member of the club got into trouble and was with her infant absolutely penniless. The girls of the club got up what they called a *lend* and actually raised eighteen shillings between them!" Rationalising on his findings here, the onlooker concluded that for such a poor clientèle. "a club like this in every part of London would keep hundreds of young girls out of the public houses, and would do more to advance the cause of women's welfare than any female suffrage bill that can be conceived".

Of course such a dictum could not be applied to those attending Toynbee Hall under the auspices of the St Ursula Association, constituting "the best class — mainly tailoresses". Fifty of them came nightly to attend classes in music, French and sewing for a subscription of one penny a week. Here he noticed a bright fire, a table full of magazines and a kind-faced lady waiting to welcome the members who were "neatly attired and seemed superior young women". He found an equally respectable clientèle supporting a club in St. Peter's Street, Hackney Road. These numbered over 100 who attended regularly popular classes in sewing and French at a cost of one penny a month. At the less salubrious Goldsmiths Row, Haggerston, club rooms were held in the Young Women's Help Society. These obviously catered for the poorest of the poor. A capital feature was the sale of old clothing on Saturday nights, and *The Echo* urged people to send cast-off clothes to them. "Boots are especially valuable. The members of this club are mostly boot machinists and are wretchedly paid and overworked, their earnings being on an average 7s or 8s a week."

As for the young girls who promenaded arm in arm along the Limehouse Causeway, he doubted whether they would abandon their evening walks. Although sympathetic to their need "to get a little air after being confined from eight o'clock in the morning to nine in the evening" he opined that they would eventually "avail themselves by degrees of the comfort, luxury and social life which the clubs offer". Here the reporter exposed his ignorance of the strict ritual played out by both sexes in the locale. Youth's a stuff that will not endure, and the young East Enders were fully cognisant of its advantages, however short-lived. For the poor lass of Poplar, Mile End or Whitechapel "keeping company" with her man was a public display of a successful catch, probably initiated by an eye-to-eye encounter between the *bloke* and his *gel* during the ceremonial stroll along the highway; and offering the girl the few heady days, when, with pride, she could show off her prize, until the prison house of marriage and child-bearing closed in. Likewise the weekly parade along the Whitechapel Road after the Sabbath (Saturday) service was common practice among the young immigrants, to end, for many a couple, under the *chupah*.[15] However, marriage for the Jewish maiden was not as hazardous a prospect as that facing her Gentile sister. Drunkenness and violence were alien to the Jewish mores, and wife-beating expressly forbidden in the Talmud.

There were various adult social clubs on offer. One of the largest was the Jewish Working Men's Club in Great Alie Street, Aldgate, catering for 1,400 members and open to women. It was strictly teetotal and offered a number of social and educational amenities. An annual event was the Purim Ball held on Saturday

3 March when 250 members danced "into the small hours of the morning to an efficient band". The following day further entertainment was given under the direction of a Miss Rose Jacob, including a vocalist, a piano solo and recitations.[16] Another active group was the Jamaica Cricket Club, Stepney, who held their third annual concert in the Limehouse Town Hall with items including a pianoforte duet and a moving rendering by girl soloist Miss Williams of two current hit tunes "Blind girl to her harp" and "Angus MacDonald". The club participated in the Challenge Cup competition held by the Victoria Park Cricket Association with other local teams named after the church or street from which they recruited their players.

Another popular leisure activity pursued by the "respectable" was dancing lessons under bona fide certified teachers. On Easter Monday we read of "some hundred and seventy ladies and gentlemen gathered together at the Town Hall, Limehouse, to participate in the annual Easter soirée in connection with Leopold Kalischer's dancing classes, and the utmost enjoyment was apparent on the part of those who "footed it so merrily" to the strains of Mr Kalischer's band".[17]

Catering for the more religious or sophisticated working men and women were a number of grand institutions enjoying a sound financial base. Charrington's Assembly Hall was given over to performances of oratorios on Saturday evenings throughout the year. On 9 January *The Echo* enthused over the choral portions of Handel's Messiah rendered "with a marvellous dash and verve" by a local troupe in front of an assemblage of more than 3,000. Choirs were trained by itinerant organist E. Day Winter, a superb professional, who drew a large weekly group of supporters including many from beyond the area. In March his conductorship of Mendelssohn's Elijah, aided by excellent principals and a chorus of 200 voices, brought a widespread reportage and acclaim. The hall was open most week-nights for speakers to entertain or instruct. On 13 October the recent sensation caused by the Ripper atrocities prompted a lecture there by a Professor Malden who "gave one of his interesting dioramic entertainments on 'London, its History and Mystery by Day and Night'" to a packed audience.

By now, universally acknowledged as two of the greatest educational and leisure centres, pioneered to serve the local "labouring classes" and prototypes for others that would follow nationally and internationally, were Toynbee Hall and the People's Palace. Toynbee set the pace and style; its warden defining its objectives as primarily "to raise man to his highest both in soul and body". The Hall, linked closely with St Jude's Church, aimed to widen educational opportunities with its addition of a free library. In connection with the University, extension courses in experimental chemistry and Shakespeare open to local mature students commenced in April. At their inception, hopes that a "teaching University for London granting all facilities for giving degrees as in Oxford and Cambridge" would develop there, were voiced by the speaker, the Marquis of Ripon.[18] This was to come about but not at Toynbee. Its rival, the People's Palace, would eventually transform itself into the Queen Mary College of the University of London.[19] However, that year, Toynbee continued to attract a galaxy of eminent speakers. On Saturday evening, 10 March, Mrs Fawcett delivered a talk on "The Social Progress of Women during the Last Century". The autumn session was inaugurated by the Master of the Clothworkers' Company, the Rev. Professor Wiltshire on 6 October. He introduced the opening speaker, M. Fyffe, who with his theme "The Revival of Teaching in the English Universities", proceeded, to chronicle in detail the growth of Oxford and Cambridge. There was a noisy eruption at the end of the year session, on Saturday 15 December, when aristocrat Baron Ferdinand de Rothschild ventured to voice his rather prejudiced views in a lecture on "The Advent of the French Revolution". The *East London Advertiser* issue of 22 December parroted his sentiments as it reported on the noisy proceedings. When commenting that "had moderation been observed in the Revolution, the French would have earned the gratitude of posterity, but moderation and common sense therefore were not qualities characteristic of Frenchmen" Rothschild was greeted by cries of Hear, Hear and No, No! There was constant interruption as he violently attacked what he listed as revolutionary excesses committed by "a small knot of persons among them mischievously indicating their sympathy with the atrocious sentiments and worst excesses of the French Revolutionaries", but the bulk of the meeting showed their disagreement with his views by counter-cheering as occasions offered. Whatever its aims and efforts it proved doubtful whether Toynbee had access to such resources as could offer the breadth of activities needed to attract and sustain the support of a maximum of respectable working-class folk in the area.

Not so its rival, the People's Palace![20] Here 1888 was certainly an eventful year, with an expansion in both facilities and public exhibitions. In January an apprentices' exhibition, opened by the Prince of Wales, was extended and followed by both a workmen's exhibition and a cat and dog show. We learn that, during New Year's week, socials and balls were held in the Queen's Hall "attended on each occasion by over 500 members with Sir Edmund Hay Currie and dance music supplied by the band of the Scots Guards". The Tuesday following "some 500 of the 1,000 odd candidates for vacancies" were admitted to membership of the Palace and entertained to a reception tea on the same evening. There was a remarkable diversification in activities. On 27 February the itinerant debating society discussed the motion "That in the opinion of this meeting, the cost compared with the uses of the royal family, is excessive and detrimental to the nation, and we consider the time has come when we all should combine to better the state of affairs by the advocacy of the absolute abolishment of the monarchy", which was quickly amended in favour of reform rather than abolition. On 8 March a further 550 members were enrolled and, again, tea in their honour was hosted by Hay Currie. ("It might be mentioned that Sir Edmund Hay Currie only arrived home the same day from Monte Carlo where he had been staying for the benefit of his health!")[21] On 9, 10 and 12 March there was another dog show in which 80 canines were exhibited by local residents of Tower Hamlets and Hackney. On 14 May a new swimming bath was opened by the Countess of Rosebery; on 26 May the *East London Observer* noted that during men's days "Curiosity among the descendants of Eve has necessitated some 'chalking up' to the effect that ladies are not to pass a certain barrier in the vicinity of the baths". The same month a workmen's exhibition was opened by the Duke of Westminster. Objects were sent from all over the country and some 70 trades were represented, the majority of the exhibits executed in the spare time and at the expense of the exhibitors themselves.[22]

There were other innovations making for the cultural uplift of local East Enders. On 16 June the People's Palace Library was opened by Princess Louise while John Morley added to the solemnity of the occasion by giving an address on literature at the express invitation of Walter Besant. A local correspondent enthused over this latest addition:

> The library (is) itself the finest and largest of its class in England. Octagon-shaped, with lofty domed tower, it measures 76 feet in diameter. The room is lighted by an eight-sided skylight in the centre of the dome, and with a triple window in each of the eight sections of the wall. In the angle between each two sections, and where the spring of the arched dome begins is placed the bust of one of England's greatest writers: so that there are eight busts: Chaucer's, Dryden's, Scott's, Wordsworth's, Byron's, Johnson's, Milton's and Shakespeare's. Of the quarter of a million volumes for which the library contains room, only a twenty-fifth, that is 10,000, have been procured.

The shape of the Palace's future was spelt out. It would prove prophetic in the sense that it laid the foundations upon which the future Queen Mary College was built:

> The Technical Schools, to which the Draper's Company have given £20,000 will not be opened before next October... These Schools are being built alongside the great hall. On the other side of the hall there will be erected buildings costing £15,000. The library itself —the bare shell of it —has cost £10,000. And £15,000 more will be spent upon the "social" rooms, which it is proposed to build right in front of the hall. The great hall, in short, is only the nucleus, or kernel, of a group of buildings. Counting 27,000 pounds for the great hall, it will be seen how quickly eighty or ninety thousand pounds can be absorbed in the mere structure of a "People's University" of the new era.[23]

A truly People's University it was not to be. An outside middle-class clientèle had already moved in to enjoy the facilities geared more to their taste. On 29 September a letter to the *East London Advertiser* by A.J.C. titled "The People's Palace Exposure" focused the issue. The writer complained that "the inheritance bequeathed by the dead, and presented by the living, to those whose existence is one long, ceaseless, soulless, hopeless round of chattel slavery, has been usurped by mainly a horde of giggling, bread-and-butter-creatures in bustles, accompanied by a mathematically equivalent number of sniggering, invertebrate, vacuum-skulled prigs in trousers, who, in any atmosphere affecting to be superior to that of a can-can college, neither get what they want nor want what they get". (He went on to suggest that these unwelcome interlopers go elsewhere and support such lesser institutions as the Bow and Bromley Club and Toynbee Hall.) However, the nature of his protest continued to be justified by events. On 6 October during a great dog show the same paper revealed that "the Palace grounds and buildings were all alive with throngs of fashionably dressed ladies and sportsmanlike men, for under Kennel Club rules, the second exhibition of sporting and other dogs was in progress... The proportion of local exhibits was small, and most of the prizes were taken by several celebrated animals in the sporting world." It was not surprising that only 50 out of upward of 450 entries were local, with alienation complete as an exhaustive catalogue, priced at 6d, was well beyond the pockets of the "poorer visitors who were unable to study the animals by book!" Yet there were other exhibitions aimed deliberately at attracting local talent. On 27 July the *East London Observer* advertised "a show of donkeys and ponies belonging to costermongers and street traders" to be held on the following Monday and Tuesday with Lord Aberdeen called upon to distribute the prizes. On 27 October the *East London Advertiser* announced a poultry show, always a popular attraction. The reporter, however, voiced his doubts when he asked, "Would it not be well for the management to make an effort to obtain more local entries, and not fill up their pens with prize birds from a distance?" On 8 December, commenting on a current chrysanthemum show at the Palace, the same commentator lamented the fact that "very little local interest... was evinced", while the large number of visitors, who "were also entertained by organ recitals and instrumental performances", were obviously well-breeched outsiders.

At the close of the year the Palace reached new heights in attractive display, as though to justify to the whole of the metropolis its cultural *raison d'etre*. On Boxing Day 15,554 visitors passed through the turnstiles; and, on this occasion, the *Advertiser's* recorder was more circumspect in his judgment:

> In the first place there was an exhibition of pictures, the result of an appeal for loans to a number of friends of the institution and comprising some very fine works by Millais, Armitage, Ansdell, Blinks, Meisonnier, Old Crome, Calderon, Giovanni Cosa, Stacy Marks, Rivieri, Seour Lucas, Orchardson, Herkomer etc. In conjunction with the exhibition of pictures the two courts

of the Show Buildings are fitted — one as a picturesque scene representing an Arctic winter; at the main entrance an old-fashioned inn covered with snow, opposite a double cottage, illustrating a show called "She" — the novelty of 1889. The court terminates with a huge snowball, entered by a rustic bridge over an artificial lake, at which are stationed Red Riding Hood in costume, and New Year, a little child seated on a white goat, dressed in all white and silver.

Only on this festive occasion were the local poor provided with a vision of high fantasy more to their taste.

The multi-variety of activities at the Palace, so widely advertised, was bound adversely to affect the intake into rival cultural clubs, particularly that of the older established Bow and Bromley Institute. This had been painfully brought to fruition as a centre of excellence, with weekly concerts and plays performed by inspired amateurs and professionals. (On 21 January the *East London Observer* noted that "this Institute had to record a diminution in its number of members and its receipts generally, no doubt partly arising from the opening of the People's Palace".) It had, in the past, attracted full audiences. A syllabus of 1888 Monday evening concerts included A.R. Gaut's new cantata Joan of Arc — with adequate choral and instrumental support — three drama performances, a dioramic entertainment, and a repertoire by the Grenadier Guards Minstrel Troupe and the Black Diamond Minstrels. On 1 and 29 February there were to be cinderella dances. The subscription of 15s or 7s 6d per annum entitled members to attend all concerts etc, to the use of the library, reading and billiard-room "as well as admission at reduced rates to evening classes". Come what may musical features of high standard were on offer to those members who remained loyal. On 10 March the art critic of the *East London Advertiser* observed:

> notwithstanding the great competition created by the People's Palace... In place of the usual organ recital, Master Charles Ewart Graveley of Brighton, a youth aged 15, but who is a brilliant genius on the pianoforte, gave a grand recital on that instrument, his selections including Beethoven's Sonata Op.26 with Funeral March. He subsequently gave in style, selections from Chopin, Heuself and Mendelssohn — which elicited the warmest appreciation from a critical audience.

On Good Friday, Handel's Messiah was rendered by the Institute Choir under the direction of host conductor Mr W.E. McNaught, Bow and Bromley continued to function that year as another cultural oasis attracting a local elite who shared their favours with the rival palace.

There was no shortage of alternative leisure facilities available across the borough. Lectures and debates were a weekly fare, and also commanded large audiences. Schools and mission halls were rarely vacant. On 21 February Women's Suffrage was debated at a smoking conference in the St Jude's School Hall, and the next day the public was invited to hear Mr H. Titchborne, "the celebrated traveller", recounting his adventures at the St. George's Mission. At Wycliffe Chapel Hall in Philpot Street throughout the whole year concerts and lectures attracted huge crowds "on some of the occasions numbering as many as a thousand, whilst they seldom reached anything beneath seven hundred".[24] On 22 May a magic-lantern show and tea was laid on for the blind (?) in St. Philip's schoolroom at the back of London Hospital.[25] On 16 July the Girls Friendly Society put on a flower show, a needlework exhibition and sale of clothing in aid of funds at the Church House, Dongola Street off Harford Street, Mile End. (In Whitechapel there were 272 active members of the branch alone, of whom 130 were in business or factory work, 50 in service, and the rest housewives, Stepney boasted 310 members who took instruction in sewing, musical drill and nursing.) Two days later 200 young women members of the Tuesday and Thursday evening classes in George Yard (where the Ripper struck eighteen days later!) were offered a grand treat "in the shape of an excursion in eight brakes to Warlies Park, the seat of Sir Thomas Foxwell Buxton, Bart., who had invited them down".[26] The great Christ Church, Spitalfields, opened its doors for public orchestral concerts, as it still does to this day. On Wednesday evening, 25 January, Handel's Messiah was rendered by the choir of the Kyrle Society in front of a large and appreciative audience "most of whom belonged to the working classes".

For the avid reader, perhaps as a result of the first generational impact of the 1870 Education Act, there was the Free Library of Bethnal Green. At the 12th annual meeting of the Committee presided over by Lord Brassey, the number of persons attending the library, lectures and classes were estimated at 42,000 for the previous year, making a grand total to date of 242,000. Such ventures were not lost on neighbouring parishes. On 18 April the Vestry of Whitechapel debated the question of implementing a free library in the district. The motion was supported by Samuel Montagu MP, who suggested that the Local Government Bill would afford such a reduction in the rates, that the penny rate would not be felt and that the Charity Commissioners... would act generously. The moving spirit, of course, was the Rev. Barnett, a dedicated advocate of public libraries.

The members of the royal family who ventured often into the East End provided street pageantry that helped to illuminate the otherwise drab lives of its inhabitants. 1888, the year after the Queen's 50th Jubilee, continued to attract a series of incursions by members of her family. On 7 February "there was a large gathering of the Royalties and the upper ten at St Andrew's Hall, Bethnal Green, the occasion being the opening of an exhibition and bazaar". Since the work carried out there was in many instances by the younger sons of peers

> this may account for the fact that no difficulty was encountered by them in securing the presence... of the Princess Mary Adelaide, Duchess of Teck, the Princess Victoria, Prince Francis Joseph, etc. The exhibition consisted of a magnificent display of local manufacture in furniture, of pianos and organs, of some exquisite lamps, etc., while in the adjoining rooms and in the galleries above were stalls devoted to the sale of fancy articles, and others where women were at work in shoe, brush, bead and lace making and silk weaving... All these articles were closely inspected and greatly admired by the distinguished party. Considerably over an hour was spent by them in the building. After having partaken of tea, the party left about 5 o'clock, amidst the cheers of some hundreds of people assembled outside.[27]

In July the Princess Beatrice, accompanied by Prince Henry of Battenberg, opened a bazaar at the Christ Church Hall, Hanbury Street, to promote aid for a purchase fund (about £750) to pay for the building opened previously by the Duchess of Teck. The hall provided a club room, which would also be hired out for public meetings, entertainments and athletics. The bazaar was the result of a local folk self-help collection to meet the debts on the building. Neither did the scale of royal operations in that area diminish during the later, inclement months. On 6 October the *East London Advertiser* enthused over a combined gift sent to the King Edward Mission Institute in Spitalfields by "four of our Royal Princesses, viz Princess Christian, the Duchess of Albany, Duchess of Connaught and Princess Mary of Teck together with over 40 members of the nobility". The visitor from afar was confronted by an extraordinary floral display in a shabby hall located in an insalubrious side-street off Brick Lane.

> Two triumphal arches had been erected, which were completely covered with foliage, interspersed with luxurious flowers (grown in the grounds of the nobility named). While suspended from these were peaches, pears, grapes, rosy apples and other rich fruit, a fine collection of vegetables including magnificent specimens of cabbage, turnips, carrots and other garden produce forming a background, while the reading desk, seats and every part of the building were smothered with flowers, ferns and flowers in pots, the whole presenting a very bright and cheerful appearance. The building was crowded, the greater part of the congregation being the very poor living in the neighbourhood who were loud in their admiration and expression of delight.

The greater pleasure was to come when the abundant produce was taken down and distributed among them.

Perhaps the most regular and welcome visitor to the East End was Mary, Duchess of Teck, who later, as Queen, was to give her name to Queen Mary College. It is interesting to note how she was received at a time when the Ripper was terrorising the neighbourhood. On 31 October she came to open the new school at the same King Edward Institute. The narrow Albert Street was "plentifully bestrewn with sand and the quiet (?) thoroughfare was hardly recognisable in its best dress". The *East London Advertiser* was full of praise, given the time and circumstance of her visit:

> Whitechapel is now under a cloud by reason of the recent murders, but it well rebounded to the honour and credit of HRH that at this particular time she could fulfil her engagement to the East End. Not only so but that HRH could come in an open carriage and — so great was her confidence in the loyalty and good will of the people — quite unattended even by a police sergeant or mounted constable. All along Baker Row and up Underwood Street, the streets were thronged with people, the road being kept clear by a constable here and there. The cheering was continuous... the spectators mostly of the lower order.[28]

On 17 December she was back again, opening and serving in a bazaar held at the Poplar Town Hall in aid of funds for the St. Saviour's Day Schools; while the following day Princess Christian ventured into Watney Street off the Commercial Road to open a bazaar in the schoolroom attached to Christ Church to raise money for the renovation of that building.[29] "Down East" royalty by now had acquired a firm base of loyal support, its popularity enhanced by the Prince of Wales, a frequent visitor, whose bluff and genial personality seems to have endeared him to the local cockney, who, notwithstanding his own deprivation, showed little envy but, on the contrary, a sort of admiration for the prince's well known extravagances.

There was always the traditional open space for a breath of fresh air and public entertainment. As we have seen, Victoria Park on a Sunday offered more than just the weekly political shenanigans. Again Margaret Harkness conveys to us an on-the-spot picture of that area around the "pond where the boats and ducks are, the stalls covered with sweets and buns, the stands holding ginger beer and lemonade, to the band". It was the orchestra that was the magnet for a large, appreciative audience.

> Victoria Park is one of the few places in which the public can indulge its Sunday taste for music. The men in high hats who play their stringed instruments at the bandstand, probably confer more pleasure than do the greatest opera singers, for their audience is less critical and more appreciative than ladies and gentlemen who can afford guineas for stalls and boxes. Tired mothers luxuriate there under the trees, listen to simple tunes, and doze over their babies; boys and girls play about; men enjoy pipes and gossip. Young men and maidens, old men and women, dream there of the future and of the past. No West End face is to be seen there, no well-dressed man or woman, only workers bent on enjoying their one day of relaxation, on making the most of the few hours they can call their own during the week.[30]

A day trip to Wanstead Park and Flats or Epping Forest the cockney countryside — was always on the cards, where, as Arthur Morrison records, on Whit Mondays

> You may howl at large... the public houses are always with you; shows, shies, swings, merry-go-rounds, fried fish stalls, donkeys are packed closer than on Hampstead Heath; the ladies' tormentors are larger, and their contents smell worse than at any other fair. Also, you may be drunk and disorderly without

being locked up — for the stations won't hold everybody — and when all else has palled, you may set fire to the turf.[31]

On Boxing Day a count of over 1,200 persons passed to and from the Great Eastern Company's Chingford line by means of the interchange station at Hackney. Yet for the East Ender there was always a longing for the smell of the sea, where the foul miasma of the slums could be, albeit temporarily, expunged. This was facilitated by the current opening of the Barking and Pitsea district line to the then "pretty and favourite Essex watering place Southend-on-Sea", with an outgoing connection at Stepney Station.[32]

Of course, for the indigent having little resources, the penny gaffs were the primary attraction — cheap theatre for the poorest of the poor. Mackay noticed a cluster along the Whitechapel Road transforming the foggy gloom of the side streets into pockets of bright lights and gaiety. Most gaffs consisted of a bare, shabby downstairs room with an improvised stage, the entrance door opening on to the street. Here could be seen

> the medicine man with his wizard oil which cures all ills no matter how taken, internally or externally — as well as the shooting stand, whose waving kerosene oil flames make the gaslights unnecessary. There we meet the powerful man and the mermaid, the cabinet of wax figures and the famous dog with the lion's claws — his forefeet have been split: all that is to be seen for a penny.[33]

Harkness caught on quickly to the fact that in these acts a human cripple was a capital investment. Entering one in the Mile End Road she observed a crude stage on which "a little girl turned the handle of an organ to keep the audience amused until a man without arms appeared on the platform. This man could shave himself, play a violin and do so many other things with his toes instead of his fingers. He was advertised at the entrance of the gaff as "A credit to his Maker"." In one of these gaffs was displayed a human mutation who would achieve international fame beyond his time and place. He was Joseph Merrick, the *Elephant Man*; by 1888 well ensconced in the London Hospital. His host and benefactor there, Dr Frederick Treves, describes the manner of his discovery four years before. Outside 259

Whitechapel Road, then a vacant greengrocer's shop, was a hanging sheet of canvas announcing that the Elephant Man was to be seen and that the price of admission was two pence.

Painted on the canvas in primitive colours was a life-size portrait of the Elephant Man. This very crude production depicted a frightful creature that could only have been possible in a nightmare. The fact that it was still human was the most repellent attribute of the creature. There was nothing about it of the pitiableness of the misshapen or the deformed, nothing of the grotesqueness of the freak, but merely the loathsome insinuation of a man being changed into an animal.

I was granted a private view on payment of a shilling. The shop was empty and grey with dust. Some old tins and a few shrivelled potatoes occupied a shelf and some vague vegetable refuse the window. The light in the place was dim, being obscured by the painted placard outside. The far end of the shop... was cut off by a curtain or rather by a red tablecloth suspended from a cord by a few rings. The room was cold and dank for it was the month of November. The showman pulled back the curtain and revealed a bent figure crouching on a stool and covered by a brown blanket. In front of it, on a tripod, was a large brick heated by a bunsen burner. Over this the creature was huddled to warm itself. It never moved when the curtain was drawn back. Locked up in an empty shop and lit by the faint blue light of the gas jet, this hunched up figure was the embodiment of loneliness...

The showman — speaking as if to a dog — called out harshly "Stand up!" The thing arose slowly and let the blanket that covered its head and back fall to the ground. There stood revealed the most disgusting specimen of humanity that I have ever seen... at no time had I met with such a degraded or perverted version of a human being... He was naked to the waist, his feet were bare, he wore a pair of threadbare trousers that once belonged to some fat gentleman's dress suit.

He was a little man below the average height and made to look shorter by the bowing of his back. The most striking feature about him was his enormous and misshapen head. From the brow there projected a huge mass like a loaf, while from the back of the head hung a bag of spongy, fungus-looking skin, the surface of which was comparable to brown cauliflower. On the top of the skull were a few lank hairs. The osseous growth on the forehead almost occluded one eye. The circumference of the head was no less than that of the man's waist. From the upper jaw there projected another mass of bone. It protruded from the mouth like a pink stump, turning the upper lip inside out and making the mouth a mere slobbering aperture. This growth from the jaw had been so exaggerated in the painting as to appear to be a rudimentary trunk or tusk. The nose was merely a lump of flesh, only recognisable as a nose from its position. The face was no more capable of expression than a block of gnarled wood. The back was horrible because from it hung, as far down as the middle of the thigh, huge, sack-like masses of flesh covered by the same loathsome cauliflower skin.

The right arm was of enormous size and shapeless. It suggested the limb of the subject of elephantiasis...[34]

And so on ad nauseam. It was a considerable financial loss for gaff exhibitor Tom Norman when he surrendered his interests in the Elephant Man.

For the respectable and the local authorities, the gaffs were a public disgrace. On 29 October the Committee of the Whitechapel Board of Works complained of penny gaff "shows and exhibitions of a very inferior character as nuisances carried on upon the premises in Whitechapel Road at the corner of Court Street (nos 106 and 107 Whitechapel Road) and in Court Street". The solicitor of the Board was called upon forthwith "to give notice to the persons engaged in carrying on such nuisance of the intention to proceed". It was, apparently, of no avail. On 10 December Board member Mr Karamelli was again protesting at the continuance of the nuisance caused by the gaffs in the Whitechapel Road, while his colleague Mr Morris Abrahams "testified to the serious injury being sustained by the tradesmen in the vicinity and how great was the annoyance caused to the respectable inhabitants of the district".[35] The "gaffs" persisted, against all legal assaults, to entertain a vast and loyal clientèle on their home ground.

Yet despite all these diverse cultural and leisure attractions open to all kinds of workers, that which commanded the greatest appeal was the music hall. Born out of the music rooms in pubs, the passing of the Theatre Regulation Act in 1843 was a signal to many East End taverns to convert and reconstruct their premises in order to promote variety acts in comedy and song. It was on the boards of these new music halls that the reputations of the greatest stars of their generation were made. Champagne Charlie (George Laybourne), The Vital Spark (Jenny Hill), Little Titch and Hoxton's own Marie Lloyd performed to packed audiences in the local music halls.

Conceived and steeped in working-class culture, the entertainers played on the tragedies and comedies, as well as the prejudices currently pertaining to that milieu. They generally operated from 7.30pm to midnight, with an entrance charge of 3d for the cheapest seats. Lavishly furnished to afford easy comfort for the stars, the orchestra and the audience, their popularity was its height during the 1880s. In 1888 there were at least half a dozen such major halls scattered across Tower Hamlets. One of the oldest was the Foresters (licensed around 1825) located at 93-95 Cambridge Road. In February a galaxy of top stars including Pat Feeney, Herbert Nicholls, Louis Gilberg and the inimitable Marie Lloyd appeared on the same bill. That year one notes the concentration on patriotic-cum-jingoistic productions. In March the *East London Observer*'s critic, commenting on the latest show, advised that "every lover of thoroughly good scenic effect should see the spectacle of Trafalgar which is being presented nightly at the Foresters... It has been put on the boards in Mr Lusby's characteristic style — utterly regardless of expense..."[36] Again Margaret Harkness, who had obviously attended such shows, got the message: "The songs were chiefly political, 'England for the English and heaven for us all' was encored over and over again... the chorus expressed a fervent wish to chuck the foreigner back to 'his own dear native land', and the galleries stood up to wave their handkerchiefs as the singer retired."[37]

A more diversified fare was preferred at perhaps the largest and most popular house of entertainment, Whitechapel's Pavilion Theatre, built in 1828 and at this time under the management of Jewish impresario Morris Abrahams. On 1 February, 500 children from the Stepney Jewish Schools were invited to a pantomime and, at the conclusion of the programme, received a free hand-out of buns and oranges. On 31 March the stage was occupied by officers of the East Lodges of the Independent Order of Good Templars presided over by Lord Robert Montagu. In such an unlikely setting was held the annual gathering of a formidable Temperance Society. It would appear that, even in light musicals, the Pavilion was careful to cater for a more elevated clientèle, and fun was rarely free from moral didacticism. Thus the pointed remarks of the *East London Advertiser*'s critic on a current production of *The Golden Ladder* by social observers E.R. Sims and Wilson Barrett:

> A domestic drama in which villainy is defeated and virtue rewarded is sure of patronage in the East End, where men and

> women are not so black as they are painted by those who do not understand their characters. This has been fully illustrated by the reception accorded to *The Golden Ladder*... by the crowds which nightly throng the Pavilion Theatre... The piece is a most healthy one, the high morality of which is unquestionable. The prison scenes are really effective... while even the sterner portion of the audience are constrained to admit the feeling usually termed lump in the throat.[39]

Such was the professionalism of the regular troupe that they were often in demand to perform in the provinces. The first week in September saw their return from one of these tours to pound "once more the boards of Mr Morris Abrahams' house, receiving each night cordial welcomes from the habitués of the East End Theatre who are not slow to respond to talent". Their new production of Rutland Barrington's *Mr Barnes of New York*, based on a popular novel by Archibald Clavering Gunter, was playing to a full house each night of that week.[40] Abrahams was constantly aiming at the spectacular. In October, notwithstanding the Ripper and the inclement fog drifts which persisted at night, there were again crowded houses at the Pavilion to enjoy the drama *A Run of Luck* and the spectacle of real live horses and hounds cavorting on the stage. On Boxing night, in lighter vein, the seasonal end-of-year pantomime *Babes in the Wood* witnessed an "auditorium holding 4,000 people, full with standing room". The production was based on the ever popular *Robin Hood and his Merry Men*; and "precisely at 10.30pm the curtain rose on a scene of wonderful beauty designed by Grimani for the 'transformation scenes'"[41] Abrahams was an exemplar of the show business entrepreneur. Earlier, in March, he was prime mover behind the formation of a Palace of Variety Company "to acquire the old established and successful property known as "The Queen's Palace of Varieties" in Poplar. According to the publicity blurb this music hall

> is the largest place of entertainment in the district; it accommodates 2,500 people... It is the only hall of the kind within easy reach of the residents of the extreme East of London and the facilities for approaching it are so ample that it draws supporters from West Ham, Canning Town... as well as from Bow, Bromley, Poplar, Limehouse, Stepney and other East End districts...

As for financial support, the company was more than optimistic since "the prospects of the enterprise appear to more than justify the anticipation of the directors of being able to pay 12½% dividend!"[42] In line with the current mores, profitability was the main aim of their world too. Yet the benefit show, in aid of a charity or even some individual or family in need known to the proprietor and the regulars, was an activity common to all, with all the money raised therefrom being handed over to the beneficiary.

Most of the halls followed a similar pattern and were sited within only a few hundred yards of each other. The Paragon Music Hall stood opposite Stepney Green and catered for a less discriminating audience (although Charlie Chaplin made his breakthrough there some years later). A few yards from the Whitechapel Bell Foundry and across the entry road into Fieldgate Street was the East London Theatre, managed by the ubiquitous Morris Abrahams and given over to Yiddish musicals and drama to accommodate the taste of its predominantly immigrant supporters. Wiltons in Graces Alley, Wellclose Square off Cable Street, and the Cambridge, Commercial Street, were regularly frequented by customers from well outside the area, notably some daring young bucks from out west. In 1888 the East End was well served by a cluster of music halls where food and drink came cheap; after which one could burst out in a euphoria of collective maudlin or the ribald chorus of a popular song. Here, always good for a belly laugh, the local cockney was, as Pearl Binder rightly contends, "adept at snatching wit from want".

In the final count the East Enders had no need to seek entertainment. It was there, daily, on their own doorstep, be it in alley, courtyard, rookery or along the main road and street market. Local mayhem and violence provided on-the-spot entertainment. "A murder gives them two sensations. Was the person poisoned or was his throat cut? Did the corpse turn black or did it keep till the nails were put in the coffin?"[43] There was always street theatre to entertain the folk. Two of many happenings that year will suffice to illustrate this. In February the "walking woman" of Bow roused an extraordinary amount of interest. A woman known as Madame Douglas Vivian had

> undertaken for a wager to walk from Sunday evening last till this (Sat.) evening, at the rate of two miles an hour, night and

day, from the Three Cups Tavern opposite Bow Church, east to Bow Bridge, then turning round to the Globe Bridge and back to the Three Cups. She continued until Tuesday evening, resting occasionally for the purpose of taking refreshments and an occasional forty winks at the Favourite coffee house. She attracted so much attention on Tuesday night that the Bow Road presented the appearance of Fairlop Friday, and as rowdyism began to show itself, Mr Superintendent Stead very properly took the matter in hand, and the "walking woman" ceased her walk much to the gratification of the tradesmen and residents, who would like to see a little more regulation of the proceedings in the Bow Road, especially on Sunday night![44]

On 12 July, a huge balloon took off from the Poplar Recreation Ground carrying an aeronaut and four local dignitaries "amidst the cheers and upturned faces of many thousand spectators". (After a hazardous flight of two hours and ten minutes it finally descended into a field at Horsebridge, near Hailsham in Sussex.)[45] Added to the antics of Old Jack, all these brought a sort of perverse relief to the labouring poor, who continued to be mythologised as a people of the abyss, festering in the gloomy somnolence of their "City of Dreadful Night".

Footnotes

[1]Brian Harrison, "Pubs" in *The Victorian City, Images and Realities* ed. H.J. Dyos and Michael Wolff, vol. 1, pp. 161-70. Harrison notes that in 1889 there were 2,309 arrests for drunkenness alone in the Whitechapel Police District.
[2]*Out of Work*, p. 136.
[3]*In Darkest London*, p. 18.
[4]Brian Harrison, "Pubs", p. 180.
[5]*The Bitter Cry of Outcast London* (London, 1883) p. 7.
[6]*ELO* 7 January.
[7]*In Darkest London*, pp. 54, 60.
[8]*Out of Work*, pp. 122-3.
[9]*Charles Booth, Life and Labour*, vol. 1, pp. 106-12. P.H.J.H. Gosden, *Self Help* (London, 1973) makes scattered references to these functions.
[10]See, for example, *ELO* 4 February, reporting on Conservative Party smoking concerts.
[11]A. Osborne Jay, *A Story of Shoreditch*, pp. 57-67. One must remember that Jay was also prone to self-publicity in order to elevate his own demands in the philanthropic stakes!
[12]P.E. Halstead, *Doctor in the Nineties* (London, 1959) pp. 30-2.
[13]According to William Potter, Thomas Jackson of Whitechapel

(Liverpool 1929) pp. 68-9.

[14] *ELO* 4 February gives details of this speech and other activities. For further examples of the Institute's operations, see *ELO* 14 and 28 April and 12 May.

[15] The marriage canopy.

[16] See Dr Harold Pollins, *A History of the Jewish Working Men's Club and Institute 1874-1912,* Ruskin College Occasional Publication no. 2 (Oxford, 1981).

[17] *ELO* 7 April.

[18] *ELO* 28 April.

[19] See C.P. Moss and M.V. Saville, *From Palace to College: an illustrated account of Queen Mary College.* Chs 1 and 2 chronicle in detail the foundation of the People's Palace.

[20] *ELO* 10 March.

[21] For the full list of exhibits, many of which were marked by creative talent, see *ELO* 26 May.

[22] *ELO* 23 June.

[23] *ELA* 29 December.

[24] For some details of the year's entertainment at Wycliffe Hall see for example *ELO* 7 January, *ELA* and *ELO* 31 March.

[25] *ELO* 26 May. "Why a magic lantern to those with no vision?" asks the reporter. The reply was "It affords a memory lesson exercising the thinking faculties in a very healthy manner. The sense of hearing and memory faculty have thus been put to the best possible use."

[26] See full report of the variety of leisure activities and entertainment held in July in *ELO* 21 July.

[27] *ELO* 11 February.

[28] *ELA* 3 November.

[29] *ELA* 22 December.

[30] *Out of Work,* pp. 44-5.

[31] Arthur Morrison, "Lizerunt" in the *National Observer,* 22 July 1893. Reprinted in *Tales of Mean Streets* (1894).

[32] *ELO* 9 June. "A Run to Southend and Back" by "An East Londoner".

[33] J.H. Mackay, *The Anarchists,* pp. 171-2.

[34] Sir Frederick Treves, *The Elephant Man and Other Reminiscences* (London, 1923) pp. 1-7.

[35] See *ELA* 3 November and 15 December on the Board's concern with the "gaffs".

[36] For newspaper comments on Foresters' shows see, for example, *ELO* 18 February, 24 March and 21 July.

[37] *Out of Work,* p. 165.

[38] *ELO* 31 March, "Temperance in a Theatre".

[39] *ELA* 22 September.

[40] *ELA* 8 September.

[41] *ELA* 29 September.

[42] *ELA* 3 March.

[43] John Law, *In Darkest London,* p. 10.

[44] *ELO* 18 February, "The Walking Woman of Bow".

[45] *ELO* 21 July, "The Poplar Balloon Ascent — 12th July".

Select Bibliography

Government Sources
House of Commons Select Committee on Alien Immigration, Report and Minutes of Evidence, Vol. I, 27 July 1988; Vol. II, 8 August 1889 (SP 1888, IX, p. 419; 1889, X, p. 265).
House of Lords Select Committee on the Sweating System, Report and Minutes of Evidence, Vol. I, 11 August 1888; Vol. II, 20 December 1888; Vol. III, 24 May 1889; Vol. IV, 17 August 1889; Vol. V, Appendix and Proceedings, 1890 (SP 1888, XX, XXI;1889, XIII, XIV;1890, XVII, p.257).

Local Government Sources
Surveyor's Department Report Whitechapel District. 32nd Annual Statement from Lady Day 1887 to Lady Day 1888.
Board of Works for the Limehouse District. Statement of Accounts, Reports etc. from Lady Day 1887 to Lady Day 1888 and from Lady Day 1888 to Lady Day 1889.
Board of Works for the Poplar District. Surveyor's Report and Summary of all contracts entered into and works commenced during the year ending Lady Day 1888.
Report of Dr F.M. Corner, Medical Officer of Health to the Board of Works of Poplar — South District, 1887, including Death Rates, Tower Hamlets Division Comparison, 1887.
Whitechapel Union Minute Book, no. 70, 1888.
Poplar Union Minute Book, 1888.
St. George's Union Minute Book, 1888.
Mile End Union Minute Book, 1888.

Contemporary Newspapers and Journals
Arbeter Fraint (in Yiddish)
City and East London Gazette
City Press
Commonweal
Criminologist
Daily Chronicle
Daily News
Daily Telegraph
East London Advertiser

East London Observer
Eastern Post
Echo
Evening News
Illustrated London News
Illustrated Police News and Weekly Record
Jewish Calendar 1888
Jewish Chronicle
Justice
Lancet
Murray's Magazine
News of the World
Nineteenth Century
Pall Mall Gazette
Penny Illustrated Paper
People's Press
Punch
Reynolds News
Star
The Times

General
(including fiction and semi-fiction)

Altick, R.D., *Victorian Studies in Scarlet*, London, 1970.
Anon., *An Oasis in the Desert: F.N. Charrington LCC and his work in the East End of London* (pamphlet), London, 1889.

Ballard, P.B., *Lux Mihi Laus: the work of the London School Board*, London, 1937.
Banks, J. & O., *Feminism and Family Planning in Victorian England*, Liverpool, 1964.
Barnardo, T.J., *Three Tracts*, London, 1888.
Barnardo, T.J., *Night and Day*, London, 1888.
Barnett, H.O., "Children of the Great City", *Atlanta*, April 1888.
Barnett, H.O., *Canon Barnett: his life, works and friends*, London, 1918.
Besant, Annie, *An Autobiography* London, 1983.
Besant, Walter, *East London*, London, 1903.

Bishop, E., *Blood and Fire*, London, 1964 (biography of William Booth)

Black, Clementina, *An Agitator*, London, 1894.

Booth, Charles, "The Inhabitants of the Tower Hamlets (School Board Division), their Conditions and Occupations, Winter 1886 to early 1887", paper read to the Royal Statistical Society, May 1887.

Booth, Charles, *Life and Labour of the People of London* (9 vols), Vol. 1, *East London*, London, 1892.

Booth, Charles, Note Books, 1888, London School of Economics.

Booth, William, *In Darkest England*, London, 1890.

Bosanquet, M., *Social Work in London 1869-1912*, London, 1914.

Buckle, G.E., *The Letters of Queen Victoria 1886-1901*, 3rd series, Vol. 1, London, 1930.

Chapman, S.D., ed., *The History of Working Class Housing*, London, 1971.

Coates, Thomas F.G., *The Prophet of the Poor: the life story of General Booth*, London, 1905.

Critchley, T.A., *A History of the Police in England and Wales*, London, 1967.

Cullen, T., *Autumn of Terror*, London, 1965.

Dyos, M.J. & Wolff, M., eds, *The Victorian City*, Vols 1 & 2, London, 1973.

Farson, D., *Jack the Ripper*, London, 1972.

Fishman, W.J., *East End Jewish Radicals 1875-1914*, London, 1975.

Fishman, W.J., *The Streets of East London*, London, 1979.

Fox, Stephen, "The Invasion of the Pauper Foreigners", *Contemporary Review* LIII, June 1888, pp. 855-67.

Fry, Herbert, *London in 1888*, London, 1888.

Gauldie, Enid, *Cruel Habitations*, London, 1974.

Halstead, D.G., *Doctor in the Nineties*, London, 1959.

Harkness, Margaret, see Law, John.

Harrison, Brian, *Drink and the Victorians*, London, 1971.

Hitchman, Janet, *They Carried the Sword*, London, 1966 (biography of Dr Barnardo).
Howard, Diana, *London Theatres and Music Halls 1850-1950*, London, 1970.

Inglis, K.S., *Churches and the Working Class in Victorian England*, London, 1963.

Jay, A. Osborne, *Life in Darkest London*, London, 1891.
Jay, A. Osborne, *A Story of Shoreditch*, London, 1896.
Jephson, Henry, *The Sanitary Evolution of London*, London, 1907.
Jones, E. & Lloyd, J., *The Ripper File*, London, 1975.
Jones, G. Stedman, *Outcast London*, Oxford, 1971.
Jones, P. d'A., *The Christian Socialist Revival 1877-1914*, Princeton, N.J., 1968.

Keating, P.J., *The Working Classes in Victorian Fiction*, London, 1971.
Keating, P.J., "Fact and Fiction in the East End", in Dyos & Wolff, eds, *The Victorian City*.
Kelly, A., *Jack the Ripper*, London, 1973.
Knight, S., *Jack the Ripper: the final solution*, London, 1976.

Lambert, B., *East London Pauperism*, London, 1868.
Law, John (pseudonym of Margaret Harkness), *Out of Work*, London, 1888.
Law, John *In Darkest London: Captain Lobo, Salvation Army*, London, 1889.
Law, John *A City Girl*, London, 1887.
Law, John *Tempted London: Young Men*, London, 1888.
Law, John *Tempted London: Toilers in London*, London, 1889 (this and the previous work consist of papers reprinted from the *British Weekly*).
Leeson, B., *Lost London*, London, 1934.
Lipman, V.D., *A Century of Social Service: the history of the Jewish Board of Guardians*, London, 1959.
London, Jack, *The People of the Abyss*, London, 1903.

Mackay, J.H., *The Anarchists*, Boston, 1891.
Macnaughton, Sir M., *Days of My Years*, London, 1914.

McCormick, D., *The Identity of Jack the Ripper*, Norwich, 1959.
Marcus, S., *The Other Victorians*, London, 1966.
Mearns, A. (pseudonym of William C. Preston), *The Bitter Cry of Outcast London*, London, 1888.
Morrison, Arthur, *A Child of the Jago*, London, 1896.
Mowat, C.L., *The Charity Organisation Society 1869-1913*, London, 1961.
Moylan, Sir John, *Scotland Yard and the Metropolitan Police*, London, 1929.

Odell, Robin, *Jack the Ripper in Fact and Fiction*, London, 1965.

Pearsall, R., *The Worm in the Bud*, London, 1969.
Pearson, M., *The Age of Consent*, London, 1972.
Pimlott, J.A., *Toynbee Hall*, London, 1935.
Potter, Beatrice, *see* Webb, Beatrice.
Potter, W., *Thomas Jackson of Whitechapel*, Liverpool, 1929.
Powell, Jessie, *The Man Who Didn't Go To China*, London, 1947 (biography of Dr Barnardo).
Preston, William C., *see* Mearns, A.
Prothero, M., *The History of the CID at Scotland Yard*, London, 1931.

Reeves, M.S., *Reflections of a School Attendance Officer*, London, 1915.
Rosen, G., "Disease, Debility and Death", in Dyos & Wolff, eds, *The Victorian City*.
Rumbelow, D., *The Complete Jack the Ripper*, London, 1975.
Russell, C. & Lewis, M.S., *The Jew in London*, London, 1901.

Sherson, Errol, *London's Lost Theatres*, London, 1925.
Simey, T.S. & M.B., *Charles Booth Social Scientist*, Oxford, 1960.
Simon, B., *Education and the Labour Movement*, London, 1965.
Sims, G., *Horrible London*, London, 1889.
Sinclair, R., *East London*, London, 1950
Stewart, W., *Jack the Ripper, a New Theory*, London, 1989.

Tarn, J.N., "The Peabody Donation Fund", *Victorian Studies* 10, September, 1966.

Tarn, J.N., *Five Per Cent Philanthropy*, Cambridge, 1973.
Tarn, J.N., *Working Class Housing in Nineteenth Century Britain*, London, 1971.
Thompson, Sir Basil, *The Story of Scotland Yard*, London, 1933.
Thorne, Guy, *The Great Acceptance: the life story of F.N. Charrington*, London, 1912.
Tillett, Ben, *A Brief History of the Dockers Union*, London, 1910.
Tillett, Ben, *Memoirs and Reflections*, London, 1931.
Tobias, J.J., *Crime and Industrial Society in the Nineteenth Century*, London, 1967.
Treves, Sir Frederick, *The Elephant Man and Other Reminiscences*, London, 1923.
Trudgill, E., "Prostitutes and Paterfamilias", in Dyos & Wolf; eds, *The Victorian City*.

Webb, Beatrice (*née* Potter), "East London Labour", *The Nineteenth Century* XXIV no. 138, August 1888, pp. 161-84.
Webb, Beatrice "Pages from a Working Girl's Diary", *The Nineteenth Century* XXV no. 139, September 1888, pp. 301-14.
Webb, Beatrice "The Lords and the Sweating System", *The Nineteenth Century* XXVII no. 160, June 1890, pp. 885-905.
Webb, Beatrice "The Tailoring Trade", ch. 3 in *Charles Booth, Life and Labour of the People of London*, Vol. 1, East London, London, 1892.
Webb, Beatrice *My Apprenticeship*, London, 1926.
Wensley, F.P., *Detective Days*, London, 1931.
White, Arnold, "The Invasion of the Pauper Foreigners", *The Nineteenth Century* XXIII no. 133, March 1888, pp. 414-22.
White, Jerry, *Rothschild Buildings*, London, 1980.
Williams, A.E., *Barnardo of Stepney*, London, 1943.
Williams, Robert, *London Rookeries and Colliers Slums*, London, 1893.
Wilson, Colin, *A Casebook of Murder*, London, 1969.
Wohl, Anthony S., "The Bitter Cry of Outcast London", *International Social History Review* 13, 1968-9.
Wohl, Anthony S., "The Housing of the Working Classes in London 1815-1914", in Chapman, ed., *The History of Working Class Housing*.

Other East End Titles *from* Five Leaves Publications

East End Jewish Radicals
William Fishman

Bill Fishman describes London's East End at a time of mass immigration from Eastern Europe to the shabby tenements of Stepney and Whitechapel. This was the birthplace of the Jewish socialist and libertarian movement. Essential reading for anyone interested in Victorian and Edwardian London, social and labour history, and Jewish and migrant history in this country.

William Fishman is the chronicler of London's East End. His other books include *The Streets of East London* and *East End 1888*. Now retired, he regularly leads East End walks and lectures in social history.
340 pages, 0 907123 457, £14.99

The London Years
Rudolf Rocker

This book had been long out of print — the autobiography of a German Catholic who moved to London to become the acknowledged leader of the Yiddish-speaking anarchists. Rocker describes the demonstrations against Russian pogroms, the establishment of Jewish trade unions and, famously, the 1912 general strike of Jewish tailors that abolished the sweatshop system.

Rocker's movement came to an end when the Government closed his journal during WWI, with Rocker being arrested and being held for several years as an "enemy alien". *The London Years* chronicles this forgotten world.
304 pages, 0 907123 309, £14.99

Choose Your Frog
Harold Rosen

In these poems a lot is being said through animals, rather than about them. There's politics too, sometimes oblique, sometimes direct. There is a strong theme of the encounter between urban East End Jew and the countryside, when once the encounters with animals were only with skinny dogs in Club Row or the eel stall in Hoxton Street Market.
36 pages, 0 907123 35 X, £4.50

Woodroffe, Kathleen, *From Charity to Social Work*, London, 1962.

Young, A.F. & Ashton, E.T., *British Social Work in the Nineteenth Century*, London, 1956.